RADICAL PHENOMENOLOGY

Essays in Honor of Martin Heidegger

Radical Phenomenology

Essays in Honor of Martin Heidegger

edited by

John Sallis

HUMANITIES PRESS

ATLANTIC HIGHLANDS, N.J.

©Copyright 1978 by Humanities Press, Inc.

ISBN 0-391-00928-1

Reprinted from RESEARCH IN PHENOMENOLOGY 1977 Volume 7. Published
in book form in the United States of America by Humanities Press, Inc. with
permission of the editors.

Printed in the United States of America

Library of Congress Cataloging in Publication Data
Main entry under title:

Radical phenomenology.

    Reprinted from v. 7 of Research in phenomenology.
    1. Heidegger, Martin, 1889-1976--Addresses,
essays, lectures. 2. Phenomenology--Addresses,
essays, lectures. I. Heidegger, Martin, 1889-
1976. II. Sallis, John, 1938-   III. Research
in phenomenology.
B3279.H49R29   193   78-12763
ISBN 0-391-00928-1

CONTENTS

In Memoriam: Martin Heidegger (1889—1976)

On May 26, 1976, Martin Heidegger died in Freiburg.

Hölderlin's words at the end of his elegy "Heimkunft" are fitting:

"Wenn wir seegnen das Mahl, wen darf ich nennen und wenn wir
    Ruhn vom Leben des Tags, saget, wie bring' ich den Dank?
Nenn' ich den Hohen dabei? Unschikliches liebet ein Gott nicht,
    Ihn zu fassen, ist fast unsere Freude zu klein.
Schweigen müssen wir oft; es fehlen heilige Namen,
    Herzen schlagen und doch bleibet die Rede zurük?
Aber ein Saitenspiel leiht jeder Stunde die Töne,
    Und erfreuet vieleicht Himmlische, welche sich nahn.
Das bereitet und so ist auch beinahe die Sorge
    Schon befriediget, die unter das Freudige kam.
Sorgen, wie diese, muß, gern oder nicht, in der Seele
    Tragen ein Sänger und oft, aber die anderen nicht."

NEUZEITLICHE NATURWISSENSCHAFT
UND MODERNE TECHNIK

MARTIN HEIDEGGER

Editorial Note

This text was addressed to the participants in the tenth annual meeting of the Heidegger Conference, which was held at DePaul University in Chicago. The meeting took place only two weeks before Heidegger's death, and this text is reported to have been the last composed by him.

Grußwort

an die Teilnehmer des zehnten Colloquiums
vom 14. - 16. Mai 1976 in Chicago

Denkende grüßen einander, indem sie sich gegenseitig Fragen stellen. Die Frage, mit der ich Sie grüße, ist die einzige, die ich bis zu dieser Stunde immer fragender zu fragen versuche. Man kennt sie unter dem Titel "die Seinsfrage."

Sie kann für uns zunächst nur auf dem Wege einer Erörterung der abendländisch-europäischen Metaphysik gefragt werden und zwar im Hinblick auf die in dieser vom Anfang her waltende Seinsvergessenheit.

Im metaphysischen Fragen nach dem Sein des Seienden verbirgt sich das Sein selbst hinsichtlich seiner Eigentümlichkeit und Ortschaft.

Dieses Sichverbergen des Seins ist in den einzelnen Epochen verschieden (vgl. Holzwege, Der Spruch des Anaximander, S. 296 ff.).

Die Seinsvergessenheit ist im Zeitalter der technologisch geprägten Weltzivilisation für das Fragen der Seinsfrage in einer besonderen Weise bedrängend. Aus der Vielfalt der hier nötigen Fragen sei die folgende genannt:

Ist die neuzeitliche Naturwissenschaft -- wie man meint -- die
Grundlage der modernen Technologie oder ist sie ihrerseits
schon die Grundform des technologischen Denkens, der
bestimmende Vorgriff und der ständige Eingriff des
technologischen Vorstellens in die ausführende und
einrichtende Machenschaft der modernen Technik?

Deren beschleunigt sich steigernde "Efficienz" treibt die
Seinsvergessenheit ins   Äußerste und läßt so die Seinsfrage als
belanglos und überflüssig erscheinen.

Sie werden diese Frage nach dem Verhältnis der neuzeitlichen
Naturwissenschaft zur modernen Technik in den wenigen Tagen des
Colloquiums nicht beantworten, vermutlich nicht einmal zureichend
stellen können.

Aber es wäre schon genug und förderlich, wenn jeder der Teilnehmer
dieser Frage auf seine Weise eine Beachtung schenkte und sie als
Anregung für seinen Arbeitsbereich aufnähme.

So könnte die Seinsfrage bedrängender und erfahrbar werden als das,
was sie in Wahrheit ist:

Das Vermächtnis aus dem Anfang der Geschichte des Seins,
das in ihm und für ihn notwendig noch ungedacht geblieben
ist-- die 'Aλήθεια als solche-- in ihrer Eigentümlichkeit zu
denken und dadurch die Möglichkeit eines gewandelten
Weltaufenthalts des Menschen vorzubereiten.

                                                        Martin Heidegger

Freiburg i. Br.
am 11. April 1976

MODERN NATURAL SCIENCE
AND TECHNOLOGY

Greetings
to the participants in the tenth colloquium
May 14 - 16, 1976, in Chicago

Thoughtful men exchange greetings by posing questions to one another. The question with which I send my greetings to you is that single question which I have persistently tried to ask in a more questioning manner. It is known as "the question of Being."

We can first ask this question only by way of a discussion of Occidental-European metaphysics, specifically, in reference to the forgottenness of Being that has prevailed therein from the beginning. In metaphysical questioning about the Being of beings, Being conceals itself as regards what is proper to it and as regards its place.

This self-concealing of Being is different in the various particular epochs (cf. *Holzwege,* "Der Spruch des Anaximander," p. 296 ff.).

In the age of a world civilization stamped by technology, forgottenness of Being is oppressive in a special way for the asking of the question of Being. From the many questions that are necessary in this regard, the following may be mentioned:

> Is modern natural science the foundation of modern technology -- as is supposed -- or is it, for its part, already the basic form of technological thinking, the determining fore-conception and incessant incursion of technological representation into the realized and organized machinations of modern technology?

The rapidly increasing efficiency of these drives the forgottenness of Being to the extreme and thus makes the question of Being appear irrelevant and superfluous.

During the few days of the colloquium you will not be able to answer, nor probably even to pose adequately, this question of the relation of modern natural science to modern technology.

But it would be sufficient and beneficial if each participant would devote his attention to this question in his own way and take it up as an intimation for his own field.

In this way the question of Being could become more compelling and could be experienced as what it in truth is:

> To think properly the legacy which derives from the beginning of the history of Being and which remained necessarily unthought in and for that beginning -- Ἀλήθεια   as such -- and thereby to prepare the possibility of a transformed abode of man in the world.

Martin Heidegger

Freiburg i. Br.
April 11, 1976

Finding Heidegger

J.L. MEHTA
Harvard University

> *"Nachdem Du mich entdeckt hast,*
> *war es kein Kunststück, mich zu*
> *finden: die Schwierigkeit is jetzt die,*
> *mich zu verlieren....."*
> *--Nietzsche*

Nobody told me about Heidegger. Not when I was a student at Banaras, back in the early thirties, nor during the following decade, when I was trying to find my way as a teacher. Nobody knew, it seems, about Heidegger. While I was a student, the British Idealists, Bergson, James and above all Freud and Jung, filled my intellectual horizon; as a teacher, it was the main stream of OxfordCambridge Positivism and Analytical philosophy that compelled attention. Husserl's *Ideen I* had appeared in English translation and there was rumor of something called Phenomenology. But nobody told me of Heidegger, until I read, around 1950, Werner Brock's *Existence and Being*, simultaneously with my discovery of Karl Jaspers as a philosopher after my own heart. Soon afterwards, I had the good fortune of being able to read with an Austrian colleague at Banaras the complete 1949 text of *Was Ist Metaphysik?*, which was something of a eureka experience for me. Now that Heidegger was discovered, it was no trick to find him. Only, it took a little over ten years to do so, and a year's stay in Germany and, above all, one year's concentrated effort to sum up my understanding of his work in English. By 1967, when this was published in book form, I had found "my" Heidegger, the Heidegger of a lone Indian, all by myself.

"Finding" Heidegger, I was to learn too well in subsequent years,

5

could never be a once-for-all affair. Nevertheless, the need for "losing" him, after that preliminary finding, was apparent to me. I proceeded to do so by immersing myself in the writings of Hans-Georg Gadamer. But, as Heidegger said in connection with Nietzsche, "And this, to lose, is harder than to find; because 'to lose' in such a case does not just mean to drop something, leave it behind, abandon it. 'To lose' here means to make ourselves truly free of that which Nietzsche's thinking has thought. And that can be done only in this way, that we, on our own accord and in our memory, set Nietzsche's thought free into the freedom of its own essential substance — and so leave it at that place where it by its nature belongs. Nietzsche knew of these relations of discovery, finding, and losing."[1] Heidegger's own life-work was a long-drawn-out exercise in finding and then losing what has been thought by Nietzsche and by the other great western thinkers. He has sought thus to arrive at the source of all that still remains to be found in past thought, and to have a glimpse of what is unlosable in it, the un-thought in these thinkers, after finding and losing that which has been thought by them. How, then, to lose Heidegger, how *"dieses Gedachte in das Freie seines eigenen Wesensgehaltes freigeben und es dadurch an dem Ort lassen, an den es von sich aus gehört"*? What is this "place" where it by its nature belongs? Is it perhaps the place where the Land of Evening, the West, is preparing a thinking which may one day transform it into the land of a new morning?[2] I have been trying hard all these years, but I have not yet found my way to losing Heidegger, for that can happen only when the unthought in all that he has thought emerges into view, some day. What he *has* thought will, meanwhile, remain for a long time to be "found", even after his entire *Nachlass* has seen the light of day.

It is one thing for a European to find a Nietzsche and for western philosophers to find Heidegger. But how does an Asiatic "find" Heidegger, and how does he set about "losing" him? It is not without significance that the *Festvortrag* at Heidegger's eighteeth birthday celebration in Messkirch was given by Koichi Tsujimura, a Japanese philosopher, or that *The Eastern Buddhist* published in 1966 two of Heidegger's less known addresses, with a long foreward by Tsujimura's teacher, Keiji Nishitani. As one can see from Heidegger's "A Dialogue on Language," other Japanese professors, approaching Heidegger from their Zen Buddhist tradition, had also begun to "find" him long before

---

[1]*What is Called Thinking?,* p. 52.
[2]See *Erläuterungen zu Hölderlins Dichtung* (4th ed.), p. 177.

that and one can perhaps understand why they all found it easier than most western scholars to find Heidegger and to begin to lose him. There are Chinese scholars who have found their way to Heidegger via Taoism, and I know at least one Iranian philosopher who is very much taken by Heidegger. In each case, this finding-and-losing seems to have been prompted by the urge to be carried to the "place" of Heidegger's thinking and, "leaving it at that place where it properly belongs," to come back to one's own tradition, seeking for *its* proper "place," and to respond creatively to the call that emanates from it. Heidegger's thinking is seen in the East, in Tsujimura's words, as "ein Sich-Erblicken des 'eigenen' des abendländischen Menschentums und seiner Welt,"[3] and therefore also a disclosure of this "ownmost" essence of the West to non-western man, calling upon him to go back and retrieve the forgotten foundations of his own spiritual tradition. In the Japanese case, the Europeanization has been more deliberate, thorough and rapid than elsewhere in Asia and in consequence the *Wesensnot,*[4] as Tsujimura calls it, is more acute and is explicitly experienced as such. The finding and the losing of Heidegger have therefore taken on there an urgency and intensity not found elsewhere in the East. The Far East is the polar opposite of the Greek and the European, and different from the Asia of the Greeks, that Asia against which and in overcoming which they defined their own identity. Hence the mutual reaching out to each other by Heidegger and Far Eastern thinkers.

India opened itself to the West around 1800, but hesitantly and with reservations, mainly to the English speaking West and without breaking, or wanting to break, with its past. Modernization without westernization, *festina lente,* has been the Indian way since Rammohun Roy. The main reason for this is its "large and daunting literate past,"[5] a massive heritage, still waiting to be freely appropriated, and the Sanskrit language, which continues to nourish its present. From this "house of Being," India cannot, would not want to, be banished. Further, its very closeness to the West, linguistically (the IndoEuropean family of languages) and in its rich and variegated tradition of discursive thought (the Indian philosophical systems), compel it to resist westernization. And its refusal to reject its religious and spiritual heritage (that same heritage which has continued to fascinate western

---

[3]*Ansprachen zum 80. Geburtstag,* p. 14.
[4]Ibid., p. 12.
[5]J.D.M. Derrett in *The Journal of Asian Studies,* 35, 4 (1976), p. 597.

scholars and poets for the last two hundred years and does so, more than ever, today), enables it to withstand, in considerable measure, the secularization and "disenchantment of the world," which have become synonymous with modernity in the West. The *"Wesensnot,"* in the Indian case, has therefore less of urgency in it, and is of a more diffuse character than in Japan or in the West itself. From the purely philosophical point of view, and admitting that "philosophy" is essentially a Greek-western phenomenon, Indian thought too begins with a concern with being and Non-Being and with a demythologization of sorts. But the "inner logic" that has determined its course has been uniquely Indian, and such that in the very process of being overtaken by and caught up in a history that, philosophically and religiously, originates in the West, it began to recover its own historical past. India cannot identify its perception of itself with the way the *Weltgeschick* is seen from Heidegger's window, for that would be to accept the ineluctability of "the Europeanization of the earth,"[6] and to ignore the possibility that while taking over western technology, the non-western world may not be related to its "essence" in the same manner in which that essence touches western man in his very core, that it may come more naturally to non-western man to say 'yes' and 'no' at the same time to technology.[7]

Nietzsche says somewhere that it was time the West tied the Gordian knot again, regained its Greek integrity and dispelled the magic of the East. Heidegger seems to have taken this to heart in his attempt to think the Greek "more Greekly,"[8] transcend the Greek *through* the Greek, and so to find a new way out of the destiny of Nihilism that emerged out of the Greek beginning. This is reflected in his remark in the *Spiegel* interview:

> It is my conviction that a reversal can be prepared only in the same place in the world where the modern technological world originated and that it cannot happen through the acceptance of Zen-Buddhism or any other Eastern experiences of the world. There is need for a rethinking which is to be carried out with the help of the European tradition and of a new appropriation of that tradition.

---

[6]See *On the Way to Language,* pp. 15-16.
[7]*Discourse on Thinking,* p. 54.
[8]*On the Way to Language,* p. 39.

> Thinking itself can be transformed only by a thinking which has the same origin and calling. (It is exactly at the same place where the technological world originated, that it must) be transcended (*aufgehoben*) in the Hegelian sense, not pushed aside, but transcended....[9]

As recommending an action of penitential un-doing and as pointing the way to a new birth to *philosophia*, this is indeed a splendid prescription. But what is the relevance of Heidegger's "preparatory thinking" to thinking men rooted in other traditions, beyond warning them (as Heidegger explicitly does in the "Dialogue on Language") against hasty, thoughtless adoption of western philosophical "concepts"?[10] Heidegger can certainly help us to glimpse the "unthought essence" of technology and so to free ourselves from the magic web of that "philosophy" which, in its ending, has entered into the social sciences. But what is its relevance in the Indian case specially, where the credentials of conceptual thought have been subjected to a thousand years of incessant questioning? Must non-western man go through the travail of deconstructing the history of "metaphysical" thinking before he can find himself in a free relationship to the technical world? That such mediation is not a desideratum seems to be admitted by Heidegger when he asks in the same interview, "And who of us can assert that someday in Russia and China the ancient traditions of a 'thought' will not awaken which will help make possible for man a free relationship to the technical world?"[11] Other traditions of the East, too, have these resources available to them in varying degrees; they are traditions, largely, of religious thinking, a thinking in which "the matter of thinking" does not receive its determination through its separation from the concern of faith (*Glaube*), or from the mythical roots of religion, as still with Heidegger. Nevertheless, for an Asiatic, the fascinating thing afoot in Heidegger's work is the appropriation of the religious into the enterprise of "pure" thinking, the preparing for the dawning of the Holy and the return of God and the gods. It is not only that the end of philosophy marks the emergence of a new "thinking," but that this thinking itself takes on the character of devotion (*Andacht*), of

---

[9] *Philosophy Today* (Winter, 1976), p. 281. Here and in note 11, the translation has been slightly modified.
[10] See *On the Way to Language*, pp. 2-3.
[11] *Philosophy Today* (Winter, 1976), p. 281.

thanking and of response to a call that comes to man from beyond himself.

The greatness of the beginning of western philosophy, Heidegger has said, "derives from the fact that it successfully faced the challenge of overcoming, that is, bringing within the framework of a truth of Being, what is its diametrical opposite, "the mythical in general and the Asiatic in particular,"[12] though in doing so it generated the metaphysical tradition of which Nihilism has constituted the "inner logic."[13] The new beginning of a no-longer-metaphysical thinking adumbrated by Heidegger does not see the mythic and the Asiatic as adversaries to be "overcome," though still as "other" to it. This makes it possible for the East, too, to accept the West in its otherness, without being swallowed up by the history that has emanated from it, and to appropriate western technology without being caught up in its "essence." The "transformation of history"[14] and the emergence of a "planetary thinking," [15] have been persuasively exhibited to be possible and needful by Heidegger. Meanwhile, since the Romantic movement in Europe, and with greater acceleration since the second world war, the Asia repressed within the western mind, "overcome" as image but never fully encountered and assimilated by the Greeks, has been emerging to the surface and is being recognized and appropriated as a reality complementary to it. The "Europeanization of the earth" is only one aspect of what is going on today, only one aspect of "the hidden necessity of history."[16] In his very attempt to prepare for the emergence of an *Abendland* that might for once become the land of a new morning, Heidegger shows to the East that, given an equally passionate concern there for the free recovery of its own traditions, the sun may yet continue to rise in the East.

That "man's ecstatic sojourn in the openness of presencing is turned only toward what is present and the existent presenting of what is present," [17] that "A liberation of man from what I called 'fallenness amidst beings (*die Verfallenheit an das Seiende*)' "[18] is possible, and that there is a truth, "above and beyond the Greek,"[19] more primordial than

---

[12]*Schelling,* p. 175.
[13]*Nietzsche II,* p. 278.
[14]See *Schelling,* p. 175.
[15]*The Question of Being,* p. 107.
[16]*Schelling,* p. 175.
[17]*On Time and Being,* p. 71.
[18]*Philosophy Today* (Winter, 1976), p. 278.

correctness, as which *aletheia* "appears to man's natural experience,"[20] all this was vividly realized by the seers of the *Upanishaḍs* in India and pondered systematically and elaborately by the thinkers of the philosophical tradition which developed there subsequently. Heidegger's thinking can help us Indians to see the contemporary relevance of that tradition and to seek to reappropriate it for a present dominated by the emergence of "the world civilization based upon western European thinking."[21] But must the Indian then not turn *away* from Heidegger and seek to enter into the unthought of his own tradition, in order to reach thinkingly into the dimension to which Heidegger points? Must he not try "to know the origin of this determination of Being (Being as presencing in the sense of calculable material)"[22] and *at the same time* turn homeward, toward the tradition from which even today he is not totally alienated, instead of looking for salvation in the poetry of Hölderlin? How else can an Indian begin to lose Heidegger except by building his own window on what is, and clear and make his own path, while continuing the adventure of "finding" Heidegger, in the assurance that even such "venturing out on a way that leads to what is questionable is not adventure but home-coming."[23]

Reflecting on the path taken by his own thinking, Heidegger said, "He who sets out on the path of thinking knows the least about that which, as the determining matter, moves him toward it, like a wind blowing from behind him and away beyond him. He who agrees to the enterprise of being on the way to a sojourn in the oldest of the old will submit to the necessity of being understood differently afterwards than he thought he understood himself."[24] He also said that "all great thinking always understands itself best of all, that is to say, *itself* within the limits set for it,[25] and that we never understand an author better than he understood himself, but always differently. Now that he is with us only in his work, and will in time *be as* his work, each of us, in the East or the West, will understand him differently, find and lose him differently, depending on what for each of us is the "oldest of the old"[26] and on the adequacy with which we seek to take up our sojourn in that.

---

[19]*On Time and Being,* p. 71.
[20]Ibid., p. 71.
[21]Ibid., p. 59.
[22]Ibid., p. 7.
[23]*Vorträge und Aufsätze,* p. 68.
[24]*Wegmarken,* p. VII.
[25]*On the Way to Language,* p. 39.
[26]See *On Time and Being,* p. 24.

Thought and Issue in Heidegger*

WERNER MARX
University of Freiburg

In the Preface to a collection of texts which were reissued in 1967 under the title *"Wegmarken"* Heidegger writes: "Whoever sets out on the way [*Weg*] of thought knows least of all about that determining issue which -- from back beyond him, as it were -- draws him on."

This acknowledgement attests that Heidegger did not regard thought as his property. As an outcome Heidegger shared this conviction with many philosophers. For Hegel, for instance, thought was the "active universal" in contrast to a conception of thought as "subjective activity." Yet, I said: "as an outcome." For the experience that led Heidegger to be convinced of the non-subjective nature of thought was a completely different one.

Heidegger also shared with others the view that what is thought, the "work," has a Being fully independent of the person of the thinker: In a work the truth of the issue itself comes forth.

Thus it would run counter to Heidegger's basic convictions for us to memorialize him today in a biographical way. We must devote ourselves rather to his thought and his work. But what does "work" mean for Heidegger? *This* work is not a self-contained whole, not a system. For Heidegger philosophy is possible only as a questioning which sets out ever anew. Therefore, it would be wrong to deal with his questions as though they were results which could be recapitulated in a summary. Nevertheless, these questions had something in common: all were ways *of thought*, all had to do with *one* issue, *one* task of thought --

*Text of a Memorial Address presented in December 1976 at the University of Freiburg under the title *"Das Denken und Seine Sache."* Also presented in April 1977 at Duquesne University and at the Western Division meeting of the American Philosophical Association.

to be sure, ways of a thought transformed over against the tradition and of a transformed issue. If one bears in mind that nothing less hinges on the transformation of thought and issue than the preparation for the advent of the "saving power" within that "highest danger" which prevails for man today, then *we* must attempt to clarify what thinking genuinely is for Heidegger and what its present and future issue and task are. These questions are at the basis of Heidegger's entire endeavor.

According to academic custom there devolves upon me the task of presenting as a whole the work of the deceased. Now, the thoughts of such an extremely difficult thinker as Heidegger cannot be simply repeated; any presentation must be the result of many years of interpretation. This is even more the case with his later writings. From them, however, I would like to take up the basic questions, because previous Heidegger-scholarship has not interpreted these texts in such a way as to show how Heidegger's entire concern can be found in them. The attempt to show this I regard as my contribution to this occasion. Through an interpretation of his later writings (suspending my own views) I hope to comply with Heidegger's demand that we carry on what he thought, that others be able to take up his questioning again at that point to which he carried it.

In this sense I see his last publication as his legacy. It is entitled "Das Ende der Philosophie und die Aufgabe des Denkens" - "The End of Philosophy and the Task of Thought". The opening sentences of this essay read: "The title designates the attempt at a reflection [*Besinnung*] which persists in questioning. Questions are pathways to an answer. The answer, once arrived at, ought rather to constitute a transformation of thought than a pronouncement upon some subject matter." And of the "task of thought," Heidegger says: "To inquire into the task of thought is, within the frame of reference of philosophy, to determine what it is that is of concern to thought, what is 'at issue.' Such is, in the German language, the connotation of the word *"Sache."*

We shall deal in this paper with these two problems: What was thought (*Denken*) for Heidegger? And what was the *"task and issue"* - *"die Sache des Denkens"*? To elucidate these two problems we pose the following three questions:

1) How did Heidegger characterize previous, that is to say, metaphysical thought?

2) In what sense was Heidegger's own thought already "transformed" or "other" than previous metaphysical thought?

3) What constituted for him the task and issue of thought, i.e., of *that* thought which has undergone transformation?

These questions are interrelated in such a way as to preclude separate treatment of them one after the other. The first may well depend upon the answer to the second, for presumably only that thought which has undergone transformation can determine the nature of thought prior to it. And can the nature of thought already transformed be determined without our having answered the third question, the question as to the task and issue? One would think that there is no such thing as thought without something that is at issue; that in that thought which, as quoted above, "persists in questioning," an interaction takes place, a mutual alteration of thought and issue. This would, however, not seem to be Heidegger's view. The issue is rather *"das Zudenkende"*: "that which has to be thought about"; and it is of the nature of an injunction (*Geheiß*) which, I quote, "puts us, questioning, on the track." The function of questioning - i.e., of thought - appears thus to be a subservient one: just to respond to the issue, the task. If we were to endorse this view of the relation between issue and thought, we should have to treat first of the *issue*. Of the issue Heidegger says in the same essay, however, that it has concealed itself from all philosophy, that is, from all metaphysics, beginning with Plato and Aristotle; it has "concealed itself at the beginning, and *through* the beginning" of metaphysics. It is that which metaphysics has left "unthought," *"das Ungedachte der Metaphysik."* And so we return after all to the first question: How does Heidegger characterize all previous, i.e., metaphysical thought?

Heidegger has attempted in numerous writings to show that the basic character of metaphysical thought was constituted by what he calls *"begründendes Vorstellen,"* a "representational act" of a "reasoning" nature. Why "representational act"? Now, of course, Heidegger does not wish to give an account of the changing views of reason in the history of thought. He wants to get at the *essence* of reason to the extent that it took on the form of *ratio*. He sees in the rationality of the *animal rationale*, in its faculty of conceiving rationally of what is, what can be, and what ought to be, a complex kind of "putting" (*Stellen*), and he is concerned to show how such "putting" develops, in modern thought, into "putting-before-oneself" (*Vor-sich-stellen*). The latter emerges with Descartes' *ego cogito* as the mode of being of the human subject. *Cogitatio qua repraesentatio* on the part of the subject means: *I* put something in front of myself, so that that which is thus put in place is an object at my disposal, my command, something I can figure out.

Heidegger's interpretation of modern philosophy is by no means uncontroversial. For Descartes a *cogitatio* is not merely the putting before oneself of an object, not merely representation to the subject that represents; it involves at the same time a relation of that which is given to its origin, to God. Similar objections can be raised in reference to the further development of the concept of representation in Spinoza, Kant, Fichte and Hegel. And yet a critique of Heidegger's view of the tradition of philosophy is not our purpose here.

What is the signifigance of the fact that Heidegger speaks of a *begründen Vorstellen*, a grounding representation? The signifigance lies in the fact that representation is determined by a demand to deliver grounds, a demand which has ruled all previous thought since the Greeks. For the latter that which is could be thought as "being" only in reference to its capacity for being grounded. And thus, according to Heidegger, all metaphysics regards the Being of that which is, of beings, as obviously ground. Being as ground has appeared in many distinct forms in metaphysics: as the transcendental condition of the possibility of the objectivity of objects, as the dialectical mediation of the movement of absolute spirit, and even as the historical process of production. To be sure, Heidegger's view leaves out of consideration the great differences between the specific determinations of the grounding nexus in the various positions within metaphysics, for instance, in Kant, Fichte, and Hegel. However only one thing has a direct bearing on the answer to our present questions: the fact that the conception of Being Itself as "*Grund*", ground, *ratio*, entailed that the "issue" of metaphysical thought was a matter of finding the *rationnes* of, of finding "grounds" for, particular beings. *Precisely* this is the reason why, according to the passage already quoted, "from the beginning and *through* its beginning" metaphysics concealed that issue from view which was for Heidegger throughout his lifetime that which has to be thought: *Being Itself.* This "obliviousness" to Being - *Seinsvergessenheit* - he regarded as a necessary consequence of the history of Western philosophy which, according to him, concerned Being Itself as ground, *ratio*. This obliviousness is ultimately the reason why all previous thought, that is, metaphysical thought, remained a "*begründendes*" *Vorstellen* - a rationalizing representational act.

Having established this, we pass from the first to the second question: To what extent had Heidegger's own thought undergone transformation into other than metaphysical thought? But was Heidegger's thought really so radically new? Was it not simply a further development of the phenomenology of Husserl, who regarded himself as carrying on the tradition of European philosophy and sought above all to bring about the culmination of the Cartesian and the transcendental approaches in his own "transcendental phenomenology"?

Heidegger, however, parted ways with Husserl's phenomenology at the point at which the latter came to regard phenomenology as a transcendental method of analysis of the intentionally structured acts of human consciousness. What allies him, nevertheless, with Husserl, even in his last works, is the motto: "to the things themselves," that is, the practice of viewing the "phenomena" themselves. Heidegger's "viewing," however, was not, as it was for Husserl, intuition, the nature of which was determined primarily by reference to external perception. Such was for Husserl the "principle of all principles." Heidegger's viewing was rather an openness for experience such as cannot be characterized with the aid of traditional designations. He tried continuously to elucidate it by means of new formulations. Thus he spoke once, puzzling as it may seem, of a "visual leap" (*Blicksprung*), in order to clarify one fact: that when we view a phenomenon that which is viewed by no means always stands over against the viewer as does the object of a representation; that what is viewed is, rather, of the nature of an element which one renders oneself, into which one *leaps*. More importantly, though, he saw this readiness for experience as the capacity of "simple kind of hearing," "*die Einfalt des Hörenkönnens*." Later on, within his reflections upon the "essence of language," he characterized such hearing as the hearing of the soundless address of that which is there to be thought about - *die Zusage dessen, was es zu denken gibt* - and called it as such the "gesture of thought" (*Gebärde des Denkens*) that precedes all questioning. For questioning is borne up by the address of that which comes into question.

There can, at all events, be no doubt that Heidegger's thought underwent an early transformation. Even prior to *Being and Time* his method was a "hermeneutics of the facticity of Dasein." With the "destruction" of the history of ontology, especially of the categories of substance and subjectivity, and with the analysis of the constitutive ontological structures of existence qua understanding of Being,

Heidegger abandoned in *Being and Time* the ontological bases of metaphysics. Yet it was two years after *Being and Time* that he first felt at liberty to pose this fundamental question: "What is Metaphysics?" - the title of his inaugural address.

I should say that only thought that had passed beyond metaphysics could possibly have taken Kant's doctrine of the origins of metaphysics in human nature as the point of departure for a demonstration of the fact that metaphysical thought originates in man's essential constitution, i.e., in that "transcendence" on the strength of which man is ever beyond particular being taken as a whole. Only thought which had already liberated itself from the ontological concepts of metaphysics could have conceived of this fundamental constitution as a transcending that leads *noi* to the *summum ens*, to God as the highest being on which human and non-human particular beings are founded, but rather into a sphere which is itself not a "being," but is altogether different from particular being, is, hence, "Nothing." Only thought which had thus severed itself from metaphysics could have seen in man's involvement in this "Nothing" the ontological meaning of Dasein as a self-encounter which is precisely not of the infinite nature of spiritual self-justification--as in Hegel--but which is rather, in its historical facticity, finite. Only thought that had dissociated itself from reasoning representation could attempt to bring to light the power of Nothingness as evidenced in the experience of dread (*Angst*), that mood over which man has no control. It was with this insight into man's own impotence that Heidegger actually passed beyond metaphysics. With it the stage was set for the "turning" (*Kehre*) which his thought underwent, such that thereafter the power of nothingness was thought to reside in the manifestation of the Being of beings.

The quintessence of this, Heidegger's "turning," is to be found in the experience that that which is thought is not the result of acts performed by human subjectivity, of thought that is of a reasoning nature or is transcendentally constitutive of what is thought; but rather that the latter imparts or, to be more exact, addresses itself to thinking. On this view, Heidegger regarded his own thinking as being in the "employ" of the issue which - I quote - "moves the thinker--behind his back, as it were--towards itself." Thought thus "turned" may remind us of such traditions within Western thought as Neoplatonism and Mysticism and of Schelling's middle period. With these, however, the issue was God and the process of His revelation. What is "at issue" in Heidegger's thought? Thus we arrive at the third and most important of our principal questions.

But before I interpret Heidegger's view of the "task and issue," I should like to interrupt the train of thought to make this remark: I myself am convinced that in the face of the current dominance of functionalistic thinking the "task and ussue" of thought is to pose the question as to a possible new conception or essence of essence and to keep this question an open one. This has nothing to do with that which is called "essentialism." The attempt in certain varieties of more recent positivism to bring the question as to essence into disrepute by branding it as "essentialistic" proceeds from the implicit presupposition that essence can only be thought of as substance. As substance it is concerned, in accordance with its derivation from the Aristotelian concept of *ousia*, with the form and content of particular beings.

I leave it for the moment an open question how the essence of essence might be conceived of differently when it is a matter of determining the essence of particular beings. In any case, where the nature of the whole of reality is to be determined, where the essence of "Being" is at issue, I regard it as the task of thought to conceive of "essence" in a manner that addresses this issue.

Further, modern historical consciousness requires that a transmutation of the whole of reality, the dawning of a "new age," be conceivable, and conceivable in such a way that man is assigned a role in this transformational process. This participation of man should be conceived in such a way as to preclude the danger of historicizing, relativising, or anthropomorphizing essence.

Now it is true that modern philosophy, by virtue of its development into transcendental philosophy and furthered by the insights gained by Hegel in the *Phenomenology of Spirit*, had already envisaged the possibility of "the birth of and transition to a new age" and had conceived also of the essence of man as that of an agent capable of effecting change. Yet on the categorical level Hegel absolutely ruled out the arising of a new spirit. For although with Hegel subjectivity as the power of negativity is capable of dissolving the fixity of substance, absolute self-knowledge must think in terms of the identity of subjectivity and objectivity and remains thus confined to that system of concepts which, because it is in itself complete, cannot be augmented by a new category.

How, then, did Heidegger view the issue of thought? An issue, it will now be clear, has with him no fixed content, it is the *task* of thought, that of present and of future thought. In determining this issue Heidegger has pursued various paths; their direction altered frequently although they all point towards *one* issue. We shall undertake to characterize the directions his path took and to discuss some of the "stops" along it. But because his thought is of the nature of a path no comprehensive definition of the "task and issue" of thought can be given.

The expressly stated issue of thought in *Being and Time* was the question as to the meaning - *der Sinn* -of the Being of particular beings. Of course, the theme of the published part was the Being only of that particular being whose essence is constituted by the understanding of Being, Dasein. In the analysis of Dasein it becomes manifest that the meaning of this understanding-of-Being resides in an horizon which Heidegger, on a new conception of time, defined as temporal.

In order to understand how the later Heidegger again took up this issue and task of thought as the problem of the meaning of the Being of all-that-is - which he did not treat of in *Being and Time* - it is important to bear in mind that he continued to think of Being in terms of time. This is true of the various ways which according to him "reasoning representation" of metaphysics conceived of Being as ground-*ratio*; and it is likewise true of the issue of "transformed thought" as well. Heidegger tried to show that in either case the temporal meaning of "a presence" is ever concurrently apprehended in Being--a kind of "presence," different from our customary understanding of it as one dimension of time, from the Aristotelian *nun* and the Scholastic *nunc stans* and changing in character throughout the history of thought.

In the German words "*Anwesen*" and "*Anwesenheit*" he saw the expression of such a temporal meaning of Being as presence and he saw the expression of the temporal meaning of "particular being" in the German word "*Anwesendes.*" The German *Anwesen* and *Anwesendes* have also the connotation of a *movement,* or an occurrence. This meaning allied itself with that of Presence. Being thus implied for Heidegger: occurring as Presence.

In order to clarify further the "task and issue" of thought we must ask next: what was the nature of the relationship of Being thus conceived as a temporal occurring and that which Heidegger quite early in his studies of Aristotle's Metaphysics saw as the underlying content of the Greek word *aletheia*, a word usually translated as "truth"?

This question we cannot answer without first having clarified Heidegger's conception of *aletheia*, "truth." Therein resides what might prove to be his most important contribution to Western thought.

In *Being and Time* the "primordial phenomenon" of truth was seen to consist in the fact that it is of the essence of Dasein to *be* its openness (*Erschlossenheit*) to be "in truth"; Dasein, however, to whose essence falling (*Verfallensein*) is proper--since concealment and hiddenness are constitutive of its facticity--is at the same time "in untruth."

In the essay "On the Essence of Truth" Heidegger went a step beyond the analysis of Dasein and proceeded to bring into view the phenomenon of an open sphere of reference, an open realm, without which no object can come to stand over against our faculty of representation which is open to it--of an open realm, which is not produced by the faculty of representation itself, the latter rather adopting or presupposing the former.

This sphere Heidegger attempted to explain by means of the German word "*Lichtung*." While "*Lichtung*" is characterized in *Being and Time* as being the illumination of the ontologically aware "Da" of Dasein, illumination of the "Da," becomes in the "Letter on Humanism" the open realm of Being itself, into which man in his ontological awareness "stands forth"--ek-sists. "*Lichtung*" comes more and more to be thought of as an occurring, both as the opening up of a sphere of openness and as the result of such opening. The image with the help of which we are supposed to be able to make the latter meaning clear to ourselves is that of a "clearing" in a thicket in the woods, which in German is indeed referred to as a *Lichtung*. In any case, one thing is readily apparent: the verb "*lichten*" no longer means "illumination" in Heidegger subsequent to *Being and Time*, and the noun "*Lichtung*" no longer means "light." A beam of light would rather be dependent upon the openness of a "Lichtung" which it can traverse. Thought of any kind and the "identity" of Being and thinking which is fundamental to traditional thought in particular presuppose the openness of the *Lichtung* in the sense of a clearing. And truth can only be what it was traditionally thought of as being, "evidence," "certainty," "correctness of propositions," in the element of and thanks to the openness of the *Lichtung*. Consequently, in his last publication Heidegger no longer referred to this "condition of the possibility" of truth in the traditional sense as "truth." Above all, this is important for our questions regarding the relationship of Being as temporal occurence and *aletheia* "clearing": Being occurs only in so far as the clearing (the *Lichtung*) "*is*"; and particular beings can only *be* and man can only *let* them be to the extent to which they stand forth into such overtness. Nonetheless, and this is Heidegger's decisive conviction: Western thought had as yet no conception either of the existence of this clearing nor of the occurrence of Being within it. To ponder this is, in a special sense, the "issue and task" of thought for the later Heidegger. It resides no longer, as at the beginning of his path, in a new delineation of *Being and Time*; the designation for the task and issue of thought is rather "clearing and Being occurring as presence"--"*Lichtung und Anwesenheit*".

Now perhaps the most important insight gained by Heidegger also characterizes the "task and issue of thought" in a significant way: clearing (*Lichtung*) is in itself concealment (*Verbergung*). In the early essay "On the Essence of Truth" Heidegger had explained this conception primarily by pointing out that in our everyday dealings with particular beings--by our very concentration on them--the *whole* of all-that-is *and* that which gives this whole an all-encompassing meaning as "Being" is concealed. Being itself conceals itself--not as a boundary, as is the case for epistemology--but as a hiddenness which is absolutely inherent in man's letting particular beings be. Progressively more in this manner, and not so much anymore on the basis of phenomenal evidence, Heidegger assumed a concealing which baffles all of man's disclosing; he assumed the existence of a dimension perpetually closed off to man. This dimension he had called in that early essay "the mystery" (*das "Geheim-nis"*).

Now this view that clearing is in itself concealment implies that whatever nonconcealment of the occurrence of Being might be dominant at a given time stays permeated by concealment, by mystery, and so does any "particular being" brought forth by virtue of such non-concealment of the occurrence of Being. Although Heidegger regards it as the vocation of man to remain cognisant of such concealment to guard this mystery, man continually turns from it--not out of neglectfulness, but because forgetting the mystery, erring (*Irre*) is constitutive of the inner nature of Dasein.

Here I should like to interrupt the train of thought again in order to further clarify by way of a reference to the history of thought wherein I see the significance of Heidegger's view.

It will be remembered that within the tradition extending from Aristotle to Hegel, the tradition which in terms of historical influence has become for us the decisive one, particular being was taken as being in principle intelligible. With Aristotle this view results from the assumption of the unconditional dominion of the principle of complete transparency, of *nous* mind. From the conception of a highest being whose actuality consists in mind's thinking itself, he proceeded to think of the essence of what is, of *ousia*, substance, as being fundamentally prone to being grasped by man's intuition and discursive, logical thought: on these grounds alone he attributed potentially to man the ability to penetrate totally the essence of things. Later on, the philosophy of subjectivity, proceeding from the "conditions of the possibility of knowledge," sought grounds for the possibility of universally valid experience of objects, and Hegel expounded the doctrine that everything-that-is is permeated by the concept "in itself," so that thought is capable of grasping it "for itself" and of demonstrating it "in and for itself." Thus the philosophy of substance and that of subjectivity took as their point of departure the view that everything-that-is is illuminated and that the source of this light is the *summum ens*, God. In this sense metaphysics was the "metaphysics of light." It can be maintained that a secularized form of this "metaphysics of light" is in evidence in the pride with which most of our contemporaries trust in the intelligibility of the universe and believe in the scientific and technical rationalization of society. A whole contingent of sciences, from cybernetics to communications theory, social and biotechnology, stand today ready to serve in controlling a completely rational society.

Over against this fundamental assumption of the tradition--the historical influence of which extends even into our own times-- Heidegger placed the view that Being occurs in a clearing which is in itself concealment, so that the nonconcealment of the occurrence of Being dominating at any given time every particular being that has come forth within such clearing, remains permeated by mystery. If some future humanity should not forget but rather experience it, it would then, indeed, abandon its faith in an ever progressing penetration of the universe.

But to return to our subject. With Heidegger it is not only that a given dominating non-concealment of the occurrence of Being remains permeated by mystery; rather, there also reigns within the sphere of "particular beings" a concealment whose nature it is to disguise (*Verstellen*). "If particular beings did not disguise other particular beings," writes Heidegger in "On the Origin of the Work of Art," "we could then never commit an oversight with regard to particular beings, nor could we make a mistake, nor go astray, nor go wrong, nor yet could we ever overstep our bounds." The capacity of particular beings to deceive, to "seem," is a necessary prerequisite for *our* being mistaken-- and not vice versa, as Heidegger expressly points out; accordingly, erring--die *Irre* as a constitutive structure of Dasein--represents in the earlier essay "On the Essence of Truth" a requisite condition of error (*Irrtum*) and this extends from "the common mistake, oversight and miscalculation to going astray and going too far in one's basic posture and decisions." Later on I shall point out an important consequence of this view of Heidegger's.

The "erring" (*Irre*) is for the later Heidegger also a decisive factor in the history of metaphysics. By "history" he means the sequence of various forms in which the meaning of Being, the meaning of what at any given time *is*, imparted itself to metaphysical thought. These forms or "impartings" (*Schickungen*) are at the same time forms of withdrawal (*Entzug*) of such impartings; in them that which imparts *holds back*. Holding back--in this sense, *epoche*--withdraws furthermore due to the obliviousness of this entire process, and impedes thus the experience of the withdrawal *as* withdrawal. In this sense metaphysics is in Heidegger's view a sequence of "epochs of erring," a sequence which involves at the same time an escalation. The current domination of erring he regards as total. We might interject this question: What is the nature of the necessity governing this escalation of "erring"? It cannot be conceived of in terms of a teleological Christian-eschatological principle. For Heidegger regards the domination of technology, the end of this historical development, not as the completion or culmination of the process, but rather as its termination or extinction. Yet, these factically diverse forms of "imparting" constitute together a coherent whole which Heidegger calls the "history of being" (*Seinsgeschichte*) and which is by no means arbitrary. However, Heidegger has, as far as I can see, failed to clarify satisfactorily the nature of that other kind of necessity which governs coherence, perhaps because this historical process, at the very point in time at which it extinguishes in total withdrawal reaches its end and

does so for an entirely different reason. It was Heidegger's thought
which attained insight into the openness of the "clearing" as well as into
the concealment proper to it, and the occurrence of Being of particular
beings within it. He took the view that he himself was the first to
perceive this "issue" of thought. This implies that the concealment no
longer concealed itself from thought--thought having now, with
Heidegger, experienced the withdrawal *as* a withdrawal. In this
experience the history of Being reaches its end. It is an almost uncanny
role which Heidegger thus felt obliged to ascribe to his own thought.

To clarify better the "task and issue" of thought, we must next ask:
How exactly did Heidegger define the occurrence of Being within the
clearing--the latter being in itself concealment? What are the
"fundamental traits" of Being thus conceived? It is possible to
distinguish two stops along the way leading to Heidegger's new
conception of fundamental traits of Being or, as one might also say,
"categories." At first, Heidegger believed his conception of these traits
resting upon the very experiences made with Being during the early
history of Western thought. The Pre-Socratic philosophers, he
believed, sedimented their experiences in such basic terms as *physis*,
logos, and *aletheia*. They did not, however, make the experiences
underlying these terms the explicit subject matter of their thought. To
do so constituted at this stop on Heidegger's way the task and issue of
thought, i.e., of recollecting (*andenken*) these experiences at the
beginning of the history of Western thought in order to "pre-think"
(*vordenken*) them towards another beginning.

The usual criticism of Heidegger's later works which regards as
"arbitrary" the fundamental traits or categories developed by him
through this recollective pre-thinking overlooks the fact that for him the
source of their legitimacy is to be found in those primordial experiences
made during the first beginning of Western thought.

It could, however, be made the objective of truly sound criticism to
investigate whether or not the categories "pre-thought" by him are,
indeed, verifiable on the grounds of being a further development of
those recollected basic terms expressing those primordial experiences.
One might furthermore raise the question: Did Heidegger, at the second
stop on his way, not entirely abandon this legitimizing reference to the
first beginning? This second stop on the way becomes only then
comprehensible when one comes to see that it represents the utmost
concentration of thought upon these basic traits of Being. If we assume

Being to be always the Being of particular beings, it becomes methodologically possible to disregard particular beings, and attend only to Being itself. We saw: Metaphysics was prevented by its preoccupation with particular being from inquiring into the meaning of Being itself. Heidegger's course is just the opposite; he inquires as to the fundamental traits of Being alone. Hereby his thought came increasingly under the sway of a key term which he cannot possibly have derived from the experiences of the early Greeks: "*Ereignis*", which Albert Hofstaedter for reasons explicated in his Introduction to *Poetry, Language, Thought* has translated as the "disclosure of appropriation." This word has the non-metaphysical signifigance which makes it possible to conceive of clearing and of the occurrence of Being within it as a "groundless bringing about" ("*grundloses Erbringen*") of particular being, as a "letting be" which is different from all "causing" to be, making and finding grounds for being; it is rather a groundless disclosing, a bringing to the fore. This exposition of the basic characteristics of letting be in terms of *Ereignis* determines henceforth the direction of the "task and issue" of thought of the latter Heidegger. The terms employed to designate it ward off all searching for grounds in the metaphysical sense. To name but a few of these designations: play (*Spielen*); imparting (*Schicken*); "giving" in the sense of "tendering an offering", the tendering itself being at once both disclosing and concealing. The expression of this groundless occurrence Heidegger sees expressed in the German phrase "*es gibt*" ("it gives"). The "*es*" (the "it") is *not* just another underlying ground or substance; it is rather the giver which withdraws in favour of its offering, giving not particular beings, but rather something which is not at all at our disposal, the occurrence of Being itself. That which by its giving sets us in each particular instance on a different course of disclosure Heidegger has called "that which grants" ("*Das Gewährende*").

It is of the greatest importance to note that this "Gewährende" ("that which grants") constitutes in the dimension of "Ereignis" the new and other "essence" which, as I have suggested, contemporary philosophy should try to conceive of as the essence--not of a particular being but of all-that-is, of the whole of reality. *Das Gewährende* gives in any given era the nonconcealment (*Unverborgenheit*) for the temporal occurrence of the Being of beings. It is an unconcealment of Being which dominates in a given era of history. It is thus an essence which has by no means the character of eternity as did the traditionally conceived essence of particular beings.

One final direction of the "task and issue of thought" can be but briefly touched upon. Heidegger envisaged a framework within which some future humanity might dwell in a primordial fashion, or, to put it as does Heidegger in Hölderlin's language, might "dwell poetically" (*"dichterisch"*). This framework was erected, on the one hand, by means of the aforementioned basic traits of Being - and it rests, on the other, upon a particular view of the "essence of language" developed by Heidegger out of his interpretations of Hölderlin's poetry. Now it will be understood that only in the element of poetic language does there emerge what he called the four regions of the "world": earth, the heavens, the divine, and the mortal. The specific significations of these terms have been set forth in the lecture "Das Ding." The inter*play* of these significations, such that each reflects the other and yet remains itself, this "groundless occurrence," the "play" of the world, different from all "grounds" and "reasons," is what lets particular beings be. "Particular being," through which the significance of each of the world regions "comes into its own," is precisely what Heidegger calls "das Ding", the "thing." Man, once cognizant of the world regions, could dwell together with things; in his dealings with them they would not show themselves only in their serviceableness and usefulness. He would live in the awareness of the significance of his mortality and aware, too, of what it means to be on earth beneath the heavens in the face of the Godhead. It is this revitalised primal form of human existence which Heidegger has called "dwelling poetically." Whether and when a world such as this and "poetic dwelling" in it will actually come about is in the present state of world-wide benightedness neither predictable nor calculable.

It is possible to show by reference to *"Ereignis"* (in the sense developed) how Heidegger's original question as to the *Being* of *beings* (and the "difference" between the two) turned into the problem of the relationship between world and thing. One might also ask whether Heidegger did not thereby bring history to a stillstand and come near to the traditional idea of a terminal point at which all the conditions of the arising and development of history are conceived of as suspended.

What is then the significance of such thought as this in the present situation, characterized as it is by the domination of technology, a situation in which, according to Heidegger, Being "is" of no concern and nihilism reigns? The meaning of world and of a possible new kind of human dwelling in it suggests to him that the salvation (*das Rettende*) might reside in the utmost peril itself. Man is today imperilled because particular beings have for him only that mode of Being which is expressed in "constantly available stock at hand" (*verfugbarer Bestand*). Out of this there arises the danger that man take himself to be no more than a "calculable constituent part of such stock" and forget entirely his true vocation.

Hitherto, we have not expressly mentioned the role of man in the occurrence of Being. Heidegger has often been understood to regard Being as an independent power reigning over man, remaining beyond his grasp in its revealing or withdrawing, a secularized God, as it were. This is, however, a total misconception. With Heidegger the problem was from the first to make apparent by means different from the metaphysical idea of identity the *"Zugehören"* (the *cor-responding* bond) between Being and man. Without actually realizing what role he plays in the occurrence of Being man is ever responding in his disclosing acts - in his *"Entbergen"* - to the given mode of non-concealment which sets him in each instance upon a new course of disclosure (*Entbergung*). Today, too, he is, responding to "that which grants" (*das Gewährende"*) by the manner in which his work and production bring particular beings to the fore as constituent parts of stock. In man's capacity to disclose, to bring to the fore particular beings, lies what Heidegger - thinking in terms of *"Ereignis"* - took to be the proper essence of man. For *"Ereignis"* (the disclosure of appropriation) means above all that Being and man are mutually appropriated (*"einander zugeeignet"*).

In the lecture "Identity and Difference," given on the occasion of the five hundredth anniversary of the University of Freiburg, Heidegger showed that and how this bond between Being and man manifests itself in the essence of technology. If man were to recognize in his relation to Being the role which is his in the occurrence of Being; if he were to "guard the non-concealment and with it the concealment of Being and beings on earth"; if he were to do so with a view to his own possibility of dwelling poetically; then *one* prerequisite for overcoming the domination of technology, for the beginning of salvation would be fulfilled. The *other,* the unforeseeable beginning of the "play of world," would, of course, have to be fulfilled as well.

We have attempted, though in a very condensed form, to present Heidegger's view of the "issue and task" of thought. A genuine philosophical exchange with Heidegger becomes possible only through constant awareness of this issue. For purposes of such an exchange one must, especially with regard to the final, the second stop on Heidegger's way, bear the following in mind: Heidegger ventured forth into a realm not yet entered by philosophy. By going back further than metaphysics he won for himself the freedom to pre-think the basic traits of a new meaning of being. Granted that this can be considered a legitimate task, the doubt arises: does not such an attempt transcend the limits of philosophy, the very range of human thought itself? What is more: is it possible to give an account of such thought in a fashion that admits of inter-subjective validity and verifiability?

In concluding, we may inquire to what extent Heidegger indeed responded to the "task of philosophy" which I had suggested before. By concentrating on the occurrence of Being itself he arrived at the conception of another essence of essence, namely the "groundless granting" that lets particular beings emerge out of concealment into the openness of a clearing which is in itself concealment. This idea of essence takes into account modern historical consciousness, concedes to it the possibility of the emergence of a new basic character of reality as a whole dominating thought only during a given era, and is thus not eternal.

Heidegger fulfilled, too, the further requirement of assigning to man a role in this occurance of essence but in such a manner that man's disclosing, be it thought, poetry or action, remains subject to the "groundless granting" essence, whereby the danger of historicizing, relativizing or anthropomorphizing of such essence is averted. Furthermore, such disclosing is no longer bound up with a total system of concepts like that attendant upon the traditional view of "identity". In place of "identity" there emerges the *Zugehörigkeit* (the bond of correspondence) of Being and man.

We alluded earlier to the possibility of an alternation in human consciousness consequent to Heidegger's view of the mysteriousness of the prevailing nonconcealment of Being. It is a matter of fact that the aggressive self-assurance of Western man has led to a blindness in regard to the bounds of knowledge and has effected, too, the loss of any sense of awe whatsoever in the face of what is in principle beyond his ken. In theory and in practice he asserts his belief in progress, the progress of his understanding of and his command over his living conditions. It would seem to me that even those current movements which are concerned to point out the bounds of human rationality and planning are not fundamental enough in their approach. In their presuppositions they betray their dependence upon what they seek to negate. In this point they might well take a lesson from Heidegger. From his insight into "what today, all over the globe, *is*," from his insight into the currently prevalent meaning of Being and into the necessity that man respond to the particular nature of non-concealed *Anwesen* being dominant at any time. From all this he concluded that the dominance of technology neither ought to be nor can be merely banished from sight. The technological age is, as it were, a phase we have to go through. But under its dominance we must, too, come to see how Being, Anwesen, occurs, and we must derive from this insight the liberty to hope that some day, suddenly, the meaning of world and thing, as envisaged by Heidegger, may dawn upon a humanity ready to receive it. In this I see no "counter-enlightenment," no "irrationalism," for Heidegger's position rests upon presuppositions that are beyond rationalism and its counter-part. One might well, on the other hand, speak of "utopianism" but, of course, not in the political sense.

At this point it becomes unavoidable to ask whether or not Heidegger did set standards, did set forth rules for thought, poetic creation and action. As a truly questionable consequence of his position I regard the fact that, with him, concealment qua "disguising" is a condition of the possibility of our being mistaken and "not vice versa"; that, according to him, the erring is a constitutive structure of human Dasein capable of leading the latter so totally astray that man "goes too far in his basic postures and decisions." Here the question must be put: Does not this view from Heidegger's middle period, a view which was not in any way qualified afterwards, entail a vindication of concrete error like the political one committed by Heidegger himself? How, the non-concealment of Being particular to a given point in time and called by Heidegger at the said stage in his thought "the truth of Being" is, indeed, of the nature of a claim; this he showed in the "Letter on Humanism" by briefly outlining his position with respect to traditional ethics. Does, however, this claim have the validity of a standard in the light of which he who hears the claim might decide whether what he has heard is in a given situation right or wrong, whether his action is good or evil? If there were no such standard for man's hearing of and response to the claim addressed to him, then it could never be discernible whether and to what extent man, in thought and action, is merely being duped by the disguising (*Verstellen*) that permeates so inexorably the clearing, deceived by the erring that governs so unalterably all human Dasein. No one could be convicted of an error the commission of which is a fact, if he had only listened and responded to a claim addressed to him. On this view all the traditional questions of responsibility, guilt, and conscience - in short the whole of the moral-ethical heritage of the Judaeo-Christian tradition - falls subject to doubt.

Seeing this as a possible consequence does not necessarily imply a rejection of the entire frame of reference of Heidegger's thought. In philosophy there can be no such clearcut decisions as to right and wrong. Without entering into the nontraditional dimensions in his thought, without readiness to meet Heidegger on his own ground, there can be no countering his ideas nor can one grasp the significance of his daring to enter a dimension more primordial than that of metaphysics by conceiving of Being itself as an occurrence of time, by bringing out its basic traits and constructing the framework for a more primordial dwelling, for a new mode of Being for humanity.

To draw this to your attention has been the aim of my remarks in memory of Martin Heidegger.

Zum Tode Martin Heideggers

OTTO PÖGGELER
Ruhr - Universität Bochum

Martin Heidegger ist am 26.5.1976 sechsundachtzigjährig in Freiburg gestorben. Seine letzte Ruhestätte fand er, seinem Wunsch gemäß, in Meßkirch beim Grab seiner Eltern. So hat die kleine Landstadt den Sohn ihres einstigen Meßners und Küfnermeisters wieder, den sie einmal ausschickte zum Gymnasium nach Konstanz und dann zum Theologiestudium nach Freiburg, der dann aber auf einem anderen Wege als Philosoph Weltgeltung errang—zuerst 1927 mit "Sein und Zeit", dann nach dem Zweiten Weltkrieg mit der Forderung einer "Kehre" des Denkens. Martin Heidegger glaubte am besten in seiner schwäbisch-alemannischen Heimat denken zu können; auch in seiner Marburger Zeit blieb er über das Ferienhaus, das er sich in Todtnauberg gebaut hatte, mit dem Schwarzwald verbunden. Es war für ihn nicht zweifelhaft, daß er Rufe nach Berlin und nach München ablehnen mußte. Sein Lebenskreis war die Universität, die stille "Hütte", die Heimatstadt (wo der Bruder lebt), die Vorträge "draußen", Reisen zu Freunden nach Frankreich und seit Anfang der sechziger Jahre zu den griechischen Inseln.

Als philosophischer Lehrer hat Heidegger den Bericht über das Leben des Aristoteles abgetan mit dem Wort: er wurde geboren, arbeitete und starb. In gleicher Weise suchte er alle biographische Neugier und Zudringlichkeit von seinem Leben fernzuhalten, von dem für die Öffentlichkeit nur das Werk zähle. Doch hat er es nicht unterlassen, den Bericht von seinem Leben auf sein Schaffen hin zu stilisieren. Hätte er nicht in einem "Hüttenbuch" in Leitworten und

Sprüchen die Fragen seines Denkens mit der Einsamkeit des
Schwarzwaldhauses verknüpft und hätte er nicht die (einstige)
Gewachsenheit bäuerlich-ländlichen Lebens ausgespielt gegen die
großstädtische Unruhe, dann hätte man sich auch nicht so darüber
erregt, daß hier ein Philosoph in ein Ferienhaus ausweicht und lieber
auf dem Gang vom Brunnen zum Tannenhang als neben dem
brodelnden Verkehr nachdenkt. "Holzwege", die jäh im Unbe-
gehbaren enden, sollten seine Gedankengänge sein, freilich auch
Feldwege, die altem Herkommen gamäß ihre Bahnen durch das
Land ziehen. Wegen eines Texts, den Heidegger über einen Weg
seiner Jugend schrieb, gibt es nun "den" Feldweg in Meßkirch; aber
im Sommer 1959 schickte Heidegger eine Photographie, die zeigte,
wie der Feldweg mit dem alten Wegstock zur Straße planiert worden
war.

In Ferdinand Christian Baur kennen wir einen Gelehrten, dessen
Leben durch den Kreis der schwäbischen Schulen und der Tübinger
Universität umgrenzt war, der aus den Schranken des hergebrachten
Lebens nie heraustrat, eine persönliche Beunruhigung durch seine
Arbeit nicht zu kennen schien und der doch die Theologie seiner Zeit
durch seine Forschung unterminierte. Deutet Heideggers Abneigung
gegen das Biographische darauf hin, daß sein Werk in Stille und
Stetigkeit gewachsen ist, oder entspringt sie der Scheu vor einem
Unmaß von persönlichen Entscheidungen, das dem abgefordert
wurde, der in einer unruhigen Zeit von dieser Zeit zur
Selbstverständigung gebraucht wurde? Heidegger hat nach dem
letzten Kriege des öfteren erzählt, sein "väterlicher Freund und
Landsmann", der spätere Freiburger Erzbischof Gröber, habe ihm
schon auf dem Gymnasium Brentanos Dissertation über die mannig-
fache Bedeutung des Seienden bei Aristoteles geschenkt und so die
einzige Frage seines Denkens, die Seinsfrage, in ihm geweckt.
"Denn wie du anfingst, wirst du bleiben", mit diesem Wort aus
Hölderlins Rheinhymne glaubte Heidegger Anfang und Ende seines
Lebensweges zusammenfassen zu können. Ist die Legende nicht
realistischer, wenn sie erzählt, Heidegger habe den Erzbischof
wieder besucht, als das Dritte Reich in Schutt und Asche gesunken
war, und als dieser seinen einstigen Schützling mit einem
"Kommscht endlich" begrüßt habe, sei der zurückgewichen mit
einem "So nit" und weggeeilt, um eine Mißdeutung seines Schritts
fernzuhalten? Die üppig wuchernde Legende glaubt freilich hinter

Türen blicken zu können, die verschlossen sind, und vieles schlicht Unwahre oder gar Verleumderische ist vorgetragen worden. Wenn Günter Grass in seinem Roman "Hundejahre" Hitlers Untergang mit der Sprache von Heideggers Freiburger Antrittsvorlesung illustriert, dann bringt auch er zusammen, was so geistesgeschichtlich nicht zusammengehört, verzerrt er die Geschichte, die auch im wirklichen Geschehen gespenstische Situationen genug gehabt haben wird.

In all den Verstrickungen, in die die weltanschaulichen und politischen Positionen einer Übergangszeit hineinnötigten, blieb es Heideggers Leidenschaft, das unvoreingenommene, sich zurückhaltende Denken und so die Kraft der Besinnung zu erproben. Für Heideggers Weg wurde entscheidend, daß im Ersten Weltkrieg Husserl nach Freiburg kam, dessen "Logische Untersuchungen" Heidegger schon früh zu studieren versucht hatte. Husserl hatte den Durchbruch seiner "phänomenologischen" Bewegung dadurch erzielt, daß er die Philosophie auf das "Sehen" verpflichtete, das von allen kurzschlüssigen Erklärungen oder überschwenglichen Spekulationen Abschied nimmt. Das Logische z.B. sollte in seinem eigenen Sinn aufgefaßt werden, nicht gleich "psychologistisch" auf eine bloße Tatsache psychischen Lebens zurückgeführt werden. In seiner Freiburger Zeit bildete Husserl diesen Ansatz zu einem transzendentalen Idealismus und einer übergreifenden Systematik fort. Seine beiden Assistenten sollten dabei helfen: Oskar Becker, vorwiegend Mathematiker und Naturwissenschaftler, und Martin Heidegger, vor allem den Geisteswissenschaften, der Theologie, der Geschichte der Philosophie zugewandt. Husserl mag sich die weitere Ausbildung der Phänomenologie so gedacht haben, daß er den Ansatz und den Rahmen des Ganzen ausarbeite, Becker den mathematisch-naturwissenschaftlichen, Heidegger den geisteswissenschaftlichen Teil konkretisiere. Mit Heideggers Arbeit "Sein und Zeit" erschienen denn auch 1927 in Husserls Jahrbuch für Philosophie und phänomenologische Forschung Beckers Untersuchungen zum damaligen mathematischen Grundlagenstreit. Heidegger brachte jedoch Geschichte und Zeitlichkeit in der Weise ins Spiel, daß er Husserls Rahmen sprengte, den Ansatz selbst verwandelte und die Phänomenologie zur "hermeneutischen" Phänomenologie weiterbildete.

Während viele Interpreten betonen, Husserl sei nicht erst durch

Dilthey oder gar durch Heidegger zur Geschichte geführt worden,
neigte Heidegger dazu, Husserl den genuinen Bezug zur Thematik
von Geschichte und Geschichtlichkeit überhaupt abzusprechen. Er
erzählte gern die Anekdote, daß er Husserl zum Freiburger Bahnhof
begleitet habe, als dieser nach England reisen mußte; Husserl habe
ihm auseinander gelegt, wie er seinen geplanten Vortrag aufbauen
und dabei die einzelnen Wissenschaften in seinem Begründungsver-
such unterbringen wolle; auf die Frage nach den historischen Wissenschaften habe er nur antworten können: "Die habe ich
vergessen." Das phänomenologische Sehen sah bei Heidegger aber
nicht nur auf die Geschichte hin; es wurde selber dynamisiert, mußte
sich erst aus den geschichtlichen Verdeckungen und Verstellungen
herausarbeiten. In Husserls Analysen ist der Phänomenologe ein
Mensch, der an einem Schreibtisch sitzt, sich Dinge vor Augen
führt, sie einmal so dreht und einmal so, der vielleicht auch einmal
aufsteht, um die Dinge von hinten zu sehen, sich daran erinnert, daß
ich hier bin und Du dort, der so mitwahrnimmt. Bei Heidegger wird
der Phänomenologe zur Existenz, die sich auf das Existierenkönnen
verstehen und Geschichte auslegen muß, dabei durch Situation,
Praxis, Angst, Tod, Gewissen bestimmt ist. Hatte Husserl noch
gemeint, die Phänomenologie könne so zur Methode ausgebildet
werden, daß er sich im Krankheitsfalle in den Vorlesungen durch
seine Assistenten müsse vertreten lassen und diese bruchlos seine
Gedanken müßten fortführen können (wie das etwa bei seinem Kol-
legen Hilbert, dem Göttinger Mathematiker, möglich gewesen
wäre), so wurde Phänomenologie bei Heidegger an eine un-
vertretbare "Erfahrung" geknüpft. Es geschah nun das Merkwür-
dige in Freiburg, daß die Studenten, die von den deutschen Universitäten oder auch aus Japan zu Husserl zum Studium kamen, von
Heidegger fasziniert wurden. In jedem Fall war es nun der heimliche
Antagonismus zwischen Husserl und Heidegger, der die Dynamik
der phänomenologischen Bewegung ausmachte.

Aristoteles, die Scholastik, der Neukantianismus und Husserls
Phänomenologie, denen Heidegger verpflichtet war, hätten freilich
nie zu den Fragen Heideggers geführt, wenn sie nicht jener Unruhe
der damaligen Zeit ausgesetzt worden wären, die im Rückgriff auf
Gestalten wie Kierkegaard und Dostojewskij, Pascal und auch
Wilhelm Dilthey artikuliert wurde. Noch in "Sein und Zeit" heißt es
ja, die mitgeteilte Analytik des Daseins sei dem Verfasser erwachsen

"im Zusammenhang der Versuche einer Interpretation der augustinischen—das heißt griechisch-christlichen—Anthropologie mit Rücksicht auf die grundsätzlichen Fundamente, die in der Ontologie des Aristoteles erreicht wurden". Eine Denkfigur kam ins Spiel, die immer weiter ausgebaut wurde (z.B. bis in Artikel des Kittelschen Wörterbuchs zum Neuen Testament); die Travestierung konnte dabei nicht ausbleiben: man führt einen hellenistischen Autor an, stellt diesem angeblich griechischen Denken etwas Ursprünglicheres, die jüdisch-christliche Zeiterfahrung gegenüber... Heidegger ging es um Anderes: um die Revision des überlieferten philosophischen Ansatzes selbst.

Man weist gern darauf hin, daß Heidegger in seiner Marburger Zeit (1923-28) durch seinen dortigen Freund Rudolf Bultmann theologisch beeinflußt worden sei. Daran ist richtig, daß Heidegger und Bultmann zusammengearbeitet haben—sie haben zusammen Seminar gehalten und sich dabei bekanntlich auch durch die Nachricht des Pedells, die Universität brenne (ein Flügel habe Feuer gefangen), nicht stören lassen, sie haben in einer Arbeitsgemeinschaft griechische Texte gelesen, sie haben zusammen das Johannesevangelium interpretiert, über das Bultmann dann später eines unserer berühmten theologischen Bücher, seinen Kommentar, geschrieben hat. Geben und Nehmen kamen aber von beiden Seiten: sieht man auf Bultmanns Arbeiten, dann zeigt sich daß es ihm erst die existenziale Interpretation ermöglicht, von der bloß auflösenden philologischen Kritik mit der neuen dialektischen Theologie zum Aufweis der Theologie des Neuen Testamentes zu kommen. Umgekehrt muß man beachten, daß Heidegger schon in Freiburg Luther studiert hat: er hat in seiner Vorlesung über Augustin und den Neuplatonismus mit Luthers Heidelberger Disputationsthesen die Theologie des Kreuzes und damit das faktisch-historische Leben gegen eine metaphysische "Theologie der Herrlichkeit" ausgespielt. "Dieses für einen Philosophierenden fremdeste, wunderlichste, existenziell kaum noch eine Sprache bedeutende, dies Lutherische in seinen schrecklichen Konsequenzen" (wie Jaspers einmal sagte) hat für Heidegger existenziell eine Sprache bedeutet, und er hat es auf seine Implikationen für eine philosophische Interpretation der Welterfahrung befragt. Manche neigen dazu, darin das theologische Engagement zu betonen ("Man muß Katholik gewesen sein, um Protestant sein zu können..."); andere finden in solchem Bezug zur

Theologie eine Zweideutigkeit, die offen läßt, ob sie nicht die ganze
Theologie nur aus den Angeln heben will. Man sollte bei solchen
Überlegungen in jedem Fall nicht zu schnell über Heideggers sehr
genaue Bestimmung des Verhältnisses von Philosophie und
Theologie hinweggehen: eine hermeneutische Phänomenologie
muß auch nach dem Sinn der Rede von Gott fragen, aber sie kann
dieses (in bloß "mitanleitender Korrektion") nur so tun, daß sie die
theologischen Antworten zurückbezieht auf Fragen, die jeder
Mensch hat, und dabei offen läßt, ob es "Gott" überhaupt gibt.

Es charakterisiert die Großzügigkeit Husserls, daß er mit Heidegger seinen besten, freilich gar nicht orthodoxen Schüler als
Nachfolger nach Freiburg holte. Die Arbeitsgemeinschaft, die man
anstrebte, ließ sich schließlich doch nicht herstellen. 1931 griff Husserl Heideggers "Anthropologismus" in einer großen Berliner Rede
öffentlich an; Heidegger hielt zwar in Freiburg zuerst noch
Lehrveranstaltungen, die er—in Huldigung an den genius loci—
phänomenologisch nannte. Aber gerade in dem Augenblick, in dem
er mit der Veröffentlichung von "Sein und Zeit" an die Spitze der
phänomenologischen Bewegung trat und an seine Heimatuniversität
zurückkehrte, geriet sein Denken in eine ganz neue Bewegung.
Heidegger drückte das später so aus, daß er sagte, Nietzsche sei ihm
zur Entscheidung geworden: Nietzsche mit seiner Lehre vom "Tode
Gottes," vom endgültigen Kraftloswerden jenes Scheins, den der
metaphysische und der christliche Gott und die Werte, die man von
ihm ableitete, noch in die Krise des Abendlandes warfen.

In dieser Situation wurde Heidegger—selber reichlich
unpolitisch—konfrontiert mit dem "Aufbruch", der sich 1933 als
national-sozialistische Revolution durchsetzte. Im April 1933 wurde
Heidegger vom Plenum der Freiburger Universität einstimmig zum
Rektor gewählt. Er nahm das Amt an, und es folgte eine hektische
Zeit—auch mit Propagandareden unter Hakenkreuzfahnen in frem-
den Städten, vor allem mit der rektoralen Bestätigung, der neue
Wille der Studentenschaft habe längst die müden Reaktionen der
Professoren überholt, usf. Doch schon in der Ruhepause der
Weihnachtsferien, zur Jahreswende 1933/34, wurde es Heidegger
klar, daß sein Engagement ein Irrtum war; die Zumutung, Dekane zu
entlassen, führte dann zum Rücktritt.

Für das Sommersemester 1934 hatte Heidegger eine
Lehrveranstaltung über das Wesen des Staates angekündigt; er las

dann—eine schneidende Absage—"Logik". Unter dem Titel "Logik" behandelte er aber die Frage nach dem Wesen des Logos und der Sprache, und diese Frage entfaltete er in der Hölderlin-Vorlesung vom Winter 34/35 weiter. Das Wesen der Dichtung, so hieß es, werde verfehlt, wenn man Dichtung auf die Erlebnisse eines Individuums (Dilthey) zurückführe oder kollektivistisch als Ausdruck einer Kulturseele (Spengler) und schließlich einer Rassenseele (Rosenberg) fasse. "Der Schriftsteller Kolbenheyer sagt: 'Dichtung ist eine biologisch notwendige Funktion des Volkes'. Es braucht nicht viel Verstand, um zu merken: das gilt auch von der Verdauung, auch sie ist eine biologisch notwendige Funktion eines Volkes, zumal eines gesunden. Und wenn Spengler die Dichtung als Ausdruck der jeweiligen Kulturseele faßt, dann gilt dies auch von der Herstellung von Fahrrädern und Automobilen. Das gilt von allem—d.h. es gilt nicht. Diese Bestimmung bringt den Begriff der Dichtung schon durch den Ansatz in einen Bereich, wo die leiseste Möglichkeit einer Wesensauffassung hoffnungslos dahin ist. Das alles ist so trostlos flach, daß wir nur mit Widerwillen davon reden." Damals öffentlich so über Rosenberg und Kolbenheyer zu sprechen, dazu gehörte wohl mehr Mut, als all den Mitläufern der Ideologie der vergangenen Jahre nötig war, die Heidegger mit Kolbenheyer zusammenstellten. Zu recht konnte Heidegger fordern, daß man nicht nur an seine kurzfristige, wenn auch verhängnisvolle Tätigkeit als Rektor erinnert, sondern auch an den bald folgenden Versuch, die "geistigen", nämlich ungeistigen Grundlagen des Nationalsozialismus aufzudecken.

Heidegger blieb damals freilich bei der Auffassung, daß ein grundsätzlicher Wandel nötig sei, daß Deutschland seinen eigenen Weg finden müsse. In einer zweiten Hölderlinvorlesung legte Heidegger 1942 dar, daß die "Antigone" des Sophokles (gemäß der Übersetzung und Deutung Hölderlins) von einer Wende der Zeit spreche, daß es in Hölderlins Hymnen wieder um diese Wende gehe, daß somit Sophokles und Hölderlin die Dichter jener "Geschichtlichkeit" seien, die die Auszeichnung "abendländischen Menschentums" ausmache. Mit Hölderlin radikalisierte Heidegger noch einmal—als die deutschen Truppen Stalingrad erreichten, die "Endlösung" der Judenfrage eingeleitet worder war—den Griechenlandmythos der Goethezeit: wenn die Deutschen ihr "Eigenes" frei gebrauchen lernten, dann könne es sein, daß den Göttern (wie Heidegger mit einer Variante des Gedichts "Der Gang aufs Land"

sagte) ein "Gast-Haus" und "Stift gestiftet und gebaut" werde,
"dem die Tempel der Griechen nicht mehr nachkommen".

Der Nationalsozialismus wurde für Heidegger zum Modellfall des
Totalitarismus, so aber zu einem bloßen Vorspiel dessen, womit die
Zukunft uns bedrohen kann. Nur ein Verwinden jener "Metaphysik", die mit Platon so groß begann und im Nihilismus endete,
könne auf andere Bahnen führen. Mit der Forderung einer "Kehre"
prägte Heidegger nach dem Zweiten Weltkrieg noch einmal für zwei
Jahrzehnte das kontinentaleuropäische Denken. Diese Wirkung ist
auch deshalb erstaunlich, weil Heidegger im wesentlichen
exoterische Arbeiten veröffentlichte: als ein Denker, der vom eigenen Denken schweigen kann, gab er allenfalls spärliche An-
deutungen jener zentralen Gedanken vom "Ereignis", die er schon
in der Einsamkeit der dreißiger Jahre ausgearbeitet hatte. Was hätten jene Jahrzehnte, in denen Europa nach einer furchtbaren Katas-
trophe sich durch den Rückgriff auf das Bewährte wieder
aufzurichten suchte und dabei Heideggers Denken in unterschied-
liche Dienste stellte, auch dazu gesagt, daß Heidegger sein
Hauptwerk aus den dreißiger Jahren (die immer noch unpublizierten
"Beiträge zur Philosophie") enden läßt mit Gedanken über den
"Vorbeigang" des "letzten Gottes"—jenes Gottes, der nicht
metaphysisch als höchstes Seiendes zum Stehen zu bringen ist, der
zwar das gewesene Göttliche in ein Letztes sammelt, aber nicht der
Letzte einer Reihe ist, sondern allein erfahren wird, wenn der
Mensch das Letzte und Äußerste des Todes aussteht? "Das Ereignis
und seine Erfügung in der Abgründigkeit des Zeit-Raumes ist das
Netz, in das der letzte Gott sich selbst fängt, um es zu zerreißen und
in seiner Einzigkeit enden zu lassen—göttlich und seltsam und das
Fremdeste in allem Seienden.

Heidegger konnte bestimmte philosophische Gedankengänge in
vorbildlicher Klarheit seinen Hörern und Lesern nahebringen; für
seine zentralen Gedanken galt das nicht. Er glaube, so konnte er
deshalb selber sagen, alles beisammen zu haben von dem, was er zu
denken suche; wie aber solle er es sagen? Man könne doch nicht
dichten, so fügte er mit halb ironischem, halb hilflosem Lächeln
hinzu. Hier aber riß der Faden zwischen Heidegger und der Zeit.
Diese Zeit konnte es nicht akzeptieren, daß Heidegger einen Band
"Unterwegs zur Sprache" mit einem bißchen Aristoteles und Humboldt und dann mit Gedicht-interpretationen und allzu schwierigen

eigenen Wendungen bestritt, aber vorbeiging an der Hermeneutik, Semiotik und Sprachanalytik, die die Zeit als ihre Leistungen glaubte vorweisen zu können. "In meiner Studentenzeit", so bemerkte Heidegger brieflich dazu, "habe ich bei der Vorbereitung meiner Dissertation Russels Principia mathematica und Frege studiert und dabei erkannt, daß hier für die mich—freilich noch sehr ungeklärt—bewegenden Fragen keine Hilfe zu erwarten sei." Der Neomarxismus, manche Motive Heideggers aufnehmend, drückte Heidegger dann ganz aus der Diskussion. Aber während man in den zwölf letzten Lebensjahren Heideggers von Heidegger in Deutschland schwieg, blieb man ihm in Frankreich oder Japan näher, zeigte sich ganz gegenläufig ein immer weiter wachsendes Interesse in den USA.

Mit Gelassenheit beobachtete Heidegger, wie man bei den deutschen Plänen für Universitätsgründungen "die Philosophie ganz hinten in die Ecke" stellte. "Es entspricht sogar dem Weltgeiste. Und die Denkenden müssen auf eine lange Zeit hinaus das Warten lernen und einsehen, daß man nicht für die 'Gesellschaft' denkt— sondern für einen Anderen, und nutzenlos dazu, und ohne weiter darüber zu sprechen." An den deutschen Universitäten selbst lehrte man seit langem, Heidegger habe sich verstiegen; aber Heidegger gab seine Weise des Fragens nicht auf. "Die Seinsfrage als 'Gratwanderung', so ist es, der Blick öffnet sich in die Höhe zum Himmel und zur Erde in die Tiefe; aber der Wanderer muß bedacht sein, nicht abzustürzen; vollends wenn es an den Abstieg geht, der schwieriger ist." Diese Formulierung von 1965 bekam 1973 noch ein Fragezeichen: "Ob die Seinsfrage eine 'Gratwanderung' ist, oder eher ein Rückgang in den Untergrund—soll offen bleiben."

Heidegger hatte sich, im Garten seines Freiburger Hauses unter den Bergen mit der Zähringer-Burg, sein "Altenteil" gebaut—ein kleines Haus, das von zwei alt gewordenen Menschen bewirtschaftet werden konnte. So sah man denn von dem kleinen Zimmer mit den nötigsten Büchern herüber zu dem großen, holzverkleideten alten Arbeitszimmer mit der Bibliothek. Immer aber war Heidegger noch voller Neugier für das, was sich philosophisch tat. Er konnte einen überraschen mit der Nachricht, daß er am Abend vorher an seinem kleinen Radio Apel gehört hatte—das "neue Chinesisch", das für ihn schließlich doch schon posthum war. Apels "Versuch der Harmonisierung verkennt doch die unüberbrückbare

Verschiedenheit der Fragestellungen''. Was hätte Heidegger gegenüber dem Versuch, sein Denken in eine zeitadäquate Transformation der Philosophie zu verrühren, auch anderes sagen können als
wiederum "So nicht"?

Heidegger hätte auch zu der Zeit, in der sein Denken in Deutschland aus der Diskussion verdrängt wurde, darauf hinweisen können,
daß er über die Wirkungen seines Philosophierens immer noch die
Diskussion mitbestimme. Er zog aber die Abgrenzung vor. Die
hermeneutische Philosophie, so sagte er, falle hinter das "Dasein"
wieder auf das "Bewußtsein" zurück, dem auch alle marxistische
"Bewußtseinsveränderung" sowie die "heute umlaufenden Phra-
sen" vom "Selbstverständnis" und der "Identität" verhaftet
blieben. Die hermeneutische Philosophie "ist ein gutes Gegenge-
wicht gegen die 'analytische Philosophie' und die Linguistik. Auf die
Dauer wird auch hier das Ge-Stell innerhalb der absterbenden 'Geisteswissenschaften' die Oberhand bekommen. Die soziologisch-
psychoanalytische Phraseologie hat sich im Journalismus bereits so
festgesetzt, daß alle noch bestehenden Dämme gegen die allgemeine
Verflachung von dieser gebrochen und von seichten Wassern
überspült werden.'' Daß auch die Frage nach der spezifischen Hermeneutik Freuds ein genuin philosophisches Anliegen sein könne,
lag außerhalb von Heideggers Gesichtskreis. Als Christen und Mar-
xisten sich in ihren Akademien anschickten, sich im Engagement für
Fortschritt und "wahren" Fortschritt zu übertreffen und gemeinsam
die Zukunft zu verehren, als man auch gegen den Stachel des Todes
glaubte löcken zu können, wenn man nur die Neuorganisation der
bestehenden, für alles Böse verantwortlichen Gesellschaft in die
Hand bekäme, war Heidegger in der Tat nicht mehr brauchbar. Es
wurde aber offenkundig, daß alles andere als eine "pessimistische"
Weltsicht im Spiel gewesen war, als Heidegger den Menschen bestimmt hatte als den "Nachbarn des Todes", der—als einziges unter
den bekannten Lebewesen—in der Nähe und aus der Nähe des
Todes leben kann, daraus auch die Freiheit gewinnen kann, sich für
eine andere Zukunft zu engagieren, ohne darin nur Frustrations
—und Aggressions—tendenzen auszuleben. Wenn im "Da-Sein"
des Menschen zusammen mit einem abgründigen Sichverbergen
jene "Lichtung" aufbricht, in der Seiendes in einem Sein stehen, der
Mensch eigens seine Zeit haben und dann auch z.B. Alter und Größe
der Welt berechnen kann, wenn auch Philosophie für das Ereignis

dieser Lichtung keinen "Grund" mehr beibringen kann, dann bleibt nach Heidegger der Dank die erste und angemessenste Antwort. Gerade in seinen letzten Lebensjahren ließ er keine Gelegenheit aus für den Hinweis, daß Dichten wie Denken mit diesem Dank zu tun haben und solches Danken dem Denken und Dichten vorausliegt.

Denken, so hatte Heidegger 1946 im "Brief über den Humanismus" geschrieben, ist selbst ein Handeln: es "vollbringt den Bezug des Seins zum Wesen des Menschen". Die Sprache—jene Zeichen, die die Wahrheit des Seins zeigen und nicht nur die Zeichen der Sprache im engeren Sinn des Wortes sind—ist das "Haus des Seins". Mit Platon (in der Betonung der freundlichen Nähe zum Dichter auch gegen ihn) werden in der Pathetik jener Jahre "die Denkenden und Dichtenden" die "Wächter dieser Behausung" genannt. Darum geht es, daß der Stein wie das Tier, der Mensch wie der Gott in der rechten Weise auch in der heutigen Welt der Menschen ihre Offenheit finden und so z.B. im Ist-Sagen der Sprache angesprochen werden können. Auf diese "Wächterschaft" konnte Heidegger auch in zurückhaltenderer Weise Hinweise geben—etwa wenn er bei Besuchen als sein Gastgeschenk zum Abschied die "Eisgeschichte" aus Stifters "Mappe meines Urgroßvaters" las. Man hat Heideggers Denken immer wieder mißverstanden als eine romantische Ablehnung der Technik, seine Seinsgeschichte als eine Verfallsgeschichte genommen, dabei aber Heideggers Hinweis überhört, daß die einzige Frage seines Denkens, die Seinsfrage, für ihn wesentlich Frage nach der Technik sei: Wie kommt es, daß der technische Bezug zum Seienden für die anbrechende Weltzivilisation noch für lange Zeit einen Vorrang hat? Wie können wir die Technik so annehmen, daß wir sie in ihre Grenzen einlassen und damit einmal wieder frei werden für ein mehr-als-technisches Weltverhältnis? Als Heidegger in seinen letzten Lebensjahren ein kurzes Vorwort zu der geplanten Gesamtausgabe seiner Werke ausarbeiten wollte, wurde daraus eine Schrift über neuzeitliche Wissenschaft und Technik im Umfang eines Buches. Dieses war immer wieder seine Mahnung: daß nicht die spektakulären Vernichtungspotentiale der Technik das Aufregende und Gefährliche sind, sondern die Weise, in der die Technik unerkannt und unscheinbar den ganzen Alltag durchdringt und alle überlieferten Lebensformen aushöhlt oder unterläuft. Auf diese Dinge macht Stifters Eisgeschichte aufmerksam—nicht durch eine Prognose, aber durch ein Bild, das zu denken gibt. Als ein

feiner Winterregen an den Bäumen vereist und ganze Wälder unter
der Eislast zusammenstürzen, kommt schließlich auch noch ein
Sturm auf. Die Leute fürchten noch schlimmere Verheerungen und
unbekannte Schrecken, aber der besonnene Arzt belehrt sie: manche Bäume würden noch fallen, die freilich in der Windstille sowieso
gefallen wären; der Wind würde aber das Eis von den Bäumen
schlagen und den Regen sich nicht an den Zweigen festsetzen lassen.
"So sei die Windstille, in der sich alles heimlich sammeln und
aufladen konnte, das Furchtbare und der Sturm, der das Zusam-
mengeladene erschütterte, die Erlösung gewesen." Diese wie jene
Möglichkeit zu sehen, auf Gefahr wie Chance in der heutigen
Veränderung des Gefüges der Welt zu achten,—für diese Aufgabe
hat Heidegger die große Tradition der abendländischen Philosophie
wieder in ein lebendiges Denken verwandelt.

The Origins of Heidegger's Thought*

JOHN SALLIS
Duquesne University

> *Delphi schlummert und wo tönet das*
> *grosse Geschik?*
> *Friedrich Hölderlin*
> *"Brod und Wein"*

Heidegger was among those for whom the untimely death of Max Scheler in 1928 brought an experience of utter and profound loss. In a memorial address, delivered two days after Scheler's death, Heidegger paid tribute to Scheler as having been the strongest philosophical force in all of Europe and expressed deep sorrow over the fact that Scheler had died tragically in the very midst of his work, or, rather, at a time of new beginnings from which a genuine fulfillment of his work could have come. Heidegger concluded the address with these words:

> Max Scheler has died. Before his destiny we bow our heads; again a path of philosophy fades away, back into darkness.[1]

Heidegger's death, however, seems different. It came not in the midst of his career but only after that career had of itself come to its

---

*Text of a memorial lecture presented at the University of Toronto on October 21, 1976 and at Grinnell College on November 12, 1977.

[1]The address is published in *Max Scheler im Gegenwartsgeschehen der Philosophie*, ed. P. Good (Bern: Francke Verlag, 1975).

conclusion. His last years were devoted to planning the complete edition of his writings, and he lived to see the first two volumes of this edition appear. The reception of his work seems likewise to have run its course, from violent criticism and misunderstanding to an appreciative assimilation of his work. Today Heidegger's thought is acknowledged as having been a major intellectual force throughout most of this century -- a force which has drastically altered the philosophical shape of things and given radically new impetus and direction to fields as diverse as psychology, theology, and literary criticism. But now, it seems, that impact is played out. Heidegger's thought, now assimilated, is being enshrined in the history of philosophy. It is as though a well-ripened fruit had finally dropped gently to the ground.

Perhaps, however, the death of a great thinker is never totally lacking in tragedy. For even if his life is lived out to its conclusion, as was Heidegger's, his work is never finally rounded out. The case of Socrates is paradigmatic, the philosopher engaged in questioning even throughout his final hours, exposing himself to the weight of the questions asked by his friends, and, most significantly, letting his positive thought, his "position," be decisively fragmented by a great myth just as it is about to be sealed forever. The work of a genuine thinker never escapes the fragmentation, the negativity, to which radical questioning exposes him; and death, when it comes, seals the fragmentation of his work. Death fixes forever the lack, the negativity, and testifies thus to the inevitable loss by casting that loss utterly beyond hope. Death brings philosophy to an end without being its end, its telos, its fulfilling completion. Death stands as a tragic symbol.

Even in its external appearance Heidegger's work is fragmentary. His book *Being and Time,* first published in 1927, remains unfinished, even though he always considered it his *magnum opus.* Moreover, its unfinished state is precisely such as to leave the entire project in suspension, for that part which remains unpublished is just the one in which Heidegger would actually have carried through the task for which the entire published part is only preparatory. Heidegger did not succeed in determining the meaning of Being in terms of time, and by ordinary standards *Being and Time*, falling short of its expressed goal, is a failure—or, at best, a torso. That failure is not redeemed by the later writings. To the extent that they take up and deepen the questioning of *Being and Time*, they do so only at the expense of still greater fragmentation. With Heidegger's death too a path of philosophy fades away, back into darkness. Though in a different way, Heidegger's work remains as tragically fragmentary as Scheler's.

Our response to Heidegger's death can be thoughtful -- rather than merely biographical -- only if we re-enact, as it were, a strand of this tragedy. To this end we need to release Heidegger's work from that seal of fragmentation brought by his death; that is, we need to let that fragmentation assume the positive aspect which it has in living thought. What is this positive aspect? It is that aspect which Heidegger designated by referring to his thought as *under way*.

If we would re-enact such thought, it is imperative that we understand what set it on its way -- that in response we might set out correspondingly. It is imperative also that we understand what sustained it on that way, what shaped the way itself -- that we too might keep to that way. We need, in other words, to understand the origins of Heidegger's thought.

This, then, is our primary question: What are the origins of Heidegger's thought? We shall deal with this question at three progressively more fundamental levels. These three levels correspond to three distinct concepts of origin. Initially, we shall take origin to mean historical origin and thus shall pursue the question of origins by asking about those earlier thinkers whose work was decisive for Heidegger's development. Secondly, we shall consider origin in the sense of original or basic issue, and accordingly shall attempt to delimit this issue and to indicate how it serves as origin. Finally, we shall understand origin in its most radical sense as that which grants philosophical thought its content. At the level of this most radical sense of origin, it is perhaps possible for death to regain a signifying power for philosophy which, despite all differences, could match that which it had among the Greeks.

I. The Historical Origins of Heidegger's Thought

Taking origin, first, in the sense of historical origin, we ask: Who are those thinkers whose work served to set Heidegger's thought on its way? If, in posing this question, we let the concept of origins expand into that of mere influences, then the question proves right away to be unmanageable. With the exception of Hegel, no other major philosopher has so persistently exposed himself to dialogue with the tradition. And if we began to count up influences, even excluding all lesser ones, we would have to name Dilthey, Nietzsche, Kierkegaard, German Idealism, Kant, Leibniz, Descartes, Medieval Scholasticism, and Greek philosophy, that is, virtually the entire philosophical tradition -- to say nothing of Heidegger's contemporaries nor of such poets as Pindar, Sophocles, Hölderlin, and Trakl, all of whom were profound influences on Heidegger. Clearly such reckoning up of influences comes to nothing unless we first grasp the basic engagement of Heidegger's thought -- that engagement on the basis of which he is then led to engage in his extended dialogue with nearly every segment of the tradition. Let us, then, pose our question in a more precise and restricted way: What are the historical origins of the basic engagement of Heidegger's thought? But the question is still inadequate. Engagement of philosophical thought involves two moments: It is an engagement *with some issue,* and it is an engagement with it *in some definite way.* In other words, engagement involves both issue and method, and it is of these that we need to consider the historical origins. Our question is: What are the historical origins from which Heidegger took over the issue and the method of his thought?

The method is that of phenomenology, and Heidegger took it over from his teacher Edmund Husserl. It was for this reason that Heidegger dedicated *Being and Time* to Husserl and therein expressed publicly his gratitude for the "incisive personal guidance" that Husserl had given him. In various later autobiographical statements Heidegger speaks of the fascination which Husserl's *Logical Investigations* had for him during his formative years and of the importance which his personal contact with Husserl had for his early development. In *Being and Time* phenomenology is explicitly identified as the method of the investigation; and in the recently published Marburg lectures of 1927 Heidegger works through almost the entire problematic of *Being and Time* under the title "Fundamental Problems of Phenomenology."

What exactly did Heidegger take over from Husserl? What is phenomenology? It is, in the first instance, the methodological demand that one attend constantly and faithfully to the things themselves. It is the demand that philosophical thought proceed by attending to things as they themselves show themselves rather than in terms of presupposed opinions, theories, or concepts. Consider the case of perception. There have been theories which claimed that, when we look at some object such as a desk, what we really see are merely impressions or sensations in our own mind. Within the framework of such a theory there can arise, then, the almost insuperable problem of trying to explain how such impressions confined within the mind can somehow be connected with real things outside the mind. This problem -- a problem arising from theory, not taken from the things themselves -- can, in turn, motivate the development of one or another version of idealism intended to preserve some sense of objectivity. By contrast, phenomenology demands that such problems and the theories by which they are generated be put aside, set out of action. The phenomenological method involves, rather, attending to the perceptual object as it shows itself; it involves granting, against all constructivism, that what we perceive when we look at such an object as a desk is just the desk itself. It involves taking seriously, for example, the fact that perception of such objects is always one-sided, that we see only one profile of the desk at a time. It involves taking such a feature so seriously as to make it a basic determinant in the very concept of external perception.

Phenomenology is thus the appeal to the things themselves. And so, in *Being and Time* we find analyses such as that which Heidegger gives of tools. A tool, for instance, a hammer, normally shows itself within a certain context, namely, as belonging with other tools all suited to certain kinds of work to be done; only through a severe narrowing of perspective can we come to regard the hammer as a mere thing. Or, take the case of hearing; and consider: What sort of things do we usually hear? We hear an automobile passing, a bird singing, a fire crackling -- whereas, as Heidegger says, "it requires a very artificial and complicated frame of mind to 'hear' a pure noise."[2] Yet, as a method, phenomenology extends beyond the sphere of things even in this enriched sense: Whatever the matter *(Sache)* to be investigated, the phenomenological method prescribes that it be investigated through an attending to it as it shows itself. Thus, *Being and Time,* dedicated primarily to the investigation of that being which we ourselves are and which Heidegger denotes by the word "Dasein," proceeds by attending to the way in which Dasein shows itself. What complicates the methodological structure of Heidegger's work is the fact that Dasein is also the investigator so that it becomes a matter of Dasein's showing itself to itself. Nevertheless, this complexity does not render the investigation any less phenomenological.

On the contrary, in that project to which his investigation of Dasein belongs, Heidegger seeks to be more phenomenological even than Husserl himself. He seeks to radicalize phenomenology by adhering even more radically than Husserl to the phenomenological demand to attend to the things themselves. As he expresses it in a later self-interpretation, he sought "to ask what remains unthought in the appeal

---

[2]*Sein und Zeit* (Tübingen: Max Niemeyer Verlag, 1960⁹), p. 164.

'to the things themselves.' "[3] This dimension, tacitly presupposed in the phenomenological appeal to the things themselves, this dimension to which Heidegger's radical phenomenology would penetrate, constitutes the basic issue of Heidegger's thought.

What is this issue? What is fundamentally at issue in Heidegger's thought? One name for this issue -- perhaps not the best -- is Being. This name betrays immediately the historical origin from which Heidegger took the issue, namely, Greek philosophy, especially Plato and Aristotle. For it was in Greek philosophy that Being was most explicitly and most profoundly put at issue, in works such as Plato's *Sophist* and Aristotle's *Metaphysics*. Heidegger considers all subsequent reflections on Being, all later ontology, as a decline from the level attained by the great Greek philosophers: Gradually Being ceased to be held genuinely at issue, and what Plato and Aristotle had accomplished, what they had wrested from the phenomena, was uprooted from the questioning to which it belonged, became rigid and progressively emptier. *Being and Time* is thus cast explicitly as an attempt to raise again the question about Being. It is cast as a renewal, a recapturing, of the questioning stance of Greek philosophy. This is why it begins as it does: The very first sentence of *Being and Time* is a statement not by Heidegger but rather by the Eleatic Stranger of Plato's *Sophist,* a statement of his perplexity regarding Being. *Being and Time* literally begins in the middle of a Platonic dialogue.

Yet, on the other hand, *Being and Time* is no mere repeating of Greek philosophy. Heidegger does not seek to reinstate the work of Plato and Aristotle, as though historicity could just be set out of action in this exceptional case; nor does he propose merely to revive the questioning in which their work was sustained. In his lectures of 1935, later published as *Introduction to Metaphysics,* his intent is clear:

> To ask 'How does it stand with Being?' means nothing less than *to recapture* [wieder-holen] the beginning of our historical-spiritual Dasein, in order to transform it into a new beginning.... But we do not recapture a beginning by reducing it to something past and now known, which need merely be imitated; rather, the beginning must be begun again, more originally, with all the strangeness, darkness, insecurity that attend a true beginning.[4]

---

[3]*Zur Sache des Denkens* (Tübingen: Max Niemeyer Verlag, 1969), p. 71.

[4]*Einführung in die Metaphysik* (Tübingen: Max Niemeyer Verlag, 1958[2]), pp. 29 f.

Heidegger would take up more originally the beginning offered by Greek philosophy, take it up by taking it back to its sustaining origin, make of that beginning a new beginning.

The historical origins of Heidegger's thought, in the restricted sense specified, are thus constituted by Husserlian phenomenology and Greek ontology. From the former Heidegger's method is taken; from the latter it receives its fundamental issue. However, method and issue are not simply unrelated. Rather, as we have already noted, Heidegger's penetration to what becomes the fundamental issue for his thought is, by his own testimony, an attempt to radicalize phenomenology, "to ask what remains unthought in the appeal 'to the things themselves.'" How is it that Being is what remains unthought in the appeal to the things themselves? How is it that a radical phenomenology must become ontology?

Let us consider again the characteristic approach prescribed by the dictum of phenomenology, "to the things themselves." What remains unthought here? What does the approach fail to take into account? The dictum prescribes that things are to be regarded as they show themselves. In thus attending to their showing of themselves — for example, in describing the one-sidedness with which external perceptual objects show themselves — what is lacking is attention to that which makes possible this showing. What remains unthought is the ground of the possibility of such showings as those to which phenomenology demands we attend.

But what kind of grounds are relevant here? In proposing to attend to the grounds of the possibility of phenomena, is Heidegger proposing that we investigate the things in themselves in order to establish, independently of their self-showing in perceptual experience, how their physical constitution makes it possible for them to show themselves — how, for example, they are capable of reflecting light which then strikes our retinas so as finally to produce sensations in us? Clearly this is *not* what he is proposing. For such an extension would amount to a relapse into pre-phenomenological investigation rather than a radicalization of phenomenology. If the advance to the grounds which make it possible for things to show themselves is to remain phenomenological, if it is to constitute a radicalization of phenomenology, then those grounds must themselves be such as can be brought to show themselves.

Consider again the example of a tool. What is required in order for a hammer to show itself, not merely as a physical thing like other physical

things, but in its specific character as a hammer? It is required that it be
linked up with a certain context of other tools, all oriented towards
certain kinds of work to be done—especially if, as Heidegger insists, the
hammer most genuinely shows itself as a hammer, not when I merely
observe it disinterestedly, but rather at the moment when I take it up
and use it for such work as it is suited to. In order for the hammer to
show itself as a hammer (when I take it up and use it), there must be
already constituted a context from out of which it shows itself—that is,
a system of involvements or references by which various tools and
related items belong together in their orientation, their assignment, to
certain kinds of work to be done. Such a system of concrete references is
an example of what Heidegger means by *world*.

So, what exactly is required in order that it be possible for the
hammer to show itself as such? What is the ground of the possibility of
the showing? It is required that there be something like a world from out
of which the tool can show itself and, more significantly, that that world
be *disclosed* in advance to the one to whom the tool would show itself.
The hammer can show itself to me in that action in which I take it up and
use it *only if* the system of involvements by which tools and tasks are
held together is one with which I am already in touch, only if it is already
disclosed to me. More generally, the ground of the possibility of things
showing themselves is a prior disclosure of a world, of an open domain
or space, for that showing. Radical phenomenology, as Heidegger
pursues it, would penetrate to the level of such disclosure.

Still, however, it is not clear why radical phenomenology must
become ontology. How is it that the investigation of such fundamental
disclosure comes to coincide with a renewal of questioning about Being?
This connection can be seen only if we consider with more precision just
how Being is put at issue in *Being and Time*. What is asked about in the
questioning of Being in *Being and Time*? It is the *meaning* of Being that
is asked about. But what is asked about in asking about meaning? What
is meaning? According to the analyses in *Being and Time* in which the
concept of meaning is worked out, meaning is that from which (on the
basis of which) something becomes understandable. To ask about the
meaning of Being is thus to ask about how Being becomes
understandable for us; it is to ask about Dasein's understanding of
Being. Yet, understanding of Being is, in general, that which makes
possible the apprehension of beings as such. Hence, to question about
the meaning of Being, about Dasein's understanding of Being, is to ask

about that understanding which makes it possible for Dasein to apprehend beings. It is to ask about that understanding which makes it possible for beings to show themselves to Dasein — that is, about that understanding which constitutes the ground of the possibility of things showing themselves. It is to ask about the opening up of the open space for such showing, about the disclosure of world, about *disclosedness.* To ask about the meaning of Being is to ask about Dasein's disclosedness.

We see, therefore, how ontological questioning and radical phenomenology converge in the basic problem of disclosedness. This matter of disclosedness is the fundamental issue. In it the issue and method which Heidegger takes over from his historical origins are brought together and radicalized. It is this issue, disclosedness, that can thus more properly be called the origin of Heidegger's thought.

II. The Original Issue of Heidegger's Thought

By thinking through the way in which Heidegger takes over his historical origins, we have come upon a second, more fundamental sense of origin, namely origin in the sense of original issue, the issue from which originates Heidegger's approach to other issues and his extended dialogue with the tradition. This issue is disclosedness.

In the various existential analyses in *Being and Time* it is readily evident that disclosedness is the original issue. For example, Heidegger's analysis of moods aims at exhibiting moods as belonging to us, i.e., to Dasein, in a way utterly different from the way in which redness belongs to a red object, different even from the way in which so-called inner states such as feelings have usually been taken to belong to man. He seeks to exhibit moods in their disclosive power, to exhibit them as belonging to Dasein's fundamental disclosedness. His analysis seeks to show that, among other functions, moods serve to attune us to the world, to open us to it in such a way that things encountered within that world can matter to us in some definite way or other — in such fashion that, for instance, they can be encountered as threatening.

Heidegger's analysis of understanding is similarly oriented. Understanding is regarded not as some purely immanent capacity or activity within a subject but rather as a moment belonging to Dasein's disclosedness. Understanding is a way in which Dasein is disclosive. In understanding, Dasein projects upon certain possibilities, comports itself toward them, seizes upon them as possibilities; and from such possibilities Dasein is, in turn, disclosed to itself, given back, mirrored back, to itself. Dasein is given to understand itself through and from these possibilities. In addition, the possibilities on which it projects are disclosive in the direction of world, most evidently in the sense that they prescribe or light up certain contextual connections pertaining to the realization of the possibilities. When, for example, I project upon the possibility of constructing a cabinet, not only do I understand myself as a craftsman but also this possibility lights up and orients the context within the workshop.

Heidegger's analysis of death also remains within the compass of the issue of disclosedness, and indeed this is why it is so revolutionary. According to this analysis death is Dasein's ownmost and unsurpassable possibility; it is that possibility which is most Dasein's own in the sense that each must die his own death, and it is unsurpassable in the sense that Dasein cannot get beyond its actualization to still other possibilities; it is the possibility in which what is at issue is the loss of all possibilities. Heidegger's analysis focuses specifically on Dasein's comportment to this possibility, its projection on it, its Being-toward-death. Such projection is an instance of understanding, that is, it is a mode of disclosedness. In Being-toward-death Dasein is, in a unique way, disclosed to itself, given back to itself from this its ownmost possibility. Precisely because it is a mode of disclosedness, Dasein's Being-toward-its-end is utterly different, for instance, from that of a ripening fruit.

Thus, **disclosedness** is the original issue in Heidegger's analyses of Dasein. Through these analyses Heidegger seeks to display the basic ways in which Dasein is disclosive and to show how these various ways of being disclosive are interconnected. Indeed, not every basic moment displayed in the analyses of Dasein is simply a way of being disclosive. Yet even those structural moments that fall outside of disclosedness proper are still related to it in an essential way. More precisely, such moments are related to disclosedness in such a way that their basic character is determined by this relation.

Consider that moment which Heidegger calls "falling." This is the moment which he seeks to display through his well-known descriptions of the anonymous mass *("das Man")* -- his descriptions of how it ensnares the individual by its standard ways of regarding things and speaking about them; how it entices the individual into a conformity in which everything genuinely original gets leveled down and passed off as something already familiar to everyone; how, more precisely, it holds Dasein from the outset in a condition of self-dispersal and opaqueness to itself. What does this moment, this falling toward the rule of the anonymous mass, have to do with disclosedness? It has everything to do with it, because it is nothing less than a kind of counter-movement to disclosedness. It is a propensity toward covering up, toward *concealment*. This counter-movement toward concealment is essentially connected with Dasein's disclosedness. The connection is best attested by the issue of authenticity: Dasein's own genuine self-disclosure, the opening up of a space for its self-understanding, takes the form of a recovery of self from that dispersal in which the self and its possibilities are concealed beneath that public self that is no one and those possibilities that are indifferently open to everyone. Dasein must wrest itself from concealment.

Thus, Dasein's disclosedness is no *mere unopposed* opening of a realm in which things can show themselves. On the contrary, there belongs to that disclosedness an intrinsic opposition; there belongs to it a contention, a strife, between opening up and closing off, between disclosing and concealing.

Disclosedness, thus understood, is the original issue not only in the Dasein-analytic of *Being and Time* but also in Heidegger's later work. In order to grasp this continuity, we must consider a basic development which Heidegger's work undergoes after *Being and Time*. We should note, first, that already in the earlier work Heidegger brings the Dasein-analytic explicitly into relation with the problem of truth. He identifies the concept of disclosedness with that of truth in its most primordial sense; he presents disclosedness or original truth as constituting the ground of the possibility of truth in that ordinary sense related to propositions and the things referred to in propositions. Hence, the strife intrinsic to disclosedness may also be termed the strife of truth and untruth. For truth in this original sense, as that opening which provides the basis on which there can be true or false propositions regarding the things that show themselves in that opening – for truth in this sense Heidegger appropriates the Greek word ἀλήθεια.

In his later work Heidegger speaks of the original issue primarily in these terms, in terms of original truth or ἀλήθεια instead of disclosedness. And, though the issue remains the same, there is, nevertheless, behind this shift in terminology a fundamental development. What is the development? It may be regarded as a progressive separation of two phenomena which in *Being and Time* tended to coalesce. Specifically, Heidegger comes in the later work to dissociate truth from Dasein's self-understanding -- that is, he dissociates the contentious opening up of a realm in which things can show themselves (i.e., truth) from the movement of self-recovery by which Dasein is given to itself. The happening of truth is set at a distance from the reflexivity of human self-understanding. But original truth remains for Heidegger the original issue; and so, with its dissociation from self-understanding, Heidegger's thought is set more decisively at a distance not only from German Idealism and the tradition which led to it but also from that idealistic path which Husserl himself followed in his later work.

Granted this development, the original issue of Heidegger's thought remains in the later work what it was from the beginning, namely, the opening up of a domain in which things can show themselves -- that is, the issue of original truth. Consider, for example, Heidegger's essay on the work of art. In this essay Heidegger opposes the modern tendency, stemming from Kant, to refer art to human capacities such as feeling that could be taken as having no connection with truth; contrary to such an approach, Heidegger seeks to show that original truth is precisely what is at issue in art. According to his analysis a work of art makes manifest the strife of truth. It composes and thus gathers into view truth in its tension with untruth. A work of art presents the strife between world, i.e., the open realm in which things can show themselves, and earth, i.e., the dimension of closure and concealment.

Heidegger's analysis of technology in his later works is similarly oriented. This analysis, which is something quite different from a sociological, political, or ethical reflection on technology, is directed, strictly speaking, not at technology as such but rather at what Heidegger calls the essence of technology. What is the essence of technology? It is simply a mode of original truth, the opening of a realm in which things come to show themselves in a certain way. It is, specifically, that opening in the wake of which nature comes to appear as a store of energy subject to human domination. It is that opening in which natural things show themselves as to be provoked to supply energy that can be accumulated, transformed, distributed, and in which human things show themselves as subject to planning and regulation. What is at issue in Heidegger's analysis of technology is that same original issue to which his thought is already addressed from the beginning. It is that issue in which converge his efforts to radicalize Husserlian phenomenology and to renew Greek ontology, the issue of disclosedness, of original truth.

III. The Radical Origin of Philosophical Thought

There is still a third sense of origin which we need, finally, to bring into play. This third sense is not such as to revoke what has been said regarding truth as the origin of Heidegger's thought. It is not a matter of discovering some origin other than truth but rather of deepening, indeed radicalizing, the concept of origin. It is a matter of grasping truth as radical origin.

In order to see how this final sense of origin emerges, we need to grasp more thoroughly the methodological character of the analyses of Dasein in *Being and Time*. Contrary to what might seem prescribed by the phenomenological appeal to the things themselves, Heidegger's analyses are not simply straight-forward descriptions of Dasein as it shows itself. Why not? Because ordinarily Dasein does not simply show itself. Rather, there belongs to Dasein a tendency toward self-concealment of the sort that Heidegger discusses, for example, in his analysis of falling. What does this entail as regards the method required of a philosophical investigation of Dasein? It entails that Dasein, rather than being merely, straightforwardly described, must be wrested from its self-concealment.

But how, then, we must ask, is the investigation to be freed of the charge of doing violence to the phenomena? How can such investigation claim to be phenomenological? How can it justify the claim of proceeding solely in accord with the manner in which the things themselves show themselves? There is only one way. The violence that is done must be a violence which Dasein does to itself rather than a violence perpetrated by the philosophical investigation. The wresting of ordinary Dasein from its concealment must be the work, not of a philosophical analysis which would inevitably distort it and impose on it something foreign, but of a latent disclosive power within Dasein itself. Heidegger is explicit about the matter: The philosophical analysis must, as it were, "listen in" on Dasein's self-disclosure; it must let Dasein disclose itself, as, for example, in anxiety. Attaching itself to such disclosure, the philosophical analysis must do no more than merely raise to a conceptual level the phenomenal content that is thereby disclosed.

This peculiar methodological structure is what determines the final sense of origin. How? By virtue of the fact that it simply traces out the connection of thought to its sustaining origin. More specifically, this structure prescribes that Dasein's self-disclosure is precisely what gives philosophical thought its content, what grants it, yields it up to thought. Dasein's self-disclosure, that self-disclosure on which philosophical thought "listens in," is thus the origin of that thought -- not just in the sense of being the central theme for that thought but rather in the sense of first granting to such thought that content which it is to think. Yet, Dasein's self-disclosure is simply a mode of Dasein's disclosedness as such -- that is, a mode of original truth. Truth is what grants to thought that content which it is to think. The origin of thought is original truth.

The genuine radicalizing of the concept of origins comes, however, only in the wake of the development that takes place in Heidegger's later work. Within the framework of *Being and Time* there is no difficulty involved in understanding how philosophical thought can attach itself to its origin, to original truth; for such truth, though perhaps merely latent, is not essentially removed from Dasein. Philosophical thought can attach itself to its origin, because that origin belongs latently to each of us, including whoever would philosophize. We are always already attached to original truth. The problem arises when, through the experience of the history of metaphysics, Heidegger comes in his later work, to dissociate truth from self-understanding. For this amounts to placing original truth at a distance from Dasein -- that is, at a distance from that thought whose origin that truth would be. Thus, Heidegger's later work has to contend with a separation between original truth and that thought to which it would grant what is to be thought. As a result, the granting becomes a problem. Truth, the origin of thought, essentially withdraws from thought, holds itself aloof. Truth is the *self-withdrawing origin of thought.* And thought, resolutely open to the radical concealment of its origin, lets itself be drawn along in the withdrawal. Here we arrive at the most radical sense of origin.

Heidegger's efforts to radicalize Husserlian phenomenology and to renew Greek ontology converge on truth, first, as the original issue or basic problem and then, finally, as the origin which grants philosophical thought as such. What is most decisive in this most radical concept of original truth is that truth so conceived withdraws from that very thought which it grants and engages. It withholds itself from thought.

What is remarkable is that the same may be said of death. It too withholds itself from thought, withdraws from every attempt to make it something familiar. In distinction from all other possibilities, death alone offers us nothing to actualize in imagination. It offers us no basis for picturing to ourselves the actuality that would correspond to it. It is sheer possibility, detached from everything actual, detached from us, self-withdrawing -- yet constantly, secretly engaging.

Death withdraws as does original truth -- withdraws while yet engaging us. And so, death has the power to signify original truth. Yet, the task of philosophy, the task to which Heidegger finally came, is to develop thought's engagement in such truth. And so, death, signifying original truth, signifies the end to which philosophy is directed. At this level death can become a positive symbol for philosophy.

Perhaps it is a more fitting memorial to Heidegger if, instead of merely dwelling on his death, we seek to restore to death its power to signify the end and thus the task of philosophy.

Heidegger and Husserl's *Logical Investigations*
In remembrance of Heidegger's last seminar (Zähringen, 1973)*

JACQUES TAMINIAUX
University of Louvain

It is known that the introduction of that work which made Heidegger famous and with respect to which he never ceased to gage the stages of his path of thinking, defined the method of investigation undertaken in that work to be phenomenological. It is also known that Heidegger recognized his debt to Husserl in the same text when he wrote at the end of the "Exposition of the Question of the Meaning of Being": "The following investigation would not have been possible if the ground had not been prepared by Edmund Husserl, with whose *Logische Untersuchungen* phenomenology first emerged."[1] In a footnote he added more specifically: "If the following investigation has taken any steps forward in disclosing the 'things themselves,' the author must first of all thank E. Husserl, who, by providing his own incisive personal guidance and by freely turning over his unpublished investigations, familiarized the author with the most diverse areas of phenomenological research during his student years in Freiburg."[2]

It is also known however that the same text combines with this recognition of debt a sense of departure from the "effective turn" taken

---

[1] *Sein und Zeit,* (Tubingen: Max Niemeyer Verlag, 8th edition, 1957, p. 38; *Being and Time,* translated by John Macquarrie and Edward Robinson (New York: Harper & Row, 1962), p. 62. Hereafter "SZ"; page-number in the English translation are given in parentheses.

[2] SZ, 389 (489).

*A French version of this article is appearing in *Revue Philosophique de Louvain* (1977).

by Husserl's investigations and from the "movement" which claimed him as authority. For example, in the following sentences: "Our comments on the preliminary conception of phenomenology have shown that what is essential in it does not lie in its *actuality* as a philosophical 'movement'. Higher than actuality stands *possibility*. We can understand phenomenology only by seizing upon it as a possibility."[3]

Heidegger's investigation alludes often to such a gratitude free of servility and to such an affinity not exempt of departure. The most explicit allusion of this kind is found in Section 10 in which Heidegger, distinguishing his analysis of Dasein from anthropology, psychology and biology, on the one hand admits that his plan for such an analysis owes much to Husserl's teachings and on the other hand deplores a certain fundamental omission in Husserl's interpretation of the "personality". The analysis of Dasein is indebted to Husserl for a two-fold teaching: "Edmund Husserl has not only enabled us to understand once more the meaning of any genuine philosophical empiricism; he has also given us the necessary tools. *'A-priorism'* is the method of every scientific philosophy which understands itself. There is nothing constructivistic about it. But for this very reason *a priori* research requires that the pheonomenal basis be properly prepared."[4] The very same analysis departs however from the literalness of Husserl's teaching. Unlike Descartes, who examines "the *cogitare* of the *ego,* only within certain limits", Husserl proposes "to grasp the kind of Being which belongs to *cogitationes."* Yet he does not see that such a grasp presupposes "the ontological question of the Being of the *sum,"* a task that he neglects just as Descartes does. Furthermore, even though Husserl requires for the unity of the person "a constitution essentially different from that required for the unity of things of nature", in spite of the fact that he distinguishes this constitution from any psychological problematic (because such a problematic consists in objectifying and in naturalizing the facts that it treats and because it does not recognize that consciousness' *Erlebniszusammenhang* is non-psychical in nature in so far as it is defined by the carrying out of those intentional acts which are called the *cogitationes*), the force of such a requirement and the sharpness of such a distinction are nonetheless harmed by a major

---

[3]SZ, 38 (62 f.).
[4]SZ, 50 (490).

weakness and indefiniteness as soon as what one calls innocently "the life of the *cogito*" or a set of *"Erlebnisse",* no matter how intentional they are recognized to be, is considered "as a 'given' whose being is not submitted to questioning."[5] Heidegger concedes that Husserl's concrete analyses of the "personality" constitution in his *Ideen* II are more rigorous and are presented in a more refined conceptual apparatus than Dilthey's analyses, whom Husserl praises for having "grasped the problems which point the way, and (for having seen) the directions which the work to be done would have to take"[6]; yet Heidegger deplores in both cases the fact that " 'life' itself as a kind of being does not become ontologically a problem".[7] Heidegger certainly does not overlook the fundamental difference between the investigations of Dilthey and of Husserl, the foundation of Husserl's problematic of the personality's constitution being pure intentional consciousness. But this difference remains inconclusive: it is not conclusive as long as the mode of being of the cogito, as well as that of the "life" for which it is characterized, are understood in accordance with a long unexamined tradition "in the sense of occuring and being-present-at-hand *(Vorhandenseins und Vorkommens)."*[8]

The traces of praise and of departure are numerous in *Sein und Zeit,* and perhaps the expression of the former takes on the whole a more modest form than that of the latter. Each commendation occurs in short footnotes, whereas every departure, even when it is only allusive, is to be found in the body of the text. Expressions of departure always refer to the same ontological blindness in Husserl's investigation, to the same lack of radicalness and to Husserl's constant acceptance of the massive and obscuring privilege of *Vorhandenheit* in his listening-in on Being.

The distance between Husserl and Heidegger is opened up in order to erode such a privilege. Thus the exposition of being-in-the-world in general as constitution of Dasein begins by posing that "because knowing has been given this priority, our understanding of its ownmost kind of being gets led astray, and accordingly being-in-the-world must be exhibited even more precisely with regard to knowing the world, and must itself be made visible as an existential 'modality' of being-in."[9] Yet

---

[5]SZ, 46-48 (71-73).
[6]SZ, 47 (489).
[7]SZ, 46 (72).
[8]SZ, 48 (74).
[9]SZ, 59 (86).

it is indisputable that Husserl associated the priority of knowledge with his idea of phenomenology, and it is precisely the anti-naturalistic, anti-psychologistic style and the lack of presuppositions in Husserl's search for an ultimate foundation in the immanence of consciousness which is alluded to in these lines: "Now the more unequivocally one maintains that knowing is proximally and really 'inside' and indeed has by no means the same kind of being as entities which are both physical and psychical, the less one presupposes when one believes that one is making headway in the question of the essence of knowledge and in the clarification of the relationship between subject and object. (...) But in any of the numerous varieties which this approach may take, the question of the kind of being which belongs to this knowing subject is left entirely unasked, though whenever its knowing gets handled, its way of being is already included tacitly in one's theme. Of course we are sometimes assured that we are certainly not to think of the subject's 'inside' and its 'inner sphere' as a sort of 'box' or 'cabinet'. But when one asks for the positive signification of this 'inside' of immanence in which knowing is proximally enclosed, or when one inquires how this 'being inside' which knowing possesses has its own character of being grounded in the kind of being which belongs to the subject, then silence reigns."[10]

Heidegger sets allusively a demarcation of the same kind over against the methodical starting point of Husserl's problematic, when he attempts to determine the starting point of the existential question: who is Dasein? An immediately understandable statement, one which is a matter of course, seems to provide a sure answer, ready to serve as starting point for the ontological interpretation of that entity which Dasein is. The statement is: the Who is none other than the "I" itself, the "subject", the "Self". Such a statement is a matter of course, self-evident. It is an ontical assertion which is understood immediately. It harbours implicitly however, concerning the Who that is being sought, an unexamined ontological interpretation, ordinary, acquired, therefore not radical and which, as such, misleads from the correct path of questioning. According to the unexamined ontological interpretation the "I" of which it has been asserted since Descartes that it is subject and to which the properties of ὑποκείμενον have long since been attributed, itself having become everyday and just as unexamined,

---

[10]SZ, 60 (87).

is conceived of as a "given" which is always already there, which persists constantly in a "closed realm," "which lies at the basis, in a very special sense, as the *subjectum*."[11] In short, only that mode of being called *Vorhandenheit* is attributed to the "I" which is supposed to be "subjective." Access to Heidegger's question, "Who is Dasein?" is consequently barred, since the question itself implies that *Vorhandenheit* is the mode of being of that entity which is not of the same kind as Dasein. The phenomenological interpretation of Dasein could only diverge from the path that the question "Who is Dasein?" recommends, in taking as starting point the "I," thus "given," being there, present, subsistant, *vorhanden*. It is at this juncture precisely that Heidegger's phenomenological method turns most deliberately away from that "effective reality," the regulations of which Husserl had established. Heidegger is fully aware of these regulations, and in fact considers and rejects the prejudicial objection of these regulations in the following lines: "But is it not contrary to the rules of all sound method to approach a problematic without sticking to what is given as evident in the area of our theme? And what is more indubitable than the givenness of the 'I'? And does not this givenness tell us that if we aim to work this out primordially, we must disregard everything else that is 'given'--not only a 'world' that is, but even the being of other 'I's? The kind of 'giving' we have here is the mere, formal reflective awareness of the 'I'; and perhaps what it gives is indeed evident. This insight even affords access to a phenomenological problematic in its own right, which has in principle the signification of providing a framework as a 'formal phenomenology of consciousness.' "[12] The effective reality of Husserl's methodical regulations is exactly what is alluded to here. Yet such regulations, no matter what guaranties of certitude Husserl pretends to associate with them, ought themselves be examined. What if this so-called "givenness" were to mask rather than to reveal Dasein? And what if Dasein were not a given? Is not being "given" what characterizes commonly *Vorhandenheit?* Even if the "I" were to be cut off from its relation to the world and its ties to others in order to assure its privileged status, it would still permit the modality of being called *Vorhandenheit* to subsist as eminent, exclusive and misleading.[13]

These considerations and citations suffice to show that the claims of

---

[11]SZ, 114 (150).
[12]SZ, 115 (151).
[13]SZ, 115 (151).

Vorhandenheit set the stage for Heidegger's debate with Husserl. Husserl's lack of vigilance with respect to the alleged universal admissibility of the traditionally evident claims of *Vorhandenheit* is what keeps him from posing the question "What does 'being' mean?" and is that which justifies in *Sein und Zeit* the numerous examples of departure from the effective turn taken by his master.

But then, how is it that the exposition of the question of the meaning of Being ends with this acknowledgment: "The following investigation would not have been possible if the ground had not been prepared by Edmund Husserl, with whose *Logische Untersuchungen* phenomenology first emerged"? If Heidegger's reasons for departing from Huserl's teaching in *Sein und Zeit* are now clear, it is on the other hand difficult to see how his working out the question of the meaning of Being can lay claim to a foundation established by Husserl, to a "ground" *(Boden)* that the author of the *Logical Investigations* is supposed to have prepared. When he mentions Husserl's first work in a kind of acknowledgment of affinity and when on the other hand all the elements of departure appear to be aimed at a problematic and a methodology of Cartesian inspiration that Husserl expressly establishes only after the *Logical Investigations,* then Heidegger seems to be claiming that the *Logical Investigations* deserve special attention. Yet even this hardly justifies the reasons for any special consideration.

If on the other hand those texts are considered in which Heidegger accounts several decades later for the situation of his thinking with respect to Husserl, then it must be asserted that the privileged role of the *Logical Investigations* in the genesis of the question of being is repeated and confirmed, even if the reasons for this priority remain obscure and enigmatic. Reminiscing in his homage to Hermann Niemeyer on his "way to phenomenology", Heidegger insists once again on the importance that the *Logical Investigations* had for the clearing of this way. The journey itself, he insists, was incited by a still imprecise question which arose out of his reading of Brentano's dissertation "On the multiple meaning of the entity according to Aristotle" (1862) in 1907. The first version of the question was: "If an entity has a multiple meaning, what then is the leading and fundamental meaning?" Moved by this question, the young student Heidegger, having meanwhile learned that Husserl was in some way a disciple of Brentano, decided already in his first semester of university studies (1909-1918) to study the *Logical Investigations,* expecting "decisive assistance for the questions arising from Brentano's dissertation."[14] It was at first a dissappointing wait and search. However, Heidegger continues, "I remained so bewildered by Huserl's work that I continued in the ensuing years to read from it over and over again, without sufficient insight into what captivated me."[15] His capitation indeed was supported by a two-fold movement of attraction and reservation: of an attraction determined by the feeling that an unprecedented insight was to be found in the book; and of a reservation determined by a "fundamental difficulty" resulting "from the discordant character *(Zwiespältigkeit)* that Husserl's work presented at first glance." The book refutes on the one hand all pretentions of psychology to found a theory of knowledge, yet then proceeds to assign an important place to a kind of psychology, *i.e.* to the description of those essential acts of consciousness upon which knowledge is founded. Heidegger maintains that this indecision in the *Logical Investigations* as to the manner in which phenomenology should be accomplished, *i.e.* as to the relation of the phenomenological task to the realms of consciousness, was removed in 1913 with the publication of the *Ideas*. Here, Heidegger says, "phenomenology consciously and resolutely fell into line with the tradition of modern philosophy," that is, with subjectivity as the proper site and proper theme of phenomenological enquiry. The famous call *Zur Sache selbst,* according to another text of approximately the same late period, subordinates the Thing towards which it directs the phenomenologist's attention to the primacy of method, in such a manner that the *Sache* is phenomenologically admissible only to the extent to which it satisfies the methodological requirements of validity which were expressed for the first time by Descartes and which deem that the only entity the presence of which is indisputably valid is the *ego cogito,* in relation to which the being of other entities can be determined.[16] But the text in homage to Niemeyer lets it be known that the *Logical Investigations* were still "philosophically neutral" as to the project of a transcendental phenomenology which leads to the "reduction" of the being of entities to an objectivity founded or constituted in and by an absolute subjectivity. The text suggests that it was only later that the *Logical Investigations* found their systematic position in such a project.[17] It was

---

[14]*Zur Sache des Denkens* (Tubingen: Max Niemeyer Verlag, 1969), p. 82. Hereafter "SD."

[15]SD, 82.

[16]"Das Ende der Philosophie und die Aufgabe des Denkens", SD, 69-71.

[17]SD, 84-85.

only later that the programmatical explanations and methodical clarifications of transcendental phenomenology, consciously and resolutely inserted by Husserl in the tradition of modern philosophy of subjectivity, would have imposed the misleading idea that phenomenology has an origin which repudiates all thinking prior to the modern era of subjectivity.

Heidegger does not say that he was aware early in his own thought of the gap between the *Logical Investigations* and Husserl's later work. He recalls rather the quandary, the helplessness, the turmoil, the disquiet that was brought about in him by the question of knowing what was appropriate to phenomenology and to the manner in which that kind of thinking should be accomplished. His direct contact with Husserl, who in the meantime had taken a post at Freiburg, was going to remove this quandary to a certain extent. But if this contact, in Heidegger's own words, permitted him through practice to gradually learn "phenomenological seeing", it did not weaken at all the sharpness of the attention paid to the *Logical Investigations,* even though its author no longer found them perfectly tuned to the systematic setting of transcendental phenomenology's programme. And it is known that Heidegger gave seminars on the *Logical Investigations* for a number of years, once he had become Husserl's assistant.

So that is a book which captivated Heidegger for at least fifteen years.

Yet Heidegger's published work remains strangely reserved about the nature of his persistent captivation by the *Logical Investigations.* The fact that they had a germinative effect must be accepted if what *Sein und Zeit* called the "ground" upon which the question of the meaning of being was able to be conceived was indeed possible only in virtue of and through such a captivation. But this fact does not explain Heidegger's reasons. It may be agreed that his captivation was in no way foreign to the still imprecise question that the reading of Brentano's dissertation had awakened, that his captivation even contributed to the specification of that question; yet this alone is not enough to see what in Husserl fostered such a refinement. It should be admitted as well that Heidegger repeatedly re-examined the *Logical Investigations,* that his captivation by Husserl's text was accompanied by a simultaneous meditation on Aristotle and the Greeks, which finally resulted in a notion of phenomenon far removed from Husserl's deliberately Cartesian position. Yet to admit this is to say that Heidegger, at the end of his long consideration of the *Logical Investigations,* had learned that "what comes to pass for the phenomenology of acts of consciousness as the self-manifestation of phenomena is thought more originally by Aristotle and generally in the thinking and existence of the Greeks as ἀ-λήθεια as the unhiddenness of what is present, of its disclosure, its showing-itself."[18] It would be to admit that his attentive meditation on Husserl's text made possible a question which is no longer Husserl's, the question of knowing "from where and how is that determined which according to the principle of phenomenology must be experienced as 'die Sache selbst.' Is it consciousness and its objectivity, or is it the being of entities in its unhiddenness and hiding [*Unverborgenheit und Verbergung*]?"[19] But then, does that imply that his long captivation by the phenomenology of the *Logical Investigations* had been nothing more than the gradual becoming aware of the truth that a phenomenon is not what Husserl thinks it to be? A negative captivation, providing for the apprentice the possibility to think in opposition to his master? Yet if that be the case, how can Heidegger's own acknowledgment be understood, that he had discovered the positive "ground" for his investigation in *Sein und Zeit* in the phenomenology of the *Logical Investigations*? Where is there an affiliation if the apprenticeship is only the gradual justification for a departure without return?

All these questions can be condensed into a single formula: Is there something in the *Logical Investigations* which anticipates in a positive sense the *Seinsfrage*? Is there in other words something like an indication of a true break from the obsession for *Vorhandenheit* in Husserl's phenomenology? There is in fact in Heidegger's published work only a fragment of an answer to this question. In *Mein Weg in die Phanomenologie* the following passage can be found: "When I myself began to practice phenomenological seeing, teaching-and-studying at Husserl's side, experimenting at the same time with a new understanding of Aristotle in seminars, my interest began to be drawn again to the *Logical Investigations,* and especially to the sixth in the first edition. The difference between sensuous and categorial intuitions, worked out in that *Investigation,* revealed to me its importance for the determination of the 'multiple meaning of the entity'."[20]

This allusion is of capital importance, and for two reasons. It indicates first of all the passage upon which Heidegger's attention

---

[18]SD, 87.
[19]SD, 87.
[20]SD, 86.

finally converged: the sixth *Investigation* with its distinction between sensuous intuition and categorial intuition. It indicates furthermore that the path which was cleared beneath Heidegger's fascinated look was the very same path which led from the determination of the theme imposed forever upon Heidegger's thinking itinerary by the reading of Brentano's dissertation, the very path upon which the *Seinsfrage* had to be articulated. If Husserl's establishment of the difference between sensuous intuition and categorial intuition had finally proven to be of decisive importance for the articulation of the question of the meaning of being, then one understands that Heidegger, at a time when Husserl no longer had a very high opinion of his own book, had his "reasons," as he states elsewhere very discreetly, "for preferring the *Logical Investigations* as an introduction to phenomenology."[21] However, nothing in Heidegger's written work shows how the difference introduced by the sixth *Investigation* established the "ground" for the *Seinsfrage*. Something, on the other hand, can be found in his oral work.

The last seminar held by Heidegger (Zähringen, 1973) proposed to attempt to find access to the *Seinsfrage* through Husserl. The starting point of the seminar was a letter by Jean Beaufret, who asked in particular: "To what extent may it be asserted that there is no question of being for Husserl?" Heidegger developed his answer along two lines. He maintained first of all that, strictly speaking, there is no *Seinsfrage* for Husserl. Because it is a property of the question of being that it be transformed into the question of truth, such a question completely eludes metaphysics. "Metaphysics is in quest of the being of entities. The *Seinsfrage* aims essentially at, if it is legitimate to speak in such a fashion, the being of being, or better: the truth of being, *Wahrheit des Seins,* where *Wahrheit* must be understood according to the protection in which being is guarded as being. In this rigorous sense, there is no *Seinsfrage* for Husserl. Husserl treats strictly metaphysical problems, for example the problem of categories."[22] Nonetheless, Heidegger concedes at once, "Husserl touches lightly, brushes the question of being in the sixth chapter of the sixth *Logical Investigation,* with the notion of categorial intuition." Particular attention was paid during the first part of the seminar to the task of understanding what it was in this

---

[21] *Unterwegs zur Sprache,* (Pfullingen: Neske, 1959), pp. 90-91.
[22] "Le seminaire de Zähringen" in *Questions IV,* pp. 310-311.

notion which was so "burning" for the articulation of the *Seinsfrage*. An accurate transcript of the seminar's proceedings has been published by François Fédier. We would like to attempt in the following pages to confront, at our own risk, the information provided by Heidegger in a necessarily allusive manner and rendered accurately in the protocol, with that text of Husserl to which reference is made. We would also like in the process to examine closely, in the course of the sixth chapter of the sixth Investigation, the grounds for the captivation that the text elicited from Heidegger at the time when he was attempting to articulate his question phenomenologically.

* *

The sixth *Logical Investigation* is entitled: "Elements of a Phenomenological Elucidation of Knowledge". Chapter Six of this Investigation begins with a section the general title of which -- "Sensibility and Understanding" -- has a Kantian ring, a fàct that Heidegger was quick to point out. But the title of the sixth chapter, he added, --"Sensuous and Categorial Intuitions"-- was not really Kantian at all. For Kant, intuition is strictly bound to sensibility and a categorial intuition would be absolutely impossible. A category, in Kant's vocabulary, deduced from the table of judgements inherited from traditional logic, is in no way given to an intuition. The phrase "categorial intuition" on the other hand refers obviously to the intuitive givenness of a category. In spite of the Kantian style of the general setting of the sixth Investigation, the notion of "categorial intuition" denotes thus a certain passing-beyond Kant's setting, a passing-beyond which supposes a broadening of Kant's notion of givenness. Heidegger maintains that something like an anticipation, a brushing of the *Seinsfrage* takes place in Husserl by means of this broadening of the notion of givenness. In order to draw an outline of this anticipation, let us attempt to follow step by step the successive stages of Husserl's examination in Chapter Six, to which the seminar referred only allusively.

Generally speaking, the sixth Investigation has the problem of truth for theme at the same time that it attempts to clarify knowledge phenomenologically. In Husserl's terminology, the problem is that of interpreting those "objectifying acts" in which the intentionality of consciousness unfolds, in so far as these acts have the function not only of signifying an object emptily, but of leading to the real manifestation of the object as well, that is, to what, according to Husserl, the intuitive givenness of the object is in its "identity." The problem of truth is therefore that of the synthesis by which the intuition fulfills the meaning-intention. It is in this setting of the problematic of synthesis and fulfilment that Husserl composes the sixth chapter.

The question which begins the chapter is formulated in the following way: "What may and can furnish fulfilment for those aspects of meaning which make up propositional form as such, the aspects of 'categorial form' to which, e.g., the copula belongs?" Such a form can be highly diverse in complexity, as is indicated by the utterances and the grammatical forms in which a proposition may be analysed (substantive, adjective, singular, plural, verb, adverb, etc.); Husserl admits that such utterances and forms refer to distinct instances of meaning. The question is precisely to know how these instances act in fulfilment. In order to answer this question, Husserl takes the simplest case, as is his custom in the *Logical Investigations,* that of a statement of perception, as provisional basis for examination.

Once it has become more specific by this simple basis, the question is transformed into "Are there parts and forms of perception corresponding to all parts and forms of meaning?"[23] If that is the case, answers Husserl, the expression, even if it is composed of a specific "matter," in other words the "stuff of meaning," would be somehow a "mirror," a twin, of the perception. A strict parallelism would reign between perception understood as fulfilling intuition and the specific matter understood as meaningful reference. It could of course be conceded that such a parallelism directs the relation of a proper meaning to its corresponding percept. In the case of proper meaning, that is of the meaning that a proper noun expresses, the meaning-intention corresponds immediately to the percept. "The direct perception" of the city of Cologne "renders the object apparent without the help of further, superordinate acts, it gives the object *which* the meaning-intention means, and *just as* the latter means it. The meaning-intention therefore finds in the mere percept the act which fulfils it with complete adequacy." But in the case of structured and articulated expressions, which therefore are no longer as simplistic as direct and proper naming, such a parallelism is according to Husserl out of the

---

[23]*Logical Investigations* tr. J.N. Findlay (New York: Humanities Press, 1970), vol. II, p. 774. Hereafter "L.I."

question. It is true that one is inclined to believe at first glance that a structured and articulated expression is merely the correctly adequate mirror of a percept: "I *see* white paper and *say* 'white paper', thereby expressing, with precise adequacy, only what I see."[24] This inclination is however deceptive. We are led astray, according to Husserl, when we believe in a coincidence of expression and perception to the extent that this coincidence leads one to think that meaning has its seat in perception, and instigates the obliteration of the complex chain of those acts inherent to vision and to meaning-intention. In the case at hand, several acts of meaning-intention are linked: that intention which refers to the white of the paper, that which refers to the paper as substance, that which refers to it as an entity, as a being. These intentions, rendered by those words used to express them, extend beyond the contents provided by pure and simple perception. As such, the contents are a rush of pure sensory givens, *Stoff* in Husserl's words in the *Logical Investigations*, a *hyle* in the terminology of his later works. Take for example the intention expressed by the word "white": "The intention of the word 'white' only partially coincides with the colour-aspect of the apparent object; a surplus of meaning remains over, a form which finds nothing in the appearance itself to confirm it." There is an excessiveness of white meant by the expression, with respect to the sensory given. Husserl calls this excessiveness a "form". Meaning has the function of a form which exceeds the contents of simple perception. Far from expressing a pure and simple seeing, a sentence expresses therefore a meaning which extends beyond what is simply seen. At the same time it is true that acts of relating, of unification, of formation are carried out on the basis of pure and simple perception, that is, the pure reception of sensory givens. Such acts, based upon the reception of the given, have a function of formal grounding with respect to the given, and they permit in virtue of this function the perception to have a cognitive essence; they perform in such a way that in perception "the apparent object announces itself as self-given."[25] The meaning-intentions denoted by the variable forms of expression are parallel to these formative, objectifying acts, and not at all to the pure and simple sensory given. The parallelism of the naive theory, which believes an expression to be the simple mirror of what is intuitively given, finds itself therefore not so

---

[24]LI, 775.
[25]LI, 776.

much repudiated as displaced. The parallelism no longer obtains "between the meaning-intention of expressions and the mere percepts which correspond to them: it is a parallelism between meaning-intentions and the above mentioned *perceptually founded acts*."[26] At the same time that it finds itself displaced, that is, re-established at another level, the parallelism is just as profoundly transformed. It no longer has the sense of a simple mirror, since now that which mirrors exceeds that which is being mirrored, since the meaning-intention is a kind of excess.

Nevertheless, this strange parallelism, in which the founded is in turn founder and excessive with respect to that upon which it is founded, in no way occasions in Hussel's investigations a questioning of the perspective which rules it. Husserl's perspective is and remains that of the synthesis of fulfilment between a meaning-intention and an intuition. Knowledge as such has for Husserl the character of fulfilment and identification, and his problem, since sensuous intuition even in the case of simple statements of perception cannot exercise the role of fulfilment, is to extricate a non-sensible intuitive realm which might exercise this role.

Such being the general perspective of the problematic and of its solution, it is first of all a matter of defining more specifically what-- as in the case of the statements of perception-- the "matter for perception" is and what the "matter for meaning" is; we need "to become aware that, *in the mere form of a judgement, only certain antecedently specifiable parts of our statement can have something which corresponds to them in intuition, while to other parts of the statement nothing intuitive possibly can correspond.*"[27]

Perceptual statements articulate utterances of varying pattern; "such as 'A is P', 'An S is P', 'This S is P', 'All S are P', etc." In such forms of judgement, it is easy to see, Husserl says, "that *only at the places indicated by letters (variables)* in such 'forms of judgement', *can* meanings be put that are themselves fulfilled in perception, whereas it is hopeless, even misguided, to look directly in perception for what could give fulfilment to our supplementary formal meanings." Yet in fact, "the same difference between 'matter' and 'form' " repeats itself even in letters (variables), as can be seen when they are replaced by the unitary

---

[26]LI, 776.
[27]LI, 778.

terms for which they are the substitutes. Once the variable (subject or predicate) is replaced by a term (this or that substantive, this or that adjective), it results that this term embraces simultaneously those elements of stuff which find their direct fulfilment in sensuous intuition and those "supplementary forms" which do not find direct fulfilment. Glancing over what Husserl calls "the whole sphere of objectifying presentation", there is therefore a fundamental difference between the sensible matter of presentation, the *Stoff* or *Hyle,* and the categorial form of presentation. In other words, the objective correlates of categorial forms are not "real" moments given as matter with the same sensible status as the perceived given.[28]

The same applies in a particularly clear manner to the category of "being", "the form-giving flexion", understood in an existential sense or in an attributive and predicative sense. Kant had always insisted that being is no real predicate. Husserl recalls and agrees with this thesis, which refers exactly to what he is trying to clarify. And he gives the following commentary: "I can see colour, but not *being*-coloured. I can feel smoothness, but not *being*-smooth. (...) Being is nothing *in* the object, no part of it, no moment tenanting it, no quality or intensity of it, no figure of it or no internal form whatsoever, no constitutive feature of it however conceived. But being is also nothing attaching *to* an object: as it is no real internal feature, so also it is no real external feature, and therefore not, in the *real* sense, a 'feature' at all. For it has nothing to do with the *real* forms of unity which bind objects into more comprehensive objects, tones into harmonies, things into more comprehensive things or arrangements of things (gardens, streets, the phenomenal external world). On these real forms of unity the external features of objects, the right and the left, the high and the low, the loud and the soft etc., are founded. Among these anything like an 'is' is naturally not to be found. (...) For all these are perceptible, and they exhaust the range of possible percepts, so that we are at once saying and maintaining *that being is absolutely imperceptible.*"[29] Absolutely imperceptible, that means that being is not something which is the "given" of sense-perception, in general, neither of external nor of internal perception.

---

[28]LI, 778 f.
[29]LI, 780 f.

Being is not the given correlate of any external sense-perception--we do not see it with our eyes, touch it with our hands, nor hear it with our ears, etc., nor furthermore is being perceived internally: it is not internally lived, it is not an *Erlebnis*. Husserl emphatically insists that, contrary to Locke and the empiricist tradition, the origin of the concept "being", like that of the other categories (the 'a' and the 'the,' the 'and' and the 'or,' the 'if' and the 'then,' the 'all' and the 'none,' the 'something' and the 'nothing,' etc.), is not in the realm of internal perception either. If a reflexion upon psychically lived experiences yields concepts such as Affirmation, Denial, Collecting, Counting, etc., if these concepts are for this reason sensible concepts, the same does not apply to categorial concepts, which are neither concepts of mental acts, nor of their real constituents. "The thought of a Judgement fulfils itself in the inner intuition of an actual judgement, but the thought of an 'is' does not fulfil itself in this manner. Being is not a judgement nor a constituent of a judgement."[30] The little word 'is' is certainly a real constituent of judgement, but the " 'is' itself" is completely different from this real constituent; it is in no way a part of the judgement; "the 'is' itself does not enter into the judgement, it is merely meant, signitively referred to, by the little word 'is.' "[31]

However, the " 'is' itself" is somehow given, even if not as a real constituent of the given correlate of external sense-perception, nor as a real constituent of internal lived experience, and in particular of judgement as mental experience. There is givenness of the " 'is' itself" when a state of affairs to which only reference is made in the meaning-intention inherent to the judgemental act *fulfils* the judgement, makes it true or adequate. "Not only what is meant in the partial meaning *gold*, nor only what is meant in the partial meaning *yellow*, itself appears before us, but also *gold-being-yellow* thus appears."[32] Such a state of affairs is not in the judgement itself; it is rather its objective correlate. The relation of this state of affairs, through which the " 'is' itself" is given to the act of *Gewahrwerdung*, of becoming aware, to which it is fitted, is conceived by Husserl according to the model of the relation of a sensible given to sensuous intuition. But the analogy preserves the notion of excessiveness obtained precisely from the case of the statement about

---

[30]LI, 782.
[31]LI, 782.
[32]LI, 782 f.

perception. The concept "red" exceeds any single red given sensorially. It is the sensible presence of any single red which founds the act of abstraction permitting the realisation of the concept, but this concept is inversely that in virtue of which such single red is recognised as red. The particular red is only given because red as such, the concept "red," is itself given, if only in a givenness which itself is not sensible. The same holds for every concept and especially the concept "being." "It is in fact obvious from the start that, just as any other concept (or Idea, Specific Unity) can only 'arise,' i.e. become *self-given* to us, if based on an act which at least sets some individual instance of it imaginatively before our eyes, so the concept of Being can arise only when *some being, actual or imaginary, is set before our eyes.*"[33]

The distinction between sensuous intuition and categorial intuition appears at this juncture in Husserl's analysis. The distinction itself is Husserl's answer to the question of knowing "where do the categorial forms of our meanings find their fulfilment, if not in the 'perception' or 'intuition' which we tried provisionally to delimit in talking of 'sensibility,'[34] that is, in "perception" or "intuition" in the sense of an affection by a given sensible matter, or a sensorial *hyle*, Husserl's thesis, in response to this question, is that the meanings of categorial form really find their fulfilment, not of course in perception understood in the strict sense of the reception of sensorial *hyle*, but in "an act which renders identical services to the categorial elements of meaning that merely sensuous perception (the reception of *hyle*) renders to the material elements (the *hyle* itself)."[35] Categorial intuition is such an act, and the recognition of this categorial intuition corrects the theory of "simple perception" with which the analysis began, for it is important to see that such an act of categorial intuition is co-present simultaneously with sensuous intuition in the limited sense of the term, whenever a perception takes place, that is, a perception in the sense of a "fulfilling act of confirmatory self-presentation."[36] Husserl pursues the same line of argument when he writes: "We have taken it for granted that forms, too, can be genuinely fulfilled, or that the same applies to variously structured total meanings, and not merely to the 'material' elements of

---

[33]LI, 784.
[34]LI, 784.
[35]LI, 785.
[36]LI, 785.

such meanings, and our assumption is put beyond doubt by looking at each case of faithful perceptual assertion."[37] In other words, the object itself is brought before us, is perceived, precisely in forms, in categorial structures. Perception, no longer understood in the strict sense as a reception of a hyletical given, but rather in its cognitive entirety as an act by which the thing itself is identified and confirmed in its identity, joins sensuous intuition to categorial intuition.

* *

It seemed useful to us to restore at length the examination that Husserl conducts in the sixth chapter according to its successive stages, because Heidegger's commentary on Husserl's theory of categorial intuition, far from being sufficiently supported by the few citations to which he drew the attention of the seminar's participants, is not fully intelligible until it is related to the movement of the chapter as a whole. What first of all is so surprising in Heidegger's commentary is his reservation, a reservation which, in the dialogic movement of the seminar, seemed to us on the one hand to indicate a kind of modesty in expressing the extent of insight that this fascinating text had exerted on him, and on the other hand to invite the participants, armed with only a few signs, to reconstruct the path which led from Husserl's text to the *Seinsfrage*. It is in this second sense at any rate that we would like to consider Heidegger's remarks.

His comments focus on the notion of categorial intuition, which according to Heidegger, "brush" the *Seinsfrage* and which constitutes the "burning point" in Husserl's thinking. Heidegger develops his commentary along two lines. The first question is to know which path led Husserl to this notion and what victory the notion represents over the tradition. The answer is suggested by the setting in which Chapter Six (second section of the sixth Investigation: "Sensibility and Understanding") is found and by the title of the chapter itself ("Sensuous and Categorial Intuitions"): Husserl started with sensuous intuition in order to arrive at categorial intuition. It is therefore first of all necessary to find out what sensuous intuition is for Husserl. Heidegger insists that sensous intuition is strictly speaking not the

---

[37]LI, 784.

perception of a thing, but rather the perception of sensory givens, the affection by the *hyle* and its givens (blue, black, extension, etc.). The thing, that is, in Husserl's view, the "object" of sense-perception, is not given in the *hyle*; it is not part of the *hyle*. And yet, the object is after all perceived: "with the sensory givens in perception comes the appearance of an object," that is, according to philosophical tradition, of a "substance." But, according to the same tradition, substance is a category, as for example in Kant's first *Critique*. Yet, contrary to Kant, for whom the category "substance" is a simple form which organises the diversity of sensibility for the understanding and which as such is not itself given, Heidegger insists that Husserl thinks of the categorial as a given: the term "catergorial intuition" itself suggests a being-present to the category. Let us refer to the text of the protocol: "I see this book. But where is the substance in the book? I do not see it at all as I see the book. And yet the book is in any case a substance that I have to see in some way, without which I can see no thing at all."[38] Here we come to Husserl's notion of *Uberschuss,* excess. Heidegger explains: the 'is'--by which I ascertain the presence of the ink-well as object or substance--is 'exceeding' among the sensible affections: the 'is' is not added to the sense-impressions, but it is 'seen', even if it is seen in a way other than that which is visible. In order to thus be seen, it is necessary that it be given."[38] This commentary is discreet. At the same time that it brings out the burning character of Husserl's notion of an excessiveness of being, it blurs to a certain extent this same excessiveness by associating it with the excessiveness coming from the category of substance. The commentary continues moreover to treat the category of substance. "Let us repeat once again: when I see this book, I see of course a substantial thing, without seeing however the substantiality the way I see the book. Yet the substantiality is what, in its non-appearance, allows what appears to appear. In this sense, it can be said that substantiality is more apparent than the apparent itself."[39]

We shall soon attempt to clarify the reasons for Heidegger's reservation. At any rate, the first stage of Heidegger's commentary consists in showing that the method that Husserl uses to arrive at the notion of categorial intuition is that of *analogy*. There is a categorial intuition analogous to sensuous intuition. The victory that this notion

---

[38]*Questions, IV,* 314.
[39]*Ibid.* 314.

represents over the tradition lies in the destruction of the setting in which the tradition, specifically that tradition which claimèd Kant as its authority, limited the given. The given, according to this tradition, is that which affects the sensibility; categories become for Husserl in turn "as encounterable as a given by the senses."[40]

Heidegger comments: "decisive discovery." And it is here that the commentary's second question arises: in what sense was this discovery an "essential stimulus" for the articulation of the *Seinsfrage*? Heidegger emphasizes in debating this question that the decisive character of Husserl's discovery did not lie in the contribution of an exhaustive answer to a question already prepared, but rather, on the contrary, consisted in the emergence of an "essential difficulty." Heidegger comments elliptically that this "difficulty stems from the two-fold meaning of the word *to see*. (...) The difficulty is that if I see some white paper, I do not see the substance 'as' I see white paper."[41] This too is a discreet commentary, for Heidegger's remarks ought to concern less the excessiveness of substance with respect to sensory givens than the excessiveness of being over that which is. This latter excessiveness is not dissociable from the first, in the sense that it grounds the ascertainment that the perceived thing is present as substance. The excessiveness of being over that which is is recognized by Husserl, as we have seen, and it is of course this excessiveness which stimulated Heidegger's imagination. Heidegger continues: "With his analysis of categorial intuition, Husserl has liberated being from its captivity in judgement. In so doing, the entire field of inquiry finds itself re-oriented. If I pose the question of the meaning of being, it is necessary for me to be already beyond being understood as the being of entities. (...) Husserl's feat lay precisely in his discovery that being (in so far as it is beyond the being of entities) is present phenomenally in categories. Because of this feat, I finally arrived at the ground: *being* is not a simple concept, a pure abstraction obtained thanks to the activity of deduction."[42]

"I finally arrived at the ground," that is, the *Boden*, the same word Heidegger used in *Sein und Zeit* when he admitted that his investigation would not have been possible without the foundation (*Boden*) established by Husserl in the *Logical Investigations*.

If one admits that Heidegger's reservation is proportional to the

---

[40]*Ibid.*, 314.
[41]*Ibid.*, 314.
[42]*Ibid.*, 315.

importance of those perspectives made possible by the long captivation
that the sixth Investigation elicited, Heidegger's commentary seems to
us to invite a consideration of the *Seinsfrage*'s articulation as a kind of
retrieval, in the sense in which Heidegger himself uses the term, of
Husserl's doctrine of categorial intuition, and to invite us to recognize
that the famous distinction between the possibility and the actuality of
phenomenology is already in Husserl's text.

Remember the structure of the *Seinsfrage*. The *Gefragtes*, that which
is posed by this question, that about which the question asks, that which
is asked in it, is the being of the entity, in so far as this being is not itself
an entity. That towards which the question is aimed, the question's
intention, its *Erfragtes*, is the meaning of being, the meaning that *Sein
und Zeit* will find in the notion of temporality. That in view of which the
questioning is presented, that to which the question is addressed, its
Befragtes, is an entity, yet not any entity whatsoever, but rather first and
foremost that entity which has a special relationship to the question,
that entity whose mode of being is to understand being: Dasein. Because
the comprehension of being is the fundamental determination of its
essence, such an entity is not merely given like one entity among others.
The analysis of Dasein will show that its mode of being consists in being
beyond what is merely given; it is a radically ecstatical mode of being
which produces in Dasein the bursting site of finite transcendance, the
thrown project where the understanding of being is tied to a dependance
with respect to entities, and where the movement by which the entity
called Dasein is made to transcend toward being is itself solicited by
being, by the openness in the heart of which that entity can manifest
itself as an entity.

This structure of the question of being together with certain essential
elements of the analysis required by that question are, in a certain sense,
anticipated in Husserl's doctrine of categorial intuition.

The main assertion of this doctrine concerns the category's excessiveness compared with what is merely given. Yet not everything is at the
same level in this categorial excessiveness. The category "substance" is
not at the same level as the category "being", which in fact founds the
objectifying function of the category "substance." When Heidegger says
discreetly that "substantiality is what, in its non-appearance, allows
what appears to appear," it may be added justifiably, in strict agreement
with Husserl's text, that it is in virtue of the category "being" that a state
of affairs can prove to be substantial and can appear as such. An entity
can appear as it is, it can let itself be seen, display its identity or its truth,

by means of an excessiveness of being over what is merely given, that is, by means of a precession of being, of an a priori of being. But, being understood in its a priori excessiveness is not less given than what is merely given, even if it is in another manner. No matter how excessive being may be, it is given nonetheless to an intuition. The category "being" is therefore apparent, it is a phenomenon, and because its function, with respect to what appears, is to found, it can be said "that it is more apparent than what appears itself," that it is the phenomenon of all phenomena, the phenomenon par excellence of phenomenology, that towards which what will soon be called the "reduction" must be directed. It is here a matter concerning a kind of duplicity of the phenomenon which is strictly interdependent with a duplicity of seeing. The excess of being over the given, far from preventing being from being as much a phenomenon as the given, bestows upon being the privileged status of primordial phenomenon: things appear as being what they are in virtue of the light of being. Correlatively, there is an excessiveness at the very heart of seeing. The seeing which grasps things in their coming-into-appearance, intentionality, is itself transfixed with excessiveness; seeing must be beyond the given in order for things to be and to be what they are. And this movement of passing-beyond is interdependent with an exposition of the entity, since, as Husserl writes, "the concept 'being' can arise only if some being is placed before our eyes." What emerges from Husserl's analysis is that the correlation of the duplicity of phenomena and of the duplicity of seeing liberates being from its imprisonment in judgement, and that this correlation constitutes that towards which knowledge knows, something which transcends both its acts and their correlates.

Heidegger's fascinated gaze found in the *Logical Investigations* the emergence of a group of themes which incite the *Seinsfrage* in *Sein und Zeit*: namely that being transcends the entity, that being is the *transcendens* par excellence, that being is in a special sense *the* phenomenon of phenomenology, that the entity's coming-into appearance requires a prior understanding of being, that this understanding, to the extent to which it is beyond, is nonetheless inseparable from an exposition of an entity, that the excessiveness of being is the cradle of truth. And it is above all Husserl's analyses, in the way in which they approach the question of being, which earn Heidegger's praise for having given to philosophy its authenticity, *empirical apriorism*.

There exists therefore a version of the ontological difference in Husserl's early work. If this difference is accounted for in the theoretical setting in which it occurs for Husserl, it can be said that it consists in founding the identification of a *Sachverhalt*, understood in its very presence, upon the excessiveness of being; it consists as well in furnishing at the same time an excessiveness to the very heart of that intentionality for which the identification takes place. The difference in consciousness between on the one hand the real contents of psychical life, the *Erlebnisse*, in so far as they are merely given, and on the other hand the objectifying acts, given in a completely different way, exceeding the *Erlebnisse* and conferring upon them an intentional status, corresponds to the difference between being, of which Husserl says that it is "absolutely imperceptible" and yet "intuited", and the given.

But the enormous difficulty, which made Heidegger's strict attention more or less obsessional, is precisely to know if these concepts and the theoretical setting which unifies them are sufficient to account for the excessiveness in question, and if this setting does not inevitably cover up again what Husserl discovers. If it is admitted that the a priorical excessiveness of being is primordial, which is what Husserl seems to anticipate when he suggests that no state of affairs could be ¡recognized for what it is without such an excessiveness, should not then the traditional language of the philosophy of consciousness, together with all the conceptual pairs which continue to circulate in Husserl's text -- subject-object, immanence-transcendance, form-contents, void-fulfilment, activity-passivity -- be destroyed? How could this language still be considered pertinent if it is true that Husserl, whatever pains he may take to distinguish the psychological from the ideal, that is, from what he will later call the transcendental, cannot avoid assigning these pairs to the very same ontical order, abolishing in the process the primordial excessiveness? Does not Husserl's thesis -- that a category is given in a way other than the way sensory contents are given with respect to which the category has the function of being the form -- lead to the levelling of the excessiveness into the sole order of *Vorhandenheit,* merely because the mode of being of categories is traced analogically from the mode of being of sensory givens? Does that not entail that being has no other meaning than that of being an object? The intrinsically relational structure of what Husserl calls intentionality is in a sense what seems to refuse such a levelling. But if, as is the case in the setting of Husserl's revival of the Cartesian *cogito sum,* intentionality is attributed to a subject which is in turn grasped as a given, as a *Vorhandenes,* then is not the excessiveness once again abolished? Can intentionality be attributed to a subject and is the strictly ontical division of interiority and exteriority still appropriate, if intentionality is essentially a relation to being, beyond entities, a relation which transfixes the perception of entities? If our relation to an entity's manifestation presupposes that being itself is a phenomenon, is it then not necessary to find names other than that of consciousness, which in itself designates merely the interiorisation of *Vorhandenheit,* the re-presentation of the given, in order to designate the site where this relation transfixed with excessiveness emerges? And why must the study of this relation become fixed in the limited area of a theory of knowledge, if it is really primordial for the entity that we are, if therefore it permeates all its dealings with things? And can this relation to the manifestation, to the extent to which the discovery of an entity presupposes the a priorical truth excessive of being, still be described in the ontical metaphors of void and fulfilment? And is not the synthesis of fulfilment, according to which Husserl interprets the self-givenness of a state-of-affairs in its identity, understood as the adjoining of one entity to another entity, covering up at the same time the excessiveness of being?

It is not our intention to follow these questions, which are far from being the only ones implied in Heidegger's captivation by the sixth Investigation and which occasion numerous departures from Husserl in *Sein und Zeit* as well as in the Marburg courses on phenomenology.[43] Our intention was solely to indicate in which direction these departures could still claim a "ground established by Husserl."[44]

---

[43]See the Marburg lectures, Winter Semester 1925-26, on *Logik, Die Frage nach der Wahrheit,* in particular the preliminary remarks concerning psychologism and the question of truth, and the questions concerning Husserl's concept of truth in the sense of identity. *Gesamtausgabe,* Band 21, section 10. See also the course for the Summer Semester 1927, *Grundprobleme der Phänomenologie,* which contains notably a "phenomenologico-critical discussion "of Kant's thesis which, as we have seen, inspired Husserl in his sixth Investigation: that being is not a real predicate. It would be easy to read this "discussion", -- during which the phrase "ontological difference" appears probably for the first time -- as a "retrieval" of the sixth *Logical Investigation,* by means of a debate with Kant.

[44]For a general view of the relationship between Heidegger and Husserl, see the excellent study by Jean Beaufret in *Dialogues avec Heidegger,* III, "Husserl et Heidegger", pp. 108-154.

* *

One final word to conclude and correct the partiality in what has just been said. The relationship between the ground and the demarcations is of course in no way that of a simple inference. It is never a question for Heidegger, as our remarks could lead one to believe, of taking one of Husserl's theses as exemplary of his entire philosophy in order to extract from it the implications from which Heidegger could arrive at the inacceptibility of Husserl's other theses. If it is tempting for an historian of philosophy to construct such logical schemes, it is nonetheless a fact that such schemes in no way encircle what occurs when a thinker's questioning awakens another thinker's questioning. When Heidegger sees the avenues of the *Seinsfrage* being outlined in Husserl's sixth Investigation, so often re-read, it is never a question of the birth of a thesis from which other theses, especially Husserl's theses, might be criticized. It is rather a matter of the birth of a question which will have no end, with which he will never cease to be associated, and whose force lies in the fact that it remains question.

In the movement of this question, ceaselessly renewed, ceaselessly displaced, it was necessary to show that the "ground" which made *Sein und Zeit* possible, thanks to Husserl and beyond him, was not something upon which something could be founded, and that the project of a scientific philosophy which understands itself, in the form of a fundamental ontology, barred access to the true listening-place of the *Seinsfrage*. The "ground" was therefore no ground at all. Or rather, yes it was. For why should "ground" mean foundation? Does not founding imply setting one entity upon another? Whereas what was the ground if not the excess of being over entities?

At the end of this movement, and from the famous *Kehre* on, Husserl is rarely mentioned, yet this silence -- another aspect of Heidegger's reservation -- does not prevent the old captivation from continuing to vibrate, and the following passage from one of Heidegger's last great texts -- "Time and Being" -- will be familiar to those who recall the sixth *Logical Investigation:* "Is being at all? If it were, then we would inevitably have to recognize it as being some entity (als etwas Seiendes) and we would consequently come upon it as one entity among the remaining.   This auditorium *is.* The auditorium *is* lighted. We shall recognize the lighted auditorium without further ado and without thinking it over as some entity. Yet where in the whole auditorium do we find the 'is'? We find being nowhere among things."[45]

And when Heidegger closed his last seminar with a re-examination of the *Sachverhalt*, of the famous ἔστι γὰρ εἶναι in Parmenides' poem, which ought to be heard with a Greek ear and understood as *anwesend-anwesen*, he ended his reading with the following words: "This thought of Parmenides is founded upon that which has appeared to seeing. As Goethe notes, the greatest difficulty perhaps is to achieve a pure remark [*reine Bemerkung*]. It is precisely a question of this difficulty for Parmenides: to achieve taking in view *das anwesend anwesen* (...) I call the thought which is asked here the tautological thought. It is the primordial meaning of phenomenology."[46] Those words -- *Sachverhalt*, pure remark, seeing, taking into view, identity -- represent the very fabric of the *Logical Investigations*. It is still the old captivation before the interdependence of seeing's excessiveness and the phenomenon's excessiveness which incites the last lesson.

(translated by Jeffrey Stevens)

---

[45]SD, 3.
[46]*Questions IV*, 336-338.

The Question of Being and Transcendental Phenomenology: Reflections on Heidegger's Relationship to Husserl

JOHN D. CAPUTO
Villanova University

The recent appearance of the first volumes of Heidegger's *Gesamtausgabe,* commencing with the publication of the Marburg lectures (1923-28), has already begun to illuminate one of the cloudier issues in Heidegger's thought.[1] I refer to the problem of how Heidegger, at least the Heidegger of *Being and Time,* is a "phenomenologist", and *a fortiori,* to the puzzling relationship of Heidegger to Husserl. We have always, it is true, been able to point to a number of brilliant phenomenological analyses in *Being and Time* -- of the tool, the world, the givenness of others, anxiety, death, primordial temporality and the like. We have always been able to refer to the definition of phenomenology in § 7 of *Being and Time* and to compare it with the principle of principles in § 24 of *Ideas I;* we have always recognized Heidegger's concern with first-hand seeing and getting back to the things themselves. Yet with all of this, there remains something deeply unsettling about Heidegger's relationship to phenomenology, so long at least as we take Husserl, to whom *Being and Time* is dedicated, as the paradigm of the phenomenologist. For where does Heidegger stand on the critical and central steps of the phenomenological method, the *epoche* and the

---

[1]Martin Heidegger, *Gesamtausgabe*, II. Abteilung: Vorlesungen 1923-44, B. 21, *Logik: Die Frage nach der Wahrheit* (Frankfurt: Klostermann, 1976), hereafter "*Logik*"; B. 24, *Die Grundprobleme der Phänomenologie* (Frankfurt: Klostermann, 1975), hereafter "GPdP". I will refer to the later title in the body of this article by its English translation. *Logik* represents the 1925-26 lectures, GPdP the lectures of the Summer semester, 1927.

phenomenological reduction? And what does Heidegger have to say about intentionality, the refutation of psychologism, or transcendental constitution?[2] And how can there be a phenomenology when the whole idea of "consciousness" has been superceded?

Heidegger's published works to date have not so much taken issue with Husserl on these points as they have totally ignored them. Heidegger makes virtually no reference to these matters in *Being and Time*. Yet he says this work would not have been possible without Husserl. The incontestable virtue of the publication of the Marburg lectures will be, I think, to illuminate these dark corners of Heidegger interpretation. As a contribution in this direction I would like to discuss the knotted problem of Heidegger's relationship to transcendental phenomenology, i.e., to Husserl's view that the objects of experience are constituted in and through transcendental consciousness. This will involve making a determination of where Heidegger stands on the question of the phenomenological reduction and the constitution of objects in consciousness. My point of departure for this discussion is provided by a section of *The Fundamental Problems of Phenomenology* (§ 5), in which Heidegger makes his own determination of the basic elements of the phenomenological method, and in which -- *mirabile dictu* -- Heidegger speaks of his own "phenomenological reduction."

To be sure, no matter is closer to Husserl's heart, no procedure more indispensable to Husserl's method, than the phenomenological reduction. Moreover it was this very question of the reduction that led Husserl to reject Heidegger's interpretation of phenomenology. In an important letter to Roman Ingarden on December 26, 1927 Husserl writes:[3]

---

[2]"Intentionality" is discussed in GPdP, §§ 9b-c, 12a, 15c, 18b. The refutation of psychologism is discussed and subjected to an anti-critique in *Logik*, §§ 6-10. See also F. Olafson, "Consciousness and Intentionality in Heidegger's Thought," *American Philosophical Quarterly*, 12, No. 2 (April, 1975), 91-103.

[3]Edmund Husserl, *Briefe an Roman Ingarden* (The Hague: Nijhoff, 1968), p.43. Cited and translated by T. Kisiel, "On the Dimensions of a Phenomenology of Science in Husserl and the Young Dr. Heidegger," *Journal of the British Society for Phenomenology* 4, no. 3 (October, 1973), p. 228, n. 48. See also Spiegelberg's account of Heidegger's relation to Husserl during the Marburg years in *The Phenomenological Movement* (The Hague: Nijhoff, 1965), Vol. 1, pp. 279-81.

I allow myself to become depressed by the kind of impact that my publications have and by the fact that my better students overlook the depth dimension that I point to and instead of finishing what I have started, time and again prefer to go their own way. So also Heidegger, this natural power of a genius, who carries all the youth away with him, so that they now consider (which is not at all his opinion) my methodic style to be out of date and my results to be part of a passing era. And this from one of the closest of my personal friends.

...the new article for the *Encyclopedia Brittannica* has cost me a great deal of effort, chiefly because I again thought through from the ground up my basic direction and took into account the fact that Heidegger, as I now must believe, has not understood this direction and thus the entire sense of the method of the phenomenological reduction.

By the reduction the phenomenological investigator is, according to Husserl, carried back (re-duction) from the hitherto naively accepted world of objects, values and other men, to the transcendental subjectivity which "constitutes" them. Without the reduction and without the operation of transcendental constitution which it uncovers, philosophy is cut off from achieving radical science. Philosophy would be, in Husserl's view, confined at best to the empirical-psychological level, to the level of "philosophical anthropology," which deals with the real experience of real men in the world, with what Husserl calls "mundane subjectivity." It is evidently in this way that Husserl understands Heidegger's talk of "existence" and "being-in-the-world." For in the *"Nachwort zu meinen "Ideen,"* in a thinly disguised reference to Heidegger, Husserl characterizes the objections that have been raised against this work in the following way:[4]

---

[4]Edmund Husserl, *Ideen III, Husserliana V* (The Hague: Nijhoff, 171), p. 140. See also Edmund Husserl "Phenomenology and Anthropology," trans. R. Schmitt in *Realism and the Background of Phenomenology*, ed. R. Chisholm (New York: The Free Press, 1960), pp. 129 ff. Cf. Heidegger's allusion to this criticism in *On the Essence of Reasons*, A Bilingual Edition Incorporating the German Text of *Vom Wesen des Grundes*, trans. T. Malick (Evanston: Northwestern, 1969), pp. 96-9, n. 59; see Malick's n. 40, pp. 140-1.

They all rest on misunderstandings and ultimately on this,
that one wishes to push my phenomenology back to the level
[anthropology, mundane subjectivity] the overcoming of
which constitutes the whole meaning of the
phenomenological reduction.

In Heidegger "consciousness" is superceded by being-in-the-world. The
world is that in which Dasein always already *(immer schon)* is, and
anything like an *"epoche"* or reduction which would free Dasein from
the world is ruled out from the start. Heidegger-interpretation has
always proceeded then with the understanding that in Heidegger there is
neither *epoche* nor reduction. As Walter Biemel said in 1950:[5]

Since Husserl's questioning leads back to the ego, his
method stands under the stamp of the reduction, through
which the totality of beings is bracketed, in order to retain
the pure ego. In Heidegger the reduction is totally absent.

We are faced then with a remarkable state of affairs. Heidegger is an
important phenomenologist --yet he has not, in the opinion of Husserl
himself, understood the basic sense of the central methodological step
in phenomenology, the reduction. In Biemel's view, Heidegger has
abandoned the reduction altogether. Yet, as if to intentionally
complicate the entire matter, Merleau-Ponty claims in his admirable
"Preface" to the *Phenomenology of Perception* that the entire
discussion of being-in-the-world in Heidegger is possible only against
the background of the phenomenological reduction.[6] Finally, in the
midst of this confusion, Heidegger himself has, in his published writings
thus far, said nothing whatever about the reduction.

Heidegger's Interpretation of the Phenomenological Method

It is then of no little interest to find that Heidegger himself, in the

---

[5]Walter Biemel, "Husserls Encyclopaedia-Brittannica Artikel und Heideggers
Anmerkungen Dazu, "*Tijdschrift Voor Philosophie*, 12 (1950), p. 276.

[6]Maurice Merleau-Ponty, *The Phenomenology of Perception*, trans. C. Smith (New
York: Humanities Press, 1962), p. xiv.

hitherto unpublished Marburg lectures, did once address himself to the question of the meaning of the phenomenological reduction for his interpretation of phenomenology. What can the "phenomenological reduction" mean to Heidegger? Let us listen to his words:

> We characterize that element of the phenomenological method which has the sense of a leading back of the investigative look from the naively grasped being to Being as the *phenomenological reduction.*
>
>   (GPdP, 29)

This is a strange saying. Every reduction is, in one way or another, a "leading back" *(züruck-fuhren, re-ducere).* In Heidegger's reduction the look of the phenomenological investigator is led back from beings to Being. Thus, by the reduction, we open up what is elsewhere in these lectures called the "ontological difference." Obviously, Heidegger is here adopting Husserl's vocabulary, but he is hardly saying the same thing as Husserl. Thus he adds:

> *For Husserl* the phenomenological reduction... is the method of leading back the phenomenological look from the natural attitude of the man who lives in the world of things and persons to the transcendental life of consciousness and to the noetic-noematic experiences in which objects constitute themselves as correlates of consciousness. *For us* the phenomenological reduction signifies the leading back of the phenomenological look from the grasp of the being, which is always something definite and determinate, to the understanding of the Being (projecting upon the manner of its unconcealment) of this being.
>
> (GPdP, 29)

For Husserl the reduction means a "leading back" from a naive consciousness, which takes the being as something 'there', as an autonomous thing in itself, to a critical consciousness which understands the hitherto anonymous life of consciousness which "constitutes" the object. It is the passage from the naive givenness of the being to the giving life of consciousness, from a world which is ready made to the creativity of transcendental consciousness. For Heidegger the reduction means the movement by which we no longer take the being naively, as something simply 'there', but discover the being *in its Being*. It is the revelation that the being, which naive common sense takes to be "given," depends upon a more original "giving." For Heidegger, the reduction discloses the hitherto anonymous operation of Being by which the being emerges as a being. The being becomes a phenomenon for Heidegger only when we grasp it in its Being. The simple and determinate grasp of a particular being is nothing phenomenological, but a mere naiveté of natural common sense.

Unfortunately, Heidegger devotes no more space to this phenomenological reduction than the paragraph that we have just quoted. For his comments occur in the "Introduction" to *The Fundamental Problems of Phenomenology*, in which he merely outlines the three parts of this lecture course. Unhappily, the whole of Part III, which was to concern itself with methodological reflections on the nature of phenomenology, was never completed. We are once again left with a Heideggerian "fragment." And our confusion is just as great as before, for this text raises more questions that it answers. The whole passage has the appearance of a rather arbitrary reinterpretation of Husserl's words which has nothing to do with the substance of the Husserlian reduction. What are we to make of this reduction? How seriously can we take it? How does it in any way illuminate the essence of Heidegger's phenomenological method? Let us reflect upon it further.

The mention of this phenomenological reduction occurs, as we said, in § 5, in which Heidegger is discussing the basic elements in the phenomenological method. He identifies three such elements: reduction, construction and destruction. This position is developed as follows. Phenomenology is radical science *(Wissens chaft)*, i.e., philosophy in its most radical sense (GPdP, 3). But a truly scientific philosophy is possible only as a philosophy--phenomenology-- of Being. For the understanding of Being is necessarily prior to the experience of any particular being, and therefore to every particular science (GPdP, 14). "Being is the genuine and only theme of phenomenology" (GPdP, 15). But this demand upon phenomenology to be a science of Being raises the methodological question of how Being is accessible to us. Now Being is given to us only in beings.[7] Thus the look of the phenomenological investigator must be directed at beings in such a way as to disclose them in their Being, i.e., to "thematize" Being. The task of thematizing Being is to be carried out in three methodic steps, the first two of which--reduction and construction-- we shall treat together. (1) *Reduction:* in this step the phenomenological look is directed negatively "away from" beings to their Being. It is, Heidegger says, a "pure turning away," a negative movement which looks away from beings. But this essentially negative element of the method must be perfected in a second and more central element: (2) *construction:* in this second step the phenomenological look is directed "towards" the Being of beings; it "leads into" Being *(Hinführung).* Being is not, Heidegger says, simply lying about like a being so that, were we to look away from beings, we would just naturally "come across" *(vorfinden)* Being. On the contrary, we must actively "project" *(entwefern)* Being; we must actively bring it into view. This projecting of the being upon its Being is what Heidegger calls phenomenological "construction".

In *Being and Time* the term "construction" is used in quite a different sense. There it referred to a dogmatic presupposition introduced from outside the *Sache* in such a way as to be imposed upon the *Sache* and to do it violence. A "construction" there is an *a priori* presupposition which, far from releasing the being and freeing it to be the thing which it is, actually does quite the opposite. It imposes determinations upon the things themselves whose effect is precisely to prevent us from seeing things as they are. Thus phenomenology is described as the opposite of all "free-floating constructions".[8] A case in point is the Cartesian projection of the things of the life-world in terms of the mathematical construction of extension and velocity and the consequent covering

---

[7]The balance of this paragraph is an exposition of GPdP, 228-30.

[8]Martin Heidegger, *Sein und Zeit* 10. Aufl. (Tübingen: Niemeyer, 1963), p. 28. Engl. Transl. *Being and Time*, trans. Macquarrie and Robinson (New York: Harper and Row, 1962), p. 50. Hereafter "SZ" with the German pagination followed by a slash and the English pagination. See also SZ, 16/37; 50, n. 1/490, n.x.; notice the shift of meaning though in SZ, 197/242. "Construction" in the positive sense used in GPdP is discussed in *Kant und das Problem der Metaphysik* 3. Aufl. (Frankfurt: Klostermann, 1965), § 42, pp. 210-11. See J.L. Mehta, *Martiñ Heidegger: The Way and the Vision* (Honolulu: University of Hawaii Press, 1976), p. 198, n. 8.

over of life-world phenomena, such as "hardness" (SZ, 97/130). The construction described in *The Fundamental Problems of Phenomenology* is precisely the opposite kind of projection, one which releases the being to be what it is, which puts the right presupposition upon the being. It is somewhat like Merleau-Ponty's example of "gearing" ourselves up in the appropriate way so that we can experience the thing as it is, finding, e.g., the right position from which to view the painting.[9] *We* find the right angle, the right distance, the right lighting in which the painting can show itself. The task of the phenomenologist is to find the right horizon, the right framework of conditions, the right structure of Being *(Seinsverfassung, Seinsart)* in which the being can be what it is. Thus the things of the *Umwelt* should be projected not in terms of extension *(Vorhandensein)* but of "instrumentality" *(Zuhandensein)* if they are to be seen for what they are.

Actually, this process of construction or projection is to be carried out for Heidegger on a two-fold level. In the first place, the being is to be projected in its Being. That process we have already briefly characterized. But secondly, and more radically, Being itself can and must be projected in terms of that which lets it be what it "is" *(west)*. Here we are referring to the process by which Being itself is projected upon temporality, which Heidegger discusses in § 20b of *The Fundamental Problems of Phenomenology* (GPdP, 395 ff.). It is also clear that what Heidegger means by construction here is identical with the projection upon "meaning" *(Sinn)* in *Being and Time* (SZ, 151/193; 324/370-1): the meaning of a thing is that upon which it must be projected in order to be understood as what it is. To understand the meaning of a thing is to put the right construction upon it. More precisely we do not "put" a construction "on" the *Sache* -- for that is precisely the procedure of construction in the bad sense. Rather, we set forth the Being-structure which the being itself suggests and evokes, and which we have learned from the being and through the being itself. The genuinely phenomenological construction is not impressed from the outside, but is prompted from within by the things themselves.

(3) The third step involved in thematizing Being phenomenologically is called by Heidegger "*destruction*" (GPdP, 30-2). In making the regress from beings to Being, Dasein must perforce begin with the actual experience of Being which is offered to it by its current historical

---

[9]Merleau-Ponty, *The Phenomenology of Perception*, p. 313.

situation. Beings are not homogeneously accessible in all ages. Indeed there is to be found in the history of Western philosophy from Plato to Hegel a tendency to level off all beings in terms of a single kind of being, particularly accessible to that particular thinker, which is then made to do service for all the differing modes and areas of beings (*Seinsarten, Seinsgebiete*). We today have inherited this vast fund of fundamental concepts which purport to disclose the Being of each of the differing regions of beings. In a radical science, which starts from the beginning, that claim cannot be accepted without further ado. Hence the reductive-constructive regress (*Rück-und Hinführung*) to Being must be at the same time an historical regress, an historical "destruction". It must in Husserl's terms be an historical-genetic phenomenology, in the manner of the *Krisis*, which re-traces the steps which the history of Western philosophy has taken and which uncovers the original and founding experiences (Husserl's *Urstiftungen*) from out of which beings first received their determination. Thus, while the first two steps of Heidegger's phenomenological method have more the appearance of the ahistorical reductions characteristic of *Ideas*, the third compares to the historical way of Husserl's later period. In *The Fundamental Problems of Phenomenology*, however, Heidegger insists that all three methodic steps must be applied together, that all three steps belong together.

Nonetheless, there remains something profoundly unsettling about the "phenomenological method" which Heidegger sketches in these pages, unsettling in the sense of how it relates to Husserl's phenomenology. For Heidegger has radically altered the terms of Husserl's reduction and recast it in the likeness of his own "ontological difference." The *terminus a quo* and the *terminus ad quem* of Heidegger's reduction are beings and Being, respectively. These categories supercede for him the terms of the Husserlian reduction: objects and consciousness, objectivity and subjectivity. Heidegger has thus replaced Husserl's "epistemological difference" with his own ontological-phenomenological reduction. For in Heidegger's view both objects and subjectivity remain within the sphere of beings and cannot claim to be ultimate categories. Indeed they themselves need to be interpreted in terms of their Being. Thus Heidegger's reduction claims to be more radical.

From Husserl's point of view, however, Heidegger appears to have emasculated the reduction by stripping from it the whole idea of a reduction to "transcendental subjectivity." Thus, while Husserl may concede that Heidegger possess the "natural power of a genius," he believes him to have struck out so thoroughly on his own path that it can no longer be called phenomenology. For what does Heidegger's reduction have to do with the constitution of objects in transcendental subjectivity? In § 59 of the *Cartesian Meditations* Husserl protested against those pretended phenomenologists who lack this most radical element of the phenomenological method. Husserl would certainly regard Heidegger's talk of his own phenomenological reduction as a bit of terminological tokenism which has nothing of substance to do with his phenomenology.

Dasein, Subjectivity and
Transcendental Phenomenology

The question to which we must next turn then in this essay is what Heidegger's reduction of Being has to do with the reduction to transcendental subjectivity. My aim in pursuing this question is not, I hasten to add, to attempt to bring Heidegger into conformity with Husserl, for there is no merit in that, nor to justify his credentials to the Husserlians of the strict observance. I am concerned simply to *understand* Heidegger's relationship to Husserl, for *Being and Time* would not have been possible "if the ground had not been prepared by Edmund Husserl" (SZ, 38/62). Heidegger and Husserl are two great and ultimately independent philosophical geniuses. I do not wish to absorb Heidegger into Husserl, nor to say that everything of worth in Husserl's thought is to be found *eminentiore modo* in Heidegger's thought. I simply want to understand better the enigmatic relationship which existed between these thinkers during Heidegger's Marburg period. This will, among other things, serve to clarify Heidegger's later development when his divergence from Husserl is even more pronounced.

I believe that the best point of departure for this question is to be found in an investigation of Heidegger's view of the relationship between Dasein and "subjectivity" during this time. Such an investigation reveals that a central idea in Heidegger's concept of phenomenology in those days lay in what he called the "regress to the subject" (*Rückgang auf das Subjekt*). Thus, in a discussion of Kant's determination of "reality" in terms of what is given to "perception",[10] Heidegger says:

> Yet the direction of the way upon which Kant enters, through the regress to the subject, is in the widest sense the only possible and correct one.
>
> (GPdP, 103)

This expression, "the regress to the subject," or its like, occurs frequently in *The Fundamental Problems of Phenomenology* (cf. pp. 156, 172, 220, 308-9, 318-9). In another important text Heidegger says:

> Accordingly, if the philosophical problematic has from the beginning of ancient philosophy. . . been oriented towards reason, soul, spirit, consciousness, self-consciousness, subjectivity, this is no accident. . . The bent (*Zug*) towards the 'subject', which is not always equally clear and unambiguous, is grounded in the fact that philosophical inquiry somehow understood that the basis for every substantive (*sachlich*) philosophical problem could and must be drawn out of an adequate elucidation of the 'subject'.
>
> (GPdP, 444)

This text substantially repeats the opening section of Heidegger's version of the *Encyclopedia* article in which Heidegger says:

> Phenomenology means: the fundamental clarification of the necessity of the regress to consciousness, the radical and expressed determination of the way of, and of the laws governing the steps of, this regress. [It means] the delimitations of principles and the systematic searching through of this field of pure subjectivity which is disclosed in this regress.[11]

---

[10]This is the second of Kant's "Postulates of Empirical Thought". Heidegger discusses it in GPdP, § 8b and again in *Logik*, § 33.

[11]Heidegger's draft of the article appears in *Husserliana IX: Phänomenologische Psychologie* (The Hague: Nijhoff, 1962), pp. 256 ff. An English translation is to be found in *The New Scholasticism* XLIV (Summer, 1970), 325-44.

There can be no doubt that Heidegger saw his fundamental ontology of Dasein, his return of the problem of Being to the being which raises the question of Being, in terms of Husserl's return to subjectivity. This regress was in keeping with the basic tendency of modern philosophy from Locke through Kant, a tradition with which at this stage Heidegger willingly aligns himself. It is furthermore, Heidegger argued, in keeping with the basic, though less easily identifiable tendency of classical thought: with Parmenides (*noein*), Heraclitus (*logos*), Plato and Aristotle (*psyche*), and the middle ages (*intellectus*, transcendental *verum*). The return to subjectivity is for the Heidegger of those days an age-old, necessary and fundamental philosophical step which, properly carried out, secures for philosophy a truly scientific status.

Nevertheless, this characterization of Heidegger's orientation in the '20's must not be left unqualified. Indeed Heidegger himself is quite careful to refine his stand. He says:

> ...in the emphasis on the subject, which has been a vital force in philosophy ever since Descartes, there does indeed lie a genuine impulse for philosophical questioning. It only sharpens what the ancients sought. Yet, on the other hand, it is just as necessary not simply to proceed from the subject, but rather also to question whether and how the Being of the subject, as the point of departure for the philosophical problematic, must be determined, [to question the subject] in such a way that the orientation to it is not *one-sidedly subjectivistic*. Philosophy must perhaps proceed from the 'subject' and with its ultimate questions go back to the 'subject', but it may not pose its questions in an one-sidedly subjectivistic way.
>
> (GPdP, 220)

Here Heidegger introduces a critical and decisive qualification upon his conception of the phenomenological return to subjectivity. The Being of the subject must not be determined subjectivistically but rather in such a way as to exhibit its Being as radically turned towards the world.

Heidegger's subject is nothing subjective because its Being consists in the concernful use of tools *(Besorgen)* and the solicitous sharing of the world with others (*Fürsorge*) and because it is itself ultimately a care for its own Being (*Sorge*). Dasein is a self not because it is self-

consciousness (*Selbstbewusstssein*) but because it must *be* itself
(*Selbstsein*), because it must decide to be its own or not its own self
(*Eigentlichkeit, Uneigentlichkeit*). One can see in Heidegger's
conception of a non-subjectivistic subject both a residual
"Cartesianism," a Cartesianism which is in truth inseparable from
transcendental phenomenology, and yet also the makings of what
Landgrebe calls the "departure from Cartesianism".[12] Dasein is in no
sense a worldless ego, but an openness towards the world, yet is a 'self',
an 'I myself'.

It is no wonder then that even in these early texts from the 1920's
Heidegger puts single quotation marks around the word 'subject'. In
connection with the supposedly Aristotelian thesis that truth belongs in
the subject, not in things, Heidegger comments:

> Being-true is revealing. Revealing is an activity of the ego.
> Thus they say being-true is something subjective. We rejoin:
> 'subjective' to be sure, but in the sense of a properly
> understood concept of the 'subject' as existing Dasein, i.e.,
> as being-in-the-world (*als des existierenden, d.h., in der
> Welt seienden Dasein*).
>   (GPdP, 308)

There is a fundamental tension in these early texts, and in *Being and
Time* itself, between Dasein as 'subject' and its unsubjectivistic
character, which is finally resolved only in the later works, in which
Descartes and Husserl, the whole philosophy of transcendental
subjectivity, and finally the entire history of Western "metaphysics" are
ultimately overcome. One can already find here the makings of the later
Heidegger out of the early.

But while this overcoming is already underway in the early works it
has not yet been carried out. If there is a tension here which needs
resolving, it is because Heidegger's work still stands within the
framework of a now more broadly conceived "transcendental
phenomenology." That is why Heidegger could say in his important

---

[12]Ludwig Landgrebe, "Husserl's Departure from Cartesianism," in *The
Phenomenology of Husserl: Selected Critical Readings,* ed. R.O. Elveton (Chicago:
Quadrangle Books, 1970), pp. 259 ff.

letter to Husserl of Oct. 22, 1927:[13]

> There is agreement between us that the being which you call
> "world" cannot be explained, in terms of its transcendental
> constitution, by a regress to a being with the same mode of
> Being.

For both Heidegger and Husserl the "world" is not constituted by
something mundane (Husserl), by something innerworldly (Heidegger),
but by a being with a radically different mode of Being (*Seinsart*), by
pure transcendental subjectivity (Husserl), by Dasein (Heidegger). The
letter continues:

> We have not thereby said, however, that that which makes
> up the place of the transcendental is not a being at all.

This is not to say, Heidegger adds, that this being is in no sense
something really existing. Here Heidegger begins to formulate his break
with Husserl, for whom the pure or absolute Being of consciousness is
opposed to the real being of the world. Husserl's brackets include both
the world and the ego. Heidegger does not wish to *bracket* the Being of
the 'subject' but to penetrate to a deeper *understanding* of its *Being*.
Husserl moves from a real-empirical to an irreal-transcendental ego.
Heidegger moves from the superficial grasp of Dasein as something
Vorhanden to the Being of man as *Existenz* and Dasein. Husserl's
subject is irreal; Heidegger's 'subject' ex-ists.

> Rather the problem precisely arises: what is the mode of
> Being of the being in which the "world" is constituted? This
> is the central problem of *Being and Time*, that is, a
> fundamental ontology of Dasein. It must be shown that the
> mode of Being of human Dasein is totally different from that
> of every other being, and that, being what it is, it harbors
> within itself the possibility of transcendental constitution.

Here *Being and Time* is cast in a startling light: it is an inquiry into the

---

[13]Heidegger's letter to Husserl appears in *Husserliana IX*, pp. 600-3. See Anlage I. For a
comment on this letter in English, see Mehta, *Way and the Vision*, p. 146, n. 4.

Being of the being which constitutes the world. Fundamental Ontology is, in its own way, transcendental constitutive phenomenology. *Being and Time* determines the Being of the 'subject' in which innerworldly beings, and other persons, are "constituted." It determines these 'subjective' processes (*Verhaltungen*) as concern and solicitude and it determines the Being of the 'subject' as care and ultimately as temporality.

> Transcendental constitution is a central possibility of the existence of the factical self. For this [= a factical self] is what concrete man is as such. Concrete man is, as a being, never a "mundane real fact" because man is never merely something present at hand. Rather he exists. And the element of "wonder" lies in the fact that the existence-structure of Dasein renders possible the transcendental constitution of every posited entity.

This is a remarkable passage in which the break with Husserl is given its sharpest formulation of all. It states what for Husserl must be a blazing paradox: transcendental constitution takes place in and through the "factical self." Whereas in Husserl the transcendental subject was separated by an "abyss" from everything factual (*Ideen* I, § 49), in Heidegger transcendental subjectivity is located in the "factiticy" of existing Dasein. The being which constitutes the world is thrown into the world and will be wrenched from it. The being which constitutes others is from the very start there, along with them, one with them, dominated by them. The being which transcends being and so is free is ever prone to be untrue to itself, to fail to be itself. This transcendental subject is radically finite and factical, and is itself separated by an abyss from the "absolute Being" of Husserl's "pure subjectivity." Still Dasein does in a meaningful sense "constitute" its world: through its moods the world is constituted *as* that into which Dasein is thrown. Without solicitude the "they" could never appear and dominate Dasein. Without anticipation my dealth would not 'be' for me. And in a word, without temporality nothing at all would be for Dasein. Temporality is the deep-structure which "gives" Dasein a world (*Logik*, § 19-20), which in Husserl's language, which Heidegger is willing to employ in this letter, "constitutes" the world. While Dasein is "factical" it is not factual and constitut*ed*. Rather, Heidegger claims, the process of factual ex-isting, the unitary process of existence-facticity-and-fallenness (ahead-of-itself-being-already-in-along-side-others) is itself the constitut*ing* process which gives Dasein its world. Husserl thought that whatever is in any way *real* is constitut*ed*. Heidegger rejoins that Husserl is being dogmatic about what Being means (if something is real it is constituted), and that a distinction needs to be made between what is real as a *Vorhandenes* and what is 'real' because it "ex-ists." The latter is in no way constituted, but rather discloses the Being of itself (*Selbstsein*), others (*Mitsein*) and innerworldly things (*Vorhandensein, Zuhandensein*).

Walter Biemel says that in this passage Heidegger's use of the word constitution arises from an attempt to be accommodating to Husserl, to cast his thought in the language of Husserl, but that the expression "constitution" is avoided in *Being and Time* because of its idealistic overtones.[14] I endorse Biemel's observation quite fully. However I would point out that the importance of the passage lies in the fact that Heidegger *can* put the problematic of *Being and Time* in the language of "constitution." This is possible I believe because Heidegger has in mind *a non-idealistic notion of constitution,* one very much like Merleau-Ponty's example of finding the right standpoint from which the painting can then "show itself from itself." If the 'subject' does not for its part do what is required of it, if it does not bring its own mode of Being to beings, then they cannot appear as what they are. Thus Heidegger, speaking of Kant's theses about reality and perception, observes:

> Perception uncovers the present-at-hand and lets it be encountered in the manner of a definite *uncovering.* Perception takes away its coveredness from the being and makes it free to show itself from itself.
> (GPdP, 98)

Or again, in discussing the 'assertion' as a mode of uncovering:

> The appropriation of the being in the true assertion about it is no ontic taking in of the present-at-hand into the subject,

---

[14]Biemel, "Husserls Encyclopaedia Brittannica Artikel," p. 276, n. 8.

> as if things were transported into the ego. ...The assertion is
> a letting be seen of the being, one which exhibits it.
>   (GPdP, 213)

In Heidegger, constituting means an uncovering, a letting be seen, which is absolutely requisite if the being is to show itself from itself. If Dasein does not build, and so hammer, then the hammer cannot be too heavy or indeed be a hammer at all. *Besorgen* constitutes the hammer as a hammer, inasmuch as it opens up the horizon within which it can show itself as a hammer. "Letting be seen" in Heidegger is no mere passive opening of our eyes so that things may just pour in upon us. It is a matter of actively projecting the being in its proper mode of Being, so as to make it accessible to us. It is letting be in the active sense of freeing the thing to show itself as what it is. Dasein constitutes the world by releasing it.

Being and Phenomenology

One might protest that our essay up to this point is disjointed and that it has made two essentially different and independent claims which do not all coincide: (1) in Heidegger's early work we find a genuine phenomenology of Being because in Heidegger there is an analogue to the phenomenological reduction, viz., the constructive-reduction to Being; (2) in *Being and Time* there is a genuine phenomenology of Being because *Being and Time* is an essay in transcendental phenomenology; it inquires into the Being of the being which constitutes the world, and so there is a reduction to (Heidegger's version of) transcendental 'subjectivity.' In the first place there is a reduction (regress) to Being (ontological reduction), in the second to the 'subject' (transcendental phenomenological reduction). Which is it? Or are these the same thing? In the first thesis there seems to be a tokenism which uses only Husserl's words, not his meaning; the second is more substantive (*sachlich*), but how is it related to the first?

The answer to this question is and must be that the two kinds of reduction--ontological and transcendental-phenomenological--belong together and are, for the Heidegger of the Marburg period, inseparable. The unity of the two claims can be expressed simply: the reduction to Being *is* a reduction to Dasein conceived as the 'subject' which harbors within itself the possibility of transcendental constitution. This is because Being for Heidegger at this point is to be interpreted in terms of

Dasein's *understanding* of Being. The reduction is made not simply to Being, Heidegger says, but to the understanding of Being possessed by Dasein. Let us listen again to the important text from *The Fundamental Problems of Phenomenology:*

> *For us* the phenomenological reduction signified the leading back of the phenomenological look from the grasp of the being, which is always something definite and determinate, to the *understanding of the Being* [these italics mine] (projecting upon the manner of its unconcealmènt) of this being.
>
> (GPdP, 29)

It is in and through Dasein's understanding of Being that it *is* able to "constitute" (uncover) the world, i.e., to free beings, to release them into being what they are. Being at this stage of Heidegger's thought is conceived after the model of an intentional phenomenology, a phenomenology of *noesis* and *noema*, in which Being is the correlate of and is accessible only through Dasein's understanding of Being:[15]

> If we have conceived the fundamental problem of philosophy to be the question into the meaning and ground of Being, then we must, if we do not wish to engage in phantasy, methodically stay with that which makes something like Being accessible to us, i.e., with the understanding of Being which belongs to Dasein.
>
> (GPdP, 319)

The regress to Being (the ontological reduction) is made possible by a regress to Dasein's understanding of Being (the transcendental phenomenological reduction). In another text Heidegger says that the uncoveredness of beings depends upon the disclosedness of Being, but that the Being of beings is disclosed only "if I understand it" (GPdP, 102). And again in the "Introduction" to *The*

---

[15]It was a failure to appreciate the intentional relationship between Dasein's understandiing and the Being which was therein understood which led in the 1930's and '40's to the popular confusion of *Sein* and Dasein (mentioned by Biemel, p. 276).

Fundamental Problems of Phenomenology:

> The Being of a being is met with by us in the understanding
> of Being. Understanding is that which first of all opens up
> or, as we say, discloses something like Being. "There is"
> Being only in the specific disclosedness which characterizes
> the understanding of Being.
>   (GPdP, 24)

Now the disclosedness of Being is that which has been called from
antiquity "truth":

> But there is truth only if a being exists which opens up,
> which discloses, and indeed in such a way that disclosing
> itself belongs to the very manner of Being of this being. We
> ourselves are such a being.
>   (GPdP, 25)

And so accordingly:

> There is Being, only if truth, that is, if Dasein exists.
>   (GPdP, 25)

These texts can also be compared with a number of similar passages in
Being and Time (SZ, 212/255, 230/272, 316/364).

Dasein is the being which harbors within itself the possibility of
transcendental constitution *because* it is the being which is
characterized by an understanding of Being. The deepest and most
fundamental reason why beings are manifest as beings, why they show
themselves as phenomena, is Dasein's understanding of Being. Dasein
discloses the being *as* a being. To be a phenomenon is to stand forth, to
emerge into presence, to show itself from itself. But it is only if presence
itself, if emerging into presence (*Anwesen, Sein*), is itself first
understood that the being *can* emerge and be present. Heidegger carries
out Husserl's demand that the phenomenon be led back into the act
which discloses and constitutes it as a phenomenon, but he identifies
that act as the pre-ontological understanding of Being. That which
discloses the being as such, which makes it possible for being to be met

with and experienced at all, is the *a priori* which discloses every being as such: Being. Thus Heidegger planned a section of *The Fundamental Problems of Phenomenology* which was to bear the title "The *A Priority* of Being and the Possibility and Structure of *A Priori* Knowledge." Heidegger rejects the idea that the *a priori* refers to some innate or inborn structure in the mind (GPdP, § 22c). Rather the *a priori* means for him the "towards which" (*das Worauf*), the horizon, upon which a thing is projected if it is to appear as such, that "in respect to which" (*in Hinblick auf, das Worauf eines Hinblicks*) a thing must be seen in order to be what it is. Being is the *a priori* in this sense: it is that in reference to which beings are manifest as beings and which must be *first understood* if beings are to be accessible. Being is prior to beings and only the prior understanding of Being (not in chronological time) makes the experience of beings possible. In this understanding the being is "constituted" in its Being, i.e., uncovered as a being.

Dasein's understanding of Being is the sole condition under which both ontology and phenomenology are possible. Not only is ontology possible only as phenomenology, but phenomenology is possible only as ontology. The regress from beings to Being and the regress from the world to the being which constitutes the world merge into one and the same regression (*Rückfuhrung, Rückgang*): the way back into Dasein's understanding of Being. It is only under the condition that Dasein understands Being that beings can be experienced as beings (phenomenology) and that they can be understood to be (ontology). The reduction to Being and the reduction to the 'subject' (Dasein) are in this sense one and the same.

Conclusion: Heidegger and Husserl

How then does Heidegger of the Marburg period stand in relationship to Husserl's "transcendental phenomenology"? Is he a revisionist whose breach with Husserl is too enormous to gap, with whom there are only incidental similarities? I think not. I see Heidegger's work in this period as an attempt to further radicalize that which Husserl had described as radical, strict, scientific philosophy. For as the world depends in Husserl upon the disclosive activity of transcendental subjectivity, so in Heidegger does it depend upon Dasein's radically temporal understanding of Being. There can be no naive acceptance of the world for either thinker. Husserl recovers the up-to-now anonymous and forgotten life of transcendental consciousness; Heidegger makes explicit the up-to-now hidden pre-ontological understanding of Being. The "anonymous" life of the ego in Husserl is paralleled in Heidegger by the "forgotten" understanding of Being. Prior to all "reflection" (Husserl), to all "listening in" (SZ, 139/179), there unfolds an activity which, wholly unknown to our natural life in the world, renders that world possible. There is for both a natural attitude which takes the world as ready-made, autonomous, objective, and there is for both a breach with this attitude which discovers the constitutive life which renders the world manifest. The breach is a breach with the world, though in quite different senses for each thinker. In Husserl the breach takes the form of an *epoche* which brackets the contingent world in order to find the necessary sphere of pure consciousness, a sphere which could survive even the destruction of the world (hardly a possibility for being-in-the-world). In Heidegger the breach consists in raising the *question* of Being, in questioning the being in its Being. This questioning--something of a Heideggerian *epoche*--discovers not a pure ego but the radically worldly Being of being-in-the-world--in whose temporal understanding of Being the world is disclosed. Heidegger's breach is perfectly described by Merleau-Ponty: it consists in slackening the bonds which tie it to the world--the broken hammer--just long enough to bring the world as such into view; it consists in attempting the *epoche* just long enough to discover the impossibility of carrying it out.[16]

What then can we say of Husserl's judgment of Heidegger--that he has not understood the basic sense of the reduction, and that he leads phenomenology back to the level of anthropology? I believe this judgment is too harsh, though it is perhaps the only judgment the author of the method could render upon such an independent appropriation of his work. Heidegger has indeed understood the reduction, but he has understood it--as he understands everything--in his own way. His version of the reduction does not lead phenomenology back to the level of natural, mundane subjectivity, but, on the contrary, to the disclosive activity in which everything natural and mundane comes to be "there" (*da*). *Being and Time* represents a brilliant

---

[16]Merleau-Ponty, *The Phenomenology of Perception*, pp. xiii-xiv.

appropriation of Husserl's thought which, while it clearly depends upon the preparation made by Husserl, also has an inspiration of its own.

The whole discussion of the early Heidegger's relationship to Husserl and so to the phenomenological movement illuminates the problem of Heidegger's path of thought. Heidegger was throughout his life moved by Husserl's call to the things themselves, to the *Sache* of all philosophical thought, and he has always adhered in his own way to the principle of direct seeing. To that extent he has always been in Husserl's debt. But in the Marburg period, in *Being and Time*, Heidegger was still profoundly affected by the transcendental motif in Husserl's phenomenology, as the numerous texts we have cited amply document. In this light his *Kehre* consists in overcoming that very "orientation towards the subject" which seemed to Heidegger in the '20's to be the very life-line of philosophy. Thus we can find something like the first reduction (to Being) which we discussed in this essay in the later Heidegger's writings but not the second (to the subject). For in the later works the regress to Being would become the "step back" (*Schritt zurück*) into Being, the regress into the ground of metaphysics (*Rückgang in den Grund der Metaphysik*).But the regress into the subject was to be overcome and identified with the history of metaphysics. We saw that even in *The Fundamental Problems of Phenomenology* Heidegger thinks that the history of Western philosophy was characterized by a return to the subject, the difference being that he was willing to associate himself with that tradition in those days. In the later works Heidegger would still conceive Dasein as "releasing" beings in their Being, but that would mean not the horizonal projection of them in their Being, but pure *Gelassenheit*. Dasein would still have an "understanding" of Being (or rather it would have Dasein!), but that would have to do not with any transcendental 'subject' but with "standing under" Being's address. The makings of the later Heidegger out of the early can be seen in these lectures by those who have the eyes to see, and who have the advantage of the hindsight afforded by the intervening years. But the special contribution of the publication of the Marburg lectures is, I believe, to throw into relief what *Being and Time* meant to and for Heidegger and his generation a half-century ago.

Destructive Retrieve And Hermeneutic Phenomenology In 'Being And Time'

JOSEPH J. KOCKELMANS
The Pennsylvania State University

I. *Introductory Reflections*

Being and Time[1] begins with an introduction which is similar to the introductions found in many classical treatises on metaphysics. The book opens with a brief description of the task to be accomplished, the road to be taken, and a provisional division of the subject matter. The goal to be achieved in the book is a critical reflection on the question concerning the meaning of Being in light of an interpretation of time as the transcendental horizon for the question of Being. (*SZ* 1, 39) Since Being is always the Being of beings, the question concerning the meaning of Being is to be approached by means of a careful study of the mode of Being of a particular kind of being. In view of the fact that some comprehension of Being is already implied in the mode of Being of that being which asks the question, namely Dasein, it is the Being of Dasein which is to be examined first. (*SZ* 5-15)

As far as the road to be taken is concerned, Heidegger makes two suggestions. The first recommends a 'destructive retrieve' of the metaphysical tradition; the other states that 'hermeneutic phenomenology' is the method of ontology. If one considers these suggestions concerning the method to be employed, it is clear that they,

---

[1] Martin Heidegger, *Being and Time*, trans. John Macquarrie and Edward Robinson (London: SCM Press Limited, 1962). All references to this work in the text are to the 7th edition of the German original whose pagination is indicated in the marginal numbering of the English translation. Following the common practice *Sein* is always translated as Being, whereas *Seiendes* is translated by being.

too, are similar to the suggestions on method made by Descartes, Kant, Hegel, and Husserl. Analysis of Heidegger's text reveals that this similarity is, indeed, intended, although one should be aware of the fact that the concrete suggestions made in each case are fundamentally different from what these authors have proposed in this regard, although there is in each case an important element of agreement, also.

From the way Heidegger determines both subject matter and method of ontology it is clear that he is trying to find and justify a personal stance in regard to the entire philosophical tradition. In the manner of the Western tradition since Plato, Heidegger subscribes to the view that ontology is a science. Like Descartes he defines the scientificity of ontology by means of the method to be employed.[2] With the entire modern tradition he admits that in a science, that which counts is not what other thinkers have already thought, but that which can be methodically justified in regard to the 'things themselves' to be studied in that science.[3] Heidegger even seems to join Descartes, Kant, and Husserl in their negative evaluation of philosophy's history, when he speaks about the need for a destruction of the traditional content of ancient ontology (*SZ* 22).[4] Finally, Heidegger is deeply aware of the intimate relationship between method and subject matter in ontology and, thus, seems to subscribe to the view that it is incorrect to conceive of method in a purely instrumental fashion. This intimate relationship appears to imply that the explicitation of the immediately given is to be mediated by what is already somehow implicitly contained in what is given immediately, without, however, being explicitly thematized there. (*SZ* 15ff., 7f., 152f., 314f.)[5]

---

[2]René Descartes, *Rules for the Direction of the Mind*, Rule IV, in *The Philosophical Works of Descartes*, trans. E.S. Haldane and G.R.T. Ross, 2 vols. (New York: Dover Publications, 1931), vol. I, p. 9.

[3]*Ibid.*, Rule III, p. 5.

[4]Cf. René Descartes, *Discourse on the Method of Rightly Conducting the Reason and Seeking for Truth in the Sciences*, Part I, *op. cit.*, pp. 85-87; *Meditations on First Philosophy*, Meditation I, *op. cit.*, pp. 144ff.; Immanuel Kant, *Prolegomena to Any Future Metaphysics*, trans. Lewis White Beck (New York: The Bobbs-Merrill Company, Inc., 1950), pp. 3ff.; Edmund Husserl, *Philosophy as Rigorous Science*, in *Edmund Husserl: Phenomenology and the Crisis of Philosophy*, trans. Quentin Lauer (New York: Harper and Row, 1965), pp. 7 iff.; *Ideas: General Introduction to Pure Phenomenology*, trans. W.R. Boyce Gibson (New York: Collier Books, 1962), 72ff.

[5]Cf. G.F. Hegel, *Phenomenology of Mind*, trans. J. Baillie (London: Allen & Unwin, 1964), Introduction, pp. 131ff.

Yet at the same time Heidegger makes it abundantly clear that he does not share any of these views without major modifications. Ontology is a 'science', indeed, but it is a science whose scientificity has nothing in common with either the formal or the empirical sciences. [6] Secondly, although it is true that as a science ontology is to be defined in its scientificity by means of the method to be employed, yet this method cannot possibly be conceived of as consisting in deduction (Descartes) or description (Husserl). Rather this method is to be conceived of as being both transcendental and hermeneutic.[7] It is true, also, that no philosopher can think without both explicitly standing in a tradition and taking a critical stance in regard to that tradition. Yet this critical attitude is not a rejection of the tradition, but rather a destructive retrieve of what was worth being thought about in that tradition. (*SZ* 22)[8] Finally, although it is true that method and content are intimately intertwined in ontology and that the mediation of the immediately given presupposes that what guides the explication takes its clues from what is already somehow present in the immediately given, the latter is not to be found in some anticipation of Hegel's absolute Truth, but rather in the finite 'truth of Being' which functions as the necessary synthesis a priori in all finite understanding.

If these reflections are correct, it is obvious that the destructive retrieve and the phenomenological method cannot be taken to be independent and unrelated procedures; rather both procedures belong intimately together[9] and the one (hermeneutic phenomenology) cannot possibly achieve its goal without the other (destructive retrieve). Just as hermeneutic phenomenology is the methical development of what is constitutive of Dasein's understanding as such (*SZ* 142-153), so destructive retrieve is no more than the methical correlate of the

---

[6]Martin Heidegger, *Die Grundprobleme der Phänomenologie* (Frankfurt am Main: Vittorio Klostermann, 1975), pp. 1-5, 15-19.

[7]Martin Heidegger, *Kant and the Problem of Metaphysics*, trans. James S. Churchill (Bloomington: Indiana University Press, 1962), pp. 211-255; cf. SZ 37-8.

[8]Cf. *Grundprobleme*, pp. 30-32.

[9]*Ibid.*, pp. 26-32. Heidegger characterizes phenomenology here with the help of the following three labels: *reduction* (the turn from a being toward its Being), *construction* (the projection of a pre-given being upon its Being and its structures), and *destruction* (the critical analysis of the concepts which are handed down to us, in light of the original sources from which they have been derived). It is important to note that in this work which is not concerned with fundamental ontology, the term 'hermeneutic' is not mentioned.

retrieve which is constitutive of Dasein's search for its authentic self. (*SZ* 316-323)

In the pages to come I plan to give an interpretation of Heidegger's view on phenomenology as the method of ontology and its inherent hermeneutic character insofar as this view is found in *Being and Time*. In so doing I shall make extensive use of Heidegger's *Die Grundprobleme der Phänomenologie* and *Kant and the Problem of Metaphysics* as well as of C.F. Gehtmann's *Verstehen und Auslegung*.[10] Yet before I can turn to a commentary on Heidegger's text I wish first to make a brief list of some important presuppositions which in my opinion play an important part in Heidegger's reflection on the method of ontology. In this section of the paper I have taken Gehtmann's work as a guideline, also.

II. *Some Presuppositions*

In *Being and Time* and other works of the same period Heidegger states explicitly that phenomenology as the method of ontology is to guarantee the scientificity of ontology. Ontology must apply the phenomenological method in order to be capable of being a *genuine science*. (*SZ* 31, 153, 230) This idea is developed much more systematically in *Kant and the Problem of Metaphysics* and *Die Grundprobleme der Phänomenologie*. In the latter work Heidegger writes that phenomenology is the label for the method of scientific philosophy[11] and that to explain what the idea of phenomenology means is tantamount to clarifying the concept of scientific philosophy.[12]

In philosophy it is impossible to develop a method independent of the subject matter to be disclosed by the method. Any genuine method is based on viewing in advance and in the appropriate manner the basic constitution of the 'object' to be disclosed and of the domain within which it is to be found. Thus any genuinely methodical consideration which is not just an empty discussion of techniques, must give information about the kind of Being of the being which is to be taken as the theme. (*SZ* 303) In the positive sciences this information follows with necessity from the a priori synthesis which each science 'freely'

---

[10]Carl Friedrich Gehtmann, *Verstehen und Auslegung. Das Methodenproblem in der Philosophie Martin Heideggers* (Bonn: Bouvier Verlag Herbert Grundmann, 1974), pp. 1-126 and passim.

[11]*Grundprobleme*, pp. 1-3.

[12]*Ibid.*, pp. 3-5, 15-19, 465-469.

projects (*SZ* 356-364); in ontology this information is to be derived from that peculiar synthesis which as the comprehension of Being is constitutive of Dasein's own Being (*SZ* 15 ff.) This is the reason why in philosophy every effort to deal with the method of philosophy itself implies a dilemma: this effort comes either too early or too late. For strictly speaking the method of ontology can be determined adequately only after the process of thought has reached its destination and its subject matter has been articulated. Yet on the other hand it is precisely this process of thought which is to be conducted methodically. Solving this dilemma is one of the basic problems of every philosophy which concerns itself explicitly with its method. Somehow the basic problems must be solved at the very beginning and yet they cannot be solved definitively except at the end. Thus at the beginning one can do no more than make some provisional and suggestive remarks; these are then to be reconsidered toward the end of the philosophical reflection. (*SZ* 303, 15ff.) Heidegger justifies this way of proceeding by means of a reference to the hermeneutic character of all finite understanding and to the hermeneutic circle which all research about ontological issues appears to imply. (*SZ* 5-8, 152ff., 314f., 436f.)

Concern for method and methodology has been a characteristic of modern philosophy since Descartes. In view of the fact that the deductive method in principle is incapable of clarifying the basic axioms of any given deductive system, from the very beginning there was the question of whether it would be possible to develop a new science which as *prima philosophia* could give an ultimate foundation to some basic insights from which then all of our theoretical knowledge could be derived according to principles and laws.

Since all rationalist and empiricist attempts in this direction had failed, Kant in his *Critique of Pure Reason* attempted to provide a theoretical framework which would lay the foundation for philosophy as well as for all other sciences. Thus the *Critique* does not contain the system of science, but is concerned primarily with its method.[13] The possibility of scientific knowledge is explained only when reason can develop for itself a method which will both guide and find reason itself in all of its theoretical endeavors. This implies that the method to be developed must be of a totally different nature than the methods employed in the formal and empirical disciplines; thus the new method

---

[13]Immanual Kant, *Critique of Pure Reason*, trans. Norman Kemp Smith (New York: St. Martin's Press, 1965), p. B *xii.*

cannot be either analytic or empirical. According to Kant the great discovery of the modern age from which philosophy and science must learn a lesson is that "reason has insights only into that which it produces after a plan of its own".[14] What is needed then in Kant's view is a *transcendental* logic, a philosophical reflection on the projective achievement of reason by which reason provides itself with an a priori framework which is the necessary condition of our theoretical knowledge of all objects.

What is completely new in this view is not the reference to the fact that there is to be an a priori of some kind, but the fact that in the question concerning our knowledge a priori the stress is placed on method, which alone can guarantee the necessity and universality of all of our scientific insights. In Kant's view the proper application of the 'transcendental' method alone is capable of closing the gap between subject and object to which Descartes had pointed and which both rationalism and empiricism had been unable to bridge. Knowledge of objects is possible only if the transcendental method is capable of showing that the objectivity of the object is projected in advance by reason itself. In the final analysis the projection of this objectivity is the reason why all of our theoretical knowledge constitutes a harmonious unity and can be developed into a system.[15]

Between Fichte and Husserl various forms of transcendental philosophy were developed. They all have Kant's basic concern in common and share his view that there is to be a highest principle of all synthetic judgments a priori which has fundamental implications for the systematicity of all genuine knowledge. The difference between the various forms of transcendental philosophy is to be found in the *concrete* manner in which each author or group of authors has tried to conceive of the a priori synthesis and the principle which founds its unity.[16]

From his earliest works it is clear that between 1914 and 1930 Heidegger conceived of himself as one who was seriously concerned with the development of transcendental philosophy as found in Kant, the neo-Kantians, and Husserl. Thus it was to be expected that in the first sections of *Being and Time* we would find an attempt by Heidegger to formulate his own position in regard to the basic problems of

---

[14]*Ibid.*, p. B *xiii.*
[15]*Ibid.*, pp. B 735-736.
[16]Gehtmann, *op. cit.*, pp. 14-21.

transcendental philosophy, even though it would not be stated explicitly in so many words.[17]

However, if we now turn to the opening sections of *Being and Time* it seems at first that Heidegger is really interested in a quite different problematic. He begins there by stating that *Being and Time* will be concerned with the question concerning the meaning of Being and with the interpretation of time as the transcendental horizon for any understanding whatsoever of Being. (*SZ* 1, 39) On several occasions he explicitly suggests that his main concern is with the categorial multiplicity of the various modes of Being which presupposes what we really mean by the expression 'Being' (*SZ* 11), the Being of beings, the 'material meaning' of Being in general (*SZ* 27), Being and its derivatives (*SZ* 35). However, on other occasions it becomes apparent that his *basic* concern is rather with the necessary and a priori condition of the categorial multiplicity of the various modes of Being (*SZ* 230; cf. 212-230, 436-7). Although the latter, transcendental problematic is less explicit in *Being and Time* than the categorial-ontological problematic described in the opening sections of the book, there cannot be any doubt that the transcendental problematic is nonetheless the one to which the expression 'the question concerning the meaning of Being' ultimately refers.[18]

It is generally known that Heidegger's concern with the Being question was influenced historically by Brentano's work on Aristotle.[19] According to Brentano, Aristotle divides 'being' in four different, but somehow related ways; and of these ways the division of 'being' into the ten categories is the most important. Yet if Being can be said in a multiplicity of significations, which one then is the guiding and basic signification? What does 'Being' really mean?[20]

One should realize that the fundamental problems with which

---

[17]Martin Heidegger, *Die Lehre vom Urteil im Psychologismus. Ein kritisch-positiver Beitrag zur Logik*, in *Frühe Schriften* (Frankfurt am Main: Vittorio Klostermann, 1972), pp. 1-119; *Kant and the Problem of Metaphysics*, Section IV, pp. 211-255; *Grundprobleme*, pp. 172-251, and passim.

[18]*Kant and the Problem of Metaphysics*, pp. 211ff.; "Mein Weg in der Phänomenologie", in Martin Heidegger, *Zur Sache des Denkens* (Tübingen: Niemeyer, 1969), pp. 81-90; Letter to Richardson, in William J. Richardson, *Heidegger: Through Phenomenology to Thought* (The Hague: Nijhoff, 1963), pp. *xiii-xiv*.

[19]F. Volpi, *Heidegger e Bretano* (Padova: Cedam, 1976).

[20]*Zur Sache des Denkens*, p. 81; Letter to Richardson, *op. cit.*, p. *xi*.

Heidegger was concerned in *Being and Time* and other works of the same period are problems which did not really exist for the entire Aristotelian tradition. In Heidegger's view these problems and their possible solutions *presuppose* the transcendental framework of modern philosophy. For according to the Aristotelian tradition the Being question which is implicit in the ontological-categorial problematic can be solved in principle by an appropriate doctrine of analogy. For Heidegger such a solution is in part inadequate. Although the classical doctrine of analogy contains part of the solution of the problem in that it is capable of explaining at least one condition to be fulfilled if any division of 'being' into categories is to be meaningful, it nonetheless leaves unanswered the basic question of what we really mean by the expression 'Being'. Secondly, without any justification all classical theories of analogy take 'natural being' as the primary analogate from which the basic meaning of Being is then to be derived.[21] Classical tradition as well as modern philosophy failed to examine the possibility of taking the very Being of man as the primary analogate.[22] But most importantly, the entire problematic is without any 'ground' as long as the transcendental problem has not been solved satisfactorily. Thus Heidegger can write "Basically, all ontology, no matter how rich and firmly constructed a system of categories it has at its disposal, remains blind and perverted from its ownmost aim, if it has not first adequately clarified the meaning of Being, and conceived of this clarification as its fundamental task". (*SZ* 11)

It is undoubtedly true that in *Being and Time* and related works Heidegger was indeed concerned with showing that the temporality of Dasein is the principle of the division of Dasein's own modes of Being, and that time as temporalized by Dasein is the principle of the division of the meaning of Being into possible significations of Being (namely Being as ek-sistence, Being as present-at-hand, Being as ready-to-hand, etc.), so that a description of the various interplayings of the three dimensions of temporality can be taken as guiding-clues for the division of the significations of Being. (*SZ* 350-366)[23] Yet one should realize also that all of this does not constitute Heidegger's *basic* concern. (*SZ* 230) Toward the end of *Being and Time* Heidegger writes: "The distinction

---

[21]*Grundprobleme*, pp. 23-25, 94ff., 140ff., 158ff., 219ff.

[22]*Ibid.*, pp. 172ff.

[23]Cf. Otto Pöggeler, "Heideggers Topologie des Seins", in *Man and World,* 2 (1969) 331-357, pp. 337-345.

between the Being of ek-sisting Dasein and the Being of beings such as reality, which do not have the character of Dasein, may appear very illuminating; but it is still only the *point of departure* for the ontological problematic; it is nothing with which philosophy may tranquillize itself." (*SZ* 436-7) And it is for that reason that the book ends with questions which point to work still to be done: Is there a way which leads from primordial time to the meaning of Being? Does time itself manifest itself as the transcendental horizon of Being? (SZ 437)

That which constitutes the determining unity of the multiplicity of the various modes of Being is something which is to be determined 'critically'; it cannot just be postulated. There is to be some final 'ground' which *as identity* of difference can be taken as the foundation of the difference. The question concerning the meaning of Being is answered adequately only when the various modes of Being with which man is confronted can be justified. This is possible only when a naive realist as well as a dogmatist position have been given up in favor of a transcendental perspective in the sense of Kant. As *Kant and the Problem of Metaphysics* clearly shows, with respect to the latter problematic, Heidegger's main concern was to substitute a 'transcendental ontology' for the Kantian and neo-Kantian transcendental logic; and this implies a fundamental re-interpretation of Kant's conception of the transcendental, a priori synthesis.[24]

Being and Time was meant to lead up to the transcendental problematic and, thus, in that book the problematic itself is not explicitly dealt with, so that the question concerning the meaning of Being remains unanswered there. Yet in the notion of Being implied in the comprehension of Being which is constitutive of Dasein's own Being, the answer to that question is already contained implicitly. What later will be called 'Being itself' is found in *Being and Time* merely in the form of 'world' in that 'Being itself' always reveals and conceals itself *concretely* in the form of a given world. From this general perspective it becomes clear why Heidegger later could say that in *Being and Time* both the classical conception of the *transcendentalia* and a new conception of truth, namely the 'truth of Being', played an important part.[25]

---

[24]*Kant and the Problem of Metaphysics*, Section 45.

[25]Martin Heidegger, *Die Kategorien - und Bedeutungslehre des Duns Scotus*, in *Frühe Schriften*, pp. 131-353, p. 344; *Kant and the Problem of Metaphysics,* pp. 119-129, 18-22, 69-72; *What is a Thing?*, trans. W.B. Barton, Jr. and V. Deutsch (Chicago: Henry Regnery

In this connection it should be noted also that the transcendental problematic plays an equally important role in Heidegger's conception of the ontological difference. The expression 'ontological difference' is not found in *Being and Time* itself, but the problematic hinted at by this expression most certainly constitutes an essential part of the book's *basic* concern; this is clear from both *Die Grundprobleme der Phänomenologie* and *Vom Wesen des Grundes*.[26] Sometimes Heidegger characterizes the difference by means of the distinction to be drawn between a being and its Being. Some authors have interpreted the meaning of this distinction as a further development of Kant's distinction of the a posteriori and the a priori.[27] Yet such an interpretation overlooks what is most typical of Heidegger's entire way of thinking, namely the attempt to reflect on the relationship between the transcendental synthesis and the categorial-ontological problematic. The *identity* presupposed by the ontological difference is first the categorial identity of those beings which have the same mode of Being; yet this identity in turn presupposes the transcendental identity of a priori synthesis as its necessary condition. Heidegger alludes to this dual principle of identity in *Vom Wesen des Grundes* where he distinguishes between the ontic and the ontological conceptions of truth.[28]

At any rate the categorial-ontological difference is the difference between a being and its Being, between the Beingness (*ousia*) of a being and this being itself (*on*). On the other hand, the transcendental-ontological difference refers to the distinction between the meaning of

---

Company, 1967), pp. 181-184, 242-243; *What Is Called Thinking?*, trans. Fred D. Wieck and J. Glenn Gray (New York: Harper and Row, 1968), pp. 242-244; Gehtmann, *op. cit.*, pp. 31-41; M. Brelage, *Transzendentalphilosophie und konkrete Subjektivität. Eine Studie zur Geschichte der Erkenntnistheorie im 20. Jahrhundert* (Berlin: de Gruyter, 1965), p. 199. For the relationship between 'world' and 'Being' cf. Joseph J. Kockelmans, *The World in Science and Philosophy* (Milwaukee: The Bruce Publishing Company, 1969), pp. 69-71 and the literature quoted there.

[26]*Grundprobleme*, pp. 452-460, and passim; *The Essence of Reasons* (*Vom Wesen des Grundes*), trans. Terrence Malick (Evanston: Northwestern University Press, 1969), pp. 26ff.; cf. Joseph J. Kockelmans, "Ontological Difference", in Joseph J. Kockelmans, ed., *On Heidegger and Language* (Evanston: Northwestern University Press, 1972), pp. 195-234. For what follows cf. Gehtmann, *op. cit.*, pp. 41-45, 344 and *Kant and the Problem of Metaphysics*, pp. 242-247.

[27]K.O. Apel, *Dasein und Erkennen*, p. 71 (quoted in Gehtmann, *op. cit.*, p. 41 and p. 342, note 45).

[28]*The Essence of Reasons*, pp. 27-29; cf. William J. Richardson, *op. cit.*, pp. 174-75.

Being, the truth of Being, Being-itself (*Sinn von Sein, einai*) on the one
hand, and the Beingness of a being (*die Seiendheit eines Seienden,
ousia*) on the other. Already in the second section of *Being and Time*
Heidegger speaks of his attempt to examine the meaning of Being (*Sein
als Sein*) by examining a being (namely Dasein) in its Being
(*Seiendheit*). (*SZ* 5ff.)[29]

In Heidegger's thought the two differences are often taken in some
combination. The essential point then is to realize that the categorial-
ontological difference is founded upon the transcendental-ontological
difference in harmony with the general thesis that *Sinn* (meaning) is that
within which the understandability of something must maintain itself.
(*SZ* 151) Finally, one should notice also that Beingness can be correctly
called the 'ground' of a being, but that Being itself can never be
conceived as ground. (*SZ* 152)[30]

These introductory reflections on some of the presuppositons which
play an important part in Heidegger's investigations concerning the
method of ontology, however incomplete and inadequate in themselves,
may suffice to put us on the 'right way' in our attempt to come to a better
understanding of what Heidegger understands by 'hermeneutic
phenomenology'.

III. *Destructive Retrieve and Hermeneutic Phenomenology*

In the Introduction to *Being and Time*, after indicating that ontology
is concerned with the Being question and is to be prepared by a
fundamental ontology which takes the concrete form of an analytic of
Dasein's Being, Heidegger turns next to the question concerning 'the
right way of access' to the primary subject of investigation, namely
Dasein. He stresses the point that this problem is a very difficult one,
because Dasein is to be taken as something already accessible to itself
and as something yet to be understood. We must thus be able to explain
how and why Dasein itself can be grasped immediately, although the
kind of Being which it possesses is not to be presented just as
immediately, but as *to be mediated by explanation and interpretation.*
(*SZ* 15)

Dasein is in such a way that it is capable of understanding its own

---

[29]Martin Heidegger, *Nietzsche*, 2 vols. (Pfullingen: Neske, 1961), vol. I, p. 654; *An
Introduction to Metaphysics*, trans. Ralph Manheim (Garden City: Doubleday and
Company, 1959), pp. 25ff.

[30]*An Introduction to Metaphysics*, pp. 70ff.

Being; yet it has the tendency to do so in terms of those beings toward which it comports itself proximally. And this means that its 'categorial structure' remains to some degree concealed. Thus the philosophical interpretation of Dasein's Being is confronted with very peculiar difficulties. Furthermore, Dasein has been made the subject of both philosophical and scientific investigations. Thus there are already many ways in which Dasein has been interpreted. It is not clear how all of these interpretations can go together. This complexity makes the problem of securing the right access which will lead to Dasein's Being even a more burning one. We have no right to resort dogmatically to constructions and to apply just any idea of Being to Dasein, however self-evident such an idea may be, nor may any of the 'categories' which such an idea prescribes be forced upon Dasein without proper ontological consideration. (*SZ* 16)

1. *Destructive Retrieve*

In Heidegger's view temporality constitutes the meaning of Dasein's Being. (*SZ* 17ff.) Temporality is also the condition which makes historicity possible as a temporal mode of Being which Dasein itself possesses. Historicity stands here for the state of Being which is constitutive for Dasein's coming-to-pass as such. Dasein is *as* it already was and it is *what* it already was. Dasein is its past, not only in the sense that it possesses its own past as a kind of property which is still present-at-hand; Dasein is its past particularly in the way of its own Being which comes-to-pass out of its future on each occasion. Regardless of how Dasein is at a given time or how it may conceive of Being, it has grown up both *into* and *in* a traditional way of interpreting itself; in terms of this tradition it understands itself proximally and, to some degree at least, constantly. Its own past, which includes the past of its generation, is thus not something which just follows along after Dasein, but something which already goes ahead of it. (*SZ* 19f.; cf. 372ff.)

But if Dasein itself as well as its own understanding are intrinsically historical, then the inquiry into the meaning of Being is to be characterized by historicity as well. The ownmost meaning of Being which belongs to the inquiry into Being as an historical inquiry, points to the necessity of inquiring into the history of that inquiry itself. Thus in working out the question concerning the meaning of Being one must take heed of this pointing, so that by positively making the past his own, he may bring himself into full possession of the very possibility of such inquiry.

When a philosopher turns to philosophy's own history he must realize that this tradition constitutes that from which he thinks as well as that from which he, to some degree at least, must try to get away. Yet Dasein is inclined to fall prey to its tradition. This tradition often keeps it from providing its own guidance whether in inquiring or in choosing. When a tradition overpowers one's own thinking it often conceals what it really tried to transmit. Dasein has the tendency to take what the tradition hands down to it as being self-evident. This blocks the access to those primordial sources from which the categories, concepts, and views handed down have been drawn. Dasein is in fact so caught in its own tradition that in philosophy it often confines its interest to the multiformity of the available standpoints of philosophical inquiry; but by this interest it seeks to hide the fact that it has no ground of its own to stand on. The state in which philosophy's concern about the Being question finds itself today, is the clearest evidence of this tendency.

Thus in the inquiry of the question concerning the meaning of Being one has to have a ground of his own and yet one's thought must carefully heed its own philosophical tradition. Both these demands are met in the 'destructive retrieve'. One must 'destroy' in the tradition what is philosophically unjustifiable and maintain those primordial experiences from which any genuine philosophical insights ultimately flow. The meaning of the retrieve is not to shake off the philosophical tradition, but to stake out the positive possibilities of a tradition and keep it within its proper limits. (*SZ* 20-23) "By the re-trieving of a fundamental problem we understand the disclosure of its original potentialities that long have lain hidden. By the elaboration of the potentialities, the problem is transformed and thus for the first time in its intrinsic content conserved. To conserve a problem, however, means to retain free and awake all those inner forces that render this problem in its fundamental essence possible."[31]

It is obvious that in these reflections Heidegger takes a critical stance with respect to Descartes, Kant, and Husserl whose positions in regard to the philosophical tradition are too negative. In this regard Heidegger's is closer to that adopted by Hegel. The only point in which he does not follow Hegel in this respect consists in the fact that Hegel saw the various philosophical perspectives developed in the past as elements of an organic unity or system and that, thus, some form of necessity is constitutive for 'the life of the Whole'. In Heidegger's view,

---

[31] *Kant and the Problem of Metaphysics*, pp. 242-243; William J. Richardson, *op. cit.*, pp. 90-93.

philosophy's history does not bind the philosopher who lives today with the necessity of the unbreakable laws of the Hegelian dialectic; rather, the philosophical tradition, like every other form of tradition, delivers and liberates man. The answer to a philosophically relevant question consists in man's authentic response to what in philosophy's history is already on the way to him. Such a response implies, at the same time, his willingness to listen to what is already said and the courage to take distance from what he has heard. This makes a *certain* criticism of the past necessary in philosophy. Yet such a criticism should not be understood as a break with the past, nor as a repudiation of philosophy's history, but as its adoption in the form of a transformation and adaptation to the requirements of the world in which we live and of what in this world has been handed down to us. Heidegger, thus, does not deny the necessity to re-think every 'experience', to mediate it and transcend it. Yet he does deny that this should be done from the perspective of the absolute knowledge of the Absolute. In his opinion, each 'experience' is to be mediated from the perspective of Being. It is in this finite perspective that man understands his own Being in its full potentialities so that he can compare each mode of Being, present in each 'experience', with the whole of possibilities and thus understand its genuine, limited meaning. Furthermore, it is within this finite perspective that one can 'let things be seen from themselves and in themselves', because within this perspective, by projecting the things upon this a priori synthesis, one can show them in their full potentialities so that the concrete mode of givenness as found in a given 'experience' can appear in its true and limited sense.[32]

Heidegger obviously maintains that the philosophical reflection should be methodical and critical. Although he rejects presuppositionlessness (Husserl) and absoluteness (Hegel), he does not reject method and rigor. The first, last, and constant task of our philosophical reflection is never to allow our pre-judgments to be dominated by merely arbitrary conceptions, but rather to make the relevant themes secure *scientifically* by working out our anticipatory conceptions in terms of 'the things themselves'. (*SZ* 153) In other words, the destructive retrieve is guided by a hermeneutic phenomenology which in each case allows for a careful comparison of the claims made

---

[32]*Grundprobleme*, pp. 30-32; cf. Joseph J. Kockelmans, *The World in Science and Philosophy*, pp. 23ff.

by thinkers of the past with the 'things' to be reflected upon.[33] I shall return to the relationship between retrieve and phenomenology in section 5.

2. *Phenomenology: The Method of Ontology*

From Heidegger's own development, as witnessed by his earliest publications (1912-1927), *Being and Time, Die Grundprobleme der Phänomenologie,* and *Kant and the Problem of Metaphysics*, it is clear that he had a solid knowledge of the history of philosophy (Plato, Aristotle, Aquinas, Scotus, Suarez, Descartes, Leibniz, Kant, Hegel, the entire neo-Kantian tradition, Husserl). We may thus expect that as far as the question concerning the method of ontology is concerned, section 7 of *Being and Time* contains a systematic attempt to determine ontology's method in reference to the authors just mentioned. Yet, at first sight at least, this expectation is not fulfilled. Section 7 makes the impression of not being thought-out as carefully as many other sections of the book. The conception of phenomenology is explained not with reference to Hegel or Husserl, but merely with the help of some enigmatic comments on the expressions *phenomenon* and *logos* of which the compound expression consists. On the other hand, Heidegger states explicitly that section 7 gives no more than a *provisional* characterization of the method which is to be re-examined and further developed at a later stage. (*SZ* 28, 34, 347)

Upon closer investigation, however, it becomes clear that this first impression is unjustified and that the Introduction to *Being and Time* contains all the information on ontology's method which may be legitimately expected at that stage of the investigation. Yet it is undoubtedly important that any commentary on the introductory reflections on method carefully heed all the methodological reflections which in harmony with the circular character of all ontological investigation are found on many pages of the book and other related works of the same period.

In Heidegger's opinion the question of the 'right approach' is a very important one in ontology. (*SZ* 15-16) Ontology must deal with its subject matter by employing the phenomenological method. The concept 'phenomenology' is no more than a methodological concept; it does not characterize the subject matter of ontology, but merely the manner in which ontology must treat its subject matter. What is meant

---

[33]*Grundprobleme*, pp. 26-32.

by phenomenology can be explained by means of a reference to the maxim: *Zu den Sachen selbst.* Thus Heidegger points to Husserl for a first specification of the method of ontology. In Heidegger's interpretation Husserl's maxim: To the things themselves, implies that ontology avoids all free-floating constructions, all artificial and accidental findings, all seemingly justified conceptions, and all adherence to pseudo-problems. Heidegger admits that this first characterization of the phenomenological method is almost trivial and that perhaps it can be applied to any method to be employed in any type of scientific research. It appears that Heidegger deliberately wished to keep his remarks on phenomenology as 'formal' as possible in order to avoid giving the impression that the term 'phenomenology' was to be taken to refer to a historical position in philosophy. In his view it is dangerous to seek help from methodological conceptions of the past. (*SZ* 27)

In his letter to Richardson (1962) Heidegger provides us with the following information. The concept of phenomenology contained in section 7 of *Being and Time* was prepared by the immediate experience of the phenomenological method which was provided to him through his conversations with Husserl. In the development which subsequently took place the two basic words of Greek thought: *logos* (to make manifest) and *phainesthai* (to show oneself) played an important part. A careful study of some sections of the works of Aristotle had led him to the view that *aletheuein* is to be understood as a process of revealment and, correspondingly, that truth is to be characterized as non-concealment, to which all self-manifestation of beings pertains. Furthermore, it became clear to him also that the question about Being under the guise of presence is to be developed into the question about Being in terms of its time-character. Once *aletheia* and *ousia* were re-interpreted in this manner, the meaning and scope of the principle of phenomenology became clear. The maxim 'to the things themselves' does not refer to intentional consciousness or the transcendental ego; instead Being is to be the first and last 'thing-itself' of thought. Meanwhile Husserl had developed his own conception of phenomenology as a distinctive philosophical position according to a pattern set by Descartes, Kant, and Fichte which leaves no room for the historicity of thought. Thus the Being-question, unfolded in *Being and Time*, had to part company with this philosophical position; yet the unfolding of that question was effected on the basis of a more faithful adherence to the very principle of phenomenology as Husserl originally conceived of it. Heidegger concludes his reflections with the remark that these developments constituted a tangled process which at that time was inscrutable even to himself.[34]

Thus from *Being and Time* as well as from his later reflections on the development of his work, it is clear that Heidegger felt that he should give tribute to Husserl, particularly to Husserl's original conception of phenomenology as contained in *Logical Investigations*; [35] yet on the other hand, he makes it quite clear also that he had to take distance from Husserl's transcendental idealism, systematically developed in the first volume of *Ideas*. Thus he could write in *Being and Time*: "Our comments on the preliminary conception of phenomenology have shown that what is essential in it does not lie in its actuality as a philosophical trend. Higher than actuality stands possibility. We can understand phenomenology only by seizing upon its possibility." (*SZ* 38) Anyone who subscribes to the historicity of all human thought and yet adheres to the view that in ontology all problems are to be examined in the light of 'the things themselves', will understand immediately that even the reflections on ontology's method necessarily imply the destructive retrieve.

At this point it is tempting to subject the relationship between Husserl's and Heidegger's conceptions of phenomenology to careful scrutiny, but I have finally decided to refrain from any attempt in that direction in that it has become clear to me that it is totally impossible to do justice to such an encompassing task within the confines of this article.[36] However, to clarify Heidegger's conception of phenomenology it is important to focus at least on one issue which

---

[34]Letter to Richardson, pp. *x-xvi*.

[35]*SZ* 38 note; *Zur Sache des Denkens*, pp. 81ff.

[36]Gehtmann, *op. cit.*, pp. 45-52, 85-92, 102-108, 123-126, 135-153, 220-236, passim; cf. Joseph J. Kockelmans, *A First Introduction to Husserl's Phenomenology* (Pittsburgh: Duquesne University Press, 1967), pp. 330-334; Ludwig Landgrebe, *Phänomenologie und Metaphysik* (Hamburg: Schröder, 1949), pp. 83-100; Walter Biemel, "Husserls Encyclopaedia Britannica Artikel und Heideggers Anmerkungen dazu", in *Tijdschrift voor Philosophie*, 12 (1950) 246-280; Paul Ricoeur, *Husserl: An Analysis of his Phenomenology* (Evanston Northwestern University Press, 1967); "Phénoménologie et herméneutique", in *Man and World* 7 (1974) 223-255; Joseph J. Kockelmans, "World-Constitution. Reflections on Husserl's Transcendental Idealism", in *Analecta Husserliana* 1 (1971) 11-35.

occupies a central position in a comparison of hermeneutic phenomenology with transcendental phenomenology. For Husserl transcendental subjectivity performs the constitution and is at the same time the ground of everything that will be so constituted. "The phenomenological explication of this monadic ego--the problem of its constitution for itself--must in general include all problems of constitution. And in the final accounting this constitution of the self for the self coincides with phenomenology as a whole."[37] If all transcendental Being is really no more than the life of the ego, the problem of Being's constitution coincides with the self-constitution of the ego.[38] Once the constituting subject is understood exhaustively, everything else is so understood as well.

Heidegger, on the other hand, does not subscribe to the view that the universal constituting force is to be found in the human subject; rather this force is to be found in 'the truth of Being', whereas Dasein merely plays a subordinate part in its constituting achievement. Dasein is that in which the constitution comes-to-pass. Thus for Heidegger the problem of man's understanding ultimately presupposes the coming-to-pass of the constituting 'truth of Being' in Dasein. In other words, the meaning of Being is not accessible to transcendental subjectivity by means of the latter's constitutive self-disclosure, but Dasein must be 'wrested' and made explicit from the comprehension of Being which comes-to-pass in Dasein's Being. (*SZ* 36) Thus to explain something phenomenologically means to make it explicitly comprehensible by means of the a priori comprehension of Being through which Dasein understands Being unthematically. Ontological investigations must be oriented first toward a being, namely Dasein; but they must then be steered away from this being and led back to this being's Being. This step of the phenomenological method is called the phenomenological reduction. Yet this turning away from being is still a negative step. In addition, a positive step is to be taken which has the character of an achievement. Being is not just found in beings as pebbles in a brook; it must be brought into view by means of a projection. To project a given being upon its Being and its structures is the task of the phenomenological construction. Such a projection presupposes that

---

[37]Edmund Husserl, *Cartesian Mediations*, trans. Dorion Cairns (The Hague: Nijhoff, 1960), p. 68.
[38]Paul Ricoeur, *op. cit.*, p. 113.

there is a transcendental a priori framework in which the projection can take place; this is the truth of Being which comes-to-pass in an implicit form in the comprehension of Being which is constitutive of Dasein's Being.[39]

The Being of being for Husserl is posited in the subject and by the subject, whereas the subject as transcendental is self-positing. For Heidegger, on the other hand, the Being of being is indeed posited in Dasein: "Only as long as Dasein *is* (that is, only as long as an understandiing is ontically possible) 'is there' Being." (*SZ* 212) Yet the Being of being is not posited by Dasein, but by the truth of Being which functions as the transcendental a priori synthesis.[40]

3. *Phenomenon*

Heidegger begins his own explanation of what is to be understood by phenomenology with the remark that the expression itself has two basic components: 'phenomenon' and 'logos'. In his view a preliminary conception of phenomenology can be developed by characterizing what one means by the term's two components and by then establishing the meaning of the name in which these two components are put together. (*SZ* 28)

The concept of phenomenon is first determined purely formally as 'that which shows itself', the manifest. Now a being can show itself in many ways, depending in each case on the kind of access one has to it. Furthermore, a being can show itself as something which in itself it is not. Then it looks like something else; but it is not this being. This kind of showing-itself is called *semblance*. It is important to observe that when phenomenon signifies 'semblance', the primordial signification of the term (namely phenomenon as the manifest) is already included as that upon which the second signification is founded. (SZ 28f.)

Both phenomenon and semblance must be distinguished from what is called *appearance*. When we speak about an 'appearance' we are not speaking about something which shows itself, but about something which announces itself in something else which shows itself, although that which so appears does not show itself. Examples of appearance are for instance: symptoms, signs, symbols, etc. In this case, too, that which announces itself is never a phenomenon, although its appearing is possible only by reason of the showing itself of something else and, thus,

---

[39] *Grundprobleme*, pp. 27-30.
[40] Gehtmann, *op. cit.*, pp. 45-52, 135-140, 185-203, and passim.

by reason of a phenomenon in the proper sense of the term. (SZ 29-31)

Until now we have limited ourselves merely to defining the purely *formal* meaning of the term phenomenon and distinguishing phenomenon from semblance and appearance. We have not yet specified which entities we consider to be phenomena and have left open the question of whether what shows itself is a being or rather some characteristic which a being has as far as its Being is concerned. In order to be able to answer this question, Heidegger makes a distinction between the ordinary and the phenomenological conception of phenomenon, both of which are then defined with an explicit reference to Kant. *Phenomenon in the ordinary sense* is any being which is accessible to us through the 'empirical intuition'. Formulated again within the perspective of the Kantian framework the *phenomenon in the phenomenological sense* is that which already shows itself in the appearance as prior to the phenomenon in the ordinary sense and as accompanying it in every case. Even though it shows itself unthematically, it can nonetheless be brought to show itself thematically. Thus the phenomena of phenomenology are those beings which show themselves in themselves, Kant's forms of intuition. In other words, the phenomena in the phenomenological sense refer to the conditions of the possibility of the objects of experience. (SZ 31) In section 5 to come I plan to clarify these references to Kant from Heidegger's own perspective.

4. *Apophantic Logos and Truth*

In the introduction to the section on method Heidegger stresses the point that the element '-logy' in the expression 'phenomenology' refers to the scientific character of the investigation concerning phenomena. (*SZ* 28) In an essay on method, therefore, the scientificity of phenomenology is to be made thematic. One may thus say that phenomenology does not merely indicate the approach to, but also the clarifying mode of determination of, the subject matter of ontology. In other words, two elements are contained in the concept of phenomenology: one dealing with the question of how the things are to be discovered and another concerned with the question of when such discovery may be taken to be adequate, i.e., when a discovery may be taken to be true. Thus we may expect that section 7 B contains a provisional analysis of the concept of truth. To this end Heidegger turns toward Aristotle who in his opinion originally conceived of truth as the unhiddenness of what is present, its unveiling, its manifesting-itself.[41] The analysis shows that the phenomenological conception of phenomenon implies a conception of truth which is notably different from the one found in Kant as well as from that developed by Husserl. Heidegger contends that the classical definition of truth as agreement is concerned with a derivative conception of truth, whereas Husserl's thesis that truth is to be defined in terms of perfect, i.e., apodictic and adequate evidence,[42] is unacceptable. (*SZ* 212-230)

Section 7 B begins with a reference to the fact that for Plato and Aristotle the concept '*logos*' has many, competing significations, none of which at first sight seems to be primordial. And yet the term appears to have a basic meaning in light of which all other, derivative meanings can be understood. One could perhaps say that the basic signification of *logos* consists in articulating discourse (*Rede*). But such a translation remains unjustified as long as one is unable to determine precisely what is meant by this expression and indicate how from this basic meaning all other significations of the term can be derived. (*SZ* 32)

Logos is related to *legein* which means to make manifest what one is talking about. As such it has the same meaning as *apophainesthai*. *Logos* lets something be seen, namely what the talk is about; and it does so for those who are somehow involved in the discourse. *Logos* furthermore lets something be seen from the very thing the talk is about. In *logos* as discourse (*apophansis*) what is said is drawn from what the talk is about, so that discursive communication, in what it says, makes manifest what the talk is about and makes it accessible to others. When in this context *logos* becomes fully concrete, then discoursing, as letting something be seen, has the character of speaking. (*SZ* 32-3)

Furthermore, because *logos* is a letting something be seen, it can therefore be true or false. But it is of the greatest importance to realize that truth cannot be understood here in the sense of an agreement between what is and what is said. Such a conception of truth is by no means the primary one. The Greek word for truth is *aletheia* and this means unconcealment. The being-true of the *logos* as *aletheuein* means that the beings about which one is talking must be taken out of their original hiddenness: one must let them be seen as something unhidden (*a-lethes*); this means, the beings must be discovered. And only because

---

[41]SZ 32 note; *Zur Sache des Denkens,* p. 87; Letter to Richardson, pp. *x-xii.*
[42]Edmund Husserl, *Cartesian Meditations,* p. 12.

the function of the *logos* as *apophansis* lies in letting something be seen by pointing it out, can it have the structural form of a synthesis. Here 'synthesis' does not mean a binding together of representations or the manipulation of psychical occurrences from which the pseudo-problem arises of how these bindings, as something inside, agree with something physical outside. Synthesis here means letting something be seen in its togetherness with something, letting it be seen *as* something. When something no longer takes the form of just letting something be seen, but always harks back to something else to which it points, so that it lets something be seen *as* something, it thus acquires a synthesis-structure, and with this it takes over the possibility of covering up. Being-false amounts to deceiving in the sense of covering-up: putting something in front of something else in such a way as to let the former be seen, thereby passing the latter off as something which it is not. (SZ 33-4)

Seen from the perspective of the enormous task in regard to the tradition, particularly in regard to Aristotle, Kant, and Husserl, which Heidegger appears to have set for himself here, section 7 B seems to be disappointing. First of all, it is not very clear precisely what the basic issue is with which Heidegger is concerned. Secondly, the section seems to suggest that *methodical* thought in ontology is not really necessary in view of the fact that a simple letting-be-seen seems to suffice.[43] Yet one should realize once more that section 7 contains merely the provisional conception of phenomenology, which later is to be developed further, once the analytic of Dasein has reached its conclusion. Secondly, what Heidegger suggests in section 7 B is to be understood from the perspective of what will be said later about the precise function of theoretical knowledge (*SZ* 59-62), about 'reality' (*SŻ* 200-212), and particularly about disclosedness and truth (*SZ* 212-230). Finally Heidegger explicitly indicates that the reflections contained in section 7 B were inspired by a careful study of Aristotle.[44]

When all of this information is taken together it becomes clear that the real meaning of section 7 B consists in the following: a being, whose ontological conception becomes manifest to Dasein (*alethes*), is, as far as its mode of becoming manifest (*logos apophantikos*) is concerned, dependent upon Dasein's disclosure. The *identity* expressed in the apophántic *logos* rests on the synthesis a priori (the truth of Being) and

---

[43]Cf. Hans Albert, *Traktat über kritische Vernunft* (Tübingen: Mohr, 1968), p. 145; cf. Gehtmann, *op. cit.*, p. 93.

[44]Aristotle, *Peri Hermeneias*, c. 1-6; *Metaphysics, Z*; and *Eth. Nicom. Z.*

at the same time presupposes a *difference* with which Dasein's disclosure is concerned and which accounts for the fact that all finite letting something be seen really is a letting something be seen *as*. It is the latter which demands methodic justification and most certainly does not exclude it.[45]

5. *The Preliminary Conception of Phenomenology*

From the interpretation of the words 'phenomenon' and 'logos' it becomes clear that there is an inner relationship between the things meant by these words. Taken as *legein* (= *apophainesthai*) *ta phainomena*, the expression 'phenomenology' means: to let that which shows itself be seen from itself the very way it shows itself. This is the formal meaning of the term phenomenology which expresses the same thing as the maxim formulated earlier: to the things themselves. (*SZ* 34-5)

But what is it that phenomenology is to 'let us see'? We have seen already that this question must be answered if we are ever to be able to go from a purely formal conception of phenomenon to the phenomenological conception. What is it, therefore, that by its very Being must be called a 'phenomenon' in a distinctive sense? What is it that is necessarily the theme whenever we try to exhibit something explicitly? Obviously, it is something that proximally and for the most part does not show itself; it is something that lies hidden in contrast to that which proximally and for the most part does show itself. Yet at the same time it must be something that belongs to what thus shows itself, and it must belong to it so essentially as to constitute its very meaning and ground.

History of philosophy shows us that that which remains hidden in a specific sense, which relapses and gets covered up time and again, is not this or that being, nor this or that kind of being, but rather the Being of these beings. Being can even be covered up so extensively that it becomes forgotten and there no longer is any question which arises about it and its ultimate meaning. In other words, that which demands that it become a phenomenon, and which demands this in a distinctive sense and in terms of its ownmost content as a thing, is precisely that which phenomenological philosophy wants to make the very subject matter and theme of its own investigations. But if phenomenology is Dasein's way of access to what is to be the theme of ontology, it is clear

---

[45]Gehtmann, *op. cit.*, pp. 113-114; cf. 107-114.

that the phenomenological conception of phenomenon as that which shows itself must refer to the Being of the beings, to its meaning, its modification, and its derivatives. (*SZ* 35,230)

For phenomenology to be possible and necessary, something must be manifest and something else, inherently connected with the manifest, must still be hidden. That which is manifest essentially implies both truth as unconcealment and immediacy. Thus being, taken as phenomenon, means being taken in immediate unconcealment. In view of the fact that each being can show itself in different ways, depending upon Dasein's manner of approach (*SZ* 28), the showing-itself always and necessarily implies some form of mediation in that the manner of approach to the things appears to be constitutive of what will show itself as the manifest. Therefore, phenomenology means the methodical mediation of the immediacy of the truth of the phenomena.

Here Heidegger takes his point of departure in the conviction that before things appear to us, they obviously 'are' already. The basic question is not whether there are 'real' things; there obviously are 'real' things, because otherwise nothing at all would appear to us. The fundamental question is connected rather with the necessary conditions which must be fulfilled in order that things can appear to us the way they do, so that it will be possible to ask the question of what their appearance precisely means. When beings appear to us, they always appear as either this or that. They can appear to us in many ways; how they in fact will appear to us depends upon the kind of access we have to them in each case (*SZ* 28). In the final analysis, the question of how a being will appear to us, depends upon the a priori synthesis from which this being is taken in each case; all letting be seen *as* presupposes some synthesis a priori (*SZ* 34). When a being appears to us in its 'genuine' mode of Being, when it appears to us 'the way it really is', it appears to us from the perspective of the *transcendental* synthesis a priori, which consists in the meaning or the truth of Being. Thus the expression 'to show itself' can be applied meaningfully in ontology to both a being and to its Being. Thus we can now determine the concept of phenomenon more adequately: phenomenon in the ordinary sense of the term is not a being, but the showing-itself of a being; phenomenon in the phenomenological sense of the term is not the Being of a being, but the showing-itself of this Being in light of the truth of Being. The immediacy of Dasein's relation to a being is to be mediated by the truth of Being; for a being to show itself to Dasein, there must be a transcendental, a priori horizon which consists in the truth of Being. In other words, the showing-itself of the beings is conditioned by the truth of Being. The showing-*itself* of a being is really a *being-brought* to show-itself on the basis of the a priori synthesis. There is a showing-itself of a being (phenomenon in the ordinary sense) if and only if there is an a priori horizon within which this being can show itself as that which it really is. This showing-itself of beings is precisely the immediacy which every methodical mediation must presuppose; that which is mediated by the method is the phenomenon in the phenomenological sense of the term. Yet there can be an explanation of phenomena (phenomenology) only if there is a transcendental ontological synthesis, i.e., the truth of Being. Thus it is clear that phenomenology is possible only as ontology.[46]

Heidegger hints at all of these implications when in defining the term phenomenon in the strict sense he does not use the expression: *das Sich-selbst-zeigende* (that which shows-itself), but *das Sich-an-ihm-selbst-zeigende* (that which shows itself with respect to itself). This '*an*' implies that in what shows-itself there is some difference; it is this difference in the immediacy of the phenomenon which requires the mediation to be brought about by the methodical approach. (*SZ* 35ff.)[47] This difference is to be determined for both the phenomenon in the ordinary sense and the phenomenon in the phenomenological sense. The phenomenon in the ordinary sense, the being, shows-itself; yet it manifests itself in such a way that the 'activity' implied in the showing is not the activity of the being itself. It shows itself in the framework of an a priori synthesis; it shows itself *as* something. The showing is accomplished with respect to it; it is constitutive for the it-self of the being that the showing is accomplished with regard to it. This occurs by means of the 'projection' of Being accomplished by Dasein; in that case the being is 'explained' *as* being from the perspective of the a priori comprehension of Being. On the other hand, the a priori structures, i.e., the Being of a being, do not show themselves from themselves either; they show themselves in their founding function only in the being which is so founded; yet they show themselves in the process of founding as that which gives it its foundation. The Being of a being again manifests itself '*an ihm*' in the sense that here, too, the immediacy of its showing is mediated by the being as well as by the truth of Being. Thus the immediacy of the phenomenon taken in both the ordinary and phenomenological sense does not exclude, but precisely requires the mediating, methodical

---

[46]*Kant and the Problem of Metaphysics*, pp. 46-7; Gehtmann, *op. cit.*, pp. 93-107.
[47]Gehtmann, *op cit.*, pp. 99-101.

explanation; nor does it presuppose that the question concerning the meaning or truth of Being be solved in advance.[48]

Heidegger thus agrees with Hegel that the necessary immediacy of the things themselves does not exclude but precisely requires the employment of method. The mediation, however, does not take place through the reflection of the subject taken as consciousness, but through Dasein for whose Being some comprehension of Being is constitutive; nor is the reflection guided by an anticipation of the absolute Truth, but merely by Being as the process of the coming-to-pass of the truth.

6. *Hermeneutic Phenomenology*

The ontological problematic which is concerned with the *conditions* of the possibility of the being's showing-itself, i.e., with the truth of Being, requires that the reflection on method not limit itself to determining the way in which the meaning of Being can be investigated (ontology); it must explain also how Dasein is to be examined in its relation to the things in the world. Thus a treatise on the method of ontology demands *on transcendental grounds* that an introductory analytic of Dasein be developed. Says Heidegger: "Because phenomena, as understood phenomenologically, are never anything but what goes to make up Being, while Being is in every case the Being of some being, we must first bring forward the beings themselves if it is our aim that Being should be laid bare; and we must do this in the right way." (*SZ* 37)

With respect to the subject matter of phenomenology one could say indeed that phenomenology is the science of the Being of beings; it is in this sense that phenomenology may be called ontology. Yet in explaining the task of ontology we have already referred to the necessity of a fundamental ontology which has to take the form of an ek-sistential analytic of Dasein. Fundamental ontology must prepare our investigation of the question concerning the meaning of Being. Thus that which phenomenology is concerned with first is the Being of Dasein. This Being which is now concealed, was once revealed; it has slipped back into oblivion; it is revealed now again, but in a distorted fashion so that man's Dasein now seems to be what in fact it is not. It is precisely inasmuch as Being is not seen that phenomenology is necessary. For Dasein to reveal itself of its own accord as that which it is

---

[48]*Ibid.*, p. 101.

and how it is, it must be submitted to phenomenological analysis in order to lay the Being of Dasein out in full view. *Such* a laying-out necessarily takes the form of an *interpretation*; this is the reason why phenomenology is essentially hermeneutical. (*SZ* 37)

The term 'hermeneutic' seems to have its historical origin in biblical exegesis. Later it was applied to the interpretation of the meaning of historical documents and works of art. As the expression is used here by Heidegger it no longer refers to documents and results of man's artistic activities, but to man's own Being. But what does it mean to interpret a non-symbolic fact such as man's Being? Interpretation focuses on the meaning of things; it presupposes that what is to be interpreted has meaning and that this meaning is not immediately obvious. Dasein obviously has meaning and this meaning allows for interpretation. For as ek-sistence Dasein is essentially related to its own Being as that which continuously is at stake for it. In view of the fact that Dasein as ek-sistence is oriented toward possibilities which reach beyond itself, Dasein is capable of interpretation. But Dasein's Being also requires interpretation. For just as Being has the tendency to fall into oblivion, so man's Being has the tendency to degenerate.

The phenomenology of Dasein is even hermeneutic in three different senses. It is hermeneutical first because (as we have just seen) in this particular case phenomenology cannot be anything but interpretation. It is hermeneutic also in the sense that by uncovering the meaning of Being and the basic structures of Dasein the conditions on which the possibility of *any* ontological investigation depends become worked-out. And finally, insofar as Dasein, because of its ek-sistence, has ontological priority over all other beings, hermeneutic, as the interpretation of Dasein's Being, has also the specific meaning of an analytic of the ek-sistentiality of Dasein's ek-sistence. And this latter is the sense which is philosophically primary. (*SZ* 37-8)

By specifying the phenomenological method with the help of the concept of hermeneutic Heidegger again makes any interpretation of his claims very difficult. Hermeneutic has a relatively long and complex history to which Heidegger does not really relate his own efforts.[49] Furthermore, hermeneutic is often taken as the method characteristic for the humanities, whereas the term is taken here to refer to the method of fundamental ontology. Yet one should note again, that in section 7

---

[49]Cf. E. Palmer, *Hermeneutics* (Evanston: Northwestern University Press, 1969).

Heidegger merely developed a preliminary conception of the method of ontology. What is said here about hermeneutic must be understood from the perspective of his view on understanding (*SZ* 142-160), temporality (*SZ* 301ff.), and the implications of all of this for the so-called hermeneutic circle (*SZ* 7, 152f., 311ff., 436-7). In an attempt to understand what Heidegger precisely means by hermeneutic, one must begin by bracketing all treatises which deal with hermeneutic as the *doctrine* of the method of explanation.[50]

Heidegger first states that hermeneutic means the business of explanation (*SZ* 148-153); explanation (*Auslegung*) determines the methodical sense of the phenomenological 'description'. We have seen that phenomenon in the phenomenological sense consists in the Being of beings; this shows itself only by means of a methodical mediation. Explanation therefore is the methodical procedure through which the Being of beings as well as the basic structures of Dasein's Being are made accessible to Dasein's understanding. (*SZ* 37) Explanation is concerned ultimately with the meaning of Being; thus the task of hermeneutic is an ontological one. Yet the meaning of Being must be made known to Dasein's understanding. Although Dasein is to be characterized by its comprehension of Being, the meaning of Being is still somehow hidden for it. This fact explains the possibility as well as the necessity of a method for ontology. Dasein's comprehension of Being does not exclude the methodical mediation, but makes it both possible and necessary. This is the reason why Heidegger can say that hermeneutic, as the interpretation of Dasein's Being, has the specific sense of an analytic of the ek-sistentiality of ek-sistence. (*SZ* 38, cf. 436)

Hermeneutic characterizes the specific character of that method which is determined by the fact that the thing to be investigated by it, always already functions as a condition for its application, so that the quest for the "thing itself" coincides with the quest for the conditions of the possibility of the investigation of the things through method. This leads us to the second characterization of hermeneutic: it becomes a 'hermeneutic' in the sense of working out the conditions on which the possibility of any ontological investigation depends. (*SZ* 37)

From all of this it follows that hermeneutic is the methodological, fundamental concept of ontology as such. Because the question

---

[50]Martin Heidegger, *On the Way to Language*, trans. Peter D. Hertz (New York: Harper and Row, 1971), pp. 29-31.

concerning the meaning of Being is oriented toward that which, as the transcendental synthesis a priori, conditions all knowledge of whatever there is, the method of the investigation concerning the meaning of Being is conditioned by the very subject matter of the investigation. And in view of the fact that the subject matter of the investigation is always already 'there' in Dasein's primordial comprehension of Being, the method must have the form of an explantation (*Auslegung*) in which what is constitutive of Dasein becomes explained by Dasein and for Dasein. The explanation found in *Being and Time* constitutes a form of man's hermeneutic-transcendental questioning.[51]

The hermeneutic character of the phenomenological method is intimately connected with the transcendental conception of the philosophical method as such. The meaning of Being for which ontology searches is knowable only through the fact that as a condition it itself must function as the a priori synthesis in that process in which a being of the mode of Being of Dasein constitutes the beings which do not have that mode of Being. Thus Being becomes methodically accessible only as that which is constituting in the effective constitution of beings which occurs in Dasein's understanding. Heidegger replaces an absolute conception of the a priori by a regulative one. The meaning or truth of Being is not something absolute from which the Being of beings can be deduced; the meaning of Being is not a universal principle of deduction or construction, but merely the universal horizon of explanation.

The reason Heidegger employed the expression 'hermeneutic' to characterize the regulative conception of the a priori, is the similarity that appears to exist between the efforts of the person who tries to discover the meaning of a text and that of the philosopher who is concerned with the question concerning the meaning of Being. Yet the determination of the phenomenological method as hermeneutical really follows from the theme itself that is to be examined. Ontology is transcendental because it conceives of the Being question in a fundamental ontological manner as the question concerning the unthematic comprehension of Being which is constitutive of Dasein's Being. Being can be comprehended thematically only on the basis of this a priori comprehension of Being. Thus in order to make the Being

---

[51]Martin Heidegger, *Nietzsche*, vol. II, p. 415; cf. Gehtmann, *op. cit.*, pp. 114-118.

question explicit, it is necessary first to develop an analytic of Dasein's ek-sistentiality which must have the form of a hermeneutic. Being itself which is 'there' in Dasein's comprehension of Being, must be explained from this Being-there. The analytic taken as a hermeneutic of facticity is thus a 'methodical' component or element of transcendental ontology. But this means that hermeneutic is really 'founded upon' ontology and not the other way around.[52]

IV. *Conclusion*

The manner in which one conceives of the reversal (*Kehre*) in Heidegger's thinking, has a decisive influence on his opinion of Heidegger's conception of the method of 'thought'. In *Being and Time* Heidegger formulated his conception of method for the first time. After the reversal on several occasions he made remarks about *Being and Time* which at first sight seemed to suggest that much of what was argued for there, and particularly the manner in which it was argued, is to be overcome in the 'thought' which is characteristic of the period after the reversal. In particular his claims about the necessity of overcoming metaphysics and ontology seem to imply that the kind of thinking still found in *Being and Time* is to be overcome as well. Expressions such as 'a universal phenomenological ontology' and 'hermeneutic phenomenology' are no longer found in the later works. In the course given in the Winter of 1931-1932 Heidegger explicitly rejected both phenomenology and ontology on the ground that they still operate in a sphere to be characterized by the forgottenness of Being typical of all Western thought since Plato. And in the second Nietzsche volume he writes that phenomenology as well as all questioning which proceeds in a 'hermeneutico-transcendental manner' does not yet question in a manner which is characteristic of an investigation concerned with Being-as-history.[53]

Löwith has construed this development to mean that Heidegger really developed two different philosophical views. Pugliese, Richardson, and Gehtmann, following Müller and Schulz, have tried to show that Heidegger's work constitutes a harmonious unity which consists of two intrinsically related phases; Heidegger's later thought necessarily presupposes *Being and Time* and related works, whereas the philosophical reflections found in those earlier works imply the

---

[52]SZ 72 note; Gehtmann, *op. cit.,* pp. 118-122.
[53]*Nietzsche*, vol. II, p. 415; Gehtmann, *op. cit.*, pp. 21-22.

necessity of the reversal.[54] Heidegger seems to have authenticated the latter view in his letter to Richardson. In it he does not deny that *Being and Time* has its inherent weaknesses; yet he maintains that without *Being and Time* the later thought would not have been possible and that investigations of the kind found in *Being and Time* are a necessary condition for genuine thought.[55]

Furthermore, although it is true that the expression 'the overcoming of metaphysics', is often taken in a negative sense, there are quite a number of passages in which Heidegger defends the thesis that to think metaphysically is a necessary element of every authentic philosophical effort.[56]

If it is true that Heidegger later maintained that *Being and Time* is and remains a necessary phase in philosophical thought, then one cannot simply claim that Heidegger abandoned the view that phenomenology is the method of ontology. True, Heidegger later no longer uses the term 'phenomenology,' but in 1963 he stated explicitly that although the word had disappeared, phenomenology remains an essential possibility of thought.[57]

It seems reasonable to assume with Gehtmann that the reversal refers not to a breach in Heidegger's thinking in either a biographical or literary sense, but rather to a decisive characteristic of Heidegger's thought as a whole; the reversal refers to the necessity of thought's turning from a concern with Being from the viewpoint of Dasein to a concern with Being itself, i.e., Being as the coming-to-pass of truth.[58] Furthermore, it is reasonable also to assume that the reversal does not imply a denial of Heidegger's earlier investigations concerning the method of ontology. On the contrary, his concern with method is a

---

[54]K. Löwith, *Heidegger, Denker in dürftiger Zeit* (Göttingen: Vandenhoeck & Ruprecht, 1965), p. 8; O. Pugliese, *Vermittlung und Kehre. Grundzüge des Geschichtsdenken bei Martin Heidegger* (Munchen: Karl Alber, 1965), pp. 13ff.; William J. Richardson, *op. cit.*, pp. 623-641, and passim; Gehtmann, *op. cit.*, pp. 21-29; M. Müller, *Existenzphilosophie im geistigen Leben der Gegenwart* (Heidelberg: Kerle, 1964), pp. 138ff.; W. Schulz, "Ueber den philosophiegeschichtlichen Ort Martin Heideggers", in Otto Pöggeler, ed., *Heidegger* (Koln: Kiepenheuer & Witsch, 1969), pp. 95-139.

[55]Letter to Richardson, pp. *xvi-xxii.*

[56]Martin Heidegger, *Was ist Metaphysik?* (Frankfurt am Main: Vittorio Klostermann, 1955), pp. 43-51, 9; *On the Way to Language*, pp. 19ff.; *What is Called Thinking?*, pp. 100-110; *Identität und Differenz* (Pfullingen: Neske, 1957), p. 47.

[57]*Zur Sache des Denkens*, p. 90.

[58]*On the Way to Language*, pp. 11-13.

necessary condition for the proper understanding of the meaning of the reversal. Finally, it seems reasonable to claim that no one will properly understand what Heidegger means by 'thought' if he does not first begin with a careful study of *Being and Time* which, as far as the question of method is concerned, constitutes Heidegger's attempt to come to an authentic stance in regard to both the classical and the modern, transcendental traditions.[59] Yet one should observe also that if in the later works there appears to be the possibility of a thinking of the truth of Being which no longer thinks in the perspective of the categorial-ontological problematic of fundamental ontology, this thinking no longer can be hermeneutical, although it can still be called phenomenological.

---

[59]Gehtmann, *op. cit.*, p. 29.

Death and Utopia
Towards a Critique of the Ethics of Satisfaction

KARSTEN HARRIES
Yale University

1

Theology and philosophy today compete with each other in celebrating death as an existential category; perverting a biological fact into an ontological essence, they bestow transcendental blessing on the guilt of mankind which they help to perpetuate--they betray the promise of utopia.[1]

Marcuse does not identify the theologians and philosophers he has in mind; but he must be thinking above all of his former teacher Martin Heidegger, for more decisively than any other philosopher Heidegger has made death constitutive of man's essence: to be for man is to be towards death.

Is Heidegger right? Or is he, as Marcuse suggests, "perverting a biological fact into an ontological essence?"[2] More is at stake here than a disagreement between two philosophers. What guides Marcuse is moral concern; his critique of those who would elevate death into an ontological essence is part of a widely shared effort to give reality to dreams of unaliented existence and "integral satisfaction" which have long haunted man. Heidegger's fundamental ontology, if correct, would

---

[1] Herbert Marcuse, *Eros and Civilization. A Philosophical Inquiry into Freud* (New York: Vintage Books, 1962), p. 216.

[2] Sartre similarly maintains that death is "a contingent fact which belongs to facticity... Death is in no way an ontological structure of my being, at least not in so far as my being is *for itself.*" *Being and Nothingness*, tr. Hazel E. Barnes (New York: Philosophical Library, 1956), pp. 545-547.

force us to dismiss such efforts; if we follow Heidegger in his interpretation of death, we have to consider what Marcuse calls "the promise of utopia" merely utopian.

2

What does Marcuse have in mind when he speaks of "the promise of utopia?" What is that promise? And why is it betrayed by any view which makes death part of man's essence?

The "promise of utopia" answers to "the tabooed aspirations of humanity."[3] Man carries within him the memory of "integral gratification, which is the absence of want and repression. As such it is the immediate identity of necessity and freedom."[4] But as long as man experiences himself as subjected to time -- and such subjection reveals itself most forcefully in the certainty that he must die -- he cannot be at peace with himself. Freedom wars with necessity; man has to exist as he does not will to exist. To accept death is thus to submit and to repress one's deepest desire. "The brute fact of death denies once and for all the reality of non-repressive existence. For death is the final negativity of time, but 'joy wants eternity'. Timelessness is the ideal of pleasure."[5]

The incompatibility of "the ideal of pleasure" and time suggests itself as soon as we understand that ideal as "integral gratification" or "integral satisfaction." "Integral" emphasizes wholeness; it suggests that we are truly satisfied only when we are entire, complete, at one with ourselves. But are we not denied such completeness by our temporality? Desire, care, anticipation -- especially the anticipation of death -- all betray a lack which appears to be inseparable from human existence. If that lack and, with it, the inability to come to rest in the present, are constitutive of the human situation, man's search for final satisfaction must be in vain; "timelessness is the ideal of pleasure."

The claim is of course hardly novel. Marcuse himself invokes the *Symposium*[6], where Plato points out that man's temporal existence is marked by lack and by a striving to overcome that lack. Aristophanes' speech describes man as fragmented being, in search of the whole; love is the desire for lost completeness. Diotima's discourse develops and deepens that analysis; the aim of love is said to be the perpetual possession of the good. If man is to gain such possession he must discover a way of escaping the destructiveness of time. Eros demands

---

[3] *Eros and Civilization*, p. 17.

[4] *Ibid.*

[5] *Ibid.*, p. 211.

[6] *Ibid.*, pp. 25, 192-193.

eternity. On its lower level it tries to achieve this by making sure that something of the individual will survive him, children for example, or fame, or works. But eros cannot finally be satisfied with such temporal counterparts of true eternity. The higher mysteries of love lead beyond time: only when the soul ascends to the vision of true beauty, is the burden of time cast off.

Such an ascent makes sense only if man is not bound to the realm of becoming, if death is not part of his essence. Plato thus maintains that the soul, while dragged by the body into the region of the changeable, yet belongs to being. Marcuse cannot follow Plato in this. He criticizes Plato for intellectualizing eros by downgrading man's sensuous and appetitive faculties and all that is connected with the body.[7] To Plato and to the tradition stemming from him he opposes Nietzsche, who is said to have been the only philosopher to surmount the ontological tradition[8]: Nietzsche was right to point to "the spirit of revenge," to "the will's ill will against time and its 'it was'," as the deepest source of self-alienation.[9] Unable to accept his temporality, unable to forgive himself his own impotence, man dreams of eternity, of realms of being beyond becoming which promise the integral satisfaction which this life denies. And yet, that promise, consoling alienated man, only compounds alienation. Not that Marcuse would have us renounce the longing for eternity, but eternity must be sought not beyond this life, but within it. Real happiness is of the earth.

To overcome "the spirit of revenge" Nietzsche turned to the doctrine of the eternal return. Marcuse cannot follow Nietzsche this far. But he, too, has to show how eternity can "become present in the here and now."[10] Something in man has to escape the tyranny of becoming if the ideal of pleasure is not to prove just another empty dream. Developing suggestions found in Freud's *New Introductory Lectures on Psychoanalysis*, Marcuse claims that "Time has no power over the id, the original domain of the pleasure principle."[11] Freud's id thus takes the place of Plato's soul. The Platonic image of man is inverted as

---

[7] *Ibid.*, p. 114.

[8] *Ibid.*, p. 108.

[9] *Thus Spoke Zarathustra*, Second Part, "On Redemption," tr. Walter Kaufmann.

[10] *Eros and Civilization*, p. 110.

[11] *Ibid.*, p. 211, cf. p. 27.

eternity is sought not above, in the realm of forms, but below, in the depths of the unconscious. Any such inversion retains much of the original picture. Most importantly, both Plato and Marcuse subscribe to what I want to call an *ethics of satisfaction,* which makes *being at one with oneself* the goal of man's striving. If this hope for satisfaction is to be more than illusory, reality, more specifically man's own reality, must transcend the power of time. The ethics of satisfaction demands an ontology which opposes being to time and asserts the primacy of being over becoming.

Already the title of Heidegger's *Being and Time* announces his disagreement with that tradition. By tying man's essence to death, Heidegger subjects man to time and denies him that pleasure which Marcuse demands.

3

Is Heidegger right to make death into an existential category? Is man's existence inseparably tied to the dreading anticipation of death? How can such a claim be supported or refuted? The appeal to our usual, everyday understanding of death cannot be decisive. For if, as Heidegger insists, man is essentially towards death, this is not to say that he will necessarily be open to his own being-towards-death. Quite the contrary: in dread of death, man will tend to hide from himself his own mortality. Of course, he knows that everyone has to die sooner or later; but for the time being his attention is claimed by more immediate concerns. Heidegger thus maintains that first of all and most of the time the phenomenon of death is covered up and with it man's essence.

Must man's usual failure to exist resolutely towards death be interpreted as a covering up of death? Why not speak instead of an authentic response to life? It is only too easy to dismiss phenonema which are difficult to reconcile with one's own "phenomenological" construction as somehow deficient. What enables Heidegger to insist that our usual understanding of death is inauthentic? He himself grants that such claims cannot be supported by an appeal to the phenomena as they present themselves "proximally and for the most part" (*zunächst und zumeist*). As he points out, his existential analysis has the "character of *doing violence*" to everyday understanding (*SZ* 311).[12]

---

[12] Page references in the text are to *Sein und Zeit*, 7th ed. (Tübingen: Niemeyer, 1953),

Such analysis must oppose itself to common sense; its insights must be wrested from our usual tendency to cover up our own being. But how can such a "violent" phenomenology distinguish itself from willful and arbitrary construction? What guiding thread leads us beyond phenomena as they present themselves "proximally and for the most part" to Heidegger's analysis of death?

Such questions become particularly urgent, given Heidegger's own appeal to everydayness. According to Heidegger, the aim of *Being and Time* "is to work out the question of the meaning of Being and to do so concretely." (*SZ* 1) Such a working out, he insists, cannot be separated from an investigation into the being of the questioner. "Therefore *fundamental ontology*, from which alone all other ontologies can take their rise, must be sought in the *existential analytic of Dasein*." (*SZ* 13) But how do we find proper access to this analytic? How can we assure that we do not read our own preconceptions into what is to be analyzed? Aware of this difficulty, Heidegger insists that we "choose such a way of access and such a kind of interpretation that this entity can show itself in itself and from itself. And this means that it is to be shown as it is *proximally and for the most part*--in its average *everydayness*." (*SZ* 16) This, however, does not establish "average everydayness" as something like a ground. The phrase "proximally and for the most part" is crucial. It indicates the brackets within which the analysis of the entire first part of *Being and Time* proceeds. Because of these brackets that analysis can have no more than a "provisional" and "preparatory" character. It is not yet "authentically ontological" and cannot claim primordiality. (*SZ* 17) In the beginning of the second part, this provisional character of the preceding analyses is re-emphasized:

> One thing has become unmistakable: *our existential analysis of Dasein up till now cannot lay claim to primordiality*. Its forehaving never included more than the *inauthentic* Being of Dasein, and of Dasein as *less* than a *whole*. If the Interpretation of Dasein's Being is to become primordial, as a foundation for working out the basic question of ontology, then it must first have brought to light

---

abbreviated *SZ*. Tr. J. Macquarrie and E. Robinson, *Being and Time* (New York: Harper and Row, 1962).

existentially the Being of Dasein in its possibilities of *authenticity* and *totality*. (*SZ* 233)

It is especially the latter notion of totality (*Ganzheit*) which must be kept in mind if we are to understand what separates the provisional analytic of Dasein offered in the first part of *Being and Time* from the primordial interpretation which makes up the second part of the work. What is meant here by "primordial"? Heidegger himself provides an answer: "If, however, the ontological Interpretation is to be a *primordial* one, this not only demands that in general the hermeneutical Situation shall be one which has been made secure in conformity with the phenomena; it also requires explicit assurance that the *whole* of the entity which it has taken as its theme has been brought into the fore-having." (*SZ* 232) A primordial interpretation of Dasein must thus reveal human existence as a whole or a totality. But to everyday understanding human existence is not given as a whole. Indeed, given such understanding, what Heidegger terms a primordial interpretation of human existence may well appear to be ruled out. Heidegger himself calls the reader's attention to the apparent incompatibility of the analysis of human existence offered in the first part of *Being and Time* with the demand for totality. "But have we not at the very outset of our Interpretation renounced the possibility of bringing Dasein into view as a whole? Everydayness is precisely that Being which is 'between' birth and death." (*SZ* 233) "Proximally and for the most part" man understands himself as incomplete. When life comes to an end he is no longer. If Heidegger is right such an understanding of the self as essentially incomplete is necessarily lacking in primordiality. The step beyond the provisional analysis of the first part and beyond the evidence which an examination of everyday existence can furnish has its foundation in Heidegger's insistence that man be understood and understand himself as a *whole*.

4

How can Dasein be understood as a whole? Is such completeness not precluded by Heidegger's understanding of care? If human existence is constituted by care, is it not inescapably ahead of itself and thus incomplete? Heidegger insists on this incompleteness.

The 'ahead-of-itself', as an item in the structure of care, tells

us unambiguously that in Dasein there is always something
still outstanding, which, as a potentiality-for-Being for
Dasein itself, has not yet become 'actual'. It is essential to the
basic constitution of Dasein that there is *constantly
something to be settled*. Such a lack of totality signifies that
there is something still outstanding in one's potentiality-for-
Being." (*SZ* 236)

To speak of something being still outstanding is to suggest that it is
missing; we do not yet have all the pieces which we need to have the
whole. Does this way of thinking do justice to human existence? Can we
judge it incomplete in the sense that there are still some pieces missing,
pieces which are finally added only by death? Just this Heidegger denies:
"The 'ending' which we have in view when we speak of death, does not
signify Dasein's Being-at-an-end, but a *Being-towards-the-end* of this
entity. Death is a way to be, which Dasein takes over as soon as it is."
(*SZ* 245) In anticipating this final possibility, man anticipates his own
being in its entirety. Only in such anticipation can man exist and
understand himself as a whole.

Heidegger is not content to show that it is *possible* for man to exist as
a whole in this sense. He wants to show that man *demands* of himself
that he exist as a whole. (*SZ* 267) This demand makes itself heard in the
call of conscience, in which man calls himself back to himself. At the
same time, this call summons him to open himself to his guilt and to
affirm it. Guilt is not to be understood here in its usual sense. We call
someone guilty if he did what should not have been done or failed to do
what should have been done. Our usual understanding of guilt thus
joins the ideas of authorship and negativity: to be guilty is to be author
of a lack. Heidegger's ontological understanding of guilt preserves the
emphasis on authorship and negativity. Man is said to be guilty because
he is called upon to be author of his own being and is yet cast into the
world, subject to death. To say that man is called upon to be author of
his own being is to point out that man is not as mere things are. In his
case, to be is to be involved in the constitution of his own being. But
such constitution is misunderstood when it is taken to be a free choosing
of what he is to be. For although man shapes, he does not create his
place. How man decides to be is not only a choice of what he is to be, but
a way of taking up and relating to what he has become and how he finds
himself in the world. Still, how we seize our being is not determined by
what is; we can grasp ourselves in different ways; thus we can resolutely

seize our own being and define what we are in response to the particular claims made on us by our situation; but we can also choose to exist as just another member of a group, letting that group define what we are to be, losing ourselves and our authorship to the community.

If Heidegger is right, this loss is not like some rare disease which now and then infects men. On the contrary, inauthenticity characterizes our normal way of being. "Proximally and for the most part" we find ourselves in the world, having already been assigned our place by the community of which we are part. In what we do and say we have already subordinated ourselves to these others. But Heidegger also emphasizes that inauthenticity is not simply something which happens to characterize everyday existence. Man's being is such that it invites him to cover it up and run away from it, more precisely from his own guilt. Man is guilty in that he is incapable of finally securing himself. If man is to exist authentically, he has to accept his guilt and thus his lack of security. It is against this background of inauthenticity as a constant temptation to which we usually have already succumbed that the call of conscience must be interpreted.

But must this call be understood as a demand that man exist as a whole, i.e., be unto death? Can man exist resolutely only by anticipating death? Heidegger himself raises doubts:

> In attempting to bring resoluteness and anticipation forcibly together, are we not seduced into an intolerable and quite unphenomenological construction, for which we can no longer claim that it has the character of an ontological projection, based upon the phenomena? (*SZ* 302)

To meet this question, Heidegger tries to show that resoluteness implies Being-towards-death. The crucial passage deserves careful analysis.

> To project oneself upon this Being-guilty, which Dasein is *as long as it is*, belongs to the very meaning of resoluteness. The existentiell way of taking over this 'guilt' in resoluteness, in its disclosure of Dasein, has become *so* transparent that Being-guilty is understood *as something constant*. But this understanding is made possible only in so far as Dasein discloses to itself its potentiality-for-Being, and discloses it 'right to its end'. Existentially, however, Dasein's "*Being-at-*

an-end" implies being-*towards*-the-end. As Being-towards-
the-end which understands--that is to say, as anticipation of
death, resoluteness becomes authentically what it can be.
Resoluteness does not just 'have' a connection with
anticipation, as with something other than itself. *It harbours
in itself authentic Being-towards-death as the possible
existentiell modality of its own authenticity.* (*SZ* 305)

Resoluteness, Heidegger maintains, demands that man understand
himself as inescapably guilty. Guilt marks my being not only now and
here, but it is "something constant" which will not leave me. To think
this constancy I have to think the self as constant. (*SZ* 322) But what
enables me to speak of myself as I have been or will be as *my* and thus as
one and the same self? How is the unity of self to be thought? Given his
ontology, Heidegger has to reject appeals to a soul substance. And
Kant,in spite of his rejection of all attempts to interpret the self as a
particular substance, is criticized for clinging to the ontological concept
of the subject which "*characterizes not the Selfhood of the 'I' qua Self,
but the selfsameness and steadiness of something that is always present-
at-hand.*" (*SZ* 320) To give unity and constancy to man's dwelling in the
world Heidegger appeals to death, to that possibility which will deny the
individual any further possibilities and which thus circumscribes his life
and gathers it together. As he himself points out, in the analysis of *Being
and Time* the anticipation of death plays a part which resembles that
given by Kant to the transcendental subject. (cf. *SZ* 318)[13] It is, however,
not quite the same part. According to Kant the unity provided by the
transcendental subject is constitutive of all possible experience. Its
realization could thus not possibly furnish man with a task. Being-
towards-death, on the other hand, can be a task, because "proximally
and for the most part" man is not transparent to himself and has
covered up his essence. "When one is absorbed in the everyday
multiplicity and the rapid succession of that with which one is
concerned,the Self of the self-forgetful 'I am concerned' shows itself as

---

[13] Sartre's claim that death is a contingent fact can therefore be defended only if it can be
shown that death is not needed to constitute the self. A Heideggerian critique of Sartre
would try to show that Sartre's conception of the self, in spite of obvious differences, owes
enough to Descartes and Kant to enable us to extend Heidegger's critique of their thought
to Sartre.

something simple which is constantly selfsame but indefinite and empty. Yet one *is* that with which one concerns oneself." (*SZ* 322) According to Heidegger's analysis it is not only possible to exist fragmented and scattered into different roles and activities, but this possibility is realized by the self-forgetful way we live most of the time. Only as a possibility is genuine being-as-a-whole or being-towards-death constitutive of human existence.

But Heidegger does not want to leave this possibility as a mere possibility uncovered by fundamental ontology. *"The question of the potentiality-for-Being-a-whole is one which is factical and existentiell. It is answered by Dasein as resolute...* The question of Dasein's totality, which at the beginning we discussed only with regard to ontological method, has its justification, but only because the ground for that justification goes back to an ontical possibility of Dasein." (*SZ* 309) It is the concretely existing human being who faces this possibility of gathering himself together by resolving to be-towards-death. Heidegger leaves no doubt concerning how he would have us choose. His entire vocabulary, especially his choice of the terms authenticity and inauthenticity, places a positive value on self-integration. Heidegger knows and insists that as long as our analysis remains purely ontological we cannot place one possibility above the other (*SZ* 42, 43); but ontological analysis is never that pure, it is always governed by ontic concern, by what Heidegger terms "a factical ideal of Dasein." (*SZ* 310)

What is this ideal? As this analysis has shown, Heidegger gives *unity a normative function*. With his emphasis on totality and being-as-a-whole, Heidegger, like Marcuse, belongs to the Platonic tradition. His account of how man can exist as a whole is of course very different from the Platonic, although for Heidegger, too, it requires an ecstatic flight which lets man recover his essence beyond the concrete and fleeting present. The possibility of this flight has its foundation in the nature of temporality itself. *"Temporality is the primordial 'outside-of-itself' in and for itself."* (*SZ* 329) Man is not lost in the here and now, but transcends it in memory, in his ability to reach out to other places, and most significantly in anticipation. This ability to transcend his present fleeting being and to anticipate his end allows man to oppose to his normal dispersed and fragmentary existence an essential constant self. In resolute being-towards-death man affirms himself as that self. Heidegger's insistence on the ecstatic character of temporality enables him thus to interpret the recovery of man's essence not as a turn away from becoming towards being but as an openness to the temporality of human existence. The only way in which it is possible for man to be-as-a-whole is by resolutely affirming himself in his being-towards-death. Like Plato in the *Phaedo*, Heidegger teaches us thus an art of dying. The reason for this is in both cases the same: both idealize being-at-one-with-oneself. This idealization makes being-towards-death a task.

5

To be open to his essence man must acknowledge how inescapably his life is his own and he himself delivered over to nothingness. Just because of this, man will tend to hide it from himself, turning away from the approaching darkness to the present: to daily routines which repeat themselves without real past or real future; to enjoyments deep enough to let him forget that they lack eternity; to the bloodless, but timeless spheres of science, philosophy, and art. Most frequently he will run to others: to the dread of nothingness and death man opposes the comforts of the community. This may take the form of the Christian conviction that as members of God's kingdom we need not fear the sting of death and the loss of community. If we can no longer hope for this heaven, we may seek comfort in another, in the community of the spirit which liberates us from this material prison and joins us with the great individuals of the past. Or we may try to derive a meaning from history as the Hegelians and Marxists do; or we may turn to the state or to the family; or to idle talk; or to love. Community and death are antagonistic forces. How impotent are words, gestures, actions to preserve the community with one who is dying. Can love create a community strong enough to defeat the power of death? If, as Heidegger says, authentic existence is towards death, are not all attempts to establish an authentic community just idle dreams?

But is Heidegger right? Or is he perhaps guilty of placing too much weight on being-as-a-whole, thus exaggerating the importance of death and, related to this, the importance of *Jemeinigkeit*, of the way in which my life is inescapably my own? Nietzsche was struck by how small a place death has in our everyday existence.[14] Heidegger would, of course, grant this and, like Nietzsche, he would seek the reason for this in our

---

[14] *Die Fröhliche Wissenschaft, Viertes Buch*, par. 278.

refusal to think the thought of death. But must this refusal be considered inauthentic? Or does it rather betray a recognition that life is more worth dwelling on? Can we turn the matter around and see in Heidegger's preoccupation with death a running away from life?

For another opposed interpretation of death we can turn to Schopenhauer. Schopenhauer sees much of what Heidegger sees. According to him, too, to exist as an individual is to exist towards death.[15] Death is constitutive of individuality. But man exists not only as an individual self, but as part of a larger whole, which Schopenhauer identifies with the species.[16] To give death the kind of primacy Heidegger gives to it is to overlook that as an essentially embodied self man is not only mortal, but also a sexual being. Sex, as Schopenhauer understands it, is misunderstood when it is reduced to an instrument which we use to amuse ourselves and others. It would be more correct to call the individual the instrument of sex and thus of the species. As this instrument the individual belongs to a larger order. Given such an interpretation, the individual who, as Heidegger's authentic man does, takes his own death to be the end which circumscribes all others, would exist inauthentically in having covered up his own *being-as-a-part*.

I do not want to place emphasis on the particulars of what Schopenhauer has to say. One could, for example, replace Schopenhauer's *species* with the *community* or with *history* and the essential point would remain the same: if, as I think we must, we deny the one sided idealization of totality and closure which is part of Heidegger's understanding of authenticity and instead demand that man affirm himself as a part, we will also find it impossible to give death quite the same significance. Hints of such a denial can be found even in *Being and Time*. Given Heidegger's claim that man exists essentially with others, must authentic self-affirmation not include affirmation of oneself as part of a community, joined to others by a common destiny?[17] But if "idle talk is the kind of Being that belongs to Being-with-one-another itself," (*SZ* 177) inauthenticity and community cannot be separated. Authentic being-with-others must then be understood as an

---

[15] Cf. especially *Die Welt als Wille und Vorstellung*, ed. Arthur Hübscher (Wiesbaden: Brockhaus, 1965), vol. I, par. 57, pp. 366-376.

[16] *Ibid.*, vol. II, chapter 44, pp. 607-651.

[17] Cf. my "Heidegger as a Political Thinker," *The Review of Metaphysics*, vol. XXIX no. 4, June 1976, pp. 648-650.

authentic way of taking up inauthenticity. (*SZ* 179) Such authentically seized inauthenticity does not allow us, however, to place being-as-a-part on a par with being-as-a-whole, let alone give it priority.

6

Do such considerations lend support to Marcuse's charge that Heidegger has perverted a biological fact into an ontological essence and thus betrayed the promise of utopia? I do not think so. If a sense of our mortality is constitutive of our sense of being an individual self, we cannot deny that death is at least part of man's essence. But if this means that we cannot reduce the significance of death to that of a mere fact, Marcuse is nevertheless right to question Heidegger's idealization of death. We may well accept Heidegger's claim that our sense of self and our mortality are intimately linked and grant that the more developed the integrity of the self, the more transparent the individual will be to himself in his being-towards-death. But how much emphasis should be placed on self-integrity? Is it not at least equally important to affirm oneself as a part? Even if we must grant that man cannot escape his mortality, this is not to say that he should exist towards death in the Heideggerian sense. Such a self-centered existence is no more than a real possibility which man may seize or reject. If getting hold of oneself is one possibility, so is letting go of oneself. Given such possibilities the question remains of how to choose among them.

Does such questioning help us to take what Marcuse calls "the promise of utopia" more seriously? Not at all. What was questioned was Heidegger's normative use of unity. In this respect his thinking, like that of Marcuse, remains tied to the Platonic tradition. Such questioning leaves large parts of Heidegger's analysis unchallenged, especially his analysis of care and guilt. Only to the extent that we can envision an alternative to that analysis, that is to say, only to the extent that we can envision a form of existence which does not involve a concernful but uncertain looking ahead, can we consider Marcuse's promise of utopia a real one.

If Heidegger's analysis of man's being makes it impossible to take seriously the promise of utopia, it does help us to understand its appeal. Consider again Heidegger's analysis of guilt. Man is guilty because it is his task to establish what he is to be, and yet such establishment is never a free choosing of his being, but is limited by how he finds himself in the world, subject to the rule of time, vulnerable and mortal. To acknowledge his guilt, man must recognize and face up to the failure of the project of pride. For him there can be no identity of freedom and necessity. Marcuse is thus quite right to suggest that thinkers like Heidegger "bestow transcendental blessing on the guilt of mankind." Authentic existence, as Heidegger describes it, accepts this guilt. Yet pride stands in the way of such acceptance. Man finds it difficult to accept his final impotence. Instead of affirming himself as he is, he looks for ways to break or to conceal the power of time. It is in such unwillingness to accept guilt that Platonism with its insistence that in his essence man is not subject to time, has its foundation. Given Heidegger's analysis, all such attempts to rescue man's being from the destructive power of time must tend to replace reality with formal abstraction or utopia, Heidegger would have to analyse Marcuse's own project as another, merely utopian and inauthentic response to man's guilt.

It is more difficult to see that Heidegger's analysis of authentic existence as being-towards-death can itself be interpreted as having its foundation in an inability to accept man's guilt. The very choice of the term "guilt," with its negative connotation, suggests such inability and is witness to what Nietzsche calls "the spirit of revenge." This, of course, is hard to reconcile with the claims made in *Being and Time*. Is not authenticity interpreted as a resolute affirmation of guilt? But, as we have seen, authenticity is also tied to being-as-a-whole. As Heidegger recognizes, such closure appears to conflict with the interpretation of human existence as care. If care is indeed constitutive of man's being, must that being not be incomplete in its very essence? (*SZ* 236) Should we not interpret this incompleteness as part of the meaning of what Heidegger terms man's guilt? If so, Heidegger's one-sided idealization of unity must be interpreted as part of an attempt to escape from guilt. To effect this escape man must take leave from himself as he finds himself in the world "proximally and for the most part." The direction of this leave-taking is indicated by Heidegger's interpretation of man's essence in terms of a resolute being-towards-death. Unfortunately our understanding of this being-towards-death and consequently of man's essence remains abstract. And this is hardly an accident: man can possess himself in his entirety only as an abstraction. Yet the power of this abstraction is great enough to isolate the individual from his world and his community.[18] In this sense one has to agree with Marcuse's charge that the glorification of death "introduces an element of surrender into life from the beginning." But the charge can be given a more general formulation so that it is directed against both Heidegger and Marcuse: The glorification of satisfaction, understood as a being-at-one-with-oneself, has to lead man away from concrete human existence and its temporality. This promise of an overcoming of alienation, when taken seriously, must alienate man from himself.

---

[18] Heidegger resists this interpretation. "Resoluteness, *as authentic Being-one's-Self,* does not detach Dasein from its world, nor does it isolate it so that it becomes a free-floating 'I'. And how should it, when resoluteness as authentic disclosedness, is *authentically* nothing else than *Being-in-the-world?* Resoluteness brings the Self right into its current concernful Being-alongside what is ready-to-hand, and pushes it into solicitous Being with Others." (*SZ* 298) Like Kierkegaard's knight of infinite resignation, the authentic individual takes leave from the world in dread and yet, paradoxically, is brought back to it. But how complete is that return? Dispersed in the world, the authentic person yet wills one thing. With others, he is yet alone.

An Inquiry Into Authenticity And Inauthenticity in *Being and Time*

JOAN STAMBAUGH
Hunter College

Near the beginning of *Being and Time*, Martin Heidegger states that the two manners of human being, authenticity and inauthenticity, are grounded in the fact that *Da-sein* is always its own being. The relation of authenticity and inauthenticity does not seem at first to be such a crucial issue in this major, classic work. The issues raised there: phenomenology; fundamental ontology; the question of Being; time and temporality; the ontic and the ontological, etc. appear as the basic problems to be explicated. This is an indisputable fact. The task of this paper will be to show that these issues are rooted in the question of the *self*, conceived in a non-traditional way, and that an elucidation of the apparent ambiguity in the relation between the self's being authentic and being inauthentic, which to my knowledge has never been pointed out, is crucial to an understanding of Heidegger's enterprise.

To begin a talk in this manner might well cause considerable confusion if the audience is unfamiliar with some of these terms and may even be confusing if they are familiar with them. To begin in this manner is, in a way, to take the Kierkegaardian leap and to plunge straight into the ontological abyss of *Being and Time*. But, as Nietzsche says: "Courage slays dizziness at the edge of abysses: and where does man not stand at the edge of abysses?"

I have set for myself here an extremely difficult task, a task of which I am only partially and imperfectly capable. But I believe that someone has to have a go at it.

Let us begin by asking what Heidegger has to say about the self. First of all, he gives an important polemic against the traditional philosophic concept of the self as substance, subject, as that which persists throughout all the multiplicity and change of our experience. The self is what remains identical throughout my life experience, it is what makes the old man fundamentally the same as the young child he once was. From Plato to Hume, the belief in the substantiality of the self was unquestioned, regardless of whether it was conceived in the Greek manner of an immortal soul imprisoned in and separable from the body, or in the Christian manner of an image of God intimately related to a body which will be resurrected. It was Hume who first challenged this belief in the substantial self, stating that the self was nothing but a behavioristically determined string of events lacking any true unity or self identity.

Heidegger does not adhere to or accept the traditional substantial view of the self, but neither, of course, does he follow Hume's empirical approach to the self as something not ascertainable materially, hence non-existent. Even Nietzsche had said of Descartes' ego in the *cogito ergo sum*: "He should have said: I think, therefore something is going on there." In other words, all that thinking yields is a *process* of thought, not a substantial soul (*res cogitans*) behind that process. With the English word "authentic" which has as its root the Greek *autos*, self, and the Sanskrit *asus*, life of the soul, the problem of the self proves to be anchored for Heidegger in the relation of authenticity and inauthenticity. The fact that the German "*eigentlich*" actually means "real" in everyday usage need not trouble us here. "*Eigen*" by itself means: "what is one's own."

Perhaps the best way to immerse ourselves in the problem of authenticity and inauthenticity is to quote the passages from *Being and Time* which present a real problematic contradition and then attempt to move in the direction of "solving" or at least softening that contradiction. In other words, I shall first document the problem and then try to state it incisively. By way of anticipation, I can say that the question here is: Which is more "primordial" -- authenticity or inauthenticity?

The passages which state that inauthenticity is more primordial are:
"The they-self is an existential and belongs to the positive constitution of *Da-sein* as an original phenomenon."

"Authentically being oneself does not consist in an exceptional state of the subject, a state detached from the they-self, but is rather an existentiel modification of the they-self which is an essential existentiel."

"Conversely, *authentic* existence is nothing which hovers over falling everydayness, but is rather existentially only a modified coming to grips with that everydayness."

"Authentically being a self is shown to be an existentiel modification of the they-self."

And the passages which state the primordiality of authenticity are:

"Inauthenticity has possible authenticity as its *ground.*"

"The they-self is an existentiel modification of the authentic self."

In order to begin to try to unravel the ambiguities inherent in Heidegger's statement on authenticity and inauthenticity, let us take a look at the two "disciplines" he is involved with in *Being and Time,* phenomenology and fundamental ontology. For Heidegger, phenomenology is a *method*, a procedure, a *way* of looking at things. It is not restricted and cannot be restricted to a particular area of things as are the other "logies" of biology which studies life, anthropology which studies man, theology which studies God, etc. Nor is it ontologically bound or committed to any definite and specific view of the world. It simply describes what is as it shows itself. Fundamental ontology, on the other hand, which is still Heidegger's main interest in this book, since it is to lead us to the *meaning* of Being, purports to analyze the conditions of the possibility of things and especially of *Da-sein* and its temporality. Here, Heidegger is still fundamentally within the Kantian framework of asking the question of what makes something possible. He has not yet reached the position of this later thought which equates metaphysics *and* fundamental ontology with onto-theo-logic, all of which he wants simply to abandon, no longer to de-struct in the sense of un-building the history of metaphysics as was his aim in *Being and Time.*

I believe that part of the ambiguity in the relation of authenticity and inauthenticity has to do with the relation of these two disciplines of phenomenology and fundamental ontology, and that one of the main questions here is rooted in what is meant by, for lack of a better term, "what comes first." In using the phenomenological method, Heidegger is analyzing the way things are most of the time in average everydayness, the way we relate to and deal with ourselves, others and the world in a fairly indifferent and matter-of-fact fashion. And this, of course, leads him to inauthenticity as the predominant mode of man's being. Thus, inauthenticity is "what comes first" in the sense of what we find first of all and most of the time. The meaning of "what comes first" here is what we inevitably and without exception start out with. Nobody is *born* authentic. This view Heidegger shares with most of the religious and philosophical traditions of the world; for example, with Plato, Christianity and Buddhism. Christianity has the myth of the fall which tells us that man cannot remain in the state of innocence and happiness, but must lose this state, collectively and individually. What is interesting here is not so much the question of *why* this is so, which in Christianity involves the ideas of sin, guilt, self-assertion, eating from the forbidden tree of knowledge, etc.; but, rather, the fact *that* it is so. Kierkegaard makes this acute question quite concrete when he says that there is no such thing as uncontested, untested innocence. Man must *lose* his innocence in order to regain it in a way that it can never be lost again. Otherwise, he will be perpetually on the brink of losing it. Only an innocence lost and regained is a tenable innocence no longer subject to radical jeopardy.

Plato gives us the myth of the cave, a subterranean cavern in which it is our natural state to live as prisoners without being aware of the fact that we are imprisoned. In fact, it is precisely man's lack of awareness that he is a prisoner which imprisons him most deeply. As Socrates remarks, to know that you do not know is the first, indispensable step toward knowledge.

What are men doing in this cave? They have been chained since childhood, their legs and necks fettered in such a way that they can only see what is in front of them, unable to turn their heads. And what they can see are shadows of stone and wooden images of men and animals, puppets, and artificial objects, shadows thrown by a fire burning behind them. They can neither see themselves nor each other except as shadows cast by the fire onto the walls of the cave. In short, the prisoners believe that reality is nothing other than shadows of artificial objects.

Plato's myth or allegory essentially presents a *process* which has four stages. The first stage we have just described, men imprisoned in a cave. In the second stage, the prisoners are unchained and are able to walk about in the cave. This new stage is accompanied by acute pain, for their limbs are stiff and unaccustomed to movement and they are blinded by the light of the fire. They can see neither shadows nor the artificial objects and are totally bewildered. They cannot see or understand clearly anything at all. Their former sense of "reality" is gone and they have as yet no sense of a new reality. In the third stage, one prisoner is forcibly dragged out of the cave into the world outside and compelled to go up a rough and steep ascent until he is finally confronted with the sun, Plato's image for the highest reality of all. The prisoner did not wish to leave the cave, for he thought that reality resided there. His ascent is even more painful and blinding than his initial release from his chains, for how much more difficult is climbing than walking, and how much more blinding is the light of the sun than that of the fire. But, finally, he grows accustomed to his new situation and is able to behold the sun, the highest reality, directly. The final stage of the process is the prisoner's return to the cave. Of course, he does not wish to return, for he is overwhelmed by joy at seeing the highest reality. True reality is joy-giving. But he must return for two reasons. He must attempt to tell his fellow prisoners of what he has seen so that they may glimpse the very *possibility* of such an intensely joyful experience. And, secondly, Plato's implication is that no one can or should dwell in contemplation of the highest reality, but one must return and live in the world where one belongs, what we would now call the "human condition."

Finally, Zen, or Buddhism in general, states that we are initially and by nature in the condition of ignorance. In contrast to Christiantiy, there is no fall from a state of innocence here. The ignorance is primordial. This ignorance is not a matter of some facts which we do not know; but rather, a matter of something already there, our true Self or Buddha nature, which we simply do not *realize*. Buddhism, in general, can explain this ignorance by saying that it is the inevitable product of deeds and actions commited in past lives, of our Karma and craving thirst for existence. But Zen, at least in the basic text called the *Mumonkan*, goes beyond that explanation without doing away with it. The name *Mumonkan* means "the gateless barrier," the barrier or obstruction to realization or enlightenment which we all face, a barrier with no gate. One passage states that it is an indisputable fact that every sentient being has its own cause of birth. But the true Self is, in some non-Western, non-Brahmanic, or non-Hindu sense, eternally free of birth and death while in the midst of birth and death, and thus cannot be merely the product of past karmic causes. The statement, "Show me your original face before you were born," also means show me your original face before your parents, the physical initiators of your existence, were born. Your original face is not subject to coming and going and is ultimately not contingent upon change and causality, although this is extremely difficult to grasp in a genuine way.

Thus, the *Mumonkan* gives us two statements which are contradictory on the surface but which are inseparable in reality. On the one hand, it emphasizes the primordiality and incredibly stubborn pervasiveness of ignorance. "If you want to see into your own nature, you must not take that nature for granted nor leave that insight to chance." "In order to row a boat, you have to use oars. In order to race a horse, you have to give it a whip." "Man, once and for all, has to be driven to the abyss of dualist contradictions and completely die to his small self in the depths of spiritual struggle. Unless he is reborn, breaking through this barrier, he cannot be really free in living his actual, everyday life." Rebirth of the true Self overcoming ignorance is absolutely crucial.

On the other hand, no one is ever totally estranged or separated from this true Self or Buddha nature since it is what truly *is* and what we truly are. In spite of ignorance, dullness, habit, distractedness, dispersedness, boredom, etc., in the most fundamental sense, we can never escape our true nature. "If you cover 'it,' trying to hide it, the very cover is nothing but 'it' (the true Self)." "It is gateless from the beginning. How can there be any barrier?"

To return to this problem formulated by Heidegger as the question of authenticity and inauthenticity, Buddhism not only presents the situation of initial inauthenticity without exception, but also lands us right in the middle of the ambiguity of authenticity and inauthenticity. We are both at once, usually without realizing it. In addition, authenticity in Heidegger or "enlightenment" in Buddhism is never something automatic, but only to be attained by some extreme experience. For Buddhism, that extreme experience is to be attained only by the utmost exertion and engagement in an intense quest for enlightenment as to one's own true nature or Self. For Heidegger, authenticity is to be attained, for example, only in the experience of dread, anticipation of one's own death, or joy. One difference here between Heidegger and Buddhism is that, whereas the Buddhist actively seeks an extreme experience, for Heidegger that experience is rather something which comes over one. It is unlikely that I seek the experience of dread or seek to anticipate my own death or even seek joy, since in the latter case I probably wouldn't know what to search for. On the contrary, in the case of dread or the anticipation of my own death, I flee from these experiences and try to refuse to face them by dispersing myself in the affairs of the world. So much for the "what comes first" with which the phenomenological method deals.

What about fundamental ontology in Heidegger? "What comes first" means in fundamental ontology what is most *primordial* and fundamental. What is being questioned is the very *ground* of man's being. This questioning can only be accomplished by analyzing man in his being as a totality and as a whole. Thus, Heidegger's initial question of the Who of *Da-sein*, the real self as opposed to the they-self, which began with inauthenticity, moves of necessity into the sphere of authenticity, of man as he is when he truly is who he is. Ultimately, this leads to an analysis of the temporal structures of his consciousness and to the description of how these structures can temporalize either an inauthentic or an authentic mode of temporal experience.

If one bears in mind that Heidegger's sole enterprise is to raise the question of the meaning of *Being* and that he is analyzing *Da-sein* only because it is that kind of being which has *access* to Being through its preontological understanding of what it means to be, then it becomes clear that it is ultimately authentic *Da-sein* which can lead us to an insight into the meaning of Being. Inauthenticity gets stuck in the things and affairs of the world, in *beings*. It is only on the level of authenticity that the insistent, prevalent claims and demands of the world recede and *Da-sein* can partially abandon things and beings, grasping itself in its *original totality*. This Heidegger emphasizes again and again. And if we consider *Being and Time* in the light of Heidegger's later writings it is not the question of authenticity and inauthenticity or even the whole "existential" emphasis that remains constitutive in the later writings. Man is considered *only* in terms of his relation to Being or the Appropriation. The very word "Appropriation" expresses the fact that man and Being are immanently and inseparably related. As I mentioned in my brief introduction to *Identity and Difference,* the *relation* is more fundamental than *what* is related. There is not much room for an analysis of inauthenticity here. Rather, Heidegger seeks a new understanding of "authenticity" by carrying out the de-structing, the unbuilding, now conceived as abandonment, of the history of western philosophy as onto-theo-logic, onto-theo-logic as the exclusive preoccupation with "Being" as the highest being (*summum ens*) and as the cause of itself (*causa sui*). "Authenticity" thus becomes the true relation to Being or the Appropriation undistorted by philosophical constructions. What remains from *Being and Time* in the later writings is the understanding of *Da-sein* as the non-spatial "place" where Being occurs or arrives. Man is truly the "place" of Being, and what corresponds to authenticity is the hope that he will take the step back out of metaphysics and allow Being to be in a new way undistorted and uncovered by the layers of metaphysical thinking.

To return in conclusion to the problem of authenticity and inauthenticity in *Being and Time*, when one considers Heidegger's analyses of these "existentials," the "categories" or ways of being of *Da-sein*, understanding, mood and discourse, these point to authenticity as Heidegger's major concern, expressed or not. Upon closer examination, the authentic is the fundamental level of *Da-sein* and the inauthentic is simply a flight from authenticity, however prevalent that inauthenticity might be. Thus, the crucial meaning of "what comes first" is what is *primordial*. Only this can lead us to the meaning of Being. Expressed in Christian terms, and in doing this I by no means intend to "Christianize" Heidegger but only to draw a perhaps misleading analogy, a consideration of the "fall" of man will not lead him to an understanding of God, but only to some kind of "theodicy." Only the kind of God-relationship expressed, for example, in Kierkegaard can lead us to God, a *relation*, an appropriation process to an objective uncertainty held fast in the most passionate inwardness. This is Kierkegaard's definition of faith *and* truth. Of course, the terms subjective and objective are out of place here, and the analogy between Kierkegaard and Heidegger breaks down to a certain degree. But the primordiality of the *relation* holds for both thinkers. It is the relation which authenticates, a relation oriented not toward the things of the world as a distraction and refuge from the possibilities of becoming authentic, but rather oriented toward those very possibilities themselves which open up the question of the meaning of *Da-sein's* own Being about which it is concerned and thus open up the question of the meaning of Being itself.

Heidegger and the New Images of Science

THEODORE KISIEL
Northern Illinois University

Heidegger and science? To some, the combination undoubtedly still sounds strange and unlikely, let alone fruitful and worthy of extended consideration. What could we possibly expect to learn about the inner workings of science from a thinker singularly and almost monotonously concerned with the time-honored and now grandiose question of Being? In the words of one astute commentator: "On the longest day he ever lived, Heidegger could never be called a philosopher of science."[1] And yet, those intimately acquainted with Heidegger's entire career can easily point to just such a day, and it must have been a long day indeed. For on July 27, 1915, the young Dr. Heidegger (age 25) held his inaugural lecture before the philosophical faculty at the University of Freiburg in order to obtain his *venia legendi*, the privilege to teach in the German university system, conceiving the lecture precisely as a logical-epistemological examination of the concept of time in natural science and in historical science.[2]

---

[1]William J. Richardson, "Heidegger's Critique of Science," *New Scholasticism* XLII (1968) 511-536. But this opening sentence of the article is moderated by a concluding paragraph suggesting how a philosophy of science could be elaborated within a Heideggerian framework.

[2]This early lecture, "Der Zeitbegriff in der Geschichtswissenschaft," is now readily available in the collection of Heidegger's major works from the period 1914-16. Cf. Martin Heidegger, *Frühe Schriften* (Frankfurt: Klostermann, 1972) pp. 355-375. This early lecture marks the high point of what I have called Heidegger's logical conception of science, as distinguished from his later existential and metaphysical conceptions. Cf, my essay, "On the Dimensions of a Phenomenology of Science in Husserl and the Young Dr. Heidegger, "*Journal of the British Society for Phenomenology*IV (1973) 217-234.

True. But after all, it must also be granted that this was long before Heidegger became *Heidegger*, by achieving international notoriety as a philosopher of existence practically overnight in 1927 with the publication of *Being and Time*. And *Being and Time* is manifestly a philosophy of being and existence and not a philosophy of science. But the examination of existential phenomena in this *magnum opus* also includes reflections on an existential conception of science, distinct from his earlier logical conception, with a promise of a thorough-going interpretation of science as a positive mode of existence to be incorporated in the as-yet-unpublished[2a] Third Division of the First Part of the project. Instead, science appears in a less positive light in the Second Part of the Heideggerian project, the part entitled "the phenomenological destruction of the history of ontology" and later elaborated under the rubric of "overcoming metaphysics." This third approach to science can be labelled the "metaphysical" or "epochal" conception of science, inasmuch as modern science is seen as a terminal epoch in the long history of metaphysics now coming to its end in the planetary dominion of technology. Note that metaphysics here does not refer to an abstract academic discipline but rather to the prevailing presuppositions and concrete interpretation of reality which uniquely stamp an age, for example, in the institutions and attitudes which that age accepts as a matter of course. In this vein, Heidegger's latest statements -- two letters to conferences on his thought in this country and the interview on German television on the occasion of his 80th birthday[3] -- make it clear that the present concretion of the question of Being is nothing less than the question of science and technology, insofar as the institutions and the attitudes they have provoked permeate the fabric of 20th century existence and thus indelibly mark the way we now live, move and have our being. In short, the question of Being now reads: What does it mean to be in a scientific-technological age?

[2a] This is no longer quite accurate in view of the recent publication of the lecture course of 1927, in which philosophy itself is taken as the "science of being." Cf. Martin Heidegger, *Die Grundprobleme der Phänomenologie*, volume 24 of the Gesamtausgabe (Frankfurt: Klostermann, 1975), pp. 15 ff.

[3] Manfred S. Frings (ed.), *Heidegger and the Quest for Truth* (Chicago: Quadrangle, 1968) pp. 17-21; John Sallis (ed.), *Heidegger and the Path of Thinking* (Pittsburgh: Duquesne UP, 1970) pp. 9-11; Richard Wisser (ed.), *Martin Heidegger im Gespräch* (Freiburg/Munich: Alber, 1970) pp. 67-77.

Science and Being? The juxtaposition sounds even more ambitious and diffuse than the thematic combination Science and Society, to which increasing attention is being devoted by a number of disciplines, including the philosophy of science. Indeed, it is difficult to think of a reflection on science more far-reaching than Heidegger's, for whom science and technology are the culmination and fulfillment of the destiny of several millenia of Western philosophy. Moreover, inasmuch as they are taken to be the mortal gasps of a tradition of metaphysics which Heidegger is striving to overcome, science and technology appear in such a negative light that some have accused Heidegger of being a reactionary romantic and even a neo-Luddite. Recall his most notorious pronouncement in this vein: "Science itself does not think."[4] The adversary relationship which has over the decades developed between Heidegger and more scientifically-oriented philosophers perhaps finds its epitome in Rudolf Carnap's debunking of what he considers to be Heidegger's "pseudo-statements," statements like "Nothing itself nothings," which have become the stock examples of meaningless metaphysical statements still circulating in neo-positivist circles. Parenthetically, it is interesting to note that Carnap's critique, which appeared in the journal *Erkenntnis* in 1913, is entitled "Overcoming of Metaphysics through Logical Analysis of Language,"[5] antedating by several years Heidegger's own adoption of the phrase "Overcoming of Metaphysics."

Heidegger's response to such critiques is characteristically sweeping. For him, the linguistic standards of clarity, formal exactness and univocity adopted by logical positivism find their natural place in the history of metaphysics in the spirit of modernity, in which 1) truth is certainty, 2) reality is objectivity, and 3) rationality finds its model in a

---

[4]Martin Heidegger, *What is Called Thinking?*, translated by Fred D. Wieck and J. Glenn Gray (New York: Harper and Row, 1968) p. 8. For an extended commentary on this remark, cf. my essay, "Science, Phenomenology, and the Thinking of Being," in Joseph J. Kockelmans and Theodore J. Kisiel (eds.) *Phenomenology and the Natural Sciences: Essays and Translations* (Evanston: Northwestern UP, 1970) pp. 173 ff.

[5]*Überwindung der Metaphysik durch logische Analyse der Sprache.* The English translation by Arthur Pap, "The Elimination of Metaphysics Through Logical Analysis of Language," appears in *Logical Positivism*, edited by A. J. Ayer (Glencoe: Fre Press, 1959) pp. 60-81.

mathesis universalis.[6] And when Heidegger asserts that science does not think, he is in fact referring to the positivistic image of science, in which logic and scientific method reign supreme over scientific content, where even the certifications of confirmation are made subservient to the so-called hypothetico-deductive method. Heidegger thus seems to make unholy alliance with his worst enemies, the positivists, in accepting their image as the ultimate upshot of modern science.

His broad historical perspective thus devolves upon an image of science oriented towards logic and the positive fact, which from the perspective of contemporary philosophy of science is now considered to be far too narrow. For the last decade or so has witnessed an anti-positivist revolt of major proportions in the philosophy of science which has challenged the positivist image of science on each of the three scores named above and, moreover, has shifted the locus of the essence of science in a direction which appears quite amenable to the direction suggested by Heidegger's existential conception of science.[7] Instead of a logical analysis of the theoretical products of science, the new philosophies of science rely more heavily on historical case studies of the actual process of science. As a result of this shift in approach, Anglo-American philosophy now definitively reflects a wholesale overhaul of the positivistic treatment of science in terms of idealized formal systems mapping empirical data. The more historical image now views science as ongoing *research* in a changing *problem-situation* which is *interpreted* and resolved according to the resources of a particular *historical* and *conceptual context.*

---

[6]These three intertwining dimensions, which will serve as touchpoints of comparison in what follows, in the Heideggerian meditation ultimately lead back to the pre-Socratic roots of the "tree of metaphysics" and correspond respectively to those most elemental of Greek words, *alethia, physics* and *logos.* Cf. Werner Marx, *Heidegger and the Tradition,* translated by Theodore Kisiel and Murray Greene (Evanston: Northwestern University Press, 1971).

[7]Cf. my essays, "Scientific Discovery: Logical, Psychological or Hermeneutical?" *Explorations in Phenomenology,* edited by David Carr and Edward S. Casey (The Hague: Nijhoff, 1973) pp. 263-284; and "Zu einer Hermeneutik naturwissenschaftlicher Entdeckung," *Zeitschrift für allgemeine Wissenschaftstheorie* II (1971) 195-221. For recent developments in the new movement, cf. Theodore Kisiel, with Galen Johnson "New Philosophies of Science in the USA: A Selective Survey," *Zeitschrift fur allegemeine Wissenschaftstheoric* V (1974) 138-191.

By way of an initial guide to what follows, permit me to underscore once again the operative terms of this new image of science and to suggest in advance the different view of truth, objectivity and rationality which this new image implies. Note first that it does not particularly mention "theory," "fact," or "method," which stood in the forefront of the positivistic image. The operative dimensions are rather 1) research or discovery, 2) the interrogative mood of a problem-situation, 3) the process of interpretation in a finite context, 4) which is a conceptual context or, more directly and simply put, a language. Finally, all of these dimensions are essentially pervaded by historical movement. Accodingly, the emphasis falls on the *dynamis* of truth *in via* rather than the *stasis* of truth once and for all, and on the holistic context rather than on an atomic objectivity. Consideration of the contextual process rather than the finished results of science suggests a more pragmatic and less syntactic and formal rationality, and, in view of the priority of the interrogative mood over the declarative mood, a more chiaroscuro and less clear and distinct rationality, more a finite sense of truth rather than the security of eternal verities.

One is immediately reminded here of Heidegger's efforts to shift the locus of truth from the proposition to the existentially rooted question, in order to view the finalization of truth against the background of the origin of truth, a background which Heidegger considers to be the more original truth. The same reversal of orientation is strikingly evident in the new philosophies of science. By tracing the termination of the scientific process, finalized in the form of theoretical and observational statements, back to its most obscure origins in the problem-situation, the new approaches bring out the inseparable unity and reciprocal interplay of the "context of justification" with the "context of discovery" to the point of insisting that judicative verification must serve the interrogative demands of discovery. This reversal of the positivist stress on the truth of verification tends to be borne out by the culture of science as it is manifested in the attitudes of scientists, who are trained and conditioned to seek new discoveries, whose professional prestige hinges on just such inventiveness, who compete vehemently to be the first to solve the most current problems of their fields, who thus become involved in the numerous bitter disputes over the priority and independence of their discoveries. And nowhere is it more evident how truncated the positivists' image was than in their attitude to the problem of scientific discovery, which they systematically excluded from any consideration whatsoever by the strategy of relegating it to the "waste basket" of "mere" psychology. According to this positivist view, discovery is a matter of intuition, strokes of genius, the workings of the unconscious and other such imponderables and therefore not a fit subject for logical minds. This most important dimension of scientific activity was thus left unexplained and accordingly left to the raconteurs of those fascinating and at once obfuscating anecdotes of discoveries made as if by "accident", and of illuminations that come from a magical "nowhere": Archimedes' bath, Newton's apple, Kekulé's dream of the dancing serpents, Poincaré's step onto an omnibus, to name only some of the better-known. A narrow area of methodological rationality populated by secure results is thus sharply demarcated from a vast enveloping jungle constituting the irrationality of creativity, which is unceremoniously dispatched to the limbo of the non-science of science.

Even the narrow realm of logically secured results, demarcated as science proper by positivism, soon proved to be a paper-thin substitute for the thick situation in which science actually takes place. The bifocal view of positivism stratifies the structure of science into a formal calculus governed by the stable laws of logic over against an independent world of fixed observations. Science proper is thus made to move in a split-level universe defined by the eternal poles of logic and fact. The time-honored metaphysical quest for stability and security thus reasserts itself in the world of science as portrayed by positivism, in spite of its loudly professed anti-metaphysical stance, now in the modern guise of a methodological subject coupling with an empirical object. Despite its reputed anti-metaphysical stance, positivism betrays its metaphysical vestiges by proclaiming both poles of its universe to be uncorrupted by becoming and change. In more epistemological terms, both formal and empirical levels are viewed as essentially uninterpreted, and interpretation becomes the act of the match maker who couples two virgins and brings them into a state of cohabitation. This is officiously executed by means of so-called "correspondence rules," "coordinating definitions," "bridge principles," or "rules of interpretation." Feigl's description of this scientific situation is particularly graphic: The postulate system of the formal calculus is like a free-floating balloon hovering over the earth of empirical facts, which must be anchored to the soil of experience and filled with empirical meaning by means of connecting tubes, which permit an "upward seepage of the empirical juice" of observational meaning to be pumped into the unvisualizable theoretical terms, thereby investing them with a partial interpretation. Interpretation is thus a matter of filling the theoretical forms of a parade of blimps by a one-way capillary pumping action skyward from the earth. This has come to be known as the Capillary Model of meaning and interpretation.[8]

In order to develop this theory of interpretation and meaning, the efforts of the logical positivists inevitably turned to linguistic reform. In the spirit of clarity and distinction aimed at expunging all vestiges of metaphysical obfuscation from the language of science, they sought to extricate from ordinary language two very non-ordinary languages, 1) an ideal language purified according to the demands of mathematical logic and 2) a neutral observation language based on the ontology of phenomenalism. But decades of effort have not yielded anything like a satisfactorily neutral observation language and it soon became apparent that only a small part of science in its most advanced theoretical efforts even approached the high degree of formality demanded by mathematical logic. Recently, not only the possibility but even the desirability of these linguistic reforms for the philosophy of science have been challenged by old-timers like Carl Hempel as well as by the new upstarts, on the grounds that they constitute a ruthless abstraction from the complex reality of scientific theorizing, in which observation is *always already* theory-laden and formal algorithms are always "*already* rich with meaning, charged with structural representations of phenomena."[9] The two extremes which positivism sought to purify out of scientific practice are *in practice* never so pristine pure, but have all along been co-habitating on the sly, in an alliance which is not only not unholy but in fact the very source of the fertility of science. To separate the two extremes and to attempt to "purify" them only serves to remove science from the profound and comprehensive reality with which it has come in contact in its formulations. Purification would mean sterilization. Science finds its proper element not in the thin clarity of extremes sifted out by the misplaced

---

[8]"New Philosophies of Science in the USA," pp. 142-4.

[9]Norwood Russell Hanson, "Logical Positivism and the Interpretation of Scientific Theories," *The Legacy of Logical Positivism: Studies in the Philosophy of Science*, edited by Peter Achinstein and Stephen F. Barker (Baltimore: The Johns Hopkins Press, 1959) pp. 67-84, esp. p. 84. This recurring reference to the *immer schon* is what Heidegger would call the facticity of science.

discreteness of logical positivism but in the already interpreted, conceptually organized context cultivated for science by a historical tradition which has been transmitted to it largely in and through the usages of ordinary language, in which theory and observation already correspond with one another in the reality about which they speak.

Explicit and formalized rules of correspondence are accordingly by and large unnecessary in scientific theorizing. It is therefore not surprising that they have been notoriously difficult to pinpoint. Instead of explicit rules bridging the chasm between formal and empirical levels, actual practice suggests more of a tacit process of mutual interpretation of a theory by its particulars and of particulars by their comprehensive theory in terms of the cues of the problem-situation to which they are addressed. The process can be described in terms of what the philological tradition has called the "hermeneutic circle," which cannot be construed as a vicious circle because it is ultimately not only logical but also and primarily ontological. For the spiral movement thus generated incessantly wends its way down toward the non-verbal frontiers of a verbally structured problem-situation, which in turn is *always already* understood according to the usages of ordinary language as well as being invested with the meanings developed by the tradition of the discipline in question. Ordinary language as well as scientific language thus always articulates the problem-situation, and solving the problem involves the ability to see the scientific linguistics of the problem *in* and *through* the ordinary language in which it is always couched. Recall the famous example of Eddington's elephant, a problem which is expeditiously solved if one knows how to translate it into the terms of the standard inclined-plane problem of physics. Viewed in this way, interpretation now is the direct perception of family resemblances between problem-situations, one already solved and the other in need of solution, without the aid of intermediate correspondence rules. If the function of correspondence rules is to correlate scientific expressions with nature, then this function is now served by these exemplar problem-solutions which one finds at the end of chapters in physics and chemistry books. One does not master his science until he "gets the knack" of how to use and apply these prototype problem-solutions,[10] which are notably expressed in the

---

[10]Which is what T.S. Kuhn means by "paradigms" in the strict sense.

language of models and metaphors, of waves, particles, hydraulic models for the flow of electric current, and the like.

This dimension of scientific language, which was forced to the periphery by positivism and downgraded to a "mere" heuristic function, now comes to the fore in the new image of science and emerges front and center as the operative language in interpretation and discovery. In the words of Heidegger, one might accordingly say that the new image of science assumes "a transformed relation to the essence of language." For the operative language is now viewed as a cultural storehouse of metaphors latent with untold possibilities for adaptation to the shifting demands of the changing problematic of science. The leading edge of scientific change is now situated in the interaction of the old language with a new situation which evokes surprising aspects from the old language not previously seen in it. The metaphoric shift ensuing from the translation of the scientific language from one problem-situation to another may at times shift the very bases of a scientific discipline, by making a hitherto peripheral metaphor into a root metaphor and thus reweaving the fabric of fundamental concepts of the scientific domain, producing as it were a re-edition of the Book of Nature. This ability of language to adapt to the changing demands of the scientific problematic constitutes a more diachronic sense of scientific rationality as compared to the synchronic concern for the form and validity of finished logical systems. This new notion of scientific rationality sees change and rationality as not only not incompatible but in fact essential to one another. In the face of a historically changing world, the most rational thing to do is to change with it.

Instead of the hermeneutic model, which focuses on the dynamics of the . linguistic change which takes place in interpretation, an evolutionary model of "variation and selective perpetuation" of concepts and hypotheses is more commonly used among philosophers of science to comprehend the rationality of scientific change. Thus, Toulmin speaks of the "ecological demands" of an "intellectual environment" imposing a "selective pressure" on the available pool of conceptual variants in order to filter out the most adaptable for perpetuation.[11] In a similar vein, the hermeneutic model underscores

---

[11]Stephen Toulmin, *Human Understanding*, Volume I: *The Collective Use and Evolution of Concepts*, (Princeton: Princeton UP, 1972) pp. 134-144, 211-212.

the importance of sensitivity to contextual determinants as guides to the appropriate interpretation of texts. The same applies to discovery. As we search for the appropriate word for a particular context, we are acutely aware that the context "demands" the recalcitrant word and no other, "rejects" the ones we do pose to it and instead "suggests" other directions of interrogation. The situation "asks" to be straightened out in certain ways while it screens out others, and we must be responsive to these interrogative solicitations and salient vectors if we are to come to an appropriate solution. Such attempts to describe the selection process seem to attribute a much more active role to the context than a more positivistic mentality, wary of anthropomorphism, would allow. But it is in fact an attempt to establish a new and more holistic sense of "objectivity" -- *Sachlichkeit und nicht Objektivität* -- oriented to the Gestalt complex of the problematic situation. Both the hermeneutic and the evolutionary model converge remarkably on such a demand-response "logic" of selection imposed by the situation itself, and in fact take us to the threshold of a reversal after the fashion of the later Heidegger, where what is said and what is talked about now not only talks back to us but even decides for us! Thus, in his meditation on the nature of thinking in *Was heisst Denken*?, Heidegger culminates in a form of this question which he formulates variously as "What calls us to thought?", "What invites (appeals to, demands, instructs, directs) us to think?" and hence "What gives directions to thought?"[12] Whence the hermeneutic maxim to which Ricoeur sometimes alludes: The context decides, and we are led to decide accordingly, as we use all available contextual determinants in order to expose the most appropriate sense of a message charged with a fluid potential of meanings. Consider, by way of example, the sentences "Man is a wolf," "Juliet is the sun," "The world is my oyster," in which the action of the context excludes the literal sense by way of its absurdity and then directs us to more metaphorical senses. It is in terms of this interplay between restrictions and latitudes that one ultimately acknowledges that meaning is interpreted by its context, i.e., in terms of what the context permits.

But the context not only determines which interpretations are appropriate and thus provide an adequate solution to our problems but

---

[12]*What is Called Thinking?*, pp. 114-117.

also, and perhaps more importantly, which problems are appropriate, in terms of both the importance of the problem and the readiness of the field to handle it. The researcher must take his cues from his historical situation in exercising "good judgment" with regard to the most promising problems as well as their adequate solutions. Prior to the right solution comes the much more subtle -- and risky -- decision of asking the right question, and in the right way, under pain of squandering years in a fruitless search for the resolution of a problem which simply will not yield. A scientific problem quite often must await its opportune time before scientific developments provide it with the resources that make it veritably "ripe" for solution. After a long incubation period, there comes a time when the potential of the field is such that the discovery of an outstanding solution cannot be postponed for long. Sometimes, precipitous events may suddenly turn a "fruitless" search into a time to "cultivate" new theoretical possibilities in order to "reap" the benefits of a recent intellectual "harvest" of "seminal" ideas from a neighboring "field."[13] When the opportune time for a problem comes, then the direction of its solution practically forces itself as "the obvious guess"[14] on the researcher steeped in his field, perhaps even leading to its simultaneous discovery by independent workers in the field. Consider, for example, the discovery of the double helical structure of DNA, prompted most proximately by the discovery of the α-helical structure of a protein molecule and supported by the opportune confluence of efforts in the disciplines of bacterial genetics, crystallographic physics and organic chemistry. The genesis and rapid blossoming of molecular biology can be specifically located at the intersection of these three domains, whose fusion was brought about by Watson and Crick's discovery, which in turn provided the key insight into the plethora of problems surrounding the genetic code or, in more popular jargon, "the secret of life." Molecular biology is just one example of a minor and peripheral specialty which suddenly and dramatically takes over the vanguard in the history of science and unfolds a new subject matter in a creative surge which makes it grow by

---

[13]The agricultural metaphors which scientists themselves use in describing their situation are reminiscent of Heidegger's treatment of poetic "Building Dwelling Thinking."

[14]James D. Watson, *The Double Helix: A Personal Account of the Discovery of the Structure of DNA* (New York: New American Library, Signet PB, 1968) p. 41.

geometric leaps and bounds from a handful of specialists to a dominant field populated by a sizable number of distinguished scientists. Other examples are x-ray crystallography and spectroscopy which played just such key roles at the turn of the century in the development of quantum physics. Such historical experiences suggest that it would be disastrous to distribute funds equitably to all fields; the task of the allocators is to play midwife to these spontaneous surges in burgeoning new fields of discovery, which are opening up at the expense of older fields in the process of being exhausted.

The unevenness of the internal history of science, with its surprising turns of events and unexpected surges in forward progress through conceptual explosions which intersperse long incubation periods of gradual development, suggests the Heideggerian model for historicity in terms of the intermittent rhythms of unconcealment and concealment, truth and error. With all the continuing emphasis on the winners of the Nobel sweepstakes, there is now also a growing recognition of the important, even essential, role of the genial error in the history of science. There comes a time when a promising idea must be followed through to an ill-fated dead-end and thus shown to be a blind alley, a *Holzwege*. Such failures may well merit the name of science just as much as those endeavors for which the Nobel prizes are awarded. Shapere suggests, for example, that Justus Liebig's search, in the early days of organic chemistry, for a mathematizable "vital force" operative in organisms, analogous to the attractive forces of matter, was just such an enterprise.[15] Of course, even the successes in science pick their way through a gauntlet of wrong turns and dead-ends. For instance, the initial steps toward the DNA discovery were marked by wrong decisions on both of the initial questions concerning the helical model, namely, the number of strands and the nature of the chemical bonding between the strands. Popper in particular has emphasized the trial-and-error character of scientific procedure and the significant role played by falsifiability in the logic of science. And Polanyi points to another kind of unavoidable error interwoven into the history of science, citing his own scientific work on physical adsorption as an example of a discovery not immediately accepted by the scientific community because it was an idea too much out of season with the

---

[15]Dudley Shapere, "Plausibility and Justification in the Development of Science," *The Journal of Philosophy* LXIII (1966), pp. 611-21.

reigning paradigm of physical chemistry at the time of its initial publication.[16]

The erratic course of the history of science is directly tied to the unspecifiability inherent in the process of scientific discovery. As noted above, the desire to eradicate this erratic dimension from science has found its extreme expression in the truncated image which equates science with the methodically controllable and verifiable and consequently excludes any consideration of the dimension of discovery. But if one refuses to exclude discovery from the essence of science and at the same time considers discovery at its fundament to outstrip all method and logic, then, for such a one, science would not be science without its profound roots in the unspecifiable, and therefore cannot be explained in terms of wholly explicit, wholly formalizable knowledge. What is to be called science would then include, for example, the unspecifiable art of "good judgment" by the scientific administrator groping in the dark in making his educated guesses on the most promising lines of research impending in his field.

Among the new philosophers of science, Michael Polanyi in particular has pursued this direction of thinking to the point of outlining the ultimately ontological character of this dimension of the unspecifiable as it makes its presence felt in every phase of the scientific endeavor. Under the rubric of "personal knowledge", he stresses the central role of a kind of intimacy between the scientist and nature, an indwelling in its harmonies by means of theoretical patterns through which the discoverer senses the presence of the hidden truth which has yet to be revealed. The scientist acquires this intimacy by entering into the inherited interpretive framework of science and passionately committing himself to learning its ways. As they say in the vernacular, it is a matter of "getting a feel for" nature in the way science currently comes in contact with it. This tacit knowledge can only be conveyed by practice and from practicing scientists, through whom the novice assimilates the subliminal premises of his science. These premises weave the framework within which all of his scientific assertions are made, and yet, for this very reason, they themselves cannot be asserted. But despite its inarticulate state, this network is known intimately as his own interpretative framework, in which he dwells "as in the garment of [his]

---

[16]Michael Polanyi, *Knowing and Being*, edited by Marjorie Grene (Chicago: The University of Chicago Press, 1969) pp. 87-96.

remarks in *Being and Time* (section 69b) on the roots of theoretical behavior in praxis, which fundamentally constitute Heidegger's existential conception of science, i.e. science as an authentic mode of Being-in-the-world.

Moreover, Polanyi's account also serves to counteract Heidegger's harsh and bleak metaphysical conception of modern science as "the absolute priority of method over its possible objects."[20] But Heidegger himself promotes a similar move in his lecture of 1954 entitled "Science and Deliberation", which I believe can be read with great profit in the light of Polanyi's exposition of the tacit dimension of science.[21] For the aim of this lecture is to promote a deliberation on a certain "inconspicuous state of affairs" latent in the heart of the matter of science. This incipient state of affairs which pervades the essence of the sciences is however by and large ignored and passed over in silence by them, since their natural orientation is more toward certified results and further progress in knowledge. Yet no matter how far removed the sciences seem to be from this incipient core, it is indispensable to them. They inevitably reside in it as a stream in its hidden source. Accordingly, the most profound way of thinking of science would seek to attune itself to this subliminal mooring in the facticity in which the sciences find their home. But such a "grass roots" thinking in proximity to the source would involve a violent reversal of the normal movement of scientific progress. Indeed, it would constitute a regress from the sciences to their presuppositional underpinning. Because of their orientation away from their source, and the momentum of their progressive movement, the sciences of their own power cannot make this leap back to the source from which they have sprung.[22] This is the task of foundational thinking.

Even more worthy of attention in the present situation is that the very spirit of modernity, seduced by the spell of certitude, guaranteed truth and assured progress, which encourages us to view science as a panacea, radically militates against such a reversal. More and more, scientific progress assumes the character of a forward project without a grounding facticity. Kant[23] thus captured the essence of modern science

---

[20]In the letter published in Sallis (ed.), *Heidegger and the Path of Thinking*, p. 10.

[21]Martin Heidegger, "Wissenschaft und Besinnung," *Vorträge und Aufsätze* (Pfullingen 1954) pp. 45-70. On the *unscheinbaren Sachverhalt*, cf. esp. pp. 59-70.

[22]*What is Called Thinking?*, p. 18.

[23]In a famous passage (B XIII) in the Preface to the second edition of the *Critique of Pure Reason*.

own skin."[17] Out of this background comes the particular but unspecifiable clues which guide the researcher from surmise to surmise, as well as providing intimations of being on the right track and drawing nearer and nearer to a solution. Even the resulting theory is more than explicit knowledge; it is a foreknowledge of things yet unknown, unforeseeable, and perhaps even inconceivable at present, and it is in anticipation of these implications that the scientist passionately commits himself to this theory. For he believes himself to have come in contact with a reality whose inexhaustible depth, independence and power will permit it to manifest itself through his theory in ways even beyond his ken. He believes his theory is true, even without confirmations, but also and primarily because of the indeterminate range of future discoveries that he expects will issue from it.

Thus Polanyi sees the entire process of discovery, from initial investiture through the explanatory phase to the final commitment to its outcome, under the sway of what he calls the "ineffable domain,"[18] which could readily be one of Heidegger's more topological names for Being. Polanyi himself explicitly acknowledges the kinship between the pretheoretical know-how that he calls "personal knowledge" and Heidegger's conception of *Seinsverständnis*.[19] Moreover, he after a fashion performs a Heideggerian kind of reversal when he espies, in and through the tacit skills, a tacit dimension of reality operative as the alpha and omega of science.

In Polanyi's account, the locus of science is clearly displaced from the image of science as method to that of science as a craft skill, an intellectual "savvy" and tacit judgment which cannot be supplanted by method, precedes and grounds it, and provides it with its viability. Put most starkly, science viewed from this side of its coin is no longer a science at all but rather an art, a *techne* in the best Greek sense of an artistic know-how capable of evoking (bringing forth, producing) truth in and through an artwork. The scientist is made a kin to the artisan-craftsman steeped in his art, responsive to his material as he attunes himself to it through his tools, and sensitive to how they relate to human existence. This emphasis provides a profound concretization to the few

---

[17]Michael Polanyi, *Personal Knowledge: Towards a Post-Critical Philosophy* (New York: Harper Torchbook, 1964) pp. 60, 64.

[18]*Ibid.*, p. 87.

[19]*Ibid.*, p. x.

when he noted that "a light broke upon all students of nature" when they realized that nature is best understood according to a project (*Entwurf*) of one's own making. Rather than subjecting ourselves to "nature's leading-strings," we must force nature to answer questions of our own choosing. In this vein, Einstein spoke of the "free inventions" of hypothesizing and Galileo readily admitted that fictional idealizations such as "freely falling body" and "frictionless plane" constituted a veritable "rape of the senses."

Yet both saw the adventures of hypothesizing counterbalanced by the security and control of method. Among the new philosophers of science, Feyerabend has reacted so violently against the image of science as method and of its truth as a security blanket that he highlights the heady willfulness of science to the point of arbitrariness. He thus proposes an anarchistic image of science based on the single methodological principle of "anything goes" (short of murder). In practice, this entails "scientific" opposition to everything which is now accepted by the scientific establishment. In short, currently accepted facts must constantly be opposed by counterinductions from experience and accepted theories countered by the proliferation of alternative theories inconsistent with the accepted point of view, whereby one not only learns by his mistakes (as Popper maintains) but also deliberately proves all rules by seeking their exceptions. Inasmuch as Feyerabend concedes the need for a certain measure of tenacity to already established theories, his recipe stops just short of the nihilistic extreme of turning scientific change into a Dionysian frenzy of activism. Though at times it may approach slapstick pandemonium, when the active interplay between tenacity and proliferation becomes pitched to its most tumultuous, so that the thick of the action appears "unreasonable, nonsensical, mad, immoral . . . when seen from the point of view of a contemporary."[24] Feyerabend's irreverent recipe of calculated willfulness and recalcitrance aims to turn science into the carefree abandon of a frolic. Against the image of the scientist as *l'homme sérieux* hard at work in the solemn and even sacred task of "the search for truth," Feyerabend would locate the sources of scientific discovery

---

[24]Paul Feyerabend, "Against Method: Outline of an Anarchist Theory of Knowledge," *Analyses of Theories and Methods of Physics and Psychology*, edited by Michael Radner and Stephen Winokur, *Minnesota Studies in the Philosophy of Science*, Volume IV (Minneapolis: University of Minnesota Press, 1970) p. 103, note 33.

as much in spontaneous play as in reasoned planning. Whence his "plea for hedonism" which would change science "from a stern and demanding mistress into an attractive and yielding courtesan who tries to anticipate every wish of her lover."[25]

But Heidegger espies a similar frenetic character to science precisely within the secure confines of its method. Willful projects continue to proliferate through the fissioning of scientific disciplines into specializations, each of whom are in turn prolific in the production of results. Each specialty imposes severe limits upon itself and the kinds of questions it wishes to pose, thereby cutting itself off all the more from an awareness of its enabling ground. The advantage of this strategy of minimizing thinking is to maximize results, so that the overall effect of the multiplication of specialties is the accumulation of a vast store of detailed, technically useful information. Here we encounter the narrower technocratic image of science as research and discovery which is wholly compatible with what Nietzsche termed the triumph of scientific method over science. "Research" in this sense is now Big Business. The proliferation in recent decades of the "think tanks" of research institutions for various and sundry purposes suggests to what extent the "knowledge industry" has replaced manual and machine labor as the most important productive force today. That the businesslike pursuit of knowledge is virtually open-ended while at the same time remaining systematic indicates how the security of method and the adventure of research can be interlocked in their progressive drift toward rootlessness. To paraphrase Victor Hugo, technical science has long sought a perpetual motion machine. It has finally found it . . . in itself.

This total mobilization of human talent as well as natural resources finds its most intense expression in the uninhibited will to power toward planetary domination through technology. By means of the power of technology, nature has been provoked into revealing hitherto unsuspected sources of electrical and nuclear energy. Recently, even outer space has been placed at our disposal as another resource to be exploited. So sure were our planners of the power of technology that the question was never whether we would land on the moon, only how soon

---

[25]Paul Feyerabend, "Consolations for the Specialist," *Criticism and the Growth of Knowlege*, edited by Imre Lakatos and Alan Musgrave (Cambridge, Mass.: Harvard UP, 1970) p. 229.

and by what means. The new cybernetic sciences appear to know no bounds in the possibilities of planetary planning and the capacity to work our will upon the entire earth. It appears that man is now in a position to assume the role of unequivocal lord and master exercising dominion over the earth.

But is the technological will really a freedom without limits? The ecology and the energy crisis dramatically testify to the contrary. And there is science-fiction's recurring nightmare of the giant computer turning the tables and overpowering its masters. In numerous ways, the technological matrix is impelled by a will to total efficiency which factors in man himself to the point of total absorption, who is after all also a natural resource to be exploited for its energy and distributed to its most effective stations in the "manpower" grid. Technology thereby takes revenge on man himself.

But in the Heideggerian perspective, all of these are but symptoms of a more radical limit to our freedom, a fundamental non-willing latent in the very will to will of the technological project. To acknowledge this most extreme limit is to take the first resolute step toward displacing this seemingly free-floating project back to its most facticitous roots. For we can always ask: What demands that we demand to the point of excess in the technological mode of existence? What provokes us to provoke nature resourcefully to the point of including our own resourceful selves? Perhaps we will then see that the thoughtless willfulness of exploitation is basically not of our own will. Our changing of the face of the earth is ultimately not of our own doing. We have long ago been led to the historical destiny of technology and can no longer turn back. No International Planning Commission or Committee of Scientists have done so, nor can they really hope to do so.

But we can turn our thoughtless willfulness around by first acknowledging the oblivion of its rootedness, as well as the oblivion of this oblivion, so that we might then come to terms with the flow of our current historical situation, what is taking place in it, the leeway it grants us and what we can start with it. This orientation of questioning thus aims to bring us "to experience the call of a more original revelation" within and through the truth of technology, to espy the harbingers of a new setting in and through the scientific-technological world, to find new roots for life in such a world, to find ways of making ourselves at home in this world, so that, in one of Heidegger's favorite expressions, we may once again learn "to dwell poetically upon this earth." Accordingly, Heidegger clearly hopes that the backtrack into and through the metaphysical conception of science and technology will be propaedeutic to a more poetic conception.

One of its central tasks would be to elaborate a new sense of the naturality of nature in and through the artifacts of science and technology, "to recast and recover the calculability and technicality of nature in the open mystery of a newly experienced naturality of nature".[26] And perhaps the time is not so far off for such a development. The ecology crisis and energy crisis suggest certain limits to our sense of nature as universally manipulable, whether as a scientifically calculable system of forces or as a technological fund of resources, and accordingly evoke the need to let it be, to cultivate, conserve, foster and cherish the Dasein of our planet in a more responsive manner. One might also hope for a measure of a poetic sense of science and technology from the more explicitly artistic endeavors to use their materials -- Heidegger might call these the "earth" of science and technology -- in the mobiles of constructivism, technological sculpture, film, perhaps even cybernetic music. Perhaps some day we may well learn to view, for example, synthesized plastics as no less natural than things found more directly in nature. Then there is the poetic-mystical strain in the Marxist tradition which sees the progressive naturalization of man through technology in mutual coordination with a progressive humanization of nature. Among others in this tradition, Marcuse, an old student of Heidegger, looks toward the emergence of a New Science and New Technology in which nature and man would no longer be related in the mutual exploitation of master and slave but rather in the mutual liberation of communicating partners, precisely to the degree that technology pacified the forces of nature by liberating them from the brutality, ferocity and blindness which has made nature our antagonist from time immemorial.[27] Astounding as it may sound to our positivistically conditioned ears, wary of all anthropomorphisms, this kind of suggestion is being seriously entertained by thinkers of the most diverse philosophical perspectives. For example, Mary B. Hesse's quest for a new form of objectivity for science prompts her to consider a more internal relationship between man and at least biological nature than an

---

[26]Martin Heidegger, *Hebel der Hausfreund* Pfullingen: Neske, 1957) p. 24.

[27]Herbert Marcuse, *One-Dimensional Man* (Boston: Beacon Press, 1964) pp. 166-7, 236-8.

epistemology based on the subject-object relationship would normally allow.[28] Others have suggested that such an intimate indwelling in wholly new dimensions of nature is acquired in our habituation to the instrumental complexes of experimental science.

So there is no lack of signs of a vigorous quest for a new habitat for man in a new, more ecological sense of the naturality of nature, a more historical and topological form of objectivity (*Sachlichkeit*), a less mathematical and more hermeneutical notion of rationality.[29] Even though science has been rendered thoughtless by the positivistic image of science, there appears to be no dearth of thinkers, scientists included, seeking to provide us with more imaginative images of a science more responsive to the most profound exigencies of the human situation. I have tried to suggest that Heidegger has blazed a trail which helps to to see how this proliferation of new images converges on the simple heart of the matter in which we live, move and are.

---

[28]Mary B. Hesse, *In Defence of Objectivity* (London/New York: Oxford University Press, 1973).

[29]Cf. my essays: "The Mathematical and the Hermeneutical: On Heidegger's Notion of the Apriori, "*Martin Heidegger: In Europe and America*, edited by Edward G. Ballard and Charles E. Scott (The Hague: Nijhoff, 1973) pp. 109-120; "Commentary on Patrick Heelan's 'Hermeneutics of Experimental Science in the Context of the Life-World'," *Zeitschrift für allgemeine Wissenschaftstheorie* V (1974) 124-135; "Hermeneutic Models for Natural Science," *Die Phänomenologie und die Wissenschaften*, edited by E. W. Orth as *Phänomenologische Forschungen 2* (Freiburg/Munchen: Alber, 1976), pp. 180-191.

Nothingness and Being
A Schelerian Comment

MANFRED FRINGS
DePaul University

Heidegger's central question, "What is the meaning of Being?", is intertwined with the concept of nothingness, as it has been since Pre-Socratic thought. I wish to articulate "nothingness" by restricting myself to three aspects of this concept given by Scheler: 1.) the meanings with which the word "nothing" is used, 2.) the moral implication belonging to the question of "nothing," and 3.) the concept of reality. It is the purpose of this selection of Schelerian thought to furnish some distinctions to be made in Heidegger's central position.

1.) Concerning the meanings of the word "nothing."

At the beginning of the final quarter of our century we can justifiably argue that at no time in the history of philosophy has there been so much talk about and concern for the theme of Being and Nothingness as in ours. While motives for such trends remain subject to speculation it does appear that the very nature of contemporary philosophy, in losing sight of the meaning, location, and value of the Divine in human Eksistenz, is horizontal, not vertical; i.e., one of its primary concerns is the horizon of the relationship between man and world, not the dimension of the Divine in man's world. This trait of twentieth centry philosophy pertains especially to Heidegger, despite attempts (including some of his own) to come to grips with this dimension or with relevant areas such as metaphysical explications of good and evil, as we find them in only a few thinkers such as Max Scheler and N. Berdyaev.

The mass references to being and nothingness we find in all of

Heidegger's works is by no means easy reading precisely because Heidegger himself did not sufficiently and clearly spell out the usages of the term "nothingness" as he has done with regard to the term "Being." It is for this reason that I wish to present some of Max Scheler's views on such distinctions to be made as to the word "nothingness," which Heidegger also observes but did not articulate. We shall see that these distinctions are of help, even if only in a technical manner, to further the understanding of what Heidegger is talking about.

There are three distinctions to be made in the uage of the term: 1.) The term "nothingness" can have the sense of a logical negation. In this sense we do not necessarily have an experience of nothingness in an onto-logical sense. The meaning of the logical negation is contained in the proposition of a judgement. I do not wish to go into details of how the phrase "contained in the proposition" poses a metaphysical problem also for the logician, a problem with which Heideggerians are all too familiar when nothingness is to be thematized. 2.) The second meaning of "nothing" is "relative nothingness." In this sense the word is used in a specific reference to "something." Thus, "I can see that there is 'nothing' on the table," says Scheler, i.e., we experience the contrariness between the *meaning* of an object (table) to which, in this case, may belong glasses (on the table), and the *existing* state of affairs revealing no glasses on the table. There is "nothing" on the table. This absense (abesse) can be taken literally, i.e., the glasses "stay away" from the table; or, as Heidegger could put it: "sie wesen ab" (absunt). But the glasses' staying away or non-presence on the table, on which there is "nothing," is relative to the being of the table. "Relative nothingness," or nothing, does, therefore, have an intermediate character which Heidegger so often assigns to Being when he speaks of its concealment and unconcealment, or emergence. Concealment or un-concealment must also be assigned to relative nothingness (which Heidegger does not articulate): while there is "nothing" on the table this nothing un-conceals not only the missing glasses but also all that could be expected to be on it. Indeed, in *Sein und Zeit* this is a character of absent things and referred to as "conspicuousness." Concealment and un-concealment permeate both Being "and" Nothingness.

Our daily experience is shot through with this usage of (relative) "nothing." We may say, for instance, that "there is nothing about this or that person," that "there is nothing we can do about this or that," or that "he or she scored, heard, said nothing."

Let us summarize the point: "Logical negation" and "relative nothingness" must be distinguished. The former is contained in the negating propositon without there being necessarily any experience of "nothingness" (e.g., the negation of my own existence). Indeed, without an experience of nothingness logicians can justifiably consider such ontological propositon as "nothingness nothings" as "non-sense." But one can put, even though in an exaggerated manner, the meaning of nothing "contained" in a logical proposition in a nutshell: the logical negation reveals itself in the printer's ink. By contrast, relative nothing relates to an existing object in the world. This "nothing" is accompanied by an experienced content with respect to which something is not-the-case, or absent. I do not wish to deal with the question concerning the extent to which the logical negation pertains to relative nothingness.

The third meaning of "nothingness" is "absolute," says Scheler. It is detached from any comprehensibility and grasp of thought. Parmenides was the first to draw this meaning to our attention in Fragments 8 and 2: "It is necessary to speak and to think what is; for Being is but nothing is not." And, "Being and Thinking are one" (i.e., to think nothing makes it already something in thought).

It is noteworthy that absolute nothingness was the first meaning of nothingness to occur in the history of philosophy.

Max Scheler relates this "absolute nothingness" to the first principle of metaphysics: "that there is something rather than nothing." According to Scheler the relationship between this metaphysical principle and absolute nothingness is the following: the Being of entities (Sein des Seienden) is "the ever astounding cover over the abyss of absolute nothingness." I wish to add a point of my own concerning this nothingness: the human accessibility to absolute nothingness in thought is, because it is un-thinkable, a minimum still of relative nothing bordering infinitely close to "absolute" (i.e., detached) nothing. This must be so because we can only attempt to grasp it in thought, albeit without complete success. For thinking and being are the same (Parmenides), not nothing and thinking.

2.) We stated above that the theme of being and nothingness much characterizes contemporary philosophy. We can now add another characteristic to it: the absence of any moral consideration in the question of nothingness. It is Scheler who apparently alone contributed to this aspect. In brief his argument runs as follows: The true philosopher is only he who has once risked coming close to the experience of horror before the abyss of absolute nothingness. This abyss surrounds the span of our transient, becoming and un-becoming life-time. Nothing is from behind this span, i.e., before our birth; and nothing is in front of this span, i.e., after death. "In between" (not taken in a logical sense) we "experience" the world and ourselves and are mostly in a state of "care-free giddiness" that keeps us away from this horror and the fact of death, states Scheler. While Heidegger later on also referred, in *Sein und Zeit*, to this as "inauthentic being-unto-death," he did not see the moral implication of the value of each moment and each thing that comes about when death would be experienced authentically. For Scheler the facing of the abyss of absolute nothingness makes every thing and moment of value, no matter how trivial they ordinarily may appear to be. This we can represent to ourselves if we dare imagine there being only one hour left for us "to be." In such a state human nature tends to cling to any thing as much and as closely as possible. Man clings to the earth when he begins to realize that soon he will see it no more. In short, man does not let things pass by him so lavishly as he does in his everyday, care-free giddiness. But it is also precisely in the face of an oncoming experience of the horror of nothingness that man's thinking is "thanking." The smallest and most humble things come to light in their openness of value while such an hour's time ticks away. And it is here, within the philosopher's thanksgiving for everything that is, that grows the most tender filigree of the human heart: *humility*.[1] The horror before nothingness generates true thanking for the worlding of entities about us, e.g., for the things along a "Path-Way," the fields and trees, people and animals, towns and clouds, seas and stars, earth and heaven. In humility the philosopher heeds the value of Being in the sphere of the heart, not the mind.

3.) A third consideration on the subject of nothingness is that of Max Scheler's concept of reality. Scheler was rather critical of Heidegger's conceptualizations of Dasein, just as he was critical of Husserl's transcendental and absolute consciousness. Indeed, it can be argued that he would have been rather critical also of all contemporary philosophy after his untimely death in 1928. From his writings we can

---

[1] For an elaboration of this subject see M.S. Frings, "Humility and Existence," *Delta Epsilon Sigma Bulletin*, Vol. 19, NO. 4, December, 1974.

safely deduce at least two reasons why he would have asserted a peculiar metaphysical stand of his own, at least against the humerous "isms" which have fragmented contemporary philosophy almost beyond recognition: 1.) the absence of a serious metaphysical explication and a hermeneutics of the Divine, and 2.) the false concepts of reality creeping through contemporary philosophy.

What then is for Scheler "reality" and what has reality to do with nothingness? Reality, we are told, is "resistance." Resistance constitutes itself whenever an entity is able to relate to something outside itself and is able to thereby relate, in whatever manner, to itself. A cell's reality, for example, is not constituted by human perception, but in the cell's own self-motion and capacity to resist and relate to something other than itself, for instance, to other cells. The factor of resistance brings about the realness and individuality of the cell. Reality always implies bi-polarity. Resistance as reality is in inorganic nature (e.g., in positive and negative charges in the atom), it is between organs and organism, it is in psychic and mental processes, and it is included even in man's capacity to relate to an unknown Deity. Needless to say, reality as resistance can have multiple intensities and forms, as in individuals and in social life among groups and classes. There is a biological, physical, individual, social, and mental reality as resistance, to mention only a few.

Moral reality, for example, is at hand in pangs of conscience. Here we experience a conflict between what we are and have done over against what we ought to have been and what we did not do that should have been done. It is what we ought to have been, but were not, and what we should have done, but did not do, that constitutes the moral reality of that for which we are in such pangs. For what we morally "ought to be" withstands "what we are," just as what we are is in conflict with what we ought to have been and failed to do.

It stands to reason that such a concept of reality, where, in other words, an entity A is really through a B (=non A) and obtains its own individual nature through this B, has very little to do, if anything, with ordinary outer "reality" that we perceive with the senses. What is important to note is, however, the notion of nothingness implied. It is here that Scheler's meta-biology is intertwined with his hitherto unpublished metaphysics. Let us try to show this in very brief terms. If reality is resistance then the world's reality must ultimately be resistance not only among its parts, but also and especially of its parts against their respective wholes and vice versa, culminating in a total "World-Resistance" experience in man. For if there is no resisting factor between the parts of the world as a whole and vice versa there is no world. The conflict of mutually resisting parts and wholes permeates, for example, organs and organism, individuals and groups, peoples and history, humanity and gods. But this universal resistance among parts and wholes must have a peculiar character. There can nowhere be a uniform relationship between them. They are never anywhere in complete agreement and balance. For this would annihilate the realizing resistance between them. Parts and wholes must always be in a state of some mutual irregularity, disharmony, and strife, bringing about their realizing resistance. Scheler emphasizes this point not only in his analysis of Husserl's *Ideas I* but also of Heidegger's *Sein und Zeit*. He argues that if everything was in total harmony, such that all parts and wholes would, as it were, fill each other out, there could not be any reality of anything. If, for instance, all human desires were to be fulfilled at any moment (as is the case in the fairy tale of the "Land of the Plenty" to which Scheler refers) then no reality of and in this world can "be," precisely because of the total lack of the dynamic factor of realizing resistance.

A similar argument can be found in Greek mythology. When Semele, mother of Dionysos by Zeus, asked Zeus to appear to her in his full and complete glory as god of light, she was struck dead by his lightning. The full and complete presence of Zeus extinguished and annihilated Semele because there was no resistance possible anymore through which Zeus could have remained real for her. Zeus ceased "to be." For Semele, both Zeus and she herself dissolved into nothing because the total completion of Zeus' presence cancelled out the disharmony and strife between her and him.

Thus the argument that "nothingness nothings," to use a Heideggerian term (avoiding the expression "there is" nothing) when there is no resistance between parts and wholes, bears on Scheler's conception of the world. The world and any entity, because its reality is in its resistance, must at any time be *evanescent* and can never be fully grasped and exhausted by any part of it, including man. At any moment of our lives not only is the world different from what we expect it to be and, therefore, resisting in the sphere of relative nothingness, but also any moment of time as factually lived is itself, however slightly, different from what it was anticipated to be. This difference makes the moment as lived real, because it withstands what it is not.

A final word may be in place as to the relationship between resistance and God. We can ask the following question: Is the Deity itself dependent for its reality on something that resists it, or can there "be" a Deity without resistance at all? The traditional notions of God, such as that of a transcendent God, would have it that the second part of the question holds true: God is almighty and omniscient. The later Scheler attacked vehemently this notion of God, indeed, with the same forcefulness as that with which Nietzsche proclaimed "God is dead." But Scheler did hold that the former part of the question must be answered in the affirmative. God's existence must be dependent on man's resistance through which God can only be real. But such a God can by no means be a perfect God, but only one who is imperfect, i.e., becoming in history. The mutual resistance between man and God in history is a unitary process of realizing resistance. "There is no less peace and war in God than there is in man," says Scheler. The question whether the idea of God will become completely fulfilled in history - i.e., whether the world process will at some time balance itself out so that no resistance and, therefore, nothing will prevail-belongs to one of the questions Scheler dealt with in his later philosophy of religion and metaphysics. The question is of importance to us when we consider the historically decreasing number of gods and their function in history in favor of a uniform idea of "a" God. But would the end of World Resistance make the world only an episode before which there was nothing and after which there will be nothing?

Indeed, Heidegger's analysis of Dasein suggests this as strongly as Dali's Surrealism does in the art of painting. For Dasein's horizontality lies not only in its "being-unto-death" but also in its "anxiety" and "care." Should these structures and others really belong to man's essence, then, Scheler held, "the world better not be." This could equally pertain to the "event" in Heidegger II. For also the "event" does not preclude its some time being extinguished into nothing.

If, however, not anxiety and care but "love" is recognized to be not only man's vertical essence, but also the ultimate lever and motor that "opens" the world up, as Scheler suggests along with Plato's "Eros" as force, our question shifts into a different light. For the essence of love lets itself be conceived as "duration" (i.e., not requiring time-sequence) and as that by which man through his "ordo amoris," is the divinizing bearer, whom the Devine needs for his resisting reality in history.

Eros can be seen to be as important a factor in the history of philosophy as truth (including its meaning of "unconcealment"). And it can be argued that Eros, too, became "covered up" in that history. For

Eros as force unites all in the Orphic cosmogonies. From these unions the immortal gods are born. In Hesoid Eros is among the first to emerge from Chaos and draws everything together. And as Proclus reports from Pherecydes, Zeus changed into Eros as soon as he wanted to create. Eros is the union and birth of mythological elements, and, in a sense, a first mover, even as such recognized by Aristotle (*Meta.* 984b). Eros maintained this function among the philosophers of nature. He remained the force conjoining opposite elements and powers. In Empedocles it is love (philia) which unites all, even from the extreme tensions brought about by hate. In Parmenides love is a daimon "uniting all." (Fr. 12). The same conception of Love we find in Plato's *Symposium*: Eryximachus shows it to be the principle of attraction. Eros, then, may have the very function Heidegger assigns to Logos, Physis, and the Heraclitian Hen: the force holding everything and all together, lest there be nothing.

Heidegger's Value-Criticism and its Bearing on the Phenomenology of Values.*

PARVIS EMAD
DePaul University

I. *Introduction*

Throughout his work Heidegger criticizes value as an idea, which, its pretensions notwithstanding, is completely unfit to guide us through the present world-historical crisis. He upholds this judgment despite the fact that phenomenology of values purports to have initiated a whole new approach to value and to have formulated a novel conception of the same.

A brief preview of the treatment of value by Heidegger is likely to bring into sharper focus his actual stance on the phenomenology of values. Already in *Being and Time* (*B&T*) Heidegger regards value as a notion whose ontological status is quite unclear. Several years later in *Nietzsche* (*N, I & II*) he subjects value to a scrupulous scrutiny, revealing its "metaphysical" nature. It is only later, in the *Letter on Humanism* (*LH*), when referring to such Schelerian theses as; "God is the highest value", and "values are either positive or negative" that he flatly rejects thinking in terms of values as "the greatest blasphemy that can be thought of in the face of Being."[1] However, nowhere does

*I wish to thank John Thornbrugh for his careful reading of the final draft of this paper. I also wish to express my gratitude to Professor John Sallis who criticized an earlier version of this paper by calling my attention to the treatment of value in Heidegger's Marburg-Lectures.

1. M. Heidegger, *Letter on Humanism,* in: *Philosophy in 20th Century* ed. W. Barret, H.D. Aiken, 1971, p. 215.

Heidegger make any effort to substantiate this rejection by critically coming to terms with the phenomenology of values.

The absence of a persuasive criticism of the phenomenological conception of value, together with its rejection by Heidegger requires an explanation. Isn't it reasonable to assume that an explicit criticism is rendered superfluous due to the peculiar affinity of the phenomenological with the "metaphysical", i.e., Nietzschean, conception of value? One passage in *NII* considerably strengthens this assumption:

> Under the influence of Nietzsche the learned philosophy of the terminating 19th and beginning 20th century turns into a "philosophy" and "phenomenology" of values. Values appear now as things-in-themselves to be arranged in "systems." Despite a tacit rejection of Nietzsche's philosophy, his writings, especially *Zarathustra*, are now examined closely. . . in order to set up an ethics of value "more scientifically" than the "unscientific philosopher-poet Nietzsche" ever could.[2]

By casting doubt on the originality of a phenomenology of values, Heidegger seems to make the assumption plausible that, in a general way, his designation of value as "metaphysical" is broad enough to include the phenomenological conception of value. Can the phenomenological conception of value be designated metaphysical in the Heideggerian sense of the term? Is the phenomenology of values vulnerable to Heidegger's criticism?

It is the purpose of this paper to attempt to answer these questions. To work our way toward the answer two steps should be taken. First, we should determine what exactly constitutes Heidegger's value-criticism. Second, we should make clear the distinctive feature of the phenomenological theory of experience which gives rise to, and supports a phenomenology of values. The first step requires that we outline the course of.Heidegger's thought on value from its inception to its culmination. The second step demands that Scheler's phenomenology of values be examined in order to see whether it is immune to Heidegger's criticism.

---

2. M. Heidegger, *Nietzsche*, Vol. II *(N, II)* Pfullingen Neske, 1961, pp. 98-99.

II. *Heidegger's Critique of Value, its Inception and Culmination*

Before reaching the conclusion that Nietzsche articulates *the* "metaphysical" conception of value, Heidegger approached value as an idea which attained philosophical prominence in close connection with Lotze's thought. To some extent this is already reflected in the way he raises the following question in *B&T:*

> What, then, does the Being of value or their validity (which Lotze took as a mode of 'affirmation') really amount to ontologically?[3]

Obviously this question points to three interrelated problems: a) the Being of value is undetermined, b) this Being is generally identified with validity, which c) Lotze took as a mode of affirmation. In contrast to *B&T,* Heidegger's recently published Marburg-Lectures shed considerable light on these three problems, specifically on Lotze's view on validity.

Central to Lotze's philosophical position is his thesis that validity is a form of actuality *(Wirklichkeit).* He further specifies actuality by indicating that it is concomitant with the act of affirmation. By stressing this concomitance Lotze minimizes the significance of distinguishing things as real or ideal. As Heidegger points out

> the universal, formal term actuality does not indicate whether what is being affirmed is real or ideal ... but only affirming as such *(Bejahtheit ueberhaupt).*[4]

Strictly speaking, actuality appears to be the point where affirmation terminates, a thesis which Lotze tries to clarify in his classification of the forms of actuality.

Actuality takes on various forms depending on the direction that affirmation takes. We affirm a thing as actual when we say that it exists as opposed to a thing which does not. Similarly, we affirm an event as actual if it takes place as distinguished from one which does not come to

---

3. M. Heidegger, *Being and Time,* tr. J. Macquarrie & E. Robinson, Harper and Row, 1963, p. 132.

4. M. Heidegger, *Gesamtausgabe,* Vol 21. V. Klostermann, 1976, p. 69.

pass. Moreover, we affirm a relation as actually holding as opposed to one which does not hold. Finally, Lotze designates a proposition as actually true when it is affirmed as valid in contrast to one whose validity is dubious.

Rethinking Lotze's classification, Heidegger finds that the term truth is carelessly introduced in it. For it is one thing to maintain that a proposition is actual when it is affirmed, quite another to say that it is actually true when it is affirmed. To be consistent, Lotze would have to designate a proposition as actual when it is affirmed: he would have to treat propositions as he did things, events and relations. Instead, he states that a proposition is actually *true* when it is affirmed. As Heidegger puts it, Lotze

> does not simply say . . . a proposition is actual when it is affirmed but a proposition is actually *true* when it is affirmed as valid.[5]

Lotze's view on affirmation is based on the assumption that by affirming a thing as actual we acknowledge the existence of what is true. A proposition which acknowledges the existence of such a thing, is a valid proposition. What distinguishes a valid from a non-valid proposition is the presence of the truth in the former and the absence of it in the latter. Validity implies constant presence of truth in a proposition. In Heidegger's words,

> Validity, as used by Lotze in determining the mode of being of true propositions, has the ontological meaning of constant presence.[6]

However, Lotze fails to account for the unprecedented ability he attributes to affirmation when he takes it to be the initiator of the constant presence of truth in a proposition. Why is a proposition suddenly affirmed as true rather than merely affirmed as actual? Simply stated, Lotze has no answer to offer to this question.

Lotze's theory of validity is, therefore, based on an unexamined

---

5. *Ibid.*, p. 73.
6. *Ibid.*, p. 78.

assumption on the nature and scope of affirmation. The neo-Kantians accept Lotze's theory without in the least questioning this assumption. Instead of critically examining Lotze's view on affirmation, that is, scrutinizing the basis of his theory of validity, the neo-Kantians merely try to interpret it more "rigorously." For they are of the opinion that what is being affirmed in a valid proposition is not primarily truth but

> . . a value, i.e., affirming a proposition as true means
> ultimately affirmation of a value.[7]

Thus the neo-Kantians subordinate truth to value. This is evident in their interpretation of Kant's work. The neo-Kantians, Rickert and Windelband, hold the three *Critiques* of Kant to deal primarily with truth, good and beauty as values. The subordination of truth to value is so exhaustive that the neo-Kantian philosophies of value "invented the value of the holy"[8] if only to prove that they have not neglected Kant's work on religion. Accordingly, they proclaimed "God as the highest value"[9], a claim which Heidegger rejects with almost the same words he was going to use two decades later in *LH*. In the Marburg-Lectures he declares the identification of God with the highest value

> a blasphemy which is no less injurious when it is proclaimed
> by some theologians as the ultimate truth.[10]

Concluding our attempt to delineate the initial stage of Heidegger's thought on value, it is profitable to stress certain points. In his Marburg-Lectures Heidegger shows how Lotze's unexamined assumptions on the nature of affirmation give rise to the neo-Kantian concept of value. Now value appears as an idea which is more readily accessible and more persistently present than the constant presence of truth in a valid proposition. Thus these Lectures clarify the position of *B&T* on the ontological status of value: when taken as a mode of affirmation, the being of value is conceived as constantly present in a valid proposition. Clearly, Lotze's account of affirmation does not

---

7. *Ibid.*, p. 82.
8. *Ibid.*, p. 84.
9. *Ibid.*, p. 84.
10. *Ibid.*, p. 84.

stand the test of Heidegger's critical analysis. However, it is one thing to disqualify Lotze's thesis on affirmation, quite another to critically assess the being of value, i.e., constant presence. Heidegger will criticize constant presence when he studies Nietzsche and reaches the conclusion that value in this philosopher's thought represents a "metaphysical" project. Only then does his critique of value become definitive and reach its culmination.

Two preliminary questions must be dealt with before we attend to Heidegger's thesis that value in Nietzsche represents a "metaphysical" project: what objectives guide Heidegger's interpretation of Nietzsche and what does he mean by the term metaphysics?

Heidegger's effort in dealing with Nietzsche is not devoted exclusively to an objective analysis of his text, but is chiefly directed at determining Nietzsche's relationship to metaphysics. It should be kept in mind that by metaphysics Heidegger does not means a philosophical discipline, but occidental thinking which throughout its history has aimed at determining the being of beings. In major periods of its history, metaphysics has demonstrated that its main concern is with the being of beings, by trying indefatigably to determine their being. However, what Being as such means in its truth (and not merely as the truth of beings) has never been the concern of metaphysics. The failure of metaphysics to concern itself with Being as such is not an indication of the shortcoming of philosophers. This failure is due to what Heidegger calls the abandonment of Being (*Seinsverlassenheit*) of which metaphysical thinking has been persistently oblivious (*Seinsvergessenheit*).

Therefore, when we say that in dealing with Nietzsche's philosophy Heidegger is basically concerned with this philosopher's relationship to metaphysics, we are saying in effect that Heidegger is interested in finding out how the being of beings shines forth through the medium of Nietzsche's thought. Furthermore, we mean that in accordance with his theses of abandonment and oblivion of Being, Heidegger is interested in determining the extent to which Nietzsche reflects this abandonment and oblivion.

Heidegger seems to attach historical significance to his work on Nietzsche because he intimates that this work fulfills a particular mission. The immediate task of discussing Nietzsche's philosophy, as he puts it, lies in

> . . . a reflection on the inner unity of Nietzsche's metaphysics
> as the completion of occidental metaphysics.[11]

This task, however, is subordinate to the far more distant goal of preparing for a strife (*Streit*) which is no longer over domination (*Meisterung*) of beings but is

> . . . the aboriginal discord (*Aus-ein-ander-setzung*) between
> the power of beings and the truth of Being.[12]

The historical significance of *N, I & II* lies ultimately in preparing for another beginning which is attainable when the current conflict between beings and beings is transformed into the latent, yet present, discord between beings and the truth of Being.

How could Nietzsche's philosophy be taken as the end and completion of Western metaphysics (the first task)? It is Heidegger's contention that Nietzsche's concept of value brings about this completion. To Heidegger, Nietzsche's concept of value is *the* most extreme expression of constant presence, *the* mode of time, to which Western metaphysical thinking has been continuously oriented. A discussion of this extreme expression entails a treatment of two interrelated questions: how does value represent the unity of Nietzsche's thought and how are we to conceive this unity?

In order to see Heidegger's critique of value culminating in his treatment of Nietzsche, we must know first what he means by the inner unity of this philosopher's thought, *mutatis mutandis* what he takes Nietzsche's concept of value to stand for. The unity of Nietzsche's thought emerges out of the five themes of will to power, eternal return, overman, nihilism, and justice (truth). According to Heidegger, the core of Nietzsche's philosophy is to be found in neither of these five basic themes alone but in their inner unity. Heidegger's treatment of will to power, eternal return and nihilism articulates this unity clearly enough to make it unnecessary to consider his views on all the major Nietzschean themes. Therefore, to see this unity we turn to Heidegger's views on will to power, eternal return and nihilism.

---

11. *N, II*, p. 262.
12. *Ibid.*, p. 262.

1. To Heidegger, will in Nietzsche is not identical with a faculty of the mind readily available to introspection. Likewise, by power Nietzsche does not mean something that the will lacks. Will, as a faculty of the mind, and power as what may or may not be wanting by this faculty are not prior to but subsequent to the will to power.

Will to Nietzsche is never without power and power is never extraneous to the will. Basically, Nietzsche does not conceive will as analogous to a wish or a desire but as identical with a command. As such it controls itself and is capable of empowering itself. By power, Nietzsche means the preservation *and* enhancement of power, which stabilizes power only to surpass this stabilization. How can will to power as command surpass its stabilization and thereby effect preservation and enhancement of power? It can do so only if it can have access to the conditions of preservation and enhancement of power. And what are these conditions? Nothing other than values:

Values as *conditions* for preservation and enhancement of power exist as conditioned due to will to power as the *exclusive* unconditioned. Values are *essentially conditioned conditions*.[13]

Heidegger sums up his views on will to power by saying, ". . the essence of will to power is empowering to power"[14], a process which is carried out through values. It is will to power itself which adopts values for the purpose of maintenance and enhancement of power. It is by its ability to surpass its own stabilization (values) that will to power reflects Nietzsche's vision of becoming.

As conceived *and* surpassed by will to power, value appears in an ambiguous light. To meet the requirement of becoming as envisioned by Nietzsche, values have to be transient. To meet the needs for maintenance and heightening of power, they have to be durable. For, only in this way can they fit a becoming which is neither altogether aimless nor knows of a definite purpose. How is such a becoming conceivable? The thought on eternal return answers this question, and it makes more intelligible the durable-transient requirement that is placed

---

13. *Ibid.,* p. 108. Italics are Heidegger's.
14. *Ibid.,* p. 236.

on values.

2. According to Heidegger, by eternal return of the same Nietzsche does not mean an observable repetition of an event which happened in the past:

> The return of the same does not mean that for an observer, whose being is not determined by the will to power, what existed formerly will exist again and again as the same.[15]

Eternal return is inconceivable without will to power and the light which this will sheds on becoming. However free from an extraneous goal, becoming is not conceived by Nietzsche as a process which goes on aimlessly. It lies in the nature of power as Nietzsche conceives it,

> . . . to be free from goal and on the whole aimless. However, this freedom from goal. . . cannot tolerate that power flows away boundlessly.[16]

For will to power to remain ultimately aimless and yet avoid flowing away boundlessly, values assume a unique role. They are structured in such a way as to allow maximum empowering of the will to power without terminating the possibility of further acquisition of power. How can this be done? Only when will to power brings together durability and transiency to such a degree as to endow values with a particular kind of constancy. By succeeding to do this, will to power turns into eternal return of the same:

> This happens to it [=will to power] when the purest constancy (*reinste Bestaendigung*) confronts it, not only once but constantly as the same. In order to secure this highest condition (value) will to power must be its own "principle for positing values".[17]

Value "links" will to power to eternal return, by making plausible a becoming which is neither mere transitoriness nor an aimless duration,

---

15. *Ibid.,* p. 287.
16. *Ibid.,* p. 285.
17. *Ibid.,* p. 290.

but "returns to the same". Value appears well suited to avoid the kind of ultimacy which is indicated in terms such as transitoriness and duration. Value appears to will to power as *the* condition for purest constancy and return to the same. However, Heidegger maintains:

> The same which returns is only relatively constant. Therefore, it is essentially inconstant. Its return, however, indicates. . . mere constancy. The eternal return is the most constant constancy of what is inconstant.[18]

Nietzsche's notion of value reflects the most fundamental trait of becoming which is neither the same as transitoriness nor mere duration. Heidegger refers to this trait as the most constant constancy of what is inconstant. Nietzsche's third basic theme, nihilism further clarifies the central significance of value in and beyond Nietzsche's thought.

3. Nihilism, according to Heidegger, means to Nietzsche a great deal more than the view, made fashionable by Turgenev, which takes as real only what is perceivable by the senses. It means to Nietzsche also a great deal more than uprootedness of a people and its lack of self-confidence, as Dostoyevsky, e.g. attributed to the Russians.[19] Nietzsche, Heidegger emphasizes, speaks of nihilism as a European phenomenon, that is as something related to occidental metaphysics. In what way is nihilism related to this metaphysics? Heidegger's answer, considerably different from Nietzsche's, centers around the notion of value as a "metaphysical" project. By discussing Heidegger's views on this project we finally arrive at his criticism of value in Nietzsche.

To be sure, Nietzsche's conception of becoming necessitates nihilism as the process of devaluation of values. For, how else could a constant rejuvenation of becoming be possible? This rejuvenation is possible because value assumes two fundamental functions: it makes accessible to thought both the nature of beings and that of becoming. The term becoming indicates Nietzsche's manner of accounting for Being as such. Therefore, his concept of value purports to make accessible to thought both the nature of beings and that of Being as such. This, however, is precisely what Heidegger refuses to concede to Nietzsche. The reason for this refusal lies in the "temporal quality" which Heidegger discerns

---

18. *Ibid.*, p. 287.
19. Cf., *N, II*, p. 31 ff.

in value as a metaphysical project. Let us see what this "temporal quality" is all about.

The most fundamental *and* elusive feature of becoming in Nietzsche is described by Heidegger as "the most constant constancy of what is inconstant". However, this elusive and fundamental feature is manifest only in values, their capability to be devalued, in short, their intrinsic nihilistic quality. Nietzsche tries to do justice to his idea of becoming by assigning to values the task of making manifest the peculiar nature of becoming. The result is the disclosure of becoming as "the most constant constancy of what is inconstant." To justify becoming then, Nietzsche finally succumbs to the fascination generated by constancy, the mode of time known to occidental metaphysics. Even though he curtails drastically the presence indicated in constancy by designating it as the curious "most constant constancy of what is inconstant" he is still under the spell of this fascination. What is constantly present, no matter how curiously inconstant, determines Nietzsche's thought as it does the thinking of other philosophers. The commitment to what is accessible to thought as constant presence, *the* pervasive trait of "metaphysical" thinking, is not relinquished in Nietzsche. His notion of value is a "metaphysical" project because it is the most extreme expression of constancy and presence.

By continuing to think in terms of constancy and presence, notwithstanding the sophisticated character which both constancy and presence assume in his thinking, Nietzsche actually exhausts the earliest possibility of metaphysical thinking. (This is the possibility that Plato took advantage of when he conceived the being of beings to be constantly present in their ideas.) However, neither the nature of beings nor that of Being is exhausted in constant presence. The task is

> . . . to meditate on the origin of presence and constancy by
> keeping the possibility open for thought that *"Being as such"*
> *on its way to "Being" could have given up its own essence in*
> *favor of a more aboriginal determination.* [20]

Constant presence is not the aboriginal determination of Being as such. Indeed, Being as such holds sway as the refusal to be present, as

---

20. *Ibid.,* p. 338. Italics are Heidegger's.

withdrawal from constant presence. Due to its refusal to be present, Being as such remains inaccessible to a thinking which is thoroughly given over to what is constantly present.

Inasmuch as value in Nietzsche requires thought to increasingly devote itself to what is present as constant inconstancy, value further enhances the oblivion of Being as what is not constantly present. The total priority of values, as advocated by Nietzsche, brings about maximum oblivion of Being as such. Hence, thinking in terms of values contributes most vigorously to the oblivion of Being. This is manifest in philosophy's increasing preoccupaion with values whereby Being's abandonment remains persistently unheeded. The competition of humanistic, secular and sacred values with each other in the contemporary philosophical scene confirms the continuing orientation of thought toward presence, constancy and accessibility.

Considering the intimate "temporal" affiliation of values with Being, it seems safe to maintain that, like any other "metaphysical" project, values too must be subjected to the scrupulous process which sums up Heidegger's relation to metaphysics and is known as its "overcoming."

At the end of this survey of the entirety of Heidegger's thought on value, it is helpful to highlight its major points. Heidegger's critique of value begins and ends by revealing the extent to which value is tied to, and embodies constant presence. Although initially he does not subject constant presence to an explicit criticism, his discussion of value in *N I & II* finally articulates such a criticism. While the neo-Kantian concept of value may be said to be rather naive (because it merely reflects a preference for value as more readily accessible than propositional truth) Nietzsche's concept of value should be characterized as extremely sophisticated. As a "metaphysical" project this conception simultaneously retains and conceals its adherence to constant presence, that is accessibility. Since the nature of Being is inaccessible (not constantly present) Heidegger regards thinking in terms of constant presence as genuine nihilism. He regards such thinking as nihilistic because it feigns the accessibility of Being as such. Consequently, such thinking hinders the coming about of a genuine relationship between thought and Being's aboriginal determination, i.e., meditation on the origin of presence and constancy. Hence, thinking in terms of value is not original, and is unfit to meet the needs of the present historical situation.

It is against this background that we have to understand Heidegger's negative stance on the phenomenology of values. To this end we must turn to this phenomenology in order to outline its manner of procedure.

III. The Objective Nature of Values in Scheler

It should be pointed out at the outset that Scheler's approach to values differs significantly from that of the neo-Kantian philosophies of value. His views on value are not derived from Lotze's theory of validity but purport to have a phenomenological basis. We see this clearly once we consider the position he occupies in the phenomenological movement.

It is generally accepted that Scheler's major contribution to the phenomenological movement is to be found in his attempt to revive the ethical consciousness via a phenomenology of values.[21] Throughout his magnum opus *Formalism in Ethics and Non-Formal Ethics of Values (Formalism),* as well as elsewhere in his writings, Scheler relentlessly advocates the objectivity and eternity of values.

To demonstrate this objectivity Scheler relies exclusively on his phenomenological theory of experience. For, as soon as he speaks of values, he emphasizes their experiential origin:

> ... there is a type of experiencing... that leads us to *genuinely* objective objects and the eternal order among them, i.e., to values...[22]

To grasp Scheler's views on the objectivity of values, we must set out from this "type of experiencing" and study its specific structure. His grandiose system of values need not detain us here, for this system rests on Scheler's phenomenological theory of experience. In order to examine his conception of value we do not need to set out from distinctions such as positivity and negativity of values, their rank and height, etc. The secondary importance of these distinctions becomes evident once we succeed in tracing Scheler's conception of value to its

---

21. Cf., H. Spiegelberg, *The Phenomenological Movement,* Vol. I, Martinus Nijhoff, The Hague, 1965, p. 251 ff. See also, L. Landgrebe, *Philosophie der Gegenwart.* 1961, Ulstein, p. 125 f.

22. M. Scheler, *Formalism in Ethics and Non-Formal Ethics of Values, (Formalism),* tr. M. S. Frings and R. L. Funk, Northwestern University Press, 1973, p. 255.

experiential origin.

Like the Husserl of the *Logical Investigations,* Scheler is of the opinion that basically experience is made up of acts and objective correlates of these acts. Using these distinctions in his theory of values he refers to the act-structure of experience as intentional feeling and specifies the objective correlates of this feeling as values. To see this clearly, it is necessary that we turn to his major work.

The section in *Formalism* which faces the task of refuting the relativity and subjectivity of values, begins by offering a brief definition of values as "irreducible basic phenomena of emotive intuition" *(fuehlende Anschauung).*[23] It is no exaggeration to maintain that this statement captures the substance of Scheler's thought on values. To understand it, however, we must know what he means by the expression "emotive intuition."

It is unfortunate that this expression omits the close ties which German *Anschauung,* intuition, has with "feeling" in the original *"fuehlende Anschauung."* This omission becomes more significant when we consider the fact that Scheler clarifies the nature of emotive intuition by addressing himself to its basic ingredient, i.e., *intentional feeling (intentionales Fuehlen).*

By feeling, Scheler does not mean a perception of something through sensation but an emotive awareness which indicates values. Intentional feeling *is* basically this awareness:

> This feeling... has the same relation to its value-correlate as "representing" has to its "object", namely, an intentional relation. It is not *externally brought together* with an object... On the contrary, feeling *originally* intends its *own* kind of objects, namely, "values."[24]

Intentional feeling is fundamentally experienced in loving and hating. As Scheler points out:

---

23. *Ibid.,* p. 265. To consult this passage in original see Vol 2 of Scheler's *Gesammelte Werke,* Franke, Bern, 1966, p. 270.

24. *Ibid.,* p. 258. Following italics are all by Scheler.

> Love and hate are acts in which the value-realm accessible to
> the feeling of a being is either *extended* or *narrowed*...[25]

According to Scheler, both love and hate are to be considered as
spiritual *acts* capable of comprehending values. Although these acts
extend or narrow the value-realm accessible to the feeling of an
individual, they do not create values. Because strictly speaking:

> Values cannot be created or destroyed. They exist
> independent of the organization of all beings endowed with
> spirit.[26]

In short, through acts of love and hate, the realm of values becomes
accessible to us. For this reason, a more adequate understanding of the
intentional feeling of values requires us to concentrate on Scheler's
conception of act. This must be done because his conception of act is the
sine qua non of his theory of love and hate. Accordingly, his thought on
act should be clearly understood in order to see equally clearly his views
on the intentional feeling of values.

It should be pointed out that the cognitive, volitive, and emotive
aspects of the mind, each emphasized in various degrees in
philosophical tradition, undergo a serious examination in Scheler. To
consider mind as primarily a cognitive agent endowed with the
capability of controlling our emotive life is as erroneous an assumption
to Scheler as is the view of the mind as a manifestation of a primordial
will. To him, mind designates generally, the execution of a variety of
acts which may have congnitive, emotive, volitive or religious
characteristics:

> ...we use the term mind [Geist] for the entire sphere of acts.[27]

In contrast to the Husserl of the *Logical Investigations*, Scheler offers
an amazingly simple account of what he means by act. He distinguishes
two major processes in the entirety of mental life. One such process
happens by itself as in the case of e.g. hearing, seeing, touching and
smelling. Scheler calls these processes functions. As distinguished from

---

25. *Ibid.*, p. 261.
26. *Ibid.*, p. 261.
27. *Ibid.*, p. 389.

these there are processes, such as thinking, willing, and "feeling", which do not happen by themselves but have to be executed. Scheler calls these processes acts and sums up the whole distinction by stating that "acts are executed; functions happen by themselves."[28]

Functions are observable and measurable. Observation of functions is carried out by execution of acts. It is, e.g. with the aid of the act of perception that the function of hearing may be analysed as to what distinguishes it, say, from seeing.

By contrast, acts are not observable nor measurable. For, unlike functions, they are not *extended* in time. Rather, they *enter* into time only to make something present:

> Acts spring from the person into time; functions are facts in phenomenal time...[29]

Moreover, functions by themselves are void of intentionality, but acts are without exception intentional. Color, e.g. is given to the act of perception which focuses on seeing, sound to the act of perception which aims at hearing. In themselves, seeing and hearing do not "intend" anything like color or sound.

The function of seeing, when modified by an act, renders present a phenomenon, color, as what is intimately connected with the modifying act. This example provides us with an insight into the relationship which holds between acts and their objective correlates. The most decisive principle of Scheler's phenomenology rests upon this insight. This principle holds that there exists an

> interconnection... between the *nature* of the *act* and the *nature* of the *object*..[30]

This principle, as Scheler is quick to point out

> excludes the possibility of "unknowable" objects and "unfeelable" values.[31]

---

28. *Ibid.*, p. 388.
29. *Ibid.*, p. 388.
30. *Ibid.*, p. 78.
31. *Ibid.*, p. 78.

In keeping with this principle, Scheler regards color as "knowable" to the act of perception which observes seeing. Likewise, this principle supports Scheler's contention that values are objective correlates of the acts of love and hate. According to Scheler, color exists independently from the function of seeing because it is rendered present by the act of perception which objectifies this function. In the same vein, values exist independently from the faculty of reasoning and thinking because acts of love and hate are not the same as the acts of thought. The objective correlates of the acts of thought are concepts not values. Unlike concepts, values are objective correlates of the acts of love and hate. These "objects" are not created by man, they are "felt" by him whenever he executes the acts of love and hate. To be sure, execution of these acts, or "intentional feeling of values", is something we come across in man. However, this does not mean that values are man's creation. As Scheler points out

> ...we do find the peculiar *essence* of ...values through *feeling;* and feeling is found *with* [am] man, ..But we do not find these in any way that differs... from the way in which we find propositions and laws of arithmetic, mechanics, physics, and chemistry...[32]

Propositions and laws of arithmetic, physics, etc. are also found "with" man without thereby becoming less objective. These propositions and laws are immune to human caprice because they are objective correlates of certain kinds of acts. Similarly, Scheler advocates the objective nature of values as correlated to the nature of certain acts.

Observations we made so far place us in a much better position to understand Scheler's basic definition of values as the irreducible basic phenomena of emotive intuition. Scheler's whole effort aims at making explicit the act-structure which is implicit in emotive intuition. The acts involved in this intuition, render values present as their objective correlates.

IV. Summary and Conclusion

Both before and after his analysis of Nietzsche's thought, Heidegger

---

32. *Ibid.*, p. 271.

considers value a notion which, in various degrees, expresses constant presence, i.e., accessibility. Because the nature of Being is inaccessible, he regards thinking in terms of values a serious impediment to achieving a genuine awareness of this inaccessibility. Devoted to beings and oblivious of Being, such thinking is unable to properly respond to the present world-historical crisis.

To be sure, value in Scheler is not derived from Lotze's theory of validity, and unlike the neo-Kantians, he can claim an independent status for his phenomenology of values. Furthermore, as objective correlates of certain acts, values in Scheler are data of emotive intentionality, hence conceived in a different way than in Nietzsche. However, notwithstanding this independence, when we examine Scheler's theory of intentional feeling we cannot fail to observe that his concept of value displays the "metaphysical" character which Heidegger found to be inseparable from the neo-Kantian and Nietzschean concepts of value. How can we discern the "metaphysical" character of value in Scheler?

Scheler conceives values as the objective correlates of certain acts. What distinguishes act in Scheler is its timeless quality. Timeless as acts are, they enter the realm of time to render values present and accessible.[33] Values in Scheler have the unmistakable characteristic of being "constantly present" in and through certain acts. It is in this temporal quality that we perceive the "metaphysical" character of value in Scheler.

Heidegger's critique of value is essentially a critique of the "metaphysical" urge to accessibility. Therefore, he characterizes as blasphemous the identification of the holy with a value only to stress the inaccessible nature of the holy. Does Scheler conceive the nature of the holy as accessible? The answer has to be in the affirmative if we consider Scheler's position, according to which

---

33. The timeless quality of act is clearly emphasized in Scheler's treatment of issues such as temporality, death, awareness of bodily states, spatiality etc. A brief discussion of some of these issues is to be found in the author's essay "Person, Death and World", published in: *Max Scheler (1874-1974) Centennial Essays,* ed. M. S. Frings, Nijhoff, the Hague, 1974, pp. 58-84. See specially pp. 66-72. Generally, the ability of acts in Scheler to render things accessible and present is not restricted to values, a point we cannot pursue here further.

...the act through which we *originally* apprehend the value
of the holy is an act of a special kind of love...[34]

This position clearly represents a case of identifying the holy with a
value. Such identification implies the constant presence of the value of
the holy in a certain kind of act as its objective correlate. This, however,
expresses the deep-rooted human propensity to conceive the holy as
something constantly present and accessible. Such propensity fails to
heed the inaccessible nature of the *Being* of the holy by mistaking it with
a being. Hence, Heidegger regards the identification of the holy with a
value (even with the highest value) as blasphemous.

---

34. *Formalism,* p. 109.

Heidegger and Merleau-Ponty: Interpreting Hegel

HUGH J. SILVERMAN
State University of New York at Stony Brook

In the last year of his life, Merleau-Ponty taught a course at the College de France entitled "Philosophy and Non-Philosophy since Hegel." These reflections, which have recently been published,[1] offer interpretations of Hegel and Marx. The first part of the study focuses on the celebrated "Introduction" to Hegel's *Phenomenology of Mind.* Curiously, however, Merleau-Ponty did not turn directly to the Hegelian text itself. Rather he worked out of Heidegger's essay "Hegel's Concept of Experience" which is collected in *Holzwege* but published for English-speaking readers as a separate volume.[2] Heidegger divides Hegel's "Introduction" into sixteen numbered paragraphs and comments upon each one in turn.[3] According to Heidegger, the 1807 title of the *Phenomenology of Mind,* i.e., "Science of the *"Experience* of Consciousness," represents "experience" as the fundamental concern of

[1]Maurice Merleau-Ponty, "Philosophy and Non-Philosophy Since Hegel," trans. Hugh J. Silverman, *Telos*, no. 29 (Fall 1976), pp. 43-105. The original French, edited by Claude Lefort, appeared in *Textures*, no. 8-9 (1974) and no. 10-11 (1975).

[2]Martin Heidegger, *"Hegels Begriff der Erfahrung"* in *Holzwege* (Frankfurt: Klostermann, 1950), pp. 105-192. The French translation by Wolfgang Brokmeier, edited by Francois Fedier as "Hegel et son concept de l'expérience": in *Chemins qui ne mènent nulle part* (Paris: Gallimard, 1962), pp. 101-172, appeared shortly after Merleau-Ponty's death. The English version is published as *Hegel's Concept of Experience* (N.Y.: Harper and Row, 1970). Although the translator of the portions by Heidegger are anonymous, the Hegel passages are translated by Kenley Royce Dove.

[3]In the German original of *Hegel's Concept of Experience*, the full text of Hegel's

the phenomenological enterprise. Indeed, the discussion of Hegel's "Introduction" develops an understanding of that very notion of "experience." Since Merleau-Ponty comments upon Hegel through Heidegger's text, it is not at all surprising that the concept of experience is also central to Merleau-Ponty's interpretation of Hegel. The confrontation of these two philosophers with Hegel is also their confrontation with each other and this encounter will be the subject of our study.

INTRODUCTION

Merleau-Ponty provides little direct commentary on Heidegger's interpretations of Hegel. Much of the dialogue is internal to Merleau-Ponty's own presentation of the Hegelian position. The absence of direct reference to Heidegger is not unusual. In fact, Merleau-Ponty rarely discusses the work of his German post-Husserlian counterpart. One of the few exceptions to this silence occurs in Merleau-Ponty's course outline for 1959 ("Philosophy as Interrogation"). He notes that through an inquiry into Being, Heidegger seeks

> to integrate truth with our capacity for error, to relate the incontestable presence of the world to its inexhaustible richness and consequent absence which it recuperates, to consider the evidence of Being in the light of an interrogation which is the only mode of expressing this eternal elusion.[4]

The passage is significant in that it embodies precisely the interchange and dialogical structure which is present throughout the two-pronged response to Hegel. By distinguishing the specific understanding which Heidegger holds toward Hegel and by contrasting that response with

---

"Introduction" is given prior to Heidegger's sixteen part paragraph by paragraph commentary. In the English version, we find not only the complete text at the beginning, but also the reproduction of each paragraph prior to Heidegger's discussion of it. Thus, in the original, one could study Hegel's text in its entirety and a reexamination of each passage would necessitate a return to the beginning. In the English version, one can readily compare Hegel's assertions with Heidegger's comments.

[4]Maurice Merleau-Ponty, *Themes from the Lectures*, trans. John O'Neill (Evanston: Northwestern University Press, 1970), p. 111.

the Merleau-Pontean position, the interrogation which Merleau-Ponty announces with respect to Heidegger can be re-directed back to Hegel and forward to contemporary thought. Hence without examining the particular statements that Merleau-Ponty has made about Heidegger or attempting to surmise how Heidegger would respond to Merleau-Ponty's incarnate philosophy and his move to visibility, our attention will be turned away from a direct confrontation. The Hegelian problematic will therefore serve as an instrument for the introduction of triangularity, as a model against which the two versions of modern phenomenology can show their differences, and as a point of inversion from the nineteenth century to the twentieth.

In order to give form to our own interrogation, it will be necessary to establish a triple tripartite set of relations. All nine terms are concerns introduced by Heidegger in his reading of Hegel's text. Yet it is precisely this text which Merleau-Ponty also reads in the move from philosophy to non-philosophy, or, as he says in the 1959 course, from "philosophy as a rigorous science" to philosophy as pure interrogation. Indeed, Merleau-Ponty cites this path as the same path "that led Heidegger from the negativist and anthropological themes to which the public reduced his early writings, to a conception of Being which he no longer calls philosophy--but which, as it has been well remarked (J. Beaufret), is certainly not extra-philosophical."[5] In a fashion similar to Heidegger's itinerary from philosophy to Being, Merleau-Ponty establishes the sojourn from philosophy to visibility, from philosophy to experience, and from philosophy to non-philosophy.[6] Just as he says of Heidegger, the result is "certainly not extra-philosophical" any more than it was for Hegel, who announced the end of philosophy before them.[7]

---

[5]*Ibid.*, p. 105

[6]This point is developed at length in my "Re-reading the Tradition with Merleau-Ponty," *Telos*, No. 29 (Fall 1976), pp. 106-129.

[7]For Hegel, the claim to the end of philosophy is the assertion that philosophy must become science. In the "Preface" to the *Phenomenology of Mind*, he puts it in the following way: "To demonstrate that the time has come for the elevation of philosophy to a science -- this would be the only true justification of the attempts which have this aim. For this would show the necessity of this aim even while accomplishing it." Translation by W. Kaufmann in *Hegel: Texts and Commentary* (N.Y.: Anchor, 1965), p. 12. Hegel restates his point near the end of the Preface: "Scientific knowledge... demands precisely that we surrender to the life of the object or -- and this is the same -- that we confront and express its inner necessity" (p. 82). In assessing this claim, Heidegger indicates that the

This retracing of steps affirms, in the first instance, the triad of (1) presence, (2) appearance, and (3) presentation; in the second case, (4) representation, (5) natural consciousness, and (6) real consciousness; and in the third account, (7) truth, (8) experience, and (9) phenomenology. The movement from presence to phenomenology follows the form of philosophy becoming experience (Merleau-Ponty) and establishes itself in the ontological difference between Being and beings (Heidegger). By detailing each of these triads, first from a Heideggerian perspective and second from a Merleau-Pontean point of view, the identity of their difference will become evident. Each element of the triple structure is thematized in Heidegger's essay "Hegel's Concept of Experience," and reformulated by Merleau-Ponty in his own terms and in his own response to Hegel.

I. THE FIRST TRIAD

(1) *Presence.* For Heidegger, the presence of that which is present establishes a difference.[8] This ontological difference, already announced above, is not only the difference between Being and beings, but also presence in that which is present *(das Anwesen in seinem Anwesende)*. The difference cannot be marked, it can only be re-marked in that which is present. The presence of the present brings Being to what is there. The 'there' simply takes the forms, shapes, and sizes that it has. As a difference that is established on the horizon of what is there, this difference (presence of the present) illustrates the philosophical

---

result of Hegel's philosophy was to become the dominant position in the nineteenth century: "The completion of metaphysics begins with Hegel's metaphysics of absolute knowledge as the Spirit of will. . . In spite of the superficial talk about the breakdown of Hegelian philosophy, one thing remains true: Only this philosophy determined reality in the nineteenth century, although not in the external form of a doctrine followed, but rather as metaphysics, as the dominance of beingness as the sense of certainty. The counter movements to this metaphysics belong *to* it." Heidegger, *The End of Philosophy,* trans. Joan Stambaugh (N.Y.: Harper and Row, 1973), p. 89. Nietzsche reiterates this completion of philosophy: "With Nietzsche's metaphysics, philosophy is completed. That means: It has gone through the sphere of prefigured possibilities... But with the end of philosophy, thinking is not also at its end, but in transition to another beginning." Ibid., p. 96.

[8]For a more extended consideration of the role of difference in its ontological character, see my article "Man and the Self as Identity of Difference," *Philosophy Today,* vol. 19, no. 2 (Summer 1975), pp. 131-136.

understanding of what is present by clarifying what needs to be known. As object of knowledge, that which is present is available for scrunity. But its availability for scrutiny is affirmed by its presence *(Anwesen)*.

A philosophical hermeneutic seeks to reveal existence as presence in its self-appearance. The enterprise, however, reveals only that which is present *(Anwesende)* and not necessarily its presence *(Anwesen)*. Philosophy, for Heidegger, examines the ontic (that which is present). Yet it continually finds itself falling into the ontic, rather than affirming its presence as the ontological character of what is there.

For Merleau-Ponty, philosophy must become the texture of existence. Just as Heidegger in *The Introduction to Metaphysics* associates the mistranslation of φύσις with the Latin *natura,* Merleau-Ponty in *The Structure of Behavior* takes the "physical order" as the first of three differentiated levels of human existence (with the vital and human orders each, in turn, fulfilling the conditons of nature). By reiterating this concept of nature *qua natura naturans* in *Phenomenology of Perception* and *qua* "concept of nature" in the Collége de France courses for 1957 and 1958, he demonstrates the "presignificatory" character of "brute being"--what Bergson viewed as "a primordial lost undividedness,"[9] and Husserl found in "the sphere of 'pure things'" *(blosse Sachen).*[10] In each of these cases, nature is present, but undifferentiated by human understanding. Nature is that to which philosophical thought must always return and that which it must become.

(2) *Appearance.* Heidegger calls for the appearance of knowledge-- thereby seeking to realize the presence of that which is present. In order for that which is present to appear, it must have a place. The place is the ontological space of the differencing of Being from beings, of presence from that which is present. In other words, an investigation of absolute knowledge requires a standard of measurement. Appearance is that standard. Knowledge of what is present can only be established through the appearance of that which is present. Its appearance, then, is the marker according to which its Being can be announced. Knowledge can be ascertained by the appearance of something. Although the

---

[9]*Themes from the Lectures*, p. 78.
[10]*Ibid.*, p. 79.

appearance cannot be regarded as static and fixed, it does require a point of emanation. In coming about (appearing), appearance realizes knowledge. Indeed, appearance depends upon performance for the realization of knowledge.

According to Merleau-Ponty, the appearance of knowledge also depends upon an investigation. However, philosophical inquiry itself makes knowledge appear. As knowledge becomes evident, philosophy is mobilized at the level of appearing. In terms of *The Visible and the Invisible,* which he was developing at the same time as "Philosophy and Non-Philosophy Since Hegel," appearance depends upon the intertwining of the visible and the invisible into pure visibility. The standard of measurement is pre-objective being itself. Appearance, for Merleau-Ponty, is philosophizing and not the standard of measurement. Philosophizing must return to pre-objective ("brute") being. Philosophy becomes non-philosophy, i.e. the fulfillment of *praxis* and the absolute, when the appearance of knowledge brings the absolute to presence.

(3) *Presentation.* According to Heidegger's interpretation, presentation aims at the appearance of knowledge. In order to achieve the presence of that which is present, knowledge must appear. Presentation is the performance according to which knowledge will appear. Presentation is the active function which brings about the appearance of that which is present in terms of its presence. The knowledge which appears according to presentation is phenomenal knowledge. Such knowledge depends entirely upon appearance taken as the standard of measurement. By checking phenomenal knowledge against appearance, that which is present becomes evident only when it is presented as an appearance. Phenomenal knowledge, as its etymology suggests, is the manifestation of beings (entities, essents, etc.) as they are brought to the fore within a particular context.

Merleau-Ponty indicates that the presentation, which is the way knowledge appears, cannot bring about the appearance as if it were an external force or condition. He would affirm Heidegger's position that "with the characterization of the science which presents phenomenal

---

[11]Heidegger, *Hegel's Concept of Experience,* p. 92.

knowledge in its appearance, we suddenly become involved ourselves in the presentation."[11] Our involvement, however, is not a conscious choice, a decision that we can or cannot make. Rather the very appearance of knowledge in the presentation is our embodied and expressive engagement with that which is present.

Merleau-Ponty would agree with Heidegger that "we are involved already, since what the presentation presents is 'for us'."[12] Yet, this 'for us' is not to be regarded as a passive involvement. Merleau-Ponty's fundamental conception of our role in the presentation prescribes our active engagement in the appearing of knowledge. No detachment is possible. The presentation is not *to* us. We effect it by presenting the appearance of the absolute, by our intentional projections throughout the phenomenal field of appearing knowledge. The presentation of that knowledge can occur only by our inhabiting it.

In this first triad, the result of the movement is phenomenal knowledge. For Heidegger, phenomenal knowledge is the presentation of that which is present as an appearance which announces its presence. The appearance differs (itself) from that which is present, while the presentation affirms its identity with the presence of that which is present. For Merleau-Ponty, the result is a phenomenal field of expression and visibility, but the result is the same as the beginning: what appears has already been presented and what has been presented is already knowledge of that which is present. At this point, what we now is only what appears to us (Heidegger) and through us (Merleau-Ponty).

II. THE SECOND TRIAD

(4)   *Representation.* A mental representation *(Vorstellen),* in Heidegger's understanding, is the basis of self-certainty. The object appears to the subject as a representation of itself to itself. Representing here means making the absolute available to itself as presence. This being present *(parousia)* is a self-presentation. In the first triad, presentation was the presentation of that which is present according to its appearance. No conditions were shown as to how the presentation takes place. In representation ("giving again" and "placing in front"),

[12]*Ibid.*

we now find that bringing to presence comes in terms of a self-presentation. The object (which is present) is brought to appearance by the object itself: the object presents itself for itself and to the subject. As a re-presentation, the object's presence to itself is self-certain. It needs no external standard of measurement apart from its appearance, through which it is given again to itself.

As the self-presentation of that which is present, representation is natural representation. In representing itself to itself, the performance is self-motivated. In this respect, it is a natural representation. Phenomenal knowledge, of which representation is a type, presents itself as true knowledge. In the mental appearance of the object, the knowledge that results is true because the truth *(a-letheia:* bringing out of concealedness) is in the belonging-together *(Zusammengehörigkeit)* of (1) that which is represented, (2) that which represents, and (3) the act of representing. As to the full understanding of truth, we must wait for the third triad, but as to the triple unity of representation, it occurs when appearance emerges from concealedness to unconcealedness, from that which is present to presence -- by an additional performance of a presentation.

Representing something in natural knowledge, that is, the knowledge of everyday awareness, maintains its own identity as mineness *(Jemeinigkeit). Qua* representation, opinion arises as belonging to someone. Such opinion takes three forms: (1) an unmediated focusing on something, (2) trusting acceptance of what is given, and (3) what is received, held and accepted as our own. In each case, what is mine is that which is represented as present, indisputably and convincingly. The presentation of phenomenal knowledge as opinion is accepted (by a subject) as the presence of what is present.

The two forms of representation, (1) self-representation as a mental appearance to the self or subject, and (2) natural representation as possessed, are both modes of rendering something cognitively present. Merleau-Ponty's approach would avoid self-representedness as a type of self-reflection. Philosophical knowledge does not come from either the mental or natural representation of an appearance to oneself. Rather philosophical knowledge is based on the move to participate in the absolute as it reveals its phenomenal character. This move is not the vision of a mystic such as Bonaventure, nor is it the pantheism of a Wordsworth. Rather the move to participate in the absolute is the intentional arching of the subject and the object, the future and the past.

This arching is a lived activity which permits neither the object to represent itself to itself by itself nor the subject to make the object represent itself to the subject by incorporating it into the subject's own sphere. For Merleau-Ponty, the incorporation must be in the representation itself. Philosophical knowledge must be the representing of what is present to the subject as an intermingling of the subject with the object and the object with the subject. Philosophical thought must enter into the self-presentation of phenomenal knowledge such that the repeated presence of the world in its various manifestations becomes the place of philosophical representation. Thus philosophy takes on the character of representation as it enters into the texture of the world's appearances, problems, and proposed solutions.

(5) *Natural consciousness.* Of the two ways in which Heidegger considers consciousness, the first, drawing upon the Husserlian conception of the natural attitude, indicates that Hegelian sense-certainty overlooks the Being of beings, the presence of that which is present. In this first instance, natural consciousness -- as a type of representation -- finds only beings, only that which is present. All presentations are simply tied to that which is present. The appearance which is the standard of measurement for the presentation, has no place in the context of the ontological difference (between Being and beings). Natural consciousness finds only beings, entities, essents. Beings appear in their everyday, existing form. Known in their ontic, rather than their ontological, character, beings do not participate in subjective experience as such. They are presented to a consciousness that treats them as objectivities, entities to be known, but not to be interpreted fully. The natural attitude in Husserl is restated in Heidegger as a consciousness incapable of articulating the Being of beings, -- the lived ontological difference by which presence can appear.

Merleau-Ponty does not accept the distinction between a natural and a phenomenological consciousness, which is implied in Heidegger's consideration of this first instance of natural consciousness. From the early *Structure of Behavior*, Merleau-Ponty shows (as we have noted in terms of "presence") that the physical order is integrated with the vital and human orders, such that nature is already consciousness of nature, life is already consciousness of life, and work is already consciousness of work.[13] Although he would agree with Heidegger that consciousness of nature (or natural consciousness) is by itself inadequate, he would also wish to point out that it cannot exist by itself in the first place. The appearance of each level of consciousness is also its self-comprehension (*Selbst-verständlichkeit*). Merleau-Ponty would deny the necessity of the distancing process: the separation of Being from beings, presence from what is present. For Heidegger, the understanding of what appears comes only with the establishment of a difference, given in the genitive form: the Being of beings. For Merleau-Ponty, nature must be lived through -- the process is one of integration. In the later philosophy, nature is united with *la chaire* (the flesh). Hence, philosophy must not separate itself from lived experience. Instead it must participate even in everyday experience *qua* non-philosophy. In that respect, even if natural consciousness is concerned only with beings, entitites, essents, it is nevertheless consciousness and it has a vocation.

The second instance of Heideggerian natural consciousness moves toward the appropriation of its own abode. With *das Ereignis* -- being as appropriation or advent -- consciousness seeks to fulfill its own horizons. For natural consciousness to appropriate its own abode, it must become fully present to itself. Such self-representation in effect goes beyond natural consciousness toward the realization of the absolute. The absolute is achieved when natural consciousness surpasses itself.

Here again, although Heidegger indicates that natural consciousness is not entirely enclosed upon itself, it does nevertheless require an act of self-overcoming in order to establish its place in the ontological difference, that is, to announce the presence of Being. For Merleau-Ponty, however, philosophizing moves into the embodied arena of practical life. The absolute is not beyond nature, it *is* nature appearing as a lived presence through the intentional experience of the individual. In suggesting a return to nature, Merleau-Ponty is closer to Nietzsche than to Hegel, - who would propose a surpassing. The Nietzschean return is the affirmation of what was as what will be. Merleau-Ponty finds that return within the interwoven flux of the presence of an incarnate consciousness of nature less *qua* natural consciousness, i.e.

---

[13]Merleau-Ponty, *The Structure of Behavior*, trans. Alden L. Fisher (Boston: Beacon Press, 1963), pp. 162 and 184.

qua presentation of the absolute in phenomenal knowledge.

(6) *Real consciousness.* Real consciousness, in Heidegger's assessment of Hegel, is different from natural consciousness. The natural is not the real, any more than natural consciousness is real consciousness. The natural stems from nature, while the real is what truly is. Nature is the ground according to which the real is understood. Real consciousness reveals what truly is, i.e. nature as a phenomenon. The representations of nature are re-interpreted according to real consciousness. The representations of natural consciousness simply return nature to itself, beings to beings, ontic to ontic. Real consciousness however, opens up the possibility of the real, of Being, and of ontological conditions in general. Yet real consciousness is natural knowledge, a real phenomen of nature. Like Husserl's phenomenological attitude, real consciousness cannot place itself in a realm that is different from that of the natural attitude.[14] Rather it is a new way of seeing, a more firmly grounded mode of interpreting what is. For Heidegger, natural consciousness is not-yet-true, since its truth is real consciousness. Real consciousness is then natural consciousness becoming its truth. In other words, real consciousness includes both the measure of truth (the real) and that which is measured (nature). As we have already seen, the standard of measurement is the appearance itself. The real as measure is opposed to nature as measured. The movement of one to the other is established according to the appearance of that which is present in nature. By examining itself (*qua* measure), consciousness shows itself to natural representation (*qua* measured). By its self-representation, consciousness combines both theoretical and practical understanding -- real knowledge is established in relation to nature, the relation in which the ontological difference is realized.

What is important here is that Heidegger points out the conditions for philosophy to develop in the context of the real, although always defining it from the natural. Merleau-Ponty, however, insists upon the presence of the real in the natural. Nature is informed by what truly is such that its realization is nature appearing as presence of the absolute

---

[14]See my discussion of these two attitudes in "The Self in Husserl's *Crisis*," *Journal of the British Society for Phenomenology*, Vol. 7, no. 1 (January 1976), pp. 24-32.

through body, speech, and political action. Interrogation is not a new mode of knowing that sets itself apart from nature and the absolute. Interrogation goes directly to nature and the absolute in order to bring out the visibility that is already there. Interrogation must therefore negate itself as a separate philosophy, as a theoretical model that distinguishes itself from what is, and what is present. Its difference occurs by becoming what is and what is present. Its negation is its affirmation. Its nature is its reality among the things of the world.

In this second triad, we have noted the self-representational character of the first triad (presence, appearance, and presentation). By representation, presentations are made available for a natural consciousness. Yet a natural consciousness can only treat what is present, it cannot account for the presence of the ontological difference. For Heidegger, the introduction of real consciousness succeeds where natural consciousness fails. For Merleau-Ponty, however, such a distinction is both artificial and mis-directed. The directionality must return real consciousness toward nature rather than away from it.

III. The Third Triad

(7) *Truth.* In order to represent the consciousness of nature to real consciousness, Heidegger claims that truth must appear. The necessity of the appearance of truth has already been noted, but without the possibility of indicating its realization. Only here, in the third triad, is there an understanding of the representational forms of presentation. In order to have an understanding of that which is present (nature), truth must appear. But truth reveals itself only for real consciousness. Truth arises out of the measure (the real) of nature (the measured). Indeed, truth is the fulfillment of the conditions of measurement in that the standard of measurement is appearance as understood by real consciousness. Truth is bringing that which is hidden in nature out of concealment (*Verborgenheit*). Truth as *a-letheia* (away from the forgotten -- the river Lethe as the veil over appearance) demonstrates the overcoming of forgetfulness (*Seinsvergessenheit*). The Being of beings, the presence of that which is present, are brought to the fore in a representational act. Natural consciousness is brought to real consciousness. That which is present is shown to be differed by Being such that its presence is known in its truth. Truth appears in the Being of beings, for truth is the self-realization of the ontological difference.

Merleau-Ponty would reserve the presence of truth for the lived phenomenon. The appearance is also the knowing. Truth cannot wait for real consciousness to bring about an understanding of the presence of that which is present. For Merleau-Ponty, truth has its origins in visibility. According to the pre-1959 working notes, what circulates as *The Visible and the Invisible* could have been entitled "The Origin of Truth" or "Genealogy of the True." Indeed, from the early 1950's Merleau-Ponty had been working on a theory of truth or at least a study of its origins and development. Truth is grounded in pre-objective Being. Its appearance is visibility itself. But truth in this sense is the fulfillment and realization of nature. Nature's visibility is called corporeality in the earlier view, and established as "inter-mondial" in the later position. Truth need not appear to a real consciousness in order to bring about this visibiity *qua* natural interworld. The sources and manifestations of truth are in the chiasm of the visible and the invisible, which corresponds to the Heideggerian ontological difference and which carries the name of visibility, but which is already present in beings and in that which is present.

For Merleau-Ponty, knowing the truth is not formalized. Consciousness is achieved in the act, as he showed with Bukharin making his choice in favor of the party and against his own objective factual condition. Here philosophical knowledge becomes true in its own self-denial. By refusing autonomy for itself, philosophy announces the truth of the world. By becoming non-philosophy, philosophical knowledge takes on the style and prose of the world.

(8) *Experience.* In Heidegger's understanding of Hegel, the appearance of truth is both experience and experienced. Experience gathers itself together by attending to the immediate present -- not to the future, nor to the past. The presence of the present when represented by natural consciousness to real consciousness as truth is experienced within the temporal present (*Gegenwart*). In other words, experience becomes the absoluteness of the absolute by bringing to presence that which is present. In this *Ereignis* -- presenting that which is present to presence or appropriating the absolute, -- experience brings truth to light.

For Heidegger, experience remains inaccessible to natural consciousness. Experience is both real and the principal activity of real consciousness. It cannot be known as an object, as an element of nature, -- nor can it be known as pure Idea. Experience is the beingness that arises out of the Being of beings. Hence, experience is the truth of the ontological difference.

In response to Heidegger's understanding of Hegel's "Introduction" to *The Phenomenology of Mind*, Merleau-Ponty emphasizes the importance of experience as *praxis*. *Praxis*, for Merleau-Ponty, *is* the absolute; and the absolute is nature, visibility, the phenomenal field. Hence, as in the case of presentation, representation, and consciousness, experience does not separate itself off from that which is present. Experience is not "in-between" (*dia*) Being and beings, but rather "throughout" it. The task of the philosopher who seeks to interrogate the world is to experience what appears in order to participate in the absolute. Where Merleau-Ponty wishes to interrogate the world, Heidegger questions Being. Just as the *Seinsfrage* crosses out the inscription of Being[15], philosophy denies itself as experience apart from the world. What is different is that, for Merleau-Ponty, philosophy moves toward and becomes the experience of the world, while for Heidegger philosophy questions the Being of beings. In other words, instead of questioning Being, Merleau-Ponty interrogates the world. In Merleau-Ponty's view, experience is the delineation of the ambiguous truth of life itself.

(9) *Phenomenology*. Since phenomenology is the study of appearances, we are returned to the question of the first triad: appearance taken as the standard of measurement. In fact, we can carry out the necessary examination only because experience is the standard. Experience, as we have seen, is the truth brought about by a real consciousness of nature. Experience, however, also depends upon a presentation of the appearance of that which is present. Seen from this third perspective, the presentation is phenomenological, but its performance does not simply present that which is. It reveals the truth of that which is in its ontological status. Indeed, phenomenology is the truth of experience.

Phenomenology, in Heidegger's understanding, is the project which seeks to know the absolute as absolute. The absolute is known through real consciousness as it represents itself in a presentation of what is generally available to natural consciousness. The real consciousness of

---

[15]See Heidegger, *The Question of Being*, trans. Jean T. Wilde and William Kluback (New Haven: College & University Publishers, 1958) and specifically Being as ~~Being~~.

the absolute establishes the truth of what appears. Phenomenology gathers together the truth of what appears in order to understand it. Thus although Heidegger speaks of the "end of philosophy" (in his interpretation of Hegel and Nietzsche), he does not, on the other hand, reject philosophizing himself. Phenomenology *qua* philosophy is that which brings knowledge of the world and the world of knowledge. Phenomenology can affirm that experience is the true experience of presence.

In "Philosophy and Non-Philosophy Since Hegel", as in *The Visible and the Invisible*, Merleau-Ponty reorients the specifically phenomenological character of his enterprise. We find claims to the appearance of the absolute and visibility, but we learn that the absolute is also the phenomenon. In *Phenomenology of Perception*, the absolute would have been the phenomenal field with its circuits of existence, its intentional arcs, and its corporeal expressivity. In his final writings, the absolute is the realization of a perceptual faith which goes by the name of pre-objective Being and which we know only by living through it. Knowledge of what appears is the experience of what appears. As consciousness unravels its truth, it does so at the level of experience. Experience, for Merleau-Ponty, is phenomenology become *praxis*. Living, expressing, and acting are philosophy at work, philosophy negating itself as separate philosophy.

This philosophy bears no resemblance to that of the tradition. We find no Platonic ideas, no Aristotelean observation, no Cartesian sceptical rationality, no Kantian critique... What appears is philosophy that has denied its theoretical stance in order to be its greatest achievement. This dialectical phenomenology is a non-philosophy, -- thought become the texture of an inter-human world of experience -- the world of Dante, Shakespeare, and Beethoven, but also of the common man.

In this third triad, truth, for Heidegger, is shown to be the full appearance of beings as presented in the relation to Being. The experience of truth is the understanding which phenomenology can bring to the study of the presence of that which is present. Merleau-Ponty's position, however, is that one need not come so far in order to recover the things themselves. Phenomenology is a return to pre-objective Being by a perceptual faith which cannot allow for a forgetting of the Being. On the contrary, phenomenology is authentic only when it negates itself and becomes the experience of the world. Its truth is in the style of the world as it makes itself visible and as we enter into its visibility. This double articulation is the intertwining of visible and invisible, Being and non-being, philosophy and non-philosophy.

Conclusion

In our tripartite triadic structure, phiosophy (questioning) follows the Heideggerian path of Hegel interpretation. Along the way we have shown (a) the inadequacy of appearance as a standard of measurement in relation to that which is measured, i.e. the ontic realm, (b) the reorientation of such presentations as representations, which natural consciousness makes available for real consciousness, and (c) the fullest understanding of that which is present as placed representationally within the ontological difference and as realized at the site of that difference. The name of this latter understanding is phenomenology. By contrast, in Merleau-Ponty's interrogation of the Hegelian dialectic, (a) the appearance of the absolute is its own standard of measurement, (b) the representation of real consciousness is visibility within nature and is distinguishable from real consciousness, and (c) philosophical self-negation becomes experience as the texture of the world. The name of this latter self-negation is non-philosophy.

The purpose of our study has been to juxtapose two readings of Hegel so that we could read the readings and so that their identical tasks could be established as the place of their difference from each other. Merleau-Ponty's continued struggle against a tradition that allows for the separation between nature and reality, objectivity and subjectivity, appearance and truth is evident in his response to Heidegger's position. Even in his later writings, Heidegger is also struggling to show that to fall into the ontic, inauthentic, realm of beings forces us to forget the ontological difference which brings the truth of our experience and demonstrates the vocation of phenomenology. The Heideggerian fall, however, is at the same time a call to stand up again in the opening (*Lichtung*), to experience what a natural consciousness does not understand. The Merleau-Pontean leap into the texture of the world, with its corporeality, and its visibility is hardly a fall. It is an achievement: the success of Western philosophy which negates itself in order to live, to understand, and to act. The truth of the ontological difference is the experience of visibility.

NATURE AND THE HOLY:
On Heidegger's Interpretation of
Hölderlin's Hymn "Wie wenn am Feiertage"

ANDRÉ SCHUWER
Duquesne University

In his essay "Hölderlin and das Wesen der Dichtung" Heidegger undertakes to indicate the essence of poetry solely through consideration of Hölderlin's work. Thus he begins the essay by asking: Why Hölderlin? Why his work alone and not also that of Homer, Sophocles, Virgil, Dante, Shakespeare, or Goethe? He answers:

> Hölderlin has been chosen, not because his work, as one among many, realizes the universal essence of poetry, but solely because Hölderlin's poetry is borne by the poetic determination expressly to poetize the essence of poetry. For us, Hölderlin is in a pre-eminent sense *the poet of the poet.*[1]

It is because Hölderlin is the poet of the poet that Heidegger takes "the risk of bringing the poetizing word of Hölderlin into the realm of thinking."[2]

In the same essay Heidegger refers to the poem "Wie wenn am Feiertage" as "the purest poetry of the essence of poetry" (HD, 44). By

---

[1]Martin Heidegger, *Erläuterungen zu Hölderlins Dichtung* (Frankfurt a.M.: Vittorio Klostermann, 1971⁴), p. 34. Hereafter "HD."

[2]Heidegger, "Was Heisst Denken?" in *Vorträge und Aufsätze* (Pfullingen: Günther Neske, 1954), p. 138.

focusing on Heidegger's interpretation of this poem we shall attempt to take some steps toward understanding what Heidegger means in calling Hölderlin the poet of the poet. Specifically, we shall elucidate Heidegger's interpretation of what, in "Wie wenn am Feiertage," Hölderlin calls *nature*. It is this which, in Heidegger's reading, "gives voice to the entire poem up to its last word" (HD, 52).

Yet, "the word" of the poem comes in the exclamation with which the third stanza begins:

> But now day breaks! I awaited and saw it come, And what I
> saw, may the holy be my word.

Heidegger writes:

> The exclamation "But now day breaks!" sounds like an
> invocation of nature. But the call certainly calls something
> that is coming. The poet's word is the pure calling of what
> the poets, always divining [*ahnend*], wait and long for. The
> poetic naming says what the called itself, from its essence,
> compels the poet to say. Thus compelled, Hölderlin names
> nature "the holy" (HD, 57 f.).

The poem "Wie wenn am Feiertage" is authentically charged to name "the holy." This word is "the word" of the poem. Because nature "unveils its own essence as the holy" (HD, 58), our elucidation of "Nature" must concentrate on nature and the holy.

1.

The first stanza reads:

> As when on a holiday, to see the field
> A countryman goes out, at morning, when
> Out of hot night the cooling lightning flashes had fallen
> The whole time and the thunder still sounds in the distance,
> The river enters its banks once more,
> And the fresh ground becomes green
> And with the gladdening rain from the sky
> The grape-vine drips and gleaming
> In quiet sunlight stands the trees of the grove:

Two remarks are here in order. The first pertains to the following interpretive statement by Heidegger:

> The first stanza transports us into a countryman's sojourn outdoors, into the fields, on the morning of a holiday. Then work is at rest. And the god is nearer to man (HD,51).

It should be observed that in the first stanza the name "God" does not occur. How, then, does Heidegger in his interpretation come upon this name? A clue is provided by a statement in "Hölderlin und das Wesen der Dichtung":

> In a letter to a friend, immediately before his departure for his last journey to France, Hölderlin writes: "O friend! The world lies before me, brighter and more serious than before! I am pleased with what happens, I am pleased as when in the summer 'the old holy father with a calm hand shakes blessing lightning-flashes out of reddish clouds.' For among all that I can see of god, this sign has become my chosen one" (HD, 43).

In the same connection the seventh stanza of "Wie wenn am Feiertage" mentions "god's lightning-flash." And since in the transition from the first stanza to the second (As when...: So...) the countryman who is exposed to the lightning flashes of the thunderstorm is compared with the poet who is, in turn, exposed to the lightning flashes of god,[3] Heidegger correctly refers in his commentary on the first stanza to "god." He does not just insert here an element that is alien to the meaning of the text.

Our second remark concerns the analogy between the countryman and the poet. The first stanza, which, so to speak, sets the stage, ends with a colon; the "So" with which the second stanza begins then indicates the movement out of the first stanza. As Heidegger says, "The 'As when...: So...' indicates a comparison that, like a brace, joins in unity the initial stanza to the second stanza, and even to all the following stanzas" (HD, 52). What is that in reference to which the countryman

---

[3]"Der Dichter ist ausgesetzt den Blitzen des Gottes" (HD, 44).

and the poet are compared? In the first stanza the countryman goes out to *see:* "As when on a holiday, to see the field a countryman goes out." In the second stanza the poets are said to be "always divining" [*doch ahnen sie immer*]; this "divining" signifies that the poet is a seer who sees visions regarding the future.[4] The countryman and the poet are compared with regard to vision. Both see.

2.

The second stanza begins by comparing the poet with the countryman. Both stand in favorable weather. The countryman lingers on his land after the thunderstorm which was a blessing for his plants and crop. In what sense do the poets stand in favorable weather? They are favored by being those,

> Whom no master alone, whom the wonderfully
> All-present educates in a light embrace,
> Powerful, divinely-beautiful nature.

Heidegger observes that the word "nature" is the key word in these lines. Also he refers to the exhaustion which this word has undergone and to the resultant need that its meaning be determined anew. And he says: What this "word 'nature' names here must be determined only through this unique poem" (HD, 55). We shall attempt to see how it is thus determined.

Heidegger excludes several senses from what is meant by the word "nature" in "Wie wenn am Feiertage." It does not mean any particular realm of beings in that sense that is operative in such current distinctions between nature and art, nature and spirit, nature and history, nature and the supernatural (HD, 55 f.). Indeed Hölderlin writes:

> For she, she herself, who is older than the ages
> And above the gods of Occident and Orient,...

---

[4]In "Andenken" Heidegger writes: "Die Dichter sind, wenn sie in ihrem Wesen sind, *prophetisch* (HD, 114).

But these words do not mean that nature is "supertemporal" in the metaphysical sense, much less that it is "eternal" in the Christian sense. Rather, as Heidegger says, "As long as it remains 'older than the ages,' it is, of course, 'older,' therefore earlier, more temporal, thus precisely more timely than the "times" with which the sons of the earth calculate" (HD, 59).

Secondly, Heidegger indicates that the "wonderfully all-present" nature of "Wie wenn am Feiertage" does not correspond to the sense which Hölderlin gave to this word in *Hyperion* and in the first drafts of *Empedocles* (HD, 56). The sense which Heidegger is here excluding is evident in the eulogies to nature in *Hyperion* - for example, in that letter of Hyperion to Bellermin which reads:

> Yet still you shine, sun of heaven! Still do you grow green, sacred earth. Still the rivers roar to the sea and shady trees rustle under the noon of day. Spring's song of bliss sings my mortal thoughts to sleep. The fullness of the living universe feeds and satisfies my starving being with its intoxication. O blessed nature! I know not how it is with me when I raise my eyes to your beauty, but all the joy of heaven is in the tears that I weep in your presence, beloved of beloveds![5]

Thirdly, Heidegger excludes that sense of nature according to which it would be posited "as identical with 'spirit' in the sense of the 'identity' which Hölderlin's friend Schelling thought of it at about the same time" (HD, 56). Clearly the reference is to Schelling's philosophy of identity, the principal statement of which was published in the year (1801) following Hölderlin's composition of "Wie wenn am Feiertage."[6]

---

[5]Hölderlin, *Hyperion or the Hermit in Greece,* tr. Willard R. Trask (New York, 1965), p. 22.

[6]Schelling's work is entitled *Darstellung meines Systems der Philosophie.* In this context reference might also be made to the so-called "System-Fragment," an early fragmentary project of a system of the kind later developed in German Idealism, of a "Philosophie des Geistes." The fragment was published by Beissner in the fourth volume of his edition of Hölderlin's works (*Gesammtliche Werke,* Vol. IV, p. 298). It is generally admitted that the text goes back to a manuscript written by Hegel in 1796. But this manuscript is a transcription of text which Franz Rosenzweig, who first published the fragment, attributed to Schelling. According to Cassirer, Schelling visited Hölderlin in the summer of 1795 in Tübingen and engaged in long discussions with him; the fragment he takes to be a protocol of these discussions. Pöggeler, disagreeing with both Rosenzweig

With the word "nature" Hölderlin does not even want, finally, to revive the ancient Greek experience of φύσις — the experience of nature as the opening up of a clearing wherein sky and earth, gods and mortals come to presence and show themselves — as the lightning flash in the night lights up things so that they shine forth in their contours, in their shapes and shadows. Indeed, what he poetizes sustains a concealed relation to what the Greeks called φύσις ; yet, nevertheless, the very word "nature," even translated back into its Greek original, is "an incongruous word in reference to what is coming, which is supposed to name" (HD, 56). In this connection, Heidegger refers to the poem "Am Quell der Donau," which Hölderlin wrote shortly after "Wie wenn am Feiertage," calling attention, specifically, to a change which Hölderlin made in the passage which reads: "We name you,we who are in need of the holy, we name you nature!" In reworking the poem Hölderlin erased the word "nature." Hellingrath explains: "from now on the name 'nature' no longer suffices for Hölderlin." Heidegger adds:

> But the name "nature," as the poetic fundamental word, is already overcome in the hymn "Wie wenn am Feiertage." This overcoming is the consequence and sign of a primordially commencing saying (HD, 58).

3.

Nature educates *(erziehet)* the poet:

> Whom no master alone, whom the wonderfully
> All-present educates in a light embrace,
> Powerful, divinely-beautiful nature.

It belongs to the essence of nature to bring the poet into the need to name it. That nature brings the poet into the need *(die Not)* to name it, is precisely the educating power of nature. Here we need to hear the word *"er-ziehen"* according to its original meaning. *"Er-ziehen,"* in Latin *"e-ducere,"* means to draw out and while drawing out to draw or raise up.

---

and Cassirer, argues that Hegel conceived the ideas expressed in the System-Fragment. For details of this controversial issue, see Otto Pöggeler's essay "Hölderlin, Hegel und das älteste System-Programm," *Hegel-Studien,* Beiheft 9 (Bonn, 1973), pp. 211-259.

Nature educates the poet in that it draws the poet into the need to name it. Although it is the poet who names nature, it is nature itself which brings the poet into the need to say it. And in naming it he says: the holy. Nature unveils itself as the holy. Nature as that unencompassable which encompasses everything encloses the poet who in his poetic word discloses it and who, in this disclosing, is raised up by it: *e-ducare*. The poets are educated by nature in a light or mild embrace, which Heidegger contrasts with the discipline of the master and his technique. Mastery is here not denied; it is simply limited or relativized because the poet is also a craftsman. As Heidegger writes:

> Mastership and instruction can only inculate something. In themselves they are not capable of anything. For another kind of education something else is needed other than the human zeal for human activity (HD, 52).

The gentle or mild educative power of nature is the origin, the source, from which the naming-power of the poet arises. However, it is not only the source of the power of the poetic word, it is also the source, the origin or the essence of the poet and of poetry as such (HD, 31).

In this connection it is appropriate to point out what, in presenting his "Erläuterungen zu Hölderlins Dichtung" (Interpretations of Hölderlin's poetry) Heidegger understands by "Erläuterung." In "Die Sprache im Gedicht" Heidegger writes that "a correct Erläuterung presupposes the Er-örterung."[7] By *"Er-örterung"* Heidegger does not mean merely a discussion such as the literary critic provides; rather *"Er-örterung"* has the sense of a pointing to the source *(Ort)* from which the poetic word originates as from its primordial beginning. This *"Ort"* is to be understood in the sense in which, as we have seen, nature brings the poet into the need to say the holy. The poet does not speak about the holy but the holy itself comes into the sound and illuminating power (what Heidegger calls *"das Lautere"*) of the poetic word.

Nature is the opening. As opening, nature arises and emerges. Emerging and arising, nature recedes into the path of its very advance. It is a coming out and a coming back. Its movement retrieves, as it were, that which it passes over as it emerges. Nature as a receding emerging is

---

[7]Heidegger, *Unterwegs zur Sprache* (Pfullingen: Günther Neske, 1959), p. 38.

a clearing; as a clearing it founds a state of clearance.[8] Nature as receding into its advance, hence into its origin or abode, is a concealing in the clearing. The clearing which emerges out of the opening of nature makes it possible for something to "appear, present itself in its outline, show itself in its aspects (eidos) and so come into presence as this or that" (HD, 56).

Nature is light and fire. In the state of clearance, founded by nature, everything gleams and radiates. The clearing, emerging from nature, is a fire which gives rise to the brightness and the ardorous glow of things. It gives to each appearing thing its distinctiveness. The ardorous glow illuminates and "sets afire in its glowing all that emerges to its appearing". (HD, 57). It is in this connection that Heidegger says of the exclamation with which the third stanza begins ("But now day breaks..."): It "names the emerging of the glowing brightness" (HD, 57). In "Vom Ursprung des Kunstwerkes" Heidegger illustrates this invocation of φύσις as Fire. He refers to a Greek temple standing on the rocky ground:

> The luster and gleam of the stone, though itself apparently glowing only by the grace of the sun, yet first brings to light the light of the day, the breadth of the sky, the darkness of the night. The temple's firm towering makes visible the invisible space of air. The steadfastness of the work contrasts with the surge of the surf, and its own repose brings out the raging of the sea.[9]

The glowing of that which is coming into the light, standing in its own contours and textures, *mirrors* the light and makes us aware of it. Nature is finally the hearth, the abode of light. φύσις as movement which recedes in its advance, φύσις as fire and light, as center and hearth, is "in" each thing which comes to presence.

4.

Nature brings the poet into the need to name it. This is nature's

---

[8]Heidegger, *Zur Sache des Denkens* (Tübingen: Max Niemeyer Verlag, 1969), pp. 71 f.
[9]Heidegger, *Holzwege* (Frankfurt a.M.: Vittorio Klostermann, 1957), p. 31.

educative power. We have seen, furthermore, that the educative power of nature is also the essence in the sense of the origin of poetry as such. The poet, who is brought by nature into the need to name it, exclaims: "May the holy be my word" *(das Heilige sei mein Wort)*. It is very important that we not overlook what the optative mood expresses in the German word "*sei*." The hymn *"Wie wenn am Feiertage"* is a hymn of a very special kind. It is a *"hymnos"* in a unique and newly formed sense. Usually we translate the Greek word ὑμνεῖν by the words "to praise" and "to celebrate"; in this sense a hymnal poem is supposed to be a hymn to something or to somebody who is celebrated and praised. But in the case of "Wie wenn am Feiertage": "The word of this song is no longer a 'hymn to' something, or a 'hymn to the poets,' or even a hymn 'to' nature, but rather the hymn 'of' the holy" (HD, 76). The expression, "the hymn of the holy" uses a genitive which is not primarily an objective genitive but first of all a subjective genitive. It is the holy itself which comes into the word rather than the poem being a word *about* the holy.

What are we to understand by "the holy"? Heidegger says of nature that it is "prior to all reality [*Wirklichkeit*] and all working [*Wirken*], prior also to the gods"; and thus nature is named as "the holy." The holy is beyond gods and men.

In his essay "Wozu Dichter?" Heidegger stresses that we should hear the word "the holy" in its original meaning: It denotes "the integralness of the whole of what is"[10] He calls it "the wholesome and sound" or "the hale and whole." "Holiness," he writes, "is in no way a property borrowed from a well established god. The holy is not holy because it is divine, rather the divine is divine because in its way it is 'holy' " (HD, 59). The holy itself is not the divine. Rather, it is that in virtue of which the divine is divine. The holy as the whole and sound, as that which is prior to and beyond gods and men, "closes off within itself, as the immediate, all fullness... and thus is precisely unapproachable by everything isolated, be this a god or a man" (HD, 63).

In the third stanza of "Wie wenn am Feiertage" the holy is brought together also with chaos — in the phrase "begotten out of holy chaos." In this connection Heidegger writes:

---

[10]*Ibid.*, p. 272.

Thought in terms of nature (φύσις), chaos remains that
gaping [*Aufklaffen*] out of which the open opens itself so
that it may grant to all that is distinct the boundaries of its
presence (HD, 63).

Holderlin therefore calls chaos "holy" because nothing real precedes
this gaping in which everything is, as it were, engulfed. And all that
appears in it and through it is already surpassed by it. Heidegger calls
nature as the holy in this context *"das Einstige."* With this word he
signifies that the holy is prior to and beyond everything, "as always"
(wie einst). He writes:

It is what is always in a double sense. It is the oldest of every
former thing and is the youngest of every subsequent thing
(HD, 63).

It remains in itself. It remains unimpaired, unharmed and whole. In this
sense Hölderlin also calls the holy "the intimate" *(die Innigheit)* and
"the eternal Heart" *(das ewige Herz)* (HD, 73).

As immediate, the holy closes off within itself all fullness. As
emerging, nature recedes into the path of its advance; it recedes into its
origin. It is therefore never anything which comes to presence within the
clearing which nature itself brings into play. In this sense Heidegger
calls nature *"das Unmittelbare,"* the immediate, that which cannot be
mediated. Since the holy is the essence of nature, Heidegger also calls
the holy the immediate (HD, 63).

It is important to mention that in "Wie wenn am Feiertage" Hölderlin
does not refer to nature and the holy as the immediate. It is rather in a
comment which Hölderlin made on a fragment by Pindar that the issue
of the immediate becomes prominent. In interpreting Hölderlin's
comment, Heidegger articulates a dialectic between nature (the holy) as
the immediate *and* the mediated.[11] Speaking of nature as the open,
Heidegger writes:

The open mediates [*vermittelt*] the relations between all that is real. The

---

[11]Ruth-Eva Schulz-Seitz, "Bevestigter Gesang," in *Durchblicke* (Frankfurt a.m.:
Vittorio Klostermann, 1970), p. 69.

latter exists only out of such mediation and is therefore something mediated. The mediate, therefore, is only by virtue of its capacity to be mediated [*Mittelbarkeit*]... The open itself, however, which first grants to all related and conjoined things the region in which they belong together, does not arise from any mediation. The open itself is the immediate [*das Unmittelbare*]. Nothing mediated, be it a god or a man, is ever capable immediately of attaining the immediate (HD, 61).

Since the holy is the immediate, in the sense that it does not and cannot arise from mediation, nature as the holy is that which can not be directly mediated. That is to say that nature as the holy never reveals itself in its immediacy. Consequently there cannot be any immediate, that is unmediated, experience of the holy. But neither can there be a mediate experience of the holy which directly attains the holy as the immediate. As Heidegger writes:

> The holy, as the unapproachable, renders every immediate intrusion of the mediate in vain. The holy expels all experience from its habituation and so withdraws it from its habitat (HD, 63).

The holy remains always unharmed and unimpaired. The holy keeps enclosed within itself all fullness. It is inaccessible to every isolated being, whether that being be a god or a man. Any intrusion upon it by the mediate, that is, by anything at all, is repelled by it as futile, as in vain. Moreover, the holy drives gods and men out of their habituation, withdrawing them from their place. In this sense the holy is called by Heidegger *"das Entsetzliche"* (HD, 63). Because the holy expels all experience from its habituation and withdraws it from its habitat or its site, it is *ent-setzend,* that is, according to the etymology of the German word, de-ranging or dislodging. In this sense the holy as *"entsetzlich"* is also the terrible.

The hope of finding the appropriate names for the holy, leaving it intact in its essential immediacy, is indeed the central problem of this poem; and it is this problem which, in effect, is expressed in the exclamation in the third stanza: "May the holy by my word." It is the central problem precisely because nature as the holy is unapproachable and inaccessible fullness, because it is that intimate which repels any intrusion upon it.

5.

We have observed that the poet is brought by nature into the need to name it. He names it "the holy." Nature discloses itself in and through the poetic word as "the holy." The self-disclosure of the holy comes to pass in the poetic words of Hölderlin's hymn "Wie wenn am Feiertage," which is the hymn of the holy in the unique sense we have explained. But how can the poet name the holy? How can the poet, in other words, mediate the holy in his naming if the holy as the immediate does not arise from any mediation and hence not from the mediation of the word or the naming of the poet? How can the poet name the holy if, furthermore, there can be no mediate experience of the holy which directly attains the immediate? Heidegger himself indicates that the word as such never offers any guarantee as to whether it is án essential word or a deception. He says that "language must constantly place itself in an illusion [*Schein*] which it has itself engendered and so endanger what is most its own, the genuine saying" (HD,37). When nature brings the poet into the need to say it, this need also means, according to an original meaning of the German word *"Not"*: danger! It is the danger that the word "the holy" as which the poet hopes to name nature when he exclaims "May the holy be my word," degenerate into something merely recited and repeated. It is thus that in the third stanza that awakening of nature which is the self-disclosure of the holy in the poetic word comes to pass "amid the clang of arms."

We have seen that nothing mediated, be it a god or a man, is ever capable of directly attaining the holy as the immediate. Yet Heidegger writes: "The poets must leave to the immediate its immediacy, and yet accept its mediation as the only one" (HD, 71). Again, he quotes from Hölderlin's Archipelagos: "Always as heroes need garlands, the hallowed elements need likewise the hearts of feeling man for their glory" (HD, 191). But how can that be? Heidegger writes: "That the holy is entrusted to a mediation by the gods and the poets and is born in the song [*Lied*] threatens to invert the essence of the holy into its opposite" (HD, 72). And: "Even the poet is never capable of attaining the holy through his own mediation or indeed of exhausting its essence and of forcing it to come to him through his own questioning" (HD, 66); for then the holy would not be left unimpaired, unharmed, its essence would be inverted. How, then, does the self-disclosure of the holy come to pass? One might suppose that there is perhaps the possibility that the poet, being enclosed in a mild embrace by nature and the holy, could attain the holy, not directly, but indirectly. But what could such indirect attaining of the holy mean? In the hymn "Wie wenn am Feiertage" the holy as the immediate becomes mediated because its self-disclosure comes to pass in the poetic word, that is, in the language of the poet. Hence, the immediate becomes mediate. But the immediate does not become mediate through an other, for there is no other, the holy as the immediate being the whole-some which is inaccessible and unapproachable. The immediate becomes mediate only if the mediating act occurs, the act of the self-disclosure of nature as the holy. The immediate mediates itself in the absolute mediation of the "song." But this is still insufficient for safeguarding the holy against perversion, against the possible perversion of language. Even when the soul of the poet is already glowing because of nature's mild embrace, a ray must still be cast into the soul of the poet. Indeed, the holy does not attain directly the soul of the divining poet. It brings itself, not directly, but indirectly into the word of the poet.

In the seventh stanza of "Wie wenn am Feiertage" are these lines:

> Yet us it behooves, you poets, to stand
> Bare-headed beneath god's thunderstorms,
> To grasp the father's ray, itself, with our hands
> And wrapt in song
> To offer the heavenly gift to the people,
> For only if we are pure in heart,
> Like children, are our hands innocent.

Heidegger comments: A god, who is nearer to the holy than is man, is that being who can hurl the holy ray into the glowing soul of the divining poet. In such an act, the god brings, collects, and shapes the holy into the impact of a single ray, through whose reception the soul of the poet is inflamed. In this sense, but in this sense only, god is dependent on man. Yet both god and man need the holy for their mediating act.

The poets await the god who will inflame their glowing souls. This waiting is the discipline of reserve, of holding back — as nature itself (the holy) holds back, remains closed up within itself, aloof.

SCHLAG DER LIEBE, SCHLAG DES TODES
On a Theme in Heidegger and Trakl

DAVID FARRELL KRELL
University of Mannheim

Historians will call them contemporaries. Martin Heidegger was born a scant two-and-a-half years later than Georg Trakl. As young men both read intently the novels of Dostoevsky and the lyric of Hölderlin. Nietzsche enthralled them. Both were caught up in fierce discussions about the purpose of art in the age of *Menschheitsdämmerung,* an age when not only gods and idols but European man himself "was submerging in the twilight..., into the night of decline..., in order to emerge again in the waxing twilight of a new day."[1]   Yet it is hard for us to think of Trakl and Heidegger as contemporaries. Trakl died of an overdose of cocaine

Tief ist der Schlummer in dunklen Giften (156)

at the age of twenty-seven; Heidegger died during the eighty-sixth year of life, so that it was difficult to cite a medically definitive

---

[1]Kurt Pinthus, *Menschheitsdämmerung: Ein Dockument des Expressionismus,* first published in 1920, reissued with new material in 1959 (Hamburg: Rowohlt), p. 25. Trakl's poetry, cited in this paper solely by page number within parentheses, is quoted from the following edition: Georg Trakl, *Die Dichtungen,* 13th printing (Salzburg: Otto Müller Verlag, 1938).

"cause." Back in 1914, while Heidegger was preparing his *Habilitationsschrift* on Duns Scotus, Trakl stood appalled by the rout of the Austrian troops at Grodek. The work on Scotus appears today in a volume of Heidegger's "early" writings; "Grodek" was the last poem Trakl wrote. After completing his doctoral work and habilitation, Heidegger taught three generations of students in Germany, dominating European thought for at least that many decades. Trakl scarcely had time to secure to himself contemporaries; the name "Heidegger," for example, meant nothing to him. But Trakl's name meant much to Heidegger, even during his student years before the War.[2] It is above all the personal significance of Trakl for Heidegger that strikes us as strange yet undeniable—though we may ask whether a poet ever signifies or sings in an impersonal way.

Nothing seems more anomalous at first than Heidegger's admiration of Trakl. Consider the bizarre oval portrait of the poet taken about 1910: hair parted aslant down the middle and pomaded flat against the skull, eyes glazed in shadow, nostrils flared, lips set in an expression of utter expressionlessness

he may smile sardonically at any moment; he may remain transfixed in silent frenzy for hours

neck and shoulders bare, pallid flesh white on black.

Two portraits of Hölderlin dominated the wall to the left of Heidegger's worktable in Freiburg, a silhouette of the twenty-year-old (original in the Stuttgart Landesbibliothek) and Louise Keller's famous sketch of the devastated seventy-two-year-old; but no portrait of the peculiar, precocious devastation Trakl embodied—ascetic sensuality, naked yet anesthetic—graced his walls. Whence the attraction to Trakl? Perhaps it was but a reminiscence of the one who in Heidegger's eyes was the poet of poetry, since Trakl "took up the lyre that slipped from Hölderlin's hands" (Klaus Mann), since he glided *"hölderlinisch* into an infinitely blue stream of fatal attenuation" (K. Pinthus), and since Hölderlin's voice resounds in so many of Trakl's verses:

---

[2]"In jener Zeit des Expressionismus waren mir diese Bereiche [Dichtung und Kunst] stets gegenwärtig, mehr jedoch und schon aus meiner Studienzeit vor dem ersten Weltkrieg die Dichtung Hölderlins und Trakls." Martin Heidegger, *Unterwegs zur Sprache* (Pfullingen: Neske, 1959), p. 92.

Der dunkle Plan scheint ohne maßen...
                              ("Melancholie des Abends,"20)
Und Brot und Wein sind süß von harten Mühn...
                              ("Der Spaziergang," 24)
Und in heiliger Bläue läuten leuchtende Schritte fort...
                              ("Kindheit," 98).

But it is belittling to both thinker and poet to speculate on the "attraction" of the one for the other. Trakl's voice is more compelling than that and Heidegger's devotion not so easily won. Rainer Maria Rilke recalls hearing that voice and describes his reaction to it in four words: *ergriffen, staunend, ahnend, und ratlos*.[3] The progression is significant: transfixed by Trakl's poetry, astounded, discerning but shadows of meaning, feeling utterly at a loss, Rilke tries to enter its mirrored space, brilliant but inaccessible. *Ratlos,* he asks Ludwig von Ficker, "Who may he have been?" Heidegger's response to Trakl's voice (though not to the question of who Trakl may have been) appears in "Die Sprache im Gedicht: Eine Erörterung von Georg Trakls Gedicht."[4]

However, by hoping to situate Trakl's poetry within the space opened by a "single unsung poem," and by claiming to hear *den einen Grundton seines Gedichts,* it seems as though Heidegger would transcend all limits in order to penetrate and occupy the Trakl-Welt.[5] But the fundamental result of Heidegger's endeavor is acknowledgment of the irreducible multiplicity of meaning in Trakl's lyric, the site of which remains *unterwegs,* in transition, transfixing but never fixed; so that discussion of its place is always out of place if it fails to listen in the way Hamlet heeds his father's ghost—*"Hic et ubique?* then we'll shift our ground.—" Within the crystalline

------

[3]R.M. Rilke, *Briefe aus den Jahren 1914 bis 1921* (Leipzig: Insel Verlag, 1938), pp. 36-37. See also the letter to L. v. Ficker immediately preceding and a later one dated 22 February 1917 to Erhard Buschbeck, pp. 126-27.

[4]See *Unterwegs zur Sprache,* pp. 35-82. This article will be cited in the text as US, with page number.

[5]So argues Karsten Harries in "Language and Silence: Heidegger's Dialogue with Georg Trakl," *boundary 2,* IV, 2(Winter 1976), 494-511, following W. H. Rey, "Heidegger-Trakl: Einstimmiges Zwiegespräch." *Deutsche Vierteljahrschrift für Literaturwissenschaft und Geistesgeschichte,* Jahrgang 30 (1956), 89-136.

space of Trakl's lyric Heidegger elucidates myriad themes and images: *der Fremdling,* the wanderer in search of the earth; *Untergang-Übergang,* the trajectory of his search; *die Abgeschiedenheit,* tentative name for the terminus of that trajectory; *der Schmerz,* the pain that nourishes the flames of spirit; *das Abendland,* the land of evening, a still undiscovered country, as the site of Trakl's lyric. Only one among such themes and images impresses itself upon us here: the generation of man, struck by love and death.[6]

Schlag der Liebe, Schlag des Todes. What do the words *Schlag, schlagen* mean? Where do they come from; what comes from them? Hermann Paul's *Deutsches Wörterbuch* (Tübingen, 1966) lists six principal areas of meaning for *der Schlag,* and for the verb *schlagen* six "proper" senses and ten "distant" meanings. Devolving from the Old High German and Gothic *slahan* (from which the English word "slay" also derives) and related to the modern German word *schlachten,* "to slaughter," *schlagen* means to strike a blow, to hit or beat. A *Schlag* may be the stroke of a hand, of midnight, or of the brain; the beating of wings or of a heart. *Schlagen* may be done with an axe or a fist. God does it through his angels and his plagues; a nightingale does it with his song. One of the most prevalent senses of *schlagen* is to mint or stamp a coin. *Der Schlag* may therefore mean a particular coinage, imprint, or type: a horse dealer might refer to *ein guter Schlag Pferde.* It is by virtue of this sense that *Schlag* forms the root of a word that is very important for Trakl, *das Geschlecht.* Paul lists three principal meanings for *Geschlecht* (Old High German *gislahti*). First, it translates the Latin word *genus,*

---

[6]It is perhaps a minor theme. Indeed the major theme of Heidegger's preoccupation with Trakl—poetic speech as such, speech which allows beings to scintillate in sheer presence, the incantatory *es ist* in Trakl's "Psalm" and "De Profundis" (57-59; 63), the Parmenidean theme of *Ereignis* and the granting of Time and Being—arises only peripherally in his major article on Trakl, only in those three places (US, 38, 65, and 73) where he speaks of "the source of the advancing wave" of Trakl's prosody, which the aesthetic tradition calls "rhythm." The theme of poetic speech and the presence of beings in Trakl's lyric, which demands a separate study, does become a central issue in three other of Heidegger's writings: "Die Sprache," US, 17-33; *Was heißt Denken?* (Tübingen: Niemeyer, 1954), p. 172, in context; and the "protocol" to the Todtnauberg Seminar on "Zeit und Sein," in *Zur Sache des Denkens* (Tübingen: Niemeyer, 1969), pp. 42-43.

being equivalent to *Gattung: das Geschlecht* is a group of people who share a common ancestry, especially if they constitute a part of the hereditary nobility. Of course, if the ancestry is traced back far enough we may speak of *das menschliche Geschlecht,* "human-kind." Second, *das Geschlecht* may mean one generation of men, dying to make way for a succeeding generation. Third, there are male and female *Geschlechter,* and *Geschlecht* becomes the root of many words for the things males and females have and do for the sake of the first two meanings: *Geschlechts-glied* or *-teil,* the genitals; *-trieb,* the sex drive; *-verkehr,* sexual intercourse; and so on. All three shades of meaning haunt Trakl's poetry. *Geschlecht* may suggest the human race as such (as in *Traum und Umnachtung,* 149-57), or that part of it which dwells in cities (as in "Der Abend," 179); in "He-lian" (80-84), glowing figure of the sun and the generative year, *Geschlecht* clearly has the sense of the generation that passes as the son "steps into the empty house of his fathers" (82; cf. "Verwandlung des Bösen," 124); while elsewhere (as in "Passion," 139) the word reflects its third sense:

Dunkle Liebe
Eines wilden Geschlechts.

Heidegger employs the words *Schlag, schlagen,* and *Geschlecht* throughout his major article on Trakl.[7] He first writes *Schlag* and *schlagen* (in the form *verschlagen*) while interpreting Trakl's line, "Es ist die Seele ein Fremdes auf Erden" (143). Such a line seems to represent the Platonistic view that the soul, a stranger on earth, is *im Sinnlichen... dahin nur verschlagen,* driven off-course and rudely cast upon the shoals of the sensuous world; here on earth she lacks *den rechten Schlag* and so is miscast. But Heidegger resists that Platonistic interpretation by reading *fremd* as the Old High German *fram* (cf. the English "from"), moving forward and away, being under way, a movement which nevertheless remains *auf Erden,* "upon the earth." Heidegger observes laconically that Trakl's

---

[7]*Der Schlag* appears at US, 40, 49-50, 66, 78-80; *das Geschlecht* at US, 49-50, 55, 65, 67, 74, 78-80.

"Frühling der Seele," of which this line is a part, mentions no other possible abode for the soul in some past or future circumstance. The wanderer soul sets out in search of its own homeland, where it must dwell.[8] But in which direction? *In den Untergang hinab* (US, 42; cf. Trakl, 101). The wanderer soul, the stranger, goes down in search of the earth—*Also,* we recall, *begann Zarathustras Untergang*—in "rest and silence." What sort of rest and silence? Heidegger does not falter: *In die des Toten,* the tranquility of those struck in death. Yet we may balk where Heidegger and Trakl do not, seeking rescue from the poor prospects such an answer affords. We discern in the words "rest" and "silence" another, presumably more congenial theme in the "later" Heidegger, one which seems to lend itself to a discussion of poetry: *Ruh und Schweigen* characterize the kind of thinking Heidegger calls *Gelassenheit.*

Like many of Heidegger's interpreters, Paul Ricoeur suggests that the basic difference between the Heidegger of *Sein und Zeit* and the Heidegger of the *Kehre* is "that the self no longer finds its authenticity in freedom unto death but in *Gelassenheit,* which is the gift of the poetical life."[9] We know what it means, the poetical life: hearts leaping over rainbows and clouds of daffodils or wallowing awhile in dejection—a mood that evaporates when poets compose odes on it: we know what it means, the poetical life. But poetry too loves to hide. In "De Profundis" (63) Trakl writes,

Auf meine Stirne tritt kaltes Metall.
Spinnen suchen mein Herz.
Es ist ein Licht, das in meinem Mund erlöscht.[10]

---

[8]Cf. Heidegger's analysis of Hölderlin's "Heimkunft" and "Andenken," in Martin Heidegger, *Erläuterungen zu Hölderlins Dichtung,* fourth, expanded edition (Frankfurt: Klostermann, 1971), pp. 13-14, "Deshalb bleibt auch der Ankommende noch ein Suchender...," and p. 150, "Das Andenken denkt an die Ortschaft des Ursprungsortes im Denken an die Wanderschaft der Wanderung durch die Fremde...." Cf. also "...Dichterisch Wohnet der Mensch..." in Martin Heidegger, *Vorträge und Aufsätze* (Pfullingen: Neske, 1954), pp. 187-204.

[9]P. Ricoeur, "The Critique of Subjectivity and Cogito in the Philosophy of Heidegger," in *Heidegger and the Quest for Truth,* ed. Manfred Frings (Chicago: Quadrangle Books, 1968), p. 74.

[10]"Across my brow cold metal creeps./Spiders seek my heart./It is a light that dies in my mouth."

It is by no means clear that "the gift of the poetical life" inaugurates or commemorates a departure from "freedom unto death" in Heidegger's thought. What is it that the thinker must let be? The tree blooming in the meadow, the pitcher, the chalice of wine, the bridge; and in each of these the presencing of the fourfold of earth, sky, mortals, and divinities. But how should mortals let mortals be? Is that mortally possible? Who are the mortals? "Mortals are men. They are called mortals because they can die. To die means to make death *as* death possible. Only man dies, and indeed continuously, so long as he remains on the earth, under the sky, before divinities. . . .Mortals *are* in the fourfold insofar as they *dwell*. But the fundamental trait of dwelling is protective cultivation."[11] Protective cultivation of mortality: such is *Gelassenheit,* the gift of the poetical life. But mortality is no invention of the "later" Heidegger. The crucial task of Heidegger's hermeneutic of Dasein in *Sein und Zeit* is to let the disclosure of finitude be. In terms of the analysis of the "whole being" of Dasein (II, 1) the endeavor is to let death be. Fulfillment of such a task requires a mode of thought and language that is alien to representational, valuative, manipulative consciousness which in its will to power obscures the dimension where the finitude of Dasein plays. To let death *be* in its disclosive power means to wrest it from the distortions of a tradition and culture which do violence to death. Both the wise and the pious, Goethe says in *Hermann und Dorothea*, drag death back into life. Heidegger's effort in §§46-53 is to release our grip on death's ears. He achieves such release by inserting himself into the circle where disclosure as such and what is disclosed are existentially selfsame, the circle of being-in-the-world and anxiety (§40). *Gelassenheit,* the protective cultivation of mortality, is and remains a thinking within anxiety. As such it is a name for Heidegger's way from start to finish, *in den Untergang hinab,* in search of the earth and the accompanying *Schlag des Todes.*

In Heidegger's discussion of Trakl's lyric the word *Schlag* next appears in the phrase "der Schlag der *verwesten* Gestalt des Menschen" (US, 49; "Siebengesang des Todes," 134): the coinage or imprint of the decomposing form of man, the type of man whose

---

[11]*Vorträge und Aufsätze,* p. 150.

essence (*Wesen*) has abandoned him. But *O, wie alt ist unser Ge-schlecht* ("Unterwegs," 96), as old as the *animal rationale* of philosophical anthropology, as old as the Christian ontotheology such anthropology serves. Of course, the genus (animal) is more troublesome to the tradition than the specific difference (rational). Of what sort is man's animality? At the end of that tradition Nietzsche says that man is the *noch nicht festgestellte Tier*.[12] Heidegger comments (US, 45-46):

> The assertion does not at all mean that man has not yet been "confirmed" as a fact. He has been so confirmed, all too decisively. The phrase means that the animality of this animal has not yet been brought to a firm ground, brought "home," brought to the indigenous character of its still veiled essence. Occidental-European metaphysics since Plato has been wrestling to gain such a firm defini-tion. Perhaps it wrestles in vain. Perhaps its way into the "under way" is still obstructed. The animal that has not yet been defined in its essence is modern man.

Perhaps it wrestles in vain: utterly unable to liberate itself from the framework of the *animal rationale*. Perhaps the *unterwegs* re-mains inaccessible to it: *unterwegs* here means "the way back down," κατάβασις, *Abstieg aus der Metaphysik, Untergang*. In his "Letter on Humanism" (1947) Heidegger argues that metaphysics does think of man in terms of *animalitas* but never succeeds in confronting with equanimity "our appalling and scarcely conceiva-ble bodily kinship with the beast."[13] It prefers to span what seems the greater distance to God. But in the historic ascent from rational-ity to subjectivity man bypasses his essence (ek-sistence). Such passing by, such oblivion, molds *die verweste Gestalt des Men-schen*. Georg Trakl seeks and finds an image to counter it: *ein blaues*

---

[12]Friedrich Nietzsche, *Jenseits von Gut und Böse,* no. 62 (Schlechta ed., II, 623): "...in Hinsicht darauf, daß der Mensch das *noch nicht festgestellte Tier ist*." Heidegger cites the phrase in his Trakl article (US, 45) and it is a salient feature of the contemporaneous lecture course *Was heißt Denken?* See p. 24 ff. of the latter.

[13]Martin Heidegger, *Wegmarken* (Frankfurt: Klostermann, 1967), p. 157.

Wild, an animal untamed but fragile, deep azure in hue, which haunts the forest rim at dark of evening. It is associated with the poet's sister (73, 184) and with the poet himself, shivering on the threshold of his dead father's house (124) or treading the dark paths of passion (139), associated too with the path of the sun and the celestial year at summer solstice (163). *Ein blaues Wild*: Heidegger hears it as a name for the mortal who wanders with the stranger down to his native soil, the earth.

Trakl contrasts *ein blaues Wild* and the decomposing, degenerate, accursed *Geschlecht* of man. The third section of *Traum und Umnachtung* begins, "O des verfluchten Geschlechts" (155). Heidegger now asks (US, 50):

> By what is this *Geschlecht* struck, i.e., cursed? The Greek word for curse is πλήγη, the German word *Schlag*. The curse of the decomposing *Geschlecht* consists in the fact that this ancient *Geschlecht* has been dispersed in the discord of *Geschlechter*. Within such discord each of them seeks the unchecked tumult of individualized and utter savagery. Not the twofold as such, but discord, is the curse. From the tumult of blind savagery, discord drives the *Geschlecht* into abscission and imprisons it in unchecked individuation. So ravaged, so severed in twain, the "fallen *Geschlecht*" can on its own no longer find its way into the right *Schlag*. It can find its way only as that *Geschlecht* whose twofold nature wanders forth out of discord into the gentleness of a confluent twofold. That *Geschlecht* is "foreign," and it follows the stranger. (Cf. the German text below.[14])

---

[14]"Womit ist dieses Geschlecht geschlagen, d.h. verflucht? Fluch heißt griechisch πλήγη, unser Wort "Schlag." Der Fluch des verwesenden Geschlechtes besteht darin, daß dieses alte Geschlecht in die Zwietracht der Geschlechter auseinandergeschlagen ist. Aus ihr trachtet jedes der Geschlechter in den losgelassenen Aufruhr der je vereinzelten und bloßen Wildheit des Wildes. Nicht das Zwiefache als solches, sondern die Zwietracht ist der Fluch. Sie trägt aus dem Aufruhr der blinden Wildheit das Geschlecht in die Entzweiung und verschlägt es so in die losgelassene Vereinzelung. Also entzweit und zerschlagen vermag das "verfallene Geschlecht"

Wildheit, Vereinzelung, Aufruhr, zerschlagen: we think of the European *Geschlecht* in late summer of 1914 as all the lights across the Continent extinguish one by one and as an Austrian medic enters a barn where ninety wounded lie in heaps and there is no doctor and not enough morphine; who next day balks at mess and cries *So kann ich nicht weiterleben!* and they take his weapons from him and lock him in the basement of a psychiatric ward. We think too of another medic and close observer of the Austrian wounded and dead during the Great War:

> The first thing that you found about the dead was that, hit badly enough, they died like animals. Some quickly from a little wound you would not think would kill a rabbit. They died from little wounds as rabbits die sometimes from three or four small grains of shot that hardly seem to break the skin. Others die like cats; a skull broken in and iron in the brain, they lie alive two days like cats that crawl into the coal bin with a bullet in the brain and will not die until you cut their heads off. Maybe cats do not die then, they say they have nine lives. I do not know, but most men die like animals, not men.[15]

Der Mensch: das noch nicht festgestellte Tier: until struck irremediably in death. In his last poem Trakl hears the "savage keen" of soldiers' "shattered mouths" (193).

    Zwietracht, Zwiefache, Zwiefalt, Entzweiung: we think of another kind of struggle, not of nation against nation but of a twosome, a kind that is halved: the race of man and woman, whom Trakl calls *die Liebenden,* the lovers. They embody the *Sanftmut einer einfältigen Zwiefalt,* as even a hasty sketch of their appearance in Trakl's poetry attests. Theirs is the mild time of gentle embrace (30, 179).

---

von sich aus nicht mehr in den rechten Schlag zu finden. Den rechten Schlag aber hat es nur mit jenem Geschlecht, dessen Zwiefaches aus der Zwietracht weg in die Sanftmut einer einfältigen Zwiefalt vorauswandert, d.h. ein "Fremdes" ist und dabei dem Fremdling folgt."

[15]Ernest Hemingway, "A Natural History of the Dead," in *The First Forty-Nine Stories* (London: Jonathan Cape, 1962), pp. 367-68.

Raising roselike eyelids under the shadow of a tree (105), breathing sighs among its branches (46), blond and beaming lovers cast darkling looks and in dark conversation come to know one another as man and woman (95, 144). Lovers glow afresh in winged things (24), embracing delicately with longing arms (95), suffering "more gently" (117). In "Heiterer Frühling" (22) the breath of lovers flows "more sweetly" through the night as they blossom toward their stars: the lovers' upsurgence in the poem mediates between two starkly contrastive lines, the first an outcry of what Nietzsche would call "Schopenhauerian pessimism,"

Wie scheint doch alles Werdende so krank!

the second a hardwon Dionysian affirmation, the subdued response to the more joyous but also crueller spring,

So schmerzlich gut und wahrhaft ist, was lebt.

For the shadow side of the lovers is never far in Trakl's poetry. They are imprisoned in disclosure (*wahrhaft*) by their very being (*ist, lebt*); they die "on their way across" (165). Their periodic resurrection is an earthly one, bound to its origins. Hear the prayer the poet utters in response to the "Nearness of Death" (73):

O die Nähe des Todes. Laß uns beten.
In dieser Nacht lösen auf lauen Kissen
Vergilbt von Weihrauch sich der Liebenden
    schmächtige Glieder.[16]

The incense is reminiscent of lines that are vital to Heidegger's reading of Trakl (US, 77-80), from the latter's "Abendländisches Lied" (133):

---

[16]"O the nearness of death. Let us pray./In this night, on pillows still warm/ Yellowed by incense, lovers' delicate limbs unravel."

> O, die bittere Stunde des Untergangs,
> Da wir ein steinernes Antlitz in schwarzen Wassern
>   beschaun.
> Aber strahlend heben die silbernen Lider die Liebenden:
> Ein Geschlecht. Weihrauch strömt von rosigen Kissen
> Und der süße Gesang der Auferstandenen.[17]

Essential to the earthly resurrection is that its radiance not dispel the shadow. In Trakl's lyric the shadow is cast by three figures: woman, brother, and sister.

Blessings of harvest are associated with woman (cf. "Frauensegen," 11) because of her blossoming womb and the fountain of her breast (24). But in the second stanza of "Die Verfluchten" (113-14) she embodies "plague," the curse of humankind as such; a tangle of scarlet snakes writhes in her tunneled womb; a child lays his brow in her hand. Yet in the third stanza of that poem woman is transfigured. *Resedenduft* now enwreathes her (cf. "Verwandlung," 60), the fragrance of mignonette or *reseda odorata,* a plant employed in folk medicine against fevers of infection and plague, administered with the incantation *reseda, morbos reseda,* heal, heal the sickness! Woman: source of the $\pi\lambda\acute{\eta}\gamma\eta$ or *Schlag;* source of the cure. Both sources well up the figure of "Sonja" (115). Her predominant qualities are *Sanftmut* and *Stille:* "gentle" is said of her three times, "quiet" four times. Yet the source of the *einfältigen Zwiefalt* in Sonja is itself a wound which Trakl locates with surgical precision:

> Wunde, rote, niegezeigte
> Läßt in dunklen Zimmern leben.[18]

"So painfully good and true is what lives." Beautifully and gently Sonja smiles as the hand of the dead reaches into the child's mouth: the roselike sighs of the lovers turn mute upon the mouth of Elis (92).

---

[17]"O the bitter hour of decline,/When we gaze on a stonelike face in black waters./But beaming lift the silver lids of lovers:/*One* Geschlecht. Incense streams from rosy pillows/And the sweet song of those resurrected."

[18]"Wound, red, never shown/Lets live in dark chambers."

Elis is that child, the brother, *frühverstorben* (129), who has gone before and so has become holy (81). Elis sings the gentle song of childhood (134), the quieter childhood of the dead (129). He appears as the victim of plague, crying the plaint of women at the crisis of birth (107, 132), and as one unborn—not so much already dead as still awaited—in any case, utterly apart, *abgeschieden* (cf. "Elis, 93, and "Gesang des Abgeschiedenen," 170-71). Yet the presence of the youth who is absent, the figure by which he haunts the poet, is called *die Schwester.* She is the counterpart of Elis (cf. *die Jünglingin,* 172), of the stranger and wanderer soul (cf. *die Fremdlingin,* 186), and of the monk (cf. *die Mönchin,* 177, 185). Her profile is not so easily adumbrated.

The sister combs her blond hair (23), plays a Schubert sonata in the next room (96), and speaks companionably with ghosts in the garden (29). She is found in an isolated forest clearing at noon amid the silence of animals (142), her mouth whispering in the black branches (25). Her white face (81, 189) stares forth strangely in someone's evil dreams (58), while her own sleep is troubled (78) perhaps by stormy melancholy (192). She appears as a beaming youth in autumn amid black corruption (104). A flaming demon (154) with eyes of stone (157), then a pallid figure with bleeding mouth, revealing a silver wound, she says, "Prick, black thorn" (187). Her lunar voice reverberates through the night of the spirit (131). Her image emerges from the blue depths of the mirror, plunging the brother into darkness, as though he were dead (151): she is perhaps a child in the summer garden whom he violates (152, 48). But when all collapses she greets the bleeding heads of fallen warriors—shadow of the Valkyries (193). Trakl dedicates the first of his "Rosary Hymns" to the sister (73). There he associates her with evening and autumn, the southerly flight of birds, and *ein blaues Wild.* He marks her slight smile, the melancholy above her brows.

Gott hat deine Lider verbogen.
Sterne suchen nachts, Karfreitagskind,
Deinen Stirnenbogen.[19]

---

[19]"God twisted the lids of your eyes./At night, Good Friday's Child,/Stars seek the curve of your brow."

Enough! Flood of images! What philosopher could snatch his thought from the inundation? Most astonishing about Heidegger's dialogue with Trakl is that he seeks no rescue from that flood: images whelm whatever formulas are launched in his own *Erörterung*.[20] One of the images that strikes Heidegger's eye—as it does that of Yeats's "Minnaloushe"—is the image of the moon. The brother treads *die mondenen Pfade* in search of the one who died young or who is yet to be born; he is entranced by *die mondene Stimme* of the sister. Heidegger recollects the way ancient Greek lyricists speak of the moon and stars (US, 48-49); in the context of *Entzweiung,* of the confluent twofold, and of σελήνη, who as Semele is the mother of Dionysos, we now recall something else.

At Agathon's drinking party Aristophanes wipes his nose and begins his encomium of Eros. He opens by explaining τὴν ἀνθρωπίνην φύσιν, "the nature of man," *den Schlag des Menschengeschlechts,* which originally consisted of three *Geschlechter* (γένη), male, female, and ἀνδρόγυνον. The male sex devolved from Helios, the sun. The female sex arose from Gaia, the earth. The third sex was truly *mondenes,* for it had as its parent σελήνη, the moon, "which participates in both sexes" (Plato, *Symposium,* 190b 3). Curious things are happening already. The two sexes we recognize as palpably true-to-life are "descended from" the sun (male) and the earth (female). But how does the earth father her children? How does the sun bear and nurse his? The only sex that makes any sense is the moonstruck androgynous. But Aristophanes does not pause to make comic capital out of that; indeed he warns Eryximachus not to try to make a joke of his speech, since he is altogether serious. However that may be, Aristophanes recounts the familiar story of the hybris and nemesis of the androgynes and of Zeus's solomonic wisdom.

> Now, when the work of bisection was complete it left each half with a desperate yearning for the other, and they ran together and flung their arms around each other's necks, and asked for nothing better than to be rolled into one. So much so, that they began to die of

---

[20]Note Heidegger's remark on the relation of poetry and prosaic formulas, US, 81.

hunger and general inertia, for neither would do anything without the other . . . .

Fortunately, however, Zeus felt so sorry for them that he devised another scheme. He moved their privates round to the front, for of course they had originally been on the outside—which was now the back—and they had begotten and conceived not upon each other, but, like the grasshoppers, upon the earth. So now, as I say, he moved their members round to the front and made them propagate among themselves, the male begetting upon the female . . . .

So you see, gentlemen, how far back we can trace our innate love for one another, and how this love is always trying to reintegrate our former nature, to make two into one, and to bridge the gulf between one human being and another.[21]

Man's nature, or at least the *Schlag* of that third of it whose descent Aristophanes can trace, is to be a σύμβολον (191d 4), a coin split down the middle, each half consigned to one of two friends; it devotes the rest of its days to the search for its fitting partner, jagged edge exposed, stirred by the tumultuous passion to become whole again. Through such passion it hopes to heal the πλήγη or *Schlag* of having been severed in twain, of having fallen into the discord of unchecked individuation which easily degenerates into the savage recklessness of ἀδικία.[22] The salutary passion of which man is the symbol is called Eros. *Schlag der Liebe*.

But it is one stroke that mints man, murderous, amatory. How are love and death to be thought together? We are prepared to answer that question. We hum along bravely as Tristan and Isolde sing their Liebestod duet or we allude to matters which psychoanalysis is said to have settled long ago. We are too well prepared. Even the most avant-garde efforts to intertwine in thought the themes of love and

---

[21]Plato, *Symposium*, 191a-d, translated by Michael Joyce.

[22]Cf. Martin Heidegger, *Early Greek Thinking*, translated by D. F. Krell and F. A. Capuzzi (New York: Harper & Row, 1975), pp. 41-47.

death fail to escape or even recognize ancient habits of representation.[23]

Are we really to look to Heidegger and Trakl for instruction in this matter? According to one experienced French critic, the Dasein of Heidegger's *Sein und Zeit* is altogether sexless. Heidegger himself took the life of Aristotle as exemplary for his own, a life that ostensibly consisted of being born, working, and dying—notwithstanding what medieval gossips intimate concerning Aristotle and Phyllis. According to ardent biographers, Trakl had an incestuous relationship with his younger sister. ("We have invented incest," say the Last Men, and they blink.) Neither Heidegger nor Trakl seems a very promising mentor. For Trakl the sister remains a terrifying embodiment of generation and corruption, a reflection of benediction and reproach. An intense ambivalence toward woman permeates his verse. As for Heidegger, it seem as though precious little is said in his work concerning matters of love. In "What Is Metaphysics?" he does refer to the joy experienced in a beloved human being, but it is a love *an der Gegenwart des Daseins—nicht der bloßen Person*—of this human being, a presence that remains formal, estranged, ghostlike, in a word, metaphysical.[24] Although Heidegger recognizes metaphysics' flight from embodiment for what it is, and although Nietzsche convinces him that *Dasein lebt, indem es leibt,*[25] Heidegger himself does not exhibit the role that the lived body plays in ek-sistence, does not make manifest the body *as* ek-sistent. As a result, "nearness to Being" remains exposed to the misinterpretation of angelic hovering, dreamy and disembodied, among the outermost spheres. It remains for Jean-Paul Sartre and Maurice Merleau-Ponty to clear a stretch of the path *unterwegs*. Yet

---

[23]See, for example, Georges Bataille, *L'érotisme* (Paris: Editions de Minuit, 1957), which abandons its one fertile idea, *la discontinuité de l'être,* and lapses into an admittedly "theological" explication of eroticism in terms of *l'interdit et la transgression,* decidedly on this side of good and evil. What at first seems the new gesture of Bataille's work turns out to be the leaden gesticulations of the dead god.

[24]*Wegmarken,* p. 8.

[25]The phrase appears often in Heidegger's early lectures on Nietzsche. See Martin Heidegger, *Nietzsche I: Will to Power as Art,* translated by D. F. Krell (New York: Harper & Row, 1978), section 14. See also the German edition of Heidegger's *Nietzsche* (Pfullingen: Neske, 1961) I, 565. Finally, see *Early Greek Thinking,* p. 65.

the long passage we read some pages back, on the discord of the
Geschlechter, the severance of man, and the "gentleness of a confluent twofold," gives the lie to our present complaint. In his
dialogue with Trakl, Heidegger looks for that *Sanftmut einer einfältigen Zwiefalt* which should transform and regenerate the decomposing *Menschengeschlecht*. He tries to follow the stranger who wanders ahead in search of gentleness and unity. In which direction?
Again the answer comes: *In den Untergang* (US, 51). Trakl celeb-
rates the gentleness of couch and grave, which are for him a kind of
childhood; such gentleness he finds in the figure of Elis, the youth
long departed, whose memory the brother sings. Such singing
should regenerate a decomposing race? A dead boy, withered before
blooming? We are incredulous. But Elis is a true child of the moon,
concealing in himself *die sanfte Zwiespalt der Geschlechter* (US, 55),
being addressed in both masculine and feminine forms, not so much
dead (as we have seen) as yet to be born. The spirit of Elis incorpo-
rates a new *Schlag des Geistes* (US, 66). *Geist* now means the flame
that feeds on persistent, gentle pain, the pain of severance, which
gathers the race to the site of its dwelling. Heidegger calls such a
spirit *das Wesen der Sterblichen*. That is what Trakl sings. It is what
Heidegger tries to think, as a friend who listens to the stranger who
died young. In that way he becomes a brother to the stranger and
thereby to the sister. Brother and sister are embraced in *ein Geschlecht,* gently, as mortals. This is what Heidegger calls "the dominant" tone of Trakl's lyric. "The unity of *the one Geschlecht* flows
from that *Schlag* which gathers in unification the discordant twofold
of *Geschlechter,* out of *Abgeschiedenheit . . . , into the more gentle
twofold" (US, 78).* Trakl sings the "sending of that *Schlag* that
forcefully casts—and that means rescues—the race of man into the
essence which remains reserved for it" (US, 80). What essence is
that? To be the race which is homeward bound, on the way under to
its earliest origins, sublunary earth.

   More than incredulous now, indignant, we dredge up names for
that kind of song or thought. "Dreamy romanticism," Heidegger
says, anticipating his critics. Others will say: If not an outright invitation to incest, hence subversive of the basic pillar of exogamous
civilization, then a sublimated wish-fulfillment of a repressed regres-
sive fixated primary choice of love-object, psychic infantilism, and
in either case unwholesome and reprobate. And others: A flagrant

example of alienated atomized impotent and decadent petit-bourgeois utopism. Still others, less eloquent, will sneer: What do you expect from poets and philosophers? We are all too well prepared.

But how would it be if for all our talk of Eros and Thanatos the single *Schlag* of love and death has not yet come home to us? Such a question is not meant as an invitation to reduce one to the other, as traditional ontology has always done; it is meant as an injunction to let the innate power of both coin our thoughts on man and woman. One thing is certain: so long as "man" remains the shuttlecock of metaphysics, batted back and forth between *animalitas* and *ratio,* such thinking cannot succeed. Neither can it succeed by means of the anthropological sciences which in their effort to emancipate themselves from metaphysics forget the origins of their most beloved presuppositions. Nor finally will it succeed at some popular level where the sciences of man carry no weight and philosophy and poetry are scorned: our cemeteries sprawl on the outskirts of town beyond the outermost tramline and our loves in photo mags with staples through their bellies. What is that? What is the distance that keeps us safely out of reach of both?

Perhaps it is time to take a second look at the sources of our thoughts on man and woman, in texts such as the following:

> Of beings, some are forever and are divine; others harbor being and nonbeing. The beautiful and divine, according to its own nature, is always the cause of what is better in whatever harbors it; whereas what does not harbor that which is forever shares in being (and nonbeing) and in the worse as well as the better. . . .Since the nature of such a genus [i.e., of living beings] is incapable of being forever, what is generated is always in the only way it can be . . . . .Hence, there is forever a genus of humans . . ., and since the dominant source of the genus is the male and the female, it is for the sake of generation that the male and the female are in the respective beings. . . .And male comes together and mingles with female in the work of generation; for this is something that concerns both in common.[26]

[26]Aristotle, *On the Generation of Living Beings,* II, 1 (73 lb 24-732a 12).

According to Aristotle, men and women share the fate of dwelling in the lower cosmos, below the circle of the moon, under the ecliptic of the sun, hence subject to periods of fertility and frigidity, γένεσις and φθορά. Considered as individuals, ἀριθμῷ, men and women are not ἀίδια. They do not last forever. Only when they are viewed εἴδει, as a "genus" that "generates" οἷον αὐτό, a likeness of itself, do men and women partake in the lasting. Their being cast in love is both a symptom of ἀδύνατος ἀίδιος, the incapacity of their φύσις or upsurgence to endure forever, and the realization of their τρόπος ἀίδιος, the way they forever are. In Aristotle's eyes that way possesses a grandeur that radiates to the rims of the stars and is reflected back again. Why and how in the development of Christian ontology that view must change, why Hegel must in the end deride generation as *schlechte Unendlichkeit,*[27] why it is that Eros must be poisoned, whereupon instead of dying he degenerates to vice,[28] why the εἶδος of man must dwindle to the *verweste Gestalt des Menschen,* are questions that still need to be asked. Answering them may demand a new kind of thinking, whose manifold nature we can only hint at here.

At the outset it may be enough to dwell on the fact that for all our readiness to confront Eros and Thanatos we have virtually nothing to say to them—whereas they have a long tale to tell us. Let our response to them therefore be coined in *Gelassenheit,* a kind of thinking that combines many ideas about masculinity and femininity so as to form a third, "foreign" strain, itself beyond the dialectics of activity-passivity, willing-notwilling, advancing-waiting. Little wonder if the foreign strain which wrests phenomena from concealment solely in order to grant their inalienable obscurity and which strikes a critical pose before every monument of traditional wisdom while resolving to remain open to it should wear a lunatic aspect; children who have abandoned their innocence gladly, suspicious of their own preparedness to cloak all things with words but encouraged to let suspicion be as well, children of the long night, but under stars. At the end of their nocturnal conversation about *Gelassenheit*

---

[27]G. W. F. Hegel, *Enzyklopädie der philosophischen Wissenschaften (1830),* ed. F. Nicolin and O. Pöggeler (Hamburg: F. Meiner, 1969), § 370.

[28]Friedrich Nietzsche, *Jenseits,* no. 168 (Schlechta ed., II, 639).

the teacher says, *Für das Kind im Menschen bleibt die Nacht die Näherin der Sterne.*[29] She who lets the stars, inconceivably remote, be near.

> Sterne suchen nachts, Karfreitagskind,
> Deinen Stirnenbogen.

Children of care (*Kar-, cura*), the generation struck by love and death, own the spectacle.

> What spectacle confronted them when they, first the host, then the guest, emerged silently, doubly dark, from obscurity by a passage from the rere of the house into the penumbra of the garden?

> The heaventree of stars hung with humid nightblue fruit.[30]

Earlier we suggested that the principal effort of Heidegger's *Sein und Zeit* and of all his later work is: to let death be. *Schlag des Todes*. Now we are asking whether the same kind of thought may induce men and women in love to let one another be. *Schlag der Liebe*. Men and women let one another be? Should they turn their backs on one another? That was tried before, Aristophanes says, and not even Zeus could make it work. For men and women *Gelassenheit* means something else, something like "a gentle confluence of the twofold," befitting mortals of both molds. There is a part of the comedian's story we did not relate:

> Now, supposing Hephaestus were to come and stand over them with his tool bag as they lay there side by side and suppose he were to ask, Tell me, my dear creatures, what do you really want with one another?

---

[29]Martin Heidegger, *Gelassenheit* (Pfullingen: Neske, 1959). p. 71.
[30]James Joyce, *Ulysses* (London: The Bodley Head, 1960), p. 819.

And suppose they didn't know what to say, and he
went on, How would you like to be rolled into one, so
that you could always be together, day and night, and
never be parted again? Because if that's what you want, I
can easily weld you together, and then you can live your
two lives in one, and, when the time comes, you can die a
common death and still be two-in-one in the lower
world . . . .

We may be sure, gentlemen, that no lover on earth
would dream of refusing such an offer, for not one of
them could imagine a happier fate. Indeed, they would be
convinced that this was just what they'd been waiting
for—to be merged, that is, into an utter oneness with the
beloved (*Symposium,* 192d-e).

Men and women: joined as mortals: who give one another whatever man can be. A minor theme, in a minor key. Yet the mode is
ancient, *aus der Frühe,* as Heidegger says. Though generations may
let it go and forget it, both Trakl and Heidegger, *unzeitgemäße
Zeitgenossen,* try to relearn it. They find it inscribed in an old
genealogy, "In ein altes Stammbuch":

Wieder kehrt die Nacht und klagt ein Sterbliches
Und es leidet ein anderes mit.

Again night comes and a mortal keens
And another suffers with him.

REVIEW ARTICLES

Some Important Themes in Current Heidegger Research

Any essay which tries to provide a survey of the numerous avenues of research now being pursued into the problems raised by the thought of Martin Heidegger is rather presumptuous, especially if it makes any claims to being exhaustive. Thus let me say immediately that the following analysis will suffer necessarily from omissions and probably from overemphasis of certain themes which I find to be of importance in Heidegger's thinking. Nevertheless, I believe that the areas discussed in the essay are generally acknowledged to be important for understanding this formidable thinker. The essay will also consider briefly how Heidegger's thinking is important for coming to terms with critical problems of modern existence; I have in mind here the question about technology. The essay will be divided into the following sections: 1) Heidegger's *Gesamtausgabe*; 2) the problem of the relation between Husserlian and Heideggerean phenomenology; 3) the question of the temporality of Dasein and the time of Being; 4) Heidegger on politics and technology; 5) other issues.

1. *Heidegger's Gesamtausgabe.* Certainly the on-going publication of Heidegger's enormous *Gesamtausgabe* ("collected works") is a very important event for Heidegger scholarship. Projected to include at least 57 volumes, the *Gesamtausgabe* is divided into four major areas: 1) published works, from 1914-1970; 2) the Marburg lectures from 1923-1928 and the Freiburg lectures from 1928-1944; 3) unpublished writings from 1919-1967; 4) "sketches and notes" (*Aufzeichnungen und Hinweise*), which are related to already published material. The publisher's flier includes the order of publication planned for the first

three years, but it is unclear that this arrangement is actually being followed. For example, an edition of *Sein und Zeit* which includes Heidegger's own marginalia was published in Spring 1977 but was not included in the brochure's projection for this year. Two volumes have already been published, *viz., Die Grundprobleme der Phänomenologie[1],* Marburg lectures from the summer semester of 1927 (just after the publication of *Sein und Zeit),* and *Logik: Die Frage nach der Wahrheit[2],* Marburg lectures from the winter semester 1925-26.

If the first two volumes are typical of those to follow, Heidegger scholars are in for several years of fascinating reading. As Friedrich-Wilhelm von Herrmann, one of the editors of the *Gesamtausgabe,* pointed out to me in the summer of 1976, Heidegger looked upon his lectures as a kind of "proving ground" for his published works. In the lectures he would try out various approaches to fundamental issues, and often in a way which was more accessible and lively than that of his published works. These lectures reveal, for example, Heidegger's personal attitude toward his own teachers and associates, including Rickert, Natorp, Scheler, and Husserl. And there are also instances of what, for Heidegger, must be understood as humorous remarks. In *Die Grundprobleme,* for example, Heidegger says that although some have called him a "Catholic phenomenologist," this makes about as much sense as the notion of "Protestant mathematics."[3] The lectures also show Heidegger to be an acerbic critic of what he considers to be philosophical foolishness, and political *misuse* of philosophy. In this regard, we find in *Die Grundprobleme's* introduction an extensive discussion of the concept of the "Weltanschuung", a discussion which explains how some "vulgar" thinkers (including politically-minded ones) spout out nonsense from every streetcorner in the attempt to reduce all fundamental thinking to some sort of life-guiding interpretation of "reality and history." These lectures will also provide fertile grounds for those concerned with tracing the "development" of Heidegger's thinking, since he himself published his writings only sporadically and often only long after they were originally written.

---

[1]Martin Heidegger, *Die Grundprobleme der Phänomenologie,* edited by Friedrich-Wilhelm von Herrmann (Frankfurt am Main: Vittorio Klostermann, 1975).

[2]Martin Heidegger, *Logik: Die Frage nach der Wahrheit,* edited by Walter Biemel (Frankfurt am Main: Vittorio Klostermann, 1976).

[3]Heidegger, *Die Grundprobleme,* p. 28.

Eventually we shall have 23 years of lectures on the most diverse topics, including the much-awaited winter semester 1930-31 lectures on "Hegel's *Phänomenologie des Geistes*," the summer semester 1925 lectures on the "Geschichte des Zeitbegriffs," and the summer semester 1933 lectures on "Die Grundfrage der Philosophie."

The new publication of the published writings will include in many instances marginalia from Heidegger's copies of his own books and essays. Such marginalia will provide further clues to deciphering Heidegger's "self-interpretation," which began immediately after the publication of *Sein und Zeit*. As Heidegger gained more insight about his own "way" he would occasionally attempt to demonstrate that *Sein und Zeit* had already anticipated (although perhaps only obliquely) the same insight formulated rather differently several years later. Such self-interpretations need to be respected, but nevertheless taken with a grain of salt. For as Heidegger himself says about the work of art, the work of philosophy is itself autonomous and must be allowed to speak out on its own -- even independently of what its author wants to say about it later.

Although the *Gesamtausgabe* will offer important insight into the mind of this remarkable thinker, there are dangers here, of which the self-critical Heidegger scholar must make himself fully aware. We recall that time and again in letters to various seminars on his thinking, Heidegger urged the participants *not* to concentrate so much on understanding *Heidegger* as on posing anew the fundamental questions about Being, technology, and so forth. Does the publication of the *Gesamtausgabe* threaten to lead to the growth of an even more intense Heidegger "scholasticism," or might it help to provoke new interest not only in Heidegger, but in the crucial themes of his thinking? Surely Heidegger himself must have been conscious of the risks involved here, but he evidently considered his writings important enough to take that risk.

2. *The Relation Between Heideggerean and Husserlian Phenomenology.* For many years now, scholars have been puzzled by Heidegger's version of phenomenology, and why it differed so markedly from Husserl's. In his essay "My Way to Phenomenology" (1962), Heidegger states plainly that he was most influenced *not* by Husserl's later writings but by the *Logische Untersuchuungen,* particularly the sixth "investigation." In his paper "Heidegger and Husserl's *Logical*

Investigations" Jacques Taminiaux (Louvain) reiterates the notion that
Heidegger believed Husserl to have caught sight of the *Seinsfrage* in the
sixth logical investigation, but to have failed to understand the
importance of this insight. This sixth investigation claims that certain
categorial structures are "given" to us in a way analagous to sensations.
The Being of a being, for example, is somehow present to us when we
perceive the being; Being is not "added" by some mental judgment, but
manifests itself. In his 1962 essay, Heidegger says:

> What occurs for the phenomenology of the acts of
> consciousness as the self-manifestation of phenomena is
> thought more originally by Aristotle and in all Greek
> thinking and existence as *aletheia*, as the unconcealedness of
> what-is-present, its being revealed, its showing itself.[4]

In an unpublished essay read to the Heidegger Conference in Waterloo,
Ontario, in May, 1975, Walter Biemel (Aachen), who has access to
Heidegger's unpublished manuscripts, remarks that "Heidegger
interprets Husserl in such a way that he attempts to keep him out of the
idealistic perspective. Expressed in an exaggerated manner: Heidegger
wants to preserve and protect the Aristotelian aspects of philosophizing
in Husserl's work."[5] This notion of phenomenology as the study of
"what shows itself from itself" is the heart of Heidegger's description of
phenomenology in *Sein und Zeit*. By distinguishing between Being and
the being which always accompanies the intuition of the categorial
structure of Being, Husserl also anticipates the "ontological difference"
so crucial to Heidegger. Of fundamental importance here is that for
Heidegger, categorial intuitions are *not* "constituted" by the ego or
subject, but are instead self-manifestations on the part of the "things
themselves." They are *discovered*, not founded or projected by the
subject.

---

[4]Cf. Martin Heidegger, *On Time and Being,* translated by Joan Stambaugh (New York:
Harper & Row, 1972), p. 79.

[5]Walter Biemel, "Heidegger and Phenomenology," unpublished manuscript, translated
by José Huertas-Jourda.

Biemel's paper also summarizes Heidegger's explicit criticism of Husserl's phenomenology, as they are found in the (unpublished) 1925 Marburg lectures on "The History of the Concept of Time." Heidegger asserts that Husserl fails to examine his own presuppositions, e.g., that consciousness is primary or even "Absolute Being." Husserl remains within an unquestioned Cartesian framework, and thus mired in the very subjectivism which Heidegger was trying to pass beyond. Husserl is said to have approached consciousness and intentionality from a stance so loaded with theoretical presuppositions, that he failed to examine lived experience. Heidegger insists upon the primacy of the question of the *Being of consciousness*, whereas Husserl affirms in advance the primacy of consciousness and suspends the ontological problematic. The notion of "Da-sein" is Heidegger's attempt to talk about man's relation to Being, without having to resort to the concept of the subject. As Dasein, we are always already open to the Being of being; there is no problem of "transcendence" from subject to its object. Heidegger clarifies this in *Die Grundprobleme's* important discussion of intentionality. Intentionality is not a thing-like relation between two things (subject and object), but is an *a priori* structure belonging to the very behavior (*Verhalten*) of Dasein. Moreover, the intentionality of Dasein is ". . . *the ontological condition for the possibility of any transcendence.*"[6] Heidegger says that the analysis of the subject gives no insight into intentionality, for intentionality is the ground of the subject!

The magnitude of the difference between Heidegger and Husserl's view of phenomenology can be seen in their differing ideas about the "phenomenological reduction." In *Die Grundprobleme*, Heidegger notes that the fundamental aspect of the phenomenological method, as the "moving-back" of the investigative glance from naively grasped being to Being, is the reduction. (Immediately, we see that here -- as in *Sein und Zeit* -- phenomenology for Heidegger is identical with ontology, the study of Being.) Heidegger first gives us a standard definition of the reduction "for Husserl," and then says that "*For us*, the phenomenological reduction means the leading-back of the phenomenological glance from the however determinate grasp

---

[6]Heidegger, *Die Grundprobleme*, p. 91. Stress in original.

(*Erfassung*) of Being, to the understanding of Being (projection on the mode of its unconcealedness) of this being."[7] It is little wonder that Husserl felt Heidegger had abandoned "authentic" phenomenology. Evidently, much work remains to be done before we understand fully the relationship between these two thinkers. But it is already apparent that phenomenology was forever bifurcated when Heidegger refused to allow Husserl back into transcendental idealism.

3. *Temporality of Dasein and Temporality of Sein.* It is well-known that *Sein und Zeit* is the "torso" of a larger, never-completed work. The most important omitted part was to be called "Zeit und Sein," which was to show how time is the "horizon" for the understanding of Being. Although Heidegger's 1962 lecture, "Zeit und Sein," bears the title of the missing portion, the lecture was nevertheless quite removed from the thinking of *Sein und Zeit*."[8] According to von Herrmann, the editor of this set of lectures, Heidegger said that this would be the only version of the missing portion ever to appear. In *Sein und Zeit*, Heidegger approached the question of the relation of time and Being by way of the analysis of human Dasein. Temporality *(Zeitlichkeit)* is there shown to be the underlying unity of Dasein's Being, "care" (*Sorge*). The major problem was how to pass beyond the idea that Dasein's temporalizing activity is constitutive for the time of Being as such. Heidegger wanted to show that Dasein's temporality has a fundamental, but *dependent* relation to the time of Being. But because he began with the analysis of Dasein's temporal Being, he remains mired within the problematic of the "subjectivity of the subject," which is probably why he never published the missing portion of *Sein und Zeit*. Years later, Heidegger admits that the way to Being through the Self is a subjectivistic-metaphysical way, which he took because he had not yet surpassed metaphysical thinking. "It is for this reason that the first way which leads away from metaphysics to the ecstatic existential nature of man must lead through the metaphysical conception of human selfhood (*S.u.Z.*, sections 63 and 64).[9]

---

[7]*Ibid.*, p. 29.

[8]Cf. Heidegger, *On Time and Being*, pp. 1-24.

[9]Martin Heidegger, "The Way Back into the Ground of Metaphysics," translated by Walter Kaufmann in his *Existentialism from Dostoevsky to Sartre* (Cleveland and New York: The World Publishing Company, 1965), p. 215.

Friedrich-Wilhelm von Herrmann handles this problem very well in his recent book, *Subjekt und Dasein*. He claims that Heidegger wants to surpass the entire subjectivistic tradition, by showing that the Being of man (as Dasein) is no longer to be considered from within the limits of the "I" and "self," but from the relation of human Dasein to the Being of beings. [10] "Dasein" thus does not mean the "subjectivity of the subject," but the ontological connection of human being with Being as such. Temporality is the key to this obscure relation. Whereas Husserl sought to "radicalize" transcendental - or consciousness-philosophy, Heidegger seeks to abandon this perspective altogether. The leading ideas in this revolution are "disclosedness" (*Erschlossenheit*) and "Dasein." According to von Herrmann, in *Sein und Zeit* disclosedness refers not only to the illuminating capacity of man (which is the chief insight of transcendental philosophy), but also to the illuminating aspect of Being as such. [11] Thus, as Da-sein, man *exists* as the "there" (*"Da-"*) of the lightedness of Being (*"-sein"*). Considerable confusion resulted from the fact that in *Sein und Zeit* Heidegger failed to make clear that Dasein refers not only to man's Being, but to the illuminating event of Being as such which takes place "in" Dasein. Thus, the "understanding of Being" is a "gift" of Being; it is the opening up of Being in the understanding-Being of human Dasein. [12] The Self of Dasein is grounded in this primordial disclosedness-understanding. Had Heidegger been a real Kantian, he would have placed primordial time *within* the Self, but this would have been to suggest that the Self somehow *is* or *constitutes* Being -- and Heidegger wanted to avoid this notion at all costs. As von Herrmann concludes, Dasein's temporal disclosedness

> . . . is no subjective structure, because in the ecstases [the three dimensions of temporality] Dasein is opened up to itself only insofar as it is opened up therein for the disclosedness of Being-in-general. The latter reaches out beyond the self-openedness of *Existenz*. In the disclosedness of Being proper, Dasein stands so little upon itself, that it

---

[10] Friedrich-Wilhelm von Herrmann, *Subjekt und Dasein* (Frankfurt am Main: Vittorio Klostermann, 1974), p. 10.

[11] *Ibid.*, p. 21.

[12] *Ibid.*, p. 31.

stands therein precisely in the disclosedness of Being-in-general, which it has not posited and which it has not brought itself, but in which it always already finds itself placed with its ecstases. [Dasein] is not abandoned to itself merely in order to circle in its own Being, but in order to hold open ecstatically by temporalizing with its own Being, the temporal (*zeithaft*) disclosedness of Being-in-general. In the same way, the temporal disclosedness of Being-in-general is no subjective time posited by the subject, because [this disclosedness] always already runs under the time of Dasein *(daseinsmässige Zeitigen)*. Only in the ecstatically held-open temporal disclosedness (executed in temporality) of Being-in-general can the "subject" reach the "object." Only on the basis of the ecstatic-temporal, held-open essential time of Being, can Dasein form the subjective and objective time oriented in the now.[13]

This probing analysis reveals how Heidegger's "realistic" tendency moved him to try to interpret Being as determinative of the Self or subject, instead of the other way around. *Die Grundprobleme*, in its attempt to overcome the objection that *Sein und Zeit* reduces Being to a property or function of man, approaches the question of time and Being *not* by way of the anlaysis of Dasein, but instead by way of a series of fundamental problems in the history of Western philosophy. The final 125 pages, which include a pentrating account of Aristotle's notion of time, do assert that time *is* the "horizon of Being." Heidegger draws the following analogy: just as we are able to deal with beings in light of our understanding of their Being, so too can we "understand" Being only in light of time. Time makes the Being of beings accessible to human understanding. Calling upon Plato's *Republic*, he even says that time illuminates the Being of beings in much the same way that the *agathon* illuminates the forms![14] The analysis of time as the horizon of Being runs briefly as follows: I can deal with a tool only insofar as I understand the Being of the tool; but further, I can only understand the

---

[13]*Ibid.*, pp. 90-91. The best book in English about Heidegger on time is Charles M. Sherover, *Heidegger, Kant, and Time* (Bloomington: Indiana University Press, 1971).
[14]Heidegger, *Die Grundprobleme*, pp. 400-401.

Being of that tool insofar as I am able to "project" this Being upon (i.e., understand it in terms of or in light of) a certain "horizon" of time. Thus to Dasein there belongs a specific temporal dimension which makes possible our understanding of the Being of tools, the ready-to-hand. The specific horizon of temporality which discloses the Being of the ready-to-hand is *Praesenz*, which denotes the specific "directionality" of Dasein's temporality. This directional horizon allows Dasein to "move out from" (transcend) itself towards things "present" as tools. A thing is able to be "present" for my use only insofar as I have been able to understand its Being in light of the dimension of the "present," which is opened up by the horizon of *Praesenz*. The power of Dasein to "transcend" itself toward Being by opening up a horizon of time is called by Heidegger an "ecstasis." But as fascinating as this account is, Heidegger still seems stuck in the neo-Kantian framework, as can be seen in the following passage:

> Each ecstasis has in itself a fully determinate schema, which modifies itself with the way in which temporality temporalizes itself, i.e., as the ecstases modify themselves. Just as the ecstases constitute in themselves the unity of temporality, so there corresponds always to the ecstatic unity of temporality such a schemata horizonal to it. The transcendence of Being-in-the-world is grounded in its specific totality in the primordial ecstatico-horizonal unity of temporality. If transcendence makes the understanding of Being possible, and if transcendence is grounded in the ecstatico-horizonal constitution of temporality, then the latter is the condition for the possibility of the understanding of Being.[15]

It is not at all clear what the relationship is between the Being of Dasein and the Being of different modes of Being (such as the present-at-hand, ready-to-hand, etc.), and between Dasein's temporalizing activity and the horizons of time which illuminate Being as such. Does not Heidegger confuse two senses of the word "Being"? On the one hand,

---

[15]*Ibid.*, p.429.

Being seems to be used in the more traditional sense of the "reality of the real." But on the other hand, Heidegger wants to suggest that Being *illuminates* (makes understandable) beings. Why must he talk of an illuminating event (time) which illuminates Being as such? Is this not a needless duplication? In *Die Grundprobleme* Heidegger seems to try to distinguish between the time of Dasein and the time of Being when he says that "The fundamental problematic of ontology, as the determination of the meaning of Being from Time, is that of *Temporalität*."[16] *Temporalität* is said to be *Zeitlichkeit* exhibited as the condition necessary for the understanding of Being.[17] Is *Temporalität* the primordial "time of Being"? If so, how is Dasein's own temporalizing activity related to this fundamental time? These are the kinds of questions which led Heidegger to abandon altogether the approach to Being and to time by way of human Dasein. Could it be that the notion of Dasein's "temporalizing activity," which *unifies* the Self and grounds the "worldhood of the world" and makes an understanding of Being possible, is later replaced by the notion of the "gathering" of the four-fold (*Geviert*) of earth, sky, gods, and mortals in Heidegger's later writings? Is this shift not also evident in Heidegger's claim that it is the *destiny* of Western man to experience the Being of beings as "present," in the sense of "re-presentedness" (*Vorgestelltheit*) of the object for the self-determinative Subject?[18] And that it is not the activity of the temporalizing self, but the *Geschick* of Being as such that allows beings to be "present" as raw-material for the all-devouring Subject? There is clearly a great deal of thinking necessary before we understand not only the "development" of Heidegger's thinking about time and Being, but before we are able to see what he was pointing to. Some of these issues may be clarified as more of the *Gesamtausgabe* becomes available.

4. *Heidegger's "Political Philosophy."* The recent publication by *Der Spiegel* of Heidegger's 1966 interview (withheld from print by his request, until after his death) will no doubt stimulate a controversy

---

[16]*Ibid.,* p. 22.

[17]*Ibid.,* pp. 388-389.

[18]Cf. Otto Pöggeler's highly instructive essay, "Being as Appropriation" ("Sein als Ereignis"), translated by Ruediger Hermann Grimm in *Philosophy Today* XIX (Summer, 1975), pp. 152-178.

which began immediately after World War II, and which has become more subtle and reflective in recent years.[19] The controversy, of course, concerns Heidegger's notorious engagement with National Socialism between 1933 and 1935, especially during his ten-month tenure as rector of the University of Freiburg. Heidegger's famous *Rektoratsrede*, called *Die Selbstbehauptung der deutschen Universität*,[20] and his various political speeches and writings from that period, show beyond any doubt that he believed National Socialism to offer the possibility of authentic existence for the German *Volk*.[21] For Heidegger scholars, and for all who admire human genius, it is depressing to read these documents, for they show that Heidegger was willing to try to mold his own thinking to the ideological demands of the NSDAP. On the other hand, it must be remembered that Heidegger resigned his position as rector because he refused to accede to Party demands that he fire two professors considered to be anti-NSDAP. Moreover, his *Rektoratsrede* was an attempt to assert the *independence* of the German university over against those who wanted to make it a mere tool of the Party will. Also, in *Der Spiegel's* interview, Heidegger confirms what many have suspected: that his lectures on Nietzsche were directed against the prevailing NSDAP exploitation of that thinker's ideas. "In 1936, I began the Nietzsche lectures. Anyone with ears to hear heard in these

---

[19]"Only a God Can Save Us: *Der Spiegel's* Interview with Martin Heidegger on September 23, 1966," translated by Maria P. Alter and John D. Caputo in *Philosophy Today*, XX (Winter, 1976), pp. 267-284. Cf. the original "Gespräch mit Martin Heidegger" in *Der Spiegel*, Issue 23, May 31, 1976, pp. 193-219. For a very helpful analysis of recently published material on Heidegger's political activity and thinking, Cf. Alexander Schwan's essay, "Martin Heidegger, Politik und Praktische Philosophie: Zur Problematick neuerer Heidegger-Literatur" in *Philosophisches Jahrbuch*, 81 (1974), pp. 148-172.

[20]Martin Heidegger, *Die Selbstbehauptung der deutschen Universitat* (Breslau: Korn, 1933).

[21]Many documents from the 1933-35 period pertaining to and by Heidegger are collected in Guido Schneeberger's *Nachlese zu Heidegger. Dokumente zu seinem Leben und Denken* (Bern, 1962). Because of Schneeberger's determination to place Heidegger in the worst possible light, the volume needs to be read critically. One of the most instructive treatments of Heidegger's relation to National Socialism is Karl Moehling's excellent work, *Martin Heidegger and the Nazi Party: An Examination* (DeKalb, Illinois: Unpublished Ph.D. Dissertation, 1972). Included here are Heidegger's statements to the de-nazification commission in 1945, as well as other previously unavailable material.

lectures a confrontation with National Socialism."[22] The interview, which is probably self-serving at some points, emphatically rejects such slanderous claims as that Heidegger (as rector) refused Husserl (born of Jewish parents) access to the university library, or that he ordered books by Jewish authors burned. But beyond insights provided into his actions from this period, the interview also reveals Heidegger's complex position concerning the relation of philosophy to "praxis." The interview deserves careful attention.

The three most important books about Heidegger's political thought and action are Alexander Schwan, *Politische Philosophie im Denken Heideggers,* [23] Jean-Michel Palmier, *Les écrits politiques de Heidegger,*[24] and Otto Pöggeler, *Philosophie und Politik bei Heidegger.*[25] Schwan's book, written in very difficult and convoluted German, focuses on the importance of Heidegger's essay, "The Origin of the Work of Art" (1936) for understanding his political thinking. Palmier's fine book is the only major work to take seriously the influence of Ernst Jünger (*Der Arbeiter*, and others) on Heidegger. And Pöggeler's largely sympathetic work tries to "rehabilitate" Heidegger's political thinking by showing the many similarities between his thinking and that of the "Frankfurt Critical School," especially with respect to the question of the will to mastery of modern technology. What may be the best *article* for some time to come is Karsten Harries', "Heidegger as a Political Thinker."[26] In this remarkable essay, which exhibits familiarity with all the appropriate sources (except *Der Spiegel's* interview which appeared too late to be consulted), Harries remarks that "It is unfortunate that Heidegger's changing political views, fragmentary as they are, have received so little attention, for it is here

---

[22]"*Der Spiegel's* Interview," p. 274.

[23]Alexander Schwan, *Politische Philosophie im Denken Heideggers* (Köln und Opladen: Westdeutscher Verlag, 1965).

[24]Jean-Michel Palmier, *Les écrits politiques de Heidegger* (Paris: l'Herne, 1968).

[25]Otto Pöggeler, *Philosophie und Politik bei Heidegger* (Freiburg und und München: Karl Alber, 1972).

[26]Karsten Harries, "Heidegger as a Political Thinker," in *The Review of Metaphysics,* XXIX (June, 1976), pp. 642-669. Of some interest here as well is my own essay, "Heidegger, and National Socialism," in the *Southwestern Journal of Philosophy,* V (Spring, 1974), pp. 97-106.

that the questionable character of his thought becomes most readily apparent--questionable in the sense of both demanding and deserving attention."[27] Harries thus reminds us that, like Nietzsche, Heidegger is a "dangerous" thinker, insofar as he discloses the *limits* of human existence.

But there remain at least three other issues raised by Heidegger's "political" thinking, besides the question of his involvement with the NSDAP: A) the notion that technology is a kind of ideology; B) the relation of Heidegger's thinking to that of Marx; and C) the question of the possibility of "praxis" arising from Heidegger's thinking. Let us treat each of these topics briefly in turn.

A) *Technology.* Perhaps the most important feature of Heidegger's later writings is their focus on modern technology as the culmination of Western man's drive to conquer Nature, by reducing the world to an object (raw material) for the all-devouring Subject. Heidegger suggests that modern totalitarianism (such as National Socialism) arises not merely from "political" motives, but primarily from the Will to Power in its widest sense as the drive by man to arrange the entire globe in light of the demands of the Subject. In his 1969 interview in *l'Expresse*, Heidegger says: "I have written in the same sense that totalitarianism was not a simple form of government, but rather the consequence of this unrestrained dominance of technology."[28] As he points out in his famous essay, "Die Frage nach der Technik," the "essence" of technology is itself nothing technical.[29] That is, technology is not equivalent to power machines and devices, but such machinery (and the mathematical projection of Nature necessary for their development) is only possible because the "withdrawal" of Being illuminates beings as objects to be disposed of according to man's requirements. The history ·of metaphysics is the history of the process whereby man makes himself the measure of all things. Once man kills God and destroys all transcendent standards, man himself becomes the source of all "values."

---

[27]Harries, "Heidegger as a Political Thinker," pp. 644-645.

[28]"Entretien avec Heidegger" in *l'Expresse,* No., 954, October 20-26, 1969, pp. 78-85. Quotation is from p. 82.

[29]Martin Heidegger, *Vorträge und Aufsätze,* Vol. I (Pfullingen: Gunther Neske, 1967), pp. 5-36. The long awaited English translation of this and other important texts on technology is supposed to appear this year.

Nihilism results from this process, for truth and value become mere *instruments* for the realization of the ceaseless Will to Power. To the extent that this technological understanding of the Being of being (as raw material) is responsible for the "total mobilization" of the world's resources (including man as the "most important raw material"[30]), technology is no "neutral" handmaiden, but the fundamental ideology of the twentieth century.[31]

It is no accident that Herbert Marcuse interprets technology in much the same way, for he was a student of Heidegger for several years, until he broke with Heidegger over the events of 1933. In both *Eros and Civilization* and *One-Dimensional Man*, Marcuse's account of the rise of technology parallels in many important ways Heidegger's idea that technology is the culmination of Western metaphysics. For both thinkers, the key to technology is the experience of the Being of being as "objectivity," i.e., as something thrown and held over against the subject which determines the object. As Marcuse says, for technological man "Nature is *a priori* experienced by an organism bent to domination and therefore experienced as susceptible to mastery and control."[32] For both Heidegger and Marcuse, only a change in our "experience of Being" can bring about a new mode of existence within technological culture. Marcuse says that "In metaphysical terms, the change is expressed by the fact that the essence of being is no longer conceived as Logos. And, with this change in the basic experience of being, the logic of domination is challenged."[33] In place of the logic of domination,

---

[30]Cf. Heidegger's powerful essay "Überwindung der Metaphysik," in *ibid.*, translated as "Overcoming Metaphysics" by Joan Stambaugh in the book of essays by Heidegger, *The End of Philosophy* (New York: Harper & Row, 1973).

[31]On the question of technology as ideology, cf. Jürgen Habermas' noted essay, "Techno Science as 'Ideology' " in *Toward a Rational Society: Student Protest, Science and Politics*, translated by Jeremy J. Shapiro (Boston: Beacon Press, 1970). Cf. also Habermas' essay, "Zur Veröffentlichung von Vorlesungen aus dem Jahre 1935," in his *Philosophische-politische Profile* (Frankfurt am Main: Suhrkamp Verlag, 1971), in which Habermas criticizes Heidegger for publishing *Einführung in der Metaphysik* (lectures from 1935), without retracting the passages which seem to praise National Socialism. Habermas, a leading figure in the Critical School, displays his admiration for Heidegger as a *thinker* when Habermas remarks that *Sein und Zeit* is "the most significant philosophical event since Hegel's *Phänomenologie*." Cf. p. 67.

[32]Herbert Marcuse, *Eros and Civilization* (Boston: Beacon Press, 1966), p. 119.

[33]*Ibid.*, p. 119.

Marcuse hopes for the emergence of a move toward "gratification," in which both man and Nature can unfold and enjoy themselves *from themselves*, and not according to the pre-figured demands of the mastering Subject. Marcuse's "solution" to the problem of technology thus seems to resemble in certain respects Heidegger's notion of "releasement" (*Gelassenheit*).[34] In a moment, we shall discuss the problem of what man can possibly *do* to help bring about this "change" in his "experience of Being."

The notion that technology is essentially a way of understanding the Being of beings as raw material for man in his drive for more power, lies in the background of much contemporary criticism of technology. Some thinkers, however--such as George Grant, in his brilliant essay, "Technology and Empire,"--say that one cannot explain the North American lust for technology solely on the basis of the "unalloyed drive to technological mastery for its own sake."[35] Grant continues:

> It is this interpretation which allows certain Europeans to consider us a wasteland with nothing seriously human among us but that self-propelling will to technology. But this interpretation underestimates the very effectiveness of North America in the world, in its forgetting that it is men who make that drive. What makes the drive to technology so

---

[34]Cf. Heidegger's *Gelassenheit* (Pfullingen: Günther Neske, 1959), translated as *Discourse on Thinking* by John M. Anderson and E. Hans Freund (New York: Harper & Row, 1966). In May, 1976, I asked Herbert Marcuse if there were any connection between his ideas in *Eros and Civilization* and elsewhere and Heidegger's notion of "releasement" *(Gelassenheit)*. He replied with a firm "no". Nevertheless, the similarity of these two thinkers on certain key themes is rather striking. On Marcuse's relation to Heidegger, cf. Martin Jay's very helpful book, *The Dialectical Imagination: A History of the Frankfurt School and the Institute of Social Research, 1923-1950* (Boston: Little, Brown, and Company, 1973). Cf. also "Technologie und Wissenschaft bei Heidegger und Marcuse," by Rolf Ahlers in *Zeitschrift fur Philosophie*, XXV (1971), pp. 575-589.

[35]George Grant, "Technology and Empire," a retitled version of "In Defense of North America," a chapter from Grant's book, *Technology and Empire*. The essay appears as one of the selections in the excellent anthology, *Philosophy and Technology*, edited by Carl Mitcham and Robert Mackey (New York: The Free Press, 1972), pp. 187-200. For an interesting criticism of Heidegger's interpretation of technology, cf. Simon Moser, "Toward a Metaphysics of Technology," translated by William Carroll, edited by Carl Mitcham and Robert Mackey, in *Philosophy Today*, XV (Summer, 1971), pp. 129-156.

strong is that it is carried on by men who still identify what
they are doing with the liberation of mankind.[36]

But Grant concludes that we are headed into the "winter of nihilism," in
which the pure will to will becomes the sole content of our actions. It is
just that our emergence into this nihilism has been slower than that of
Europe!

Growing concern over the destruction of the environment as a result
of man's heedless drive for total domination of Nature has also given
rise to criticisms of technology which remind one of Heideggerean
themes. Two excellent articles in this vein are "The Paradox of Man and
Nature: Reflections on Man's Ecological Predicament"[37] by Hwa Yol
Jung, and "Anthropocentrism and the Environmental Crisis"[38] by
George S. Sessions. These authors, along with Heidegger, recognize
that a really *radical* attitude toward the eco-crisis calls for a
fundamental change in our way of existence, or in our way of
understanding man and Nature. Those ecologists who are interested
only in "husbanding" Nature more efficiently (or in such a way as to
enhance man's existence, without using up or destroying the natural
environment), remain within the anthropocentric standpoint.

In his last letter, written on April 19, 1976, to the members of the
Heidegger Conference about to meet at DePaul University, Heidegger
urged those present to concentrate attention on the problem of science
and technology, and in particular on this question: "Is modern science
the foundation of modern technology, as many claim, or is science
already the basic form of technological thinking, that is, the foregone
determining factor and the continuous intervention of technological
representations in the performing and arranging machinations of
modern technology?"[39] In response to Heidegger's appeal the entire
meeting of the Heidegger Conference held at Tulane University in 1977

---

[36]*Ibid.*, p. 193.

[37]Hwa Yol Jung, "The Paradox of Man and Nature: Reflections on Man's Ecological
Predicament" in *The Centennial Review,* XVIII (Winter, 1974), pp. 1-28. Cf. also by Hwa
Yol Jung and Petee Jung, "To Save the Earth" in *Philosophy Today,* XIX (Summer,
1975), pp. 108-117.

[38]George S. Sessions, "Anthropocentrism and the Environmental Crisis" in *The
Humboldt Journal of Social Relations,* II (Fall/Winter, 1974), pp. 1-12.

[39]Translated by Manfred S. Frings.

was devoted to consideration of the questions of science and technology. It may be that Heidegger's most important legacy will be his fundamental insights into the nature and problem of technology. Certainly, no Heidegger scholar can fully understand Heidegger's thinking if he fails to come to terms with this crucial theme.

B) *Marxism*. Ever since Heidegger's "Letter on Humanism" praised Marx's concept of history, considerable attention has been paid to the relation between the two thinkers. Leftist thinkers have usually interpreted Heidegger as a "right wing intellectual," but Heidegger's thinking is far too complicated to be so easily categorized. One of the major figures in the interpretation of Heidegger's relation to Marx is Kostas Axelos. In his recently translated work, *Alienation, Praxis, and Techné in the Thought of Karl Marx*, [40] Axelos provides a Heideggerean critique of Marx's thinking. He shows that for Marx, man is still the focus for everything; history is the story of man's quest to develop the technological capabilities which will enable man to achieve his real, material, human possibilities. Heidegger considers such "humanism" to be the high point of Western subjectivism and metaphysics. As Axelos says, this humanism constitutes

...the culminating point of Western metaphysics; for this metaphysics is what gives birth to science and technique with their readiness to conquer the entire planet in the name of man laboring to satisfy his needs.[41]

He remarks further that

The absolutely productive subject, in the form of the subjects who devote themselves to total social praxis, makes up the (metaphysical) foundation of Marxism and of the planetary technique in the course of which all that is comes to appear more and more as a product, as the result of a *production*, the world itself being simply that which is disclosed through *human activity*.[42]

---

[40]Kostas Axelos, *Alienation, Praxis, and Techné in the Thought of Karl Marx*, translated by Ronald Bruzina (Austin: The University of Texas Press, 1976).
[41]*Ibid.*, p. 226.
[42]*Ibid.*, p. 275.

Axelos thus achieves the *Auseinandersetzung* with Marx which Heidegger never undertook. For Axelos, Marx fails to understand that technology is *not* neutral or value-free, but poses dangers to man in capitalist as well as socialist society. In his work, *Einführung in ein kunftiges Denken,* Axelos notes that "Marx reduces the world to the production of Technik; Heidegger demands that we hold ourselves open to the essence of Technik." [43] But the "essence" (*Wesen*) of technology is the way in which beings are "present" to us in light of Being. Thus, Marx culminates metaphysics because he brings human subjectivism to its pinnacle--and because he is wholly closed to the question of Being.[44]

The Marxist, of course, would respond by saying that Heidegger develops a new "myth of the twentieth century" and merely urges a kind of "receptivity" or "attentiveness" in the face of exploitation of man by man. The means of production (or technology) are said by the Marxist to be destructive only because they are organized as private property. But Heidegger is not unaware of the economic forces at work in the technological world. We read in "What Are Poets For?":

> In place of all the world-content of things that was formerly perceived and used to grant freely of itself, the object-character of technological dominion spreads itself over the earth ever more quickly, ruthlessly, and completely. Not only does it establish all things as producible in the process of production; it also delivers the products of production by means of the market. In self-assertive production, the humanness of man and the thingness of things dissolve into the calculated market value of a market which not only spans the whole earth as a world market, but also, as the Will to Will, trades in the nature of Being and thus subjects all beings to the trade of a calculation that dominates most

---

[43] Kostas Axelos, *Einführung in ein künftiges Denken* (Tübingen: Max Niemeyer, 1966), p. 41. Cf. also the essay by Jean Beaufret, "Le 'Dialogue avec le Marxisme' et la 'Question de la Technique," dedicated to Axelos, in Beaufret's *Dialogue avec Heidegger,* Vol II. *Philosophie moderne* (Paris: Les Editions de Minuit, 1973), pp. 143-181.

[44] As Heidegger says in the interview in *l'Expresse,* "The question of Being is not Marx's question." p. 82.

tenaciously in those areas where there is no need of numbers.[45]

Those familiar with Georg Lukács' brilliant revision of Marx, *History and Class Consciousness,*[46] will detect important similarities between the modes of expression of these two thinkers with regard to the "objectification" of the modern world by capitalist man. Lucien Goldmann, in his recent work, *Lukács et Heidegger,*[47] makes the controversial claim that *Sein und Zeit* is in important ways an attempt to show the inadequacy of Lukács' work (which appeared about four years before *Sein und Zeit*). According to Goldman, Heidegger claims that Lukács' ideas about reification and false-consciousness are ontologically groundless.[48] The concept of *Sorge* (Care) is supposed to provide the ontological underpinning for many Marxist concepts. Herbert Marcuse, in his 1928 essay, "Beiträge zu einer Phänomenologie des Historischen Materialismus,"[49] also makes the claim that *Sein und Zeit* provides the ontological grounding for Marx's theory of history. In the *l'Expresse* interview, Heidegger learns that in 1969 Goldmann was giving a course on the points of convergence between Lukács and Heidegger, and remarks: "I am astonished. And it makes me want to smile. In an issue of *Der Spiegel* from March, 1966, Lukács treated me as a fascist philosopher. Moreover, I don't recall having read Lukács before writing *Being and Time*. No, I did not read it."[50]

It seems to me that interest in the relation between Heidegger and Marx will continue to grow, especially insofar as more and more people

---

[45]Martin Heidegger, "What Are Poets For?", translated by Albert Hofstadter in *Poetry Language, Thought* (New York: Harper & Row, 1971), pp. 114-115. Cf. also p. 135.

[46]George Lukács, *History and Class Consciousness,* translated by Rodney Livingstone (Cambridge: MIT Press, 1971). Cf. in particular the essay "Reification and the Consciousness of the Proletariat," pp. 83-222.

[47]Lucien Goldmann, *Lukács et Heidegger,* posthumous fragments edited by Youssef Ishaghpour (Paris: Editions Denoël, 1973).

[48]*Ibid.,* p. 73.

[49]Herbert Marcuse, "Beiträge zu einer Phänomenologie des Historischen Materialismus," *Philosophische Hefte,* Vol. 1 (1928), pp. 45-68.

[50]*l'Expresse* interview, p. 83. Two writers from Eastern Europe provide their views of the relation of Heidegger to Marx in *Durchblicke* (Frankfurt am Main: Vittorio Klostermann, 1970). Cf. Jan Patočka, "Heidegger vom anderen Ufer," pp. 394-411, and Gajo Petrović, "Der Spruch des Heideggers," pp. 412-436.

become conscious of the problems of technological culture and interested in Marx's claim that technology is only detrimental when misused by greedy human beings. Heidegger, on the other hand, suggests that *human* action to alleviate the situation only tends to strengthen the grip of technological domination; technology (as metaphysical subjectivism) is not within the control of man, but instead man is within the sway of the essence of technology. That is, man is *not* master of his own destiny. But this brings us to the question: what *is* man to *do* in the face of the possible destruction of himself and the planet?

C) *The Question of Praxis.* Many readers of Heidegger eventually become frustrated because they find within his thinking no guidelines for how to act to bring about the new understanding of Being necessary to take us beyond the grip of one-dimensional, technological existence. Heidegger's primary response to such considerations is twofold: 1) technology itself is the *Geschick* (destiny) of Being and to that extent, beyond man's ability to control; but 2) man can at least prepare himself for a new revelation of beings, or for the "return of the gods," by attending to the silent mysteries of what is. Man needs somehow to "will" himself into "releasing" himself from the pure Will to Will. Although Being is primary, man is nevertheless the "shepherd" of Being and can thus try to co-operate in receiving a new destiny. Reinhart Maurer's exceptional essay, "From Heidegger to Practical Philosophy,"[51] provides a penetrating discussion of all of these themes, including the problem of developing an "ethics" in technological culture.

As Maurer remarks:

> After the end of philosophy the "thinking of being" grows out of the difficulty that no satisfactory theory, especially no satisfactory normative theory, of human existence and action can develop within the boundaries of that metaphysic which has become manifest... How one comports himself towards things and men which are not objects and co-

---

[51]Reinhart Maurer, "From Heidegger to Practical Philosophy," translated by Walter E. Wright, in *Idealistic Studies* III (May, 1973), pp. 133-162.

workers in social labor remains undetermined, indeed the danger threatens that the universal manufacture will fill this vacuum. That would mean the total self-alienation of man in the process of the mastery and/or destruction of nature for the purpose of the satisfaction and boundless expansion of human needs, a consumption of things with the corresponding enslavement of man to this process of consumption.[52]

In the interview in *Der Spiegel,* Heidegger tries to explain the task of thinking in effecting change within the world, when he says:

It is not a matter simply of waiting until something occurs to man within the next 300 years, but of thinking ahead (without prophetic proclamations) into the time which is to come, of thinking from the standpoint of the fundamental traits of the present age, which have scarcely been thought through. Thinking is not inactivity but is in itself the action which stands in dialogue with the world mission (*Weltgeschick*). It seems to me that the distinction, which stems from metaphysics, between theory and praxis, and the representation of some kind of transmission between the two, blocks the way to an insight into what I understand by thinking.[53]

The interview shows that Heidegger himself is unwilling to offer man any specific program as a "way out" of the present predicament; nor does he offer much hope that thinking adequate to the situation will be forthcoming. But at least it is clear here and elsewhere in his writings that it is only in a confrontation with the essence of technology, i.e., a full disclosure of this mode of "presencing" of beings, that a satisfactory new way of "dwelling" within the technological world will present itself. Insofar as technology is the destiny and fate of the West, then Western man must learn somehow to exist within this destiny. The task which

---

[52]*Ibid.,* p. 157.
[53]"Only a God Can Save Us." *Der Spiegel* interview, p. 280.

remains for us -- as writers, thinkers, and doers -- is to open ourselves up to whatever insight is made available to us to guide us in entering the new age. The formidable question, posed by Heidegger so often in *What Is Called Thinking?*, is suggested by Nietzsche: is man ready to become the Overman, to assume planetary domination?[54]

5. *Other Developments.* This sketch of certain major themes of particular interest to Heidegger scholars at this time is by no means exhaustive. For those who would like to pursue this matter further, I recommend highly the recently published Heidegger bibliography by Winfried Franzen.[55] Although Franzen's book is not as complete as the *Heidegger-Bibliographie* by Peter Sass,[56] Franzen's book is more valuable because he organizes the great number of cited works topically, *not* chronologically. The bibliography includes numerous references to works dealing with Heidegger and psychology, psychoanalysis, literature, theology, Wittgenstein, Marxism, Japan, France and Italy, the Heidegger "school", and so forth. Of particular help are Franzen's short essays which sketch out the research themes and directions for each of the fields he demarcates. Because he devotes an entire book to the topic, Franzen succeeds in providing fuller coverage of more themes than I have been able to do in this little essay.

Heidegger research continues to grow, in part because of the growing accessibility of translations of his work. There is not time here to discuss upcoming translations, or to provide a critical assessment of existing ones. But interest in Heidegger's thinking is growing primarily because he offers a way of understanding and interpreting the difficulties of being a human being in late twentieth century technological culture. The themes of human authenticity and the problems of achieving that authenticity run through his work even after he goes "beyond" humanism. Each of us is still an issue for himself, particularly in the face of a culture designed to conceal that issue. If we as scholars take

---

[54]Martin Heidegger, *What is Called Thinking?*, translated by Fred D. Wieck and J. Glenn Gray (New York: Harper & Row, 1972).

[55]Winfried Franzen, *Martin Heidegger* (Stuttgart: J. B. Metzlersche Verlagsbuchhandlung, 1976).

[56]Hans-Martin Sass, *Heidegger-Bibliographie* (Meisenheim am Glan: Anton Hain Verlag, 1968).

Heidegger seriously, this means that we must try in our work to surpass mere scholarship. We must *think* the problems he has summoned us to think. We must try to respond to the possibilities of a new understanding of what is. And we must recall that for Heidegger, the distinction between "thinking" (theory) and "acting" (practice) is largely a pseudo-distinction. That means that the Heidegger scholar must learn to *exist* in a way which corresponds to the new understanding *of what* is, especially if we maintain hope for deliverance from the current situation. But who among us is equal to the task?

Michael E. Zimmerman
Newcomb College
Tulane University

TO RE-AWAKEN THE MATTER OF BEING

Martin Heidegger. *Sein und Zeit.* Martin Heidegger
Gesamtausgabe, Band 2. Vittorio Klostermann Verlag
Frankfurt a. M., 1977. 583 pages.*

This new edition of *Sein und Zeit,* published as volume 2 of the
Gesamtausgabe, contains (1) the unchanged text of the separate edition
of *Sein und Zeit,* (2) some 180 marginal notes from Heidegger's own
working copy, (3) some minor corrections of the text (not marked in this
new edition, at Heidegger's direction), and (4) the removal of various
typographical errors, which have remained in the many editions up
until now. The new edition of *Sein und Zeit* was prepared by
FriedrichWilhelm von Herrmann (who will edit the entire first division
of the *Gesamtausgabe:* Published Writings, 1914-1970).

The philosophically significant part of the new edition are the
marginal notes. These are taken solely from Heidegger's copy of the
second edition (1929). Heidegger considered this working copy the most
important among the various copies which he himself used from time to
time; it is the copy which he always used at his "Todtnauberger Hütte"
and which he thus called the "Hüttenexemplar." When he gave
guidelines for selecting the marginal notes in already published works,
he explicitly requested that only this "Hüttenexemplar" be used for the
editing of *Sein und Zeit.* Thus all marginal notes printed in the new
edition are from this copy.

---

*References to *Sein und Zeit* appear in parentheses and include the following
information, in this order: (1) the page number of the work in the *Gesamtausgabe,* (2)
when applicable, the letter of the marginal note in question, and (3) the page number and,
in the case of a marginal note, the appropriate line in the separate edition of *Sein und Zeit*
(Tübingen: Max Niemeyer Verlag, 1967¹¹).

The marginal notes, stretching from 1929 until his death in 1976, are not dated in any way; and there is no external evidence available for any chronological ordering of them, so that any dating of these notes, should that be considered appropriate, would have to emerge from the philosophical *content* of each note.

The notes fit into four groups:

1. explanations and clarifications of the text itself, in which Heidegger improves formulations, clarifies some obstruse expressions, and above all makes more precise some statements that were vague or less thought out,
2. self-critical notes, in which he corrects his own earlier way of expression or criticizes the linguistic-conceptual framework in which his words were indeed embedded,
3. marginal notes made in the context of the turning in his thinking and
4. notes from a later standpoint, in which he rethinks in terms of later insights what was said at this earlier stage.

This division of the marginal notes into four groups is, in some sense, artificial and the fruit of an over-simplification; for none of the notes belongs exclusively to any one of these groups. Rather they are four aspects of a single movement, parts of the one movement of an initial rounding out of the fragmentary work *Sein und Zeit*.[1]

These marginal notes can be seen as an attempt by Heidegger to re-awaken the matter of being. This despite the fact that *Sein und Zeit* already originally, and explicitly, opened with the question of being as central (Do we know what we mean by the word *seiend*? Do we understand the expression "Sein"? -- from the first page of *Sein und Zeit*) and despite the fact that genuine thinking was to be made aware that the whole matter of being, in addition to its not being understood, was wholly forgotten in this age (3;2). Thus Heidegger's notes highlight

---

[1]These notes form only an initial rounding out, for Heidegger's many and prolonged attempts to come to grips with *Sein und Zeit* and its thinking are in the form of sketches and commentaries which he wrote expressly for the purpose of coming to grips with the matter of *Sein und Zeit*. They will appear in a volume of Division IV of the *Gesamtausgabe*. Set against this wealth of notes yet to be published, the ado that we make here and now about this relatively small number of notes may be justified only in that *that* volume of Division IV will probably not be available until the next century!

his own driving concern that the matter of being get re-awakened, that thinking come to grips with it, that it be again at-work in thinking. The marginal notes reveal Heidegger's lifelong preoccupation with *Sein, Seyn, Wahrheit des Seins, Da-sein.*

Why, even after the appearance of *Sein und Zeit,* does the matter of being need to be re-awakened in us? Why does thinking not easily become or remain awake to the issue? (1) The matter of being~~was~~ (is) actually forgotten. It remained hard to get a hold on it even after the appearance of *Sein und Zeit* in 1927, for that work did not (could not) of itself automatically change the situation in which men and thinkers find themselves. (2) The published work of *Sein und Zeit* was left unfinished, so that the balance or roundness intended for the work never came about within the work. The work did not unfold fully, in order (partially) to take care of apparent pitfalls--into existentialistic, ethical, or anthropological interpretation. What was said in *Sein und Zeit* remained too cryptic for the thinker who was less capable of what in Heidegger's thought was at issue for Heidegger's own thinking as he started on the pathway of thinking. *Sein und Zeit* was not (could not be) totally explicit; for he was a pathfinder in thinking: he had to forge new ways through the jungle of encrusted philosophical tradition. He through his thinking had to light up the landscape and make it visible for the first time. We today forget that the pathways of thinking which we have as a result of Heidegger's thinking *were not there at all* for him. Philosophical thought was shaped anew by Heidegger's thinking, and this new shaping did not have a pre-scribed mold.[2]

From this we gain insight into the necessarily fragmentary character of *Sein und Zeit,* then and now, stemming from an insight into the fragmentary character of Heidegger's whole "unified" thinking. This fragmentary character has major philosophical implications.

Granted this fragmentary character, the marginal notes do not portray any fulfillment or completion of what was started on the early part of Heidegger's itinerary of thinking. Nor do they portray any revolutionary alterations-- in the literal sense of "changing into an *other (alter)*" -- in what he said, i.e. thought, in *Sein und Zeit* as originally

---

[2]Cf. in this regard Walter Biemel, *Martin Heidegger in Selbstzeugnissen und Bilddokumenten* (Reinbek bei Hamburg: Rowohlt Taschenbuch Verlag, 1973), p. 8.

published. In my judgment there is no major revelation of a character other than that of his whole effort of thinking; there is nothing to shock us, to set us back on our heels.[3] Rather the marginal notes contain signifigant clarifications, which portray a continuation of his thought and in which new turns are made and his one guiding question gets reshaped in accordance with the matter for thinking as it calls to him along the way. These significant clarifications, in turn, call on us to think.

What does Heidegger say, i.e. think, in the marginal notes which can (1) shed light on our understanding of the work *Sein und Zeit* as published and (2) help us toward an insight into the pathway of this thinking as a whole, i.e. involving his own re-reading of *Sein und Zeit* from a perspective gained further along on his way? How can we gain a grasp of these marginal notes as more than 180 words, phrases, or sentences somehow dumped together, as more than just so many appendages to an already difficult philosophical text?

Carefully staying with these at first quite isolated notes, our thinking in measured pace discovers a double thread revealed in them. This double thread pulls them together without binding them. One strand of this thread is their common character of making distinctions: their immediate purpose seems to be to make distinctions, to show differences, in an attempt to clarify the text and the issues therein. For the most part the marginal notes make distinctions in what was originally undistinguished or unclearly distinguished. But within the distinguishing, along with it, the other strand of the thread emerges: a

---

[3]There is at first glance one notable exception to this (117c; 87,1. 31), where Heidegger notes that what he originally wrote about langugage is "untrue," that the founding (grounding) of the being of words and language on meanings (Bedeutungen) is not a correct structuring of the issue.In *Sein und Zeit* in 1927 Heidegger identified *Sprache* with the secondary order, expressing already given significations: Significance (Bedeutsamkeit) is the ontological condition for the possibility of Dasein's disclosing "significations (Bedeutungen)"; "these in their turn found the possible being of words and language." The marginal note reads: "Untrue. Language is not stacked up [as in building a house one story is stacked on another], but *is* the originary and essential unfolding (Wesen) of truth as *Da*." If we understand that the thinking on language -- on *Rede* in *Sein und Zeit* and on *Sprache* later -- is always in light of the question of being, then we gain "insight into" Heidegger's note as a deeper understanding of the matter of being, a clarification of an issue that was for the most part unthought earlier, rather than thought otherwise.

gathering of the import of the distinctions into that one matter that unifies all of Heidegger's work of thinking: "To head for one star, that alone."[4]

To understand the marginal notes of *Sein und Zeit* is to understand the dialectic (interplay) between this distinguishing and this gathering. This thread -- of the distinguishing and gathering, of the distinguishing that gathers, of the gathering within the distinguishing -- takes us from the beginning of Heidegger's thinking to the place where it came to a close and then back again to the beginning.

With these reflections in mind we now focus on a series of distinctions for the sake of what is gathered in each distinction and what is gathered in all of them, taken as a whole.

(1) *Dasein and subject.* Heidegger's analytic of Dasein is not at all intended to make more concrete the acts of pure consciousness as thought in the transcendental phenomenology of Husserl. On the contrary: all determination of subject and subjectivity rests in Dasein. Thinking man as Dasein -- or, in accord with the language of these notes, man as in Da-sein -- is fundamental and essentially different from any determination of man as subject.

The ground for the whole matter expressed in the analytic of Dasein cannot be gained by a phenomenological correction of the concept of subject, made (makeable) only after the conceptual structure belonging to subject has already been set up.[5] Rather the thinking of Dasein is a leap, a breakthrough; the "leap into Da-sein" (274a; 207, 1.10) is necessary, for otherwise the analytic of Dasein gets reduced to something needing that firm and unshakeable (i.e. clear and distinct) foundation which contemporary science and "intellectual thought" have come to expect, even to demand, of all knowledge. The leap wants to say that man is always already in the world, belonging to being. The "scandal of philosophy" is that it has become satisfied to begin by

---

[4]"Auf einen Stern zugehen, nur dieses." *Aus der Erfahrung des Denkens* (Pfullingen: Verlag Günther Neske, 1965), p. 7.

[5]This is precisely how Husserl himself understood Heidegger's analytic of Dasein: as a concrete, phenomenological anthropology thought on the basis of his own phenomenology of transcendental consciousness. Cf. Friedrich-Wilhelm von Herrmann, *Subjekt und Dasein* (Frankfurt a.M.: Vittorio Klostermann Verlag, 1974), p. 20.

establishing a subject and then "knowing" everything in terms of the subject, to think subject as measure for all things. This radical leap shows that "subject" is not as such, but is always already Dasein: being. in the world and Da-sein: belonging to being.

Although Husserl's phenomenology offers a more in-depth understanding of the matter of the Cartesian *cogito,* it still remains a philosophy of consciousness with man the subject as measure. What Heidegger did not explicitly state in this regard in 1927 gets expressly said in the course of making these marginal comments. The establishing of subject as measure is essentially what takes place in Husserl's philosophy: the transcendental subject is the basis for whatever is, the outer world. What Heidegger writes in *Sein und Zeit* about Descartes, putting Descartes's attempt to solve the problem of the "I and the world" into question, he means to say also about all of Husserl's works, that at work within them is basically a reduction of the being of what is in the world to something on hand (vorhanden), whose being-character is determined by a prior and already established subject (132a; 98, 1.35).

That is to say, Heidegger already at the beginning of his encounter with Husserl (primarily through *Logische Untersuchungen* and throughout his years of daily personal contact with Husserl) differed fundamentally with him. In none of its shapes can Heidegger's analytic of Dasein be identified with Husserlian phenomenology.

Specifically, Husserl's construction of "ontologies" reduces all being to *something* that is, i.e. a something in the perceived world, something "on hand" (213a; 160, 1.25). The essential problematic of transcendental phenomenology is "the transcendental problem of world,"[6] i.e. the constitution of world on the basis of transcendental subjectivity. For Husserl phenomenology is analysis of phenomena, which get disclosed in acts of transcendental consciousness. For Heidegger, on the other hand, Dasein names a way of being before any distinction of world as innerwordly phenomena and of transcendental consciousness. This way of being, that is always already there, is understood first as being-in-the-world and then as belonging to (in) being (Da-sein, cf. third distinction below).

---

[6]Eugen Fink, "Die phänomenologische Philosophie E. Husserls in der gegenwärtigen Kritik," *Studien zur Phänomenologie 1930-1939* (Den Haag: Martinus Nijhoff, 1966), p. 119.

Whenever Heidegger calls Descartes and modern philosophy of subjectivity into question, he is also calling Husserl's phenomenology into question, insisting that it is essentially within that tradition. "Both titles, 'subjectivity' and 'transcendental,' show that 'phenomenology' falls deliberately and decisively within the tradition of modern philosophy..."[7]

The being of Dasein is, first, to be always already in the world; Dasein is "historical being in the world" (56b; 41,1.21). Dasein is always already directed toward world, "but not as an I-oriented action of the subject, rather: Dasein and Sein" (117b; 87,1.25). Dasein does not exist as subject or individual (194b; 146,1.8).

In several notes Heidegger clarifies that it is not "through" man that the lighting up of what is is possible.[8] Man is not the producer (177b; 133,1.5) or the measure for what is (10b and 11b; 7,1.27 and 8,1.25); rather Dasein is the region in which what is gets revealed. (All these references which Heidegger makes in the marginal notes show up the extraordinary difficulty that thinking has when it tries to understand the dimension of Dasein and tries to grasp how this dimension is more originary than that of all philosophies of subjectivity or consciousness.) This distinction, and especially saying what Dasein really is, calls for a more precise thinking of how the revealing takes place, of what it means to be "Da" (cf. third distinction below).

(2) *Dasein and man.* But first thinking must focus on a very important distinction belonging to the heart of philosophy itself. *Dasein* is the name for the being who is man. But what gets expressed in the word *Dasein* is precisely not man as a being who simply is, but rather man in terms of his ownmost being, his essential character as man, or: man in his belonging together with being. *Dasein* is then not the word for man, but the word for being.

Man lives in the world without always being appropriately man: man is not always engaged in his own being, in his proper way of being as man. Man is not always, Heidegger says, a being "of" Da-sein (W 112a).

---

[7]Martin Heidegger, "Mein Weg in die Phänomenologie," *Zur Sache des Denkens* (Tübingen: Max Niemeyer Verlag, 1969), p. 84.

[8]Cf. note in "Was ist Metaphysik?" *Wegmarken,* Martin Heidegger Gesamtausgabe, IX (Frankfurt a.M.: Vittorio Klostermann Verlag, 1976), 115e. Hereafter "W."

Dasein is man who cultivates his ownmost being, who is engaged in his own way of being. Man who is not a man "of" Dasein gets off the track (derailed) in the midst of the world that is. Man "out of" Dasein takes a rest, becomes static (194a; 145, last line). For man who is not in or of Dasein, everything is taken for granted. Nothing is uncanny. Man who is not of Dasein is "at home," at rest (125a; 93, last line). He finds everything, including the meaning of that by which everything is, to be a matter of course. When asked about understanding it, his reply is: "Of course!" He finds everything, including the most questionable matter, understandable without hesitation or explanation. He is unsuspecting, and the matter (every matter) is harmless.

It is central to the whole movement of Dasein, both as initially understood in *Sein und Zeit* and as later thought in terms of Ereignis, that man as Dasein (man of Dasein) feels himself *not* at home, that man is restless, is continually called upon to think.

Man becomes man of Dasein -- or man is as Dasein -- when he is awake to the matter, when he is restlessly not yet something that is his to become, when he is on the way, when being on the way is at work in his very character.[9]

"Become what you are," but "you are as *becoming*" (194a; 145, last line): become one who is becoming. The crucial movement, then, is: If man as Dasein is to become, is on the way, then the measure by which he becomes what he is not yet and is to be is outside himself. That is, Dasein -- or man "of" Dasein -- is in the movement of which man is not the measure.

(3) *Dasein and Da-sein.* There are two meanings for the words "being of Dasein" as used in *Sein und Zeit,* and they are not at all clearly distinguished in the original work. To distinguish them now serves to focus squarely on the matter of Dasein, which is: Da-sein. So the matter of Dasein is the matter of being.

Perhaps the most significant distinction that Heidegger makes throughout the many years during which he wrote these marginal notes

---

[9]*Sein und Zeit,* 310 (233): "Im Dasein steht, solange es ist, je noch etwas aus, was es sein kann und wird." "As long as Dasein is, there is something in it that remains open, something that it can and will be (become)."

is his regular and consistent use of a hyphen in the word *Da-sein*. One might ask (1) whether this is a wholly new thought, alien to the original work *Sein und Zeit*, or (2) whether it is a clarification of the original work and was originally meant in each case. To speak dramatically: Should *Sein und Zeit* now be re-written (reprinted) always using a hyphen in the word *Da-sein*?

Before answering such a question, we are called upon to understand the meaning of the hyphen. First, it is a clarification of the matter of Dasein in *Sein und Zeit*. Secondly, it makes distinct the ontological character of man's being in Da-sein. Thirdly, it serves to show that the three matters of man, Dasein, and Da-sein are to be distinguished.

"Man is delivered up to Da-sein, is born into its hold," that means: "into the belonging to being itself" (179a; 134,1.20). Da-sein is that "in which man unfolds essentially" (117a; 87,1.18). Finally, in a note to "Vom Wesen des Grundes," Heidegger writes: "Dasein undergoes... the essential unfolding of truth and thus establishes the possibility of being man as being man *in* Dasein!" (W 164a).

As a matter for thinking, Dasein is never merely being-in-the-world, but always already points beyond to the belonging together with being, i.e. Dasein points beyond to Da-sein. Being-in-the-world includes within it the relation to being as a whole (16a; 12,1.11). When Dasein is engaged in its ownmost way to be (its essential character as Dasein), then it belongs-together with that realm we call up to now: being. Man and being belong together, belong to each other, and are held thus.

Whereas this meaning of Dasein was always in the background and was always meant along with the meaning of Dasein as historical being in the world, it was not always explicit. The first distinction that the analytic of Dasein made was that Dasein is not of the character of subjectivity, that Dasein meant an "intentionality" always already there before consciousness. This character of Dasein was named being-in-the-world or disclosedness (Erschlossenheit) whereby the world of things at hand bore significance before consciousness or subjectivity: Dasein's commerce with things was in terms of a whole of significations already there *within* the handling of things in the world. This is the character of Daesin as always already before consciousness.

But the analytic of Dasein has always to do with the disclosure that being is, with man's engaging himself in his own being, which takes in more than man is, which goes beyond the realm of man, which cannot be grasped either positively or negatively in terms of consciousness; for this "being" does not have the character of a something. This is the only way in which our inherited way of thinking can handle any matter.

Sein und Zeit has clearly visible in it the first meaning of Dasein as historical being in the world prior to consciousness. In the marginal notes, then, Heidegger tries again and again to bring to light the second, more essential meaning of Da-sein as the place for the disclosure of being, as belonging to/with being. He does this by writing *Da-sein* with a hyphen. This relatively new way of speaking brings into words that man's being (as Dasein) does not rest in Dasein (man) alone, but rather that its full meaning consists in his holding open the disclosure of being itself (Da-sein).

Since the matter of being has yet to be re-awakened, we have little understanding of this being-in-being that Da-sein is. Therefore thinking tends to grasp it in terms of something it already knows, i.e. in terms of man. This can be done if thinking focuses on the finitude of man, for the belonging-in-being says precisely that: that man is not his own measure. In this regard, Heidegger's notes focus on the being-toward-death that is Dasein's essential finitude, in order to clarify that the finitude of Dasein is not the finitude of man (W 175a). Man's finitude is indeed his dying; Dasein's finitude is being-toward-death, is belonging-together with the being of not being, or with the possibility of not being (311c; 234,1.9). Da-sein is man as he stands in the full closure that being is, as he gains insight into that beyond himself which is his measure. Da-sein is not the name for something from which the matter of being can be "deduced," but rather is the place (Statte) for understanding being (11b; 8,1.25). Dasein has a special role in the unfolding of the matter of being beyond being the one who can ask the question (ascertain the problem); Dasein has a special role in being the one who, at-play with being, brings being into play, into the play of resonance (9c; 7,1.7). Heidegger writes: Da-sein: as held in being, as the relationship (10a; 7,1.22); for if Dasein is the being to be explicated in terms of the matter of being (the purpose of *Sein und Zeit* as expressed in 1927), it is not the measure of being -- being is not "read off" Dasein (10b; 7,1.27). Da-sein is *Instandigkeit:* penetration, standing into (being) (295a; 223,1.5).[10]

---

[10]Many other marginal notes repeat this same thought. Cf. 56c (42,1.1); 57a (42,1.22); 58a (43,1.25); 204a (153,1.31); 190a (143,1.1); 244b (183, 1,36); 275b (207, 1.33); W 169.

We can perhaps return now to the question raised earlier: Should *Sein und Zeit* be rewritten with Da-sein everywhere? No, because the meaning of the word *Dasein* as it appears in *Sein und Zeit* is not always explicitly that of Da-sein (in this profound sense). The movement from subject to Dasein as being in the world was somehow first necessary before the movement from Dasein to Da-sein, a movement that gets accomplished, at least partially, in the marginal notes to the original work.

Granted our uneasiness in speaking about being thus, i.e. not knowing very well what we are doing, one thing becomes clear: When we speak of man as in Da-sein, we are in no way speaking of man in terms of himself or as his own measure -- as in speaking of I, *cogito,* subject, or consciousness. The matter of being and of Da-sein breaks through the conceptual structure of subjectivity. Man's proper understanding of being makes of him more than the man who will die; his understanding of being is his being in Da-sein: being in being.

As invariably happens when any thinking grapples with Heidegger's thought, we are confronted with the matter of being and the virtual impossibility of letting the word say the richness and originary character of the matter of being. Not that the word is wrong (it isn't) or has been surpassed (it hasn't been), but rather that the encroachment of traditional (even philosophical) prejudices is almost too strong. (Even Husserl in his attempt at the greatest possible philosophical rigor could not think being aside from its being a something -- 213a; 160,1.25).

(4) *Being and the being of what is (Sein and Sein des Seienden).* Usually we have understood the meaning of the ontological difference as a difference between being and that which is (Seiendes). Two marginal notes to the first pages of *Sein und Zeit* question any such conceptual scheme which we "Heidegger scholars" have adopted in order to understand the matter of "being." "Being" as the most general concept (Tò ὄν) is not that being of Da-sein just brought into words above, as that which is man's measure and into which man penetrates, with which man is engaged. It is rather the being of what is (die Seiendheit des Seienden) (4a; 3,1.9).

Òυσία has a twofold meaning: (1) that which is (das Seiende) and (2) the being of that which is (das Seiend-sein des Seienden, Sein des Seienden) (120a; 90,1.3). Being as the being of what is is not something like what is (Seiendes). But -- and here is Heidegger's thoughtprovoking clarification -- it is also not something like that rich and originary being that gets called *Anwesenheit, Lichtung;* ἀλήθεια or *Ereignis.* To understand *this* matter of being, such conceptualization of *Sein* and *Seiendes* is of no help (5a; 4,1.9). The "difference" here is in terms of this more originary realm (named also: *Seyn*), "no longer as the being *of what is* (des Seienden)" (W 134c).

Being (Seyn) does not lend itself to -- i.e. we cannot think the matter with -- the conceptual structure of *Sein* and *Seiendes.* The ontological difference in its static form -- naming the difference between being and what is -- is not applicable when thinking the more originary being (Seyn).

(5) *The truth of being.* What must this being mean? What is the truth of being? The ontological difference between "being" and what is gives way in fundamental thinking to the matter of the truth of being, the being which belongs-together with Dasein (and constitutes Da-sein), being which grants or gives forth the phenomenon, while itself remaining hidden.

In this being there is a new character; a movement of granting and withdrawing. It is the onefold of revealing-hiding. It is named ἀλήθεια, *Anwesenheit, Lichtung, Ereignis.*

What is the theme of phenomenology in the originary sense given to it in Heidegger's thinking? What is the phenomenon, that which gets seen from out of itself for what it is of itself, in that thinking lets it be seen as such? This phenomenon, Heidegger writes in the original text of *Sein und Zeit,* is something "which for the most part and initially does *not* show itself, which in opposition to what shows itself initially and for the most part is *hidden;* but at the same time it is something which belongs essentially to what shows itself for the most part and initially, belongs to it to such an extent that it constitutes its meaning and ground" (47; 35). A note in the margin reads: "Wahrheit des Seins." The truth of being images what does not show itself in the "phenomenon" or the showing, but which belongs essentially to it as that which gives it its meaning. The truth of being is that which allows or gives forth what is shown, but which never shows *itself.*

This, then, is the matter of being that needs to be re-awakened in thinking. It is called the truth of being -- and then simply, but enigmatically: Ereignis. The marginal notes make two brief references to Ereignis: (1) truth of being as Ereignis (51a; 38,1.12) and (2) Anwesenheit (Ankunft und Ereignis): "presence (coming and Ereignis)" (312a; 235,1.16).

(6) *Ereignis.* Given the central place that the thought of Ereignis has in Heidegger's thinking, it is of great importance that the matter of Ereignis be dealt with here, (1) in order to gather the several moments of the "unified" thinking expressed in the marginal notes, (2) in order to understand *Sein und Zeit* within the perspective of the thinking of Ereignis, and (3) in order to highlight what Heidegger's published works have shown: a dilemma and ambiguity in the word *being.* Should we speak of being or not? Should we rather say Anwesenheit, ἀλήθεια Ereignis? Or can we think -- does Heidegger think -- the matter while still using the word *being?*

Heidegger focuses on the *matter* of being with the *word* Ereignis more in the marginal notes to *Brief über den Humanismus* than in those to *Sein und Zeit.* We therefore turn to the marginal notes of that essay. Heidegger writes there that a way was begun in 1936 which tried simply to say the truth of being (W 313a). The leading word for that way of thinking, the leading word for his thinking since 1936, is: Ereignis (W 316a). This new way was to think the truth of being, to think the nearness, the ec-static standing within the truth of being. That is the meaning of *Eigentlichkeit:* being appropriately (as one's ownmost way to be) in terms of Ereignis.

Nearness is being; being shows itself as nearness. *This* way to think being is: being as Ereignis (W 342a).

> This turn [taken in 1936] is not a change of the standpoint of *Sein und Zeit* [viz. the question of being -- marginal note 328c], but rather within the turn the thinking attempted there first gets to the place of the dimension from which *Sein und Zeit* is experienced -- and indeed experienced in the fundamental experience of the forgetting of being (W328).

Here Heidegger adds the note: "Forgetting -- Λήθη -- hiding - withdrawal -- Enteignis: Ereignis" (W 328d).

Heidegger deliberately refrained at first from this way of speaking (in terms of Ereignis) (W 313a, 321a). There is no reason given. Perhaps it was his conviction that an undue focus on the word by non-hearers would only misplace the matter for thinking. Or perhaps his own thinking needed to grow ripe for getting said in terms of Ereignis.

There are several moments in the thinking of Ereignis which must be thought as carefully and as precisely as possible in order to gather those moments in the marginal notes into their one unifying source.

(a) Man is not his own measure. Rather, his own finitude, expressed in the closed-off character of death as the possibility of not being at all, leads him to think that which is beyond himself and by which he is appropriately man. The state of affairs, viz. his own finitude and the appropriateness of a measure outside himself, calls on man to think. When he heeds this measuring by which he is measured, then there is opened up a region in which man, awakened and awake, is drawn along toward the accomplishing of what is his to become.

Man's experience of not being his own measure is an originary aspect of Ereignis: The experience of not-being-at-home is that primordial step man takes out of his usual blindness into the possibility of becoming what it is his to become essentially. This experience of the not-settled character in man Heidegger calls in a marginal note. Enteignis (252a; 189,1.33). Man's not fitting is an original characteristic of his being. Man is to become fitting, to befit himself in terms of Ereignis. It belongs to Ereignis as its proper mark "that it brings man as the one who hears (undergoes) being, in that he stands within proper time, into his own. Thus befitted, man belongs in Ereignis."[11]

Man's true character is in Ereignis, in the character that is his own as being appropriately fitted in Ereignis. Thus fitted, man cultivates his own being, i.e. is at work in the being of Ereignis.

(b) This belonging that belongs to the awake man's work of befitting is the belonging character that belongs to Ereignis. Therefore: Ereignis cannot be conceptualized or set up over against us, even only as something to be thought. Thinking remains preparatory in that it cannot ever gain the kind of comprehension of Ereignis that it

---

[11]"Zeit und Sein," *Zur Sache des Denkens*, p. 24.

(thinking) in its calculative mode tends toward. Given its rootedness in metaphysical and subjectivistic thinking, all thinking is limited in its attempt to think, i.e. say, Ereignis. *And yet Ereignis is.* Therefore thinking is directive, not encompassing.

(c) Ereignis is not "Ereignis itself," for what is thought in Ereignis is precisely some realm that cannot be singled out like that. Such singularization leads to an absolutizing -- and a concretizing as something (a being, even the highest); this is precisely what happened as long as Heidegger tried to say the matter with "Sein" and "Sein selbst." The singularization of the absolute was unavoidable as long as the matter was said in terms of being, being itself, and man's relation to being (W 321a). Ereignis is (1) non-sayable in this way, but also (2) non-perfectible, although our thinking wants perfection.

(d) Ereignis grants and appropriates. (1) It grants to man to be as he is to become. It is at work in the befitting that takes place as man, growing aware of his finitude and becoming uneasy about his own blind accepting of what is, gets into a movement that takes him to his ownmost character as man. (2) It grants also the being of what is, in its many shapes throughout the history of thinking. It is at work in the emergence of that by which things are; it is the difference that opens up.

(e) Ereignis at the same time withdraws, keeps to itself. Ereignis is never revealed as such; it only reveals, lets be seen. In a sense all that we can say is that we know it by its works. In another sense "it" isn't at all. *Ereignis ereignet.*

(f) To get any foothold in the realm in question, we turn, as Heidegger does at the end of the essay "Zeit und Sein," to the chronologically first way of saying the same: ἀλήθεια, coming out of hiddenness, remaining hidden, from this hidden shelter showing what is in its true character, as revealed. The task at the end of philosophy is to experience ἀλήθεια as disclosure in the Greek sense, and then beyond the Greek sense, to think ἀλήθεια as the lighting of the self-hiding. Such a thinking, Heidegger says, ought to be "nüchtern," nocturnal, as the night, reflective, not being torn away and blinded by passion (e.g. the passion of reason), reticent.[12]

The difference between analytical (calculative) thinking and genuine thinking is discovered in the enigma of Ereignis. For in that enigma there is almost always the danger of contradiction. When we think calculatively, we hang on one horn of the dilemma, i.e. we remain on one side of the matter. This is the movement in thought that we as men inaugurate and carry out. But when we are moved by the matter itself (when we respond to the matter's call upon us), then the enigmatic "contradiction" gets resolved, by thinking's being at the same time on both horns of the dilemma and on no horn at all -- yet remaining in accord with the matter. For example, calculative analyzing wants to resolve the tension in the matter and can do so only by removing, in analysis, the twofold and by unduly focusing exclusively on the one. But for genuine thinking, genuinely carried out, the dilemma ceases to matter.

This paper comes appropriately to a close by calling to mind a somewhat poetic, pregnant note which was written in the margin in conjunction with the *project* of "Zeit und Sein" as it is listed at the end of the Introduction of *Sein und Zeit* (53a; 39, last line). This note, imaging the many convolutions of Heidegger's way, can be seen as one way to say the whole of Heidegger's way of thinking.

> Die transzendenthafte Differenz.
> Die Überwindung des Horizontes als solchen.
> Die Umkehr in die Herkunft.
> Das Anwesen aus dieser Herkunft.

> Difference in terms of transcendence (as man's
>   ecstatic standing within being).
> Overcoming horizon as such.
> Turning back into the source.
> Presencing from out of this source.

(Source: that from which thinking and being is accomplished and upon

---

[12]"Das Ende der Philosophie und die Aufgabe des Denkens," *Zur Sache des Denkens*, p. 79.

which it is, must be, built. Origin: beginnings.)

The turn that thinking takes is to the source, to the beginnings which upholds thinking, but which is not itself revealed. Ereignis is Heidegger's way of somehow gathering up and ordering the matter for thinking. That is, we thinkers must stay with the matter of Ereignis, as giving the "matter of being" the particular structure and constellation which it had for Heidegger since 1936.

But what of the call to think the matter of being as $\dot{\alpha}\lambda\dot{\eta}\theta\epsilon\iota\alpha$? Must thinking turn to $\dot{\alpha}\lambda\dot{\eta}\theta\epsilon\iota\alpha$ only to turn back necessarily to Ereignis? Perhaps, for Ereignis is the same and yet not the same as $\dot{\alpha}\lambda\dot{\eta}\theta\epsilon\iota\alpha$ (for it is also a *return* from $\dot{\alpha}\lambda\dot{\eta}\theta\epsilon\iota\alpha$). In the same sense we learn that we are not to get tangled up in the *Ereignis,* but rather to think and respond to the matter of being. What word it may have remains open. It is rather the issue that matters. All thinking remains preparatory.

Exegetically, is the new edition of *Sein und Zeit* the beginning of a new work? Do the notes show a new interpretation that was not present at all in *Sein und Zeit* as originally published? Do the notes comprise a new thought, essentially other than the thought of *Sein und Zeit* of 1927? Or are the marginal notes more for clarification/elucidation of what was there in *Sein und Zeit,* but veiled, vague and less precisely thought? Do the marginal notes want to say what was meant but not stated in *Sein und Zeit?* This exegetical question is external to the genuinely philosophical matter at issue and as such cannot receive an appropriate answer. For the answer to the question lies within the genuinely philosophical, and in the philosophical realm the question has no bearing. The question for philosophical thinking then and now is: How must we think the matter of being?

Kenneth Maly

GETTING TO THE TOPIC:
THE NEW EDITION OF *WEGMARKEN*

Martin Heidegger, *Wegmarken,* second expanded edition
with marginal notes, edited, Friedrich-Wilhelm von
Herrmann (*Gesamtausgabe, I. Abteilung: Veröffentliche
Schriften 1914-1970, Band 9*). Vittorio Klostermann
Verlag, Frankfurt/Main, 1976. 487 pages.

Apart from the editor's epilogue this volume has three main features which distinguish it from the first edition of *Wegmarken*
(1967).[1] First and of greatest interest, it bears some 180 (lettered)
footnotes gleaned from the margins of Heidegger's personal copies
of the essays. Whereas the actual selection of these marginalia was
left to the editor, Heidegger himself laid down the rules, namely,
that those glosses were not to be printed which either have meaning
only for Heidegger or are not understandable by his readers. Secondly, the volume duly notes the changes which Heidegger quietly
and controversially made in the 1949 edition of his 1943 *"Nachwort
zu 'Was ist Metaphysik?'"* and which he publically acknowledged

---

[1] Apparatus: (1) All abbreviations of Heidegger's works follow the standard "List of
Symbols" in Richardson, *Heidegger: Through Phenomenology to Thought,* p. xxxi.
(2) Numbers in parentheses indicate pages in the two editions of *Wegmarken.* For
example, (485) or (124, 159) refer to pages in the new edition; (316=148.3) means that
on page 316 of the new edition there is a footnote which glosses page 148 *line 3* of the
old edition. (3) In the Appendix, e.g., "114=12.4: vor das Seiende → vor Sein des
Seienden" means that on page 114 of the new edition there is a note which glosses
page 12, line 4 of the old, specifically, "vor das Seiende" is annotated by "vor Sein
des Seienden."

only in the 1975 edition. The later changes remain embodied in the text, but the original phrases are recorded in nine (numbered) footnotes. Thirdly, this new edition contains three additional essays which have appeared elsewhere: the *"Anmerkungen zu Karl Jaspers 'Psychologie der Weltanschauungen' "* (1919/21) published in 1975 and the two theology essays from 1927 and 1964 published in 1970 as *Phänomenologie und Theologie*. There are other, minor changes in this volume. The list of sources has some new but insignificant information; the essays are arranged in chronological order (exception: theology-1964 appears as an appendix to theology-1927); and the pagination of the first edition is given in the margins for easy cross-reference. A warm dedication to the late Rembrandt scholar, Kurt Bauch, Heidegger's colleague at Freiburg since 1933, graces the volume.

There is another kind of change which scholars may find troubling. In his epilogue the editor writes: "Several small textual changes which serve only for clarification were taken over from [Heidegger's] personal copies, but on the author's instructions were not to be expressly noted" (485). Without combing the text, I have no way of reporting which these are.[2] But I found another change, hardly of any significance, but an unstated change nonetheless. Note "b" on p. 134 refers to § 22 of *Die Grundprobleme der Phänomenologie* for discussion of the ontological difference. However, in Heidegger's autograph of that course, which he personally showed me on 12 May 1971, that section is numbered § 16. The discrepancy is due to the fact that in Heidegger's autograph the numbered sections begin only *after* the Introduction, whereas in von Herrmann's published edition of that course the Introduction itself gets divided into six more sections so that § 16 of the autograph becomes § 22 of the published text. This is trivial, but what might the other changes be?

This is a difficult book to review. For one thing, most of the essays have been available for some time, all but two—the Jaspers piece and *"Hegel und die Griechen"*—in English translation.[3] To discuss

---

[2]I have since found two: (1) The word "wesenhaft" is added before "weiter" (331=162.4); (2) to the phrase "Das Wesen der Wahrheit" is added "als Richtigkeit der Aussage verstanden" (186=81.20).

[3]An excellent new anthology, Martin Heidegger, *Basic Writings,* ed. David Farrell Krell (New York, Harper and Row, 1977) contains new translations of WM, WW, and

the Jaspers essay would require a whole article, and David Krell's excellent commentary on it ("Towards *Sein und Zeit*" JBSP, VI, 1975) is readily available. That leaves the footnotes, 180 of them, unindexed, most of them not complete sentences, many as suggestively enigmatic as the oracles of Delphic Apollo, who "neither shows nor hides but gives a sign" (Heraclitus, Fr. 93). Nor are these marginalia accurately datable (cf. 486 f.). Supposedly any mention of *Ereignis* places a marginal note later than 1936, but I will show below that the word begins to emerge as early as 1928 (cf. also US 260 n.). One could offer statistics on the marginalia. Four essays have none at all (the Jaspers essay, theology-1927, the lecture on Leibnitz from the 1928 course of that name, and the 1939 essay on *physis* in Aristotle). Three essays have a minimum of glosses, none important (*"Zur Seinsfrage"* has one, *"Hegel und die Griechen"* has two, theology-1964 has one). The Plato and the Kant essays have nine and eleven notes respectively, *"Vom Wesen der Wahrheit"* has fourteen. The five most heavily noted are *"Vom Wesen des Grundes,"* *"Was ist Metaphysik?"* as well as the *Nachwort* and *Einleitung,* and the *"Humanismusbrief,"* all with about thirty notes apiece. The glosses concerning the alterations in the *Nachwort* clarify very little for this reader.

I shall reserve an appendix at the end for a listing of selected marginalia. Within this essay I shall attempt to place some of the important glosses into a reading of Heidegger's overall project, and I shall concentrate particularly on how and whence Heidegger derives the word and concept *"Ereignis."* First, then, what Heidegger's topic is *not*, secondly, what it *is*, and finally, why it is called *Ereignis*.

I shall risk saying that there is almost nothing in these marginalia which cannot be found more substantially and clearly in the published writings. (And after reading transcripts of Heidegger's courses from 1920 through 1952, I predict the same for a good deal of the *Gesam-*

HB. *The Piety of Thinking,* ed. and trans. James Hart and John Maraldo (Bloomington: Indiana U.P., 1976) brings the two theology essays into English. I have translated the Aristotle essay: "On the Being and Conception of *Physis* in Aristotle's *Physics* B, 1" in *Man and World* IX (1976) 219-270, and I have completed a new translation of the Plato essay which I am happy to supply to interested scholars in dittographed form.

tausgabe.) But if the glosses in this volume will satisfy no treasure hunter searching for the "secret" of Heidegger's thought, they will help scholars to test their hypotheses about that scandal of all scandals: Just what was Heidegger talking about? For the longest time it has been customary to say that Heidegger's topic is the Being or Being-question left forgotten by the tradition. But for one thing, neo-Thomists regularly publish articles proving irrefutably that Being (*esse*) is not forgotten in Aquinas (just as Protestants maintain it is not forgotten in Luther[4]), and for another, Heidegger himself said in 1966 that he no longer liked to use the word *das Sein* (*Heraklit*, p. 18). He even took to crossing it out (~~*Sein*~~: 369 f.) or substituting the older form *Seyn* (124, 159, 169, 237 etc.), and in this volume he even crosses *Seyn* out (306)! If to name Heidegger's subject matter we fall back on *"Ereignis"* (*"seit 1936 das Leitwort meines Denkens,"* 316=148.3; cf. US 260 n.), we only explain *ignotum per ignotius*. What then can we do? I suggest the employment of a heuristic device to designate what Heidegger was after. Let us call it simply "the topic" (as in the phrase "Get to the topic!"—*'Zur Sache selbst!''*), and only later shall I enlist words like *Ereignis, physis* or *alētheia* to explicate it.

At the outset it is worth saying the obvious: that the topic, *die Sache,* is not *das Sein* in the traditional sense of the Being of beings. For that, Heidegger generally uses the word *Seiendheit,* beingness (132, 134, 306)—hardly something forgotten by metaphysics, which thematized it under such titles as *idea, energeia, ipsum esse,* absolute spirit, will to power, and so on. These historical transformations of the beingness of beings may or may not exhibit development among themselves. The point of a "history of Being" is not necessarily to demonstrate some kind of evolution, for if anything, linear progression is swallowed up in a grand circularity whereby these modes of beingness revolve around, and in the process hide, that which renders them possible. Insofar as they "bracket out" (*epechein*) the central topic, each of them constitutes an "epoch" (*epochē*) in the "history of Being."[5] The end of this history would

---

[4]Cf. the anecdote in Helmut Franz, "Das Denken Heideggers und die Theologie," p. 262 f. in Gerhard Noller, ed., *Heidegger und die Theologie* (München: Kaiser, 1967).

[5]Note that the *Seinsgeschichte* may have two meanings. "Negatively" it is a history of various epochs of beingness, each forgetful of the central topic so that "Diese

consist in removing the brackets and "seeing" what has lain hidden: *"Sein, Wahrheit, Welt, ~~Sein~~, Ereignis"* (369=199.16). But what do these titles mean? The disconcerting habit that some Heideggerians have of answering the question by blindly repeating the master's language with its rustic imagery of "forest paths" and "regioning"—as if they too walked the woods above Todtnauberg instead of fighting traffic in Paris and New York—is a sign of the deplorable state of the hermeneutical art.

Such a charge obliges its author to put up or shut up, and at some risk I shall put up, i.e., try to say what Heidegger's topic is. For openers I invoke Aron Gurwitsch's insistence that the *only* topic for philosophy is sense (*Sinn*).[6] I wish to carry on a discussion of Heidegger's so-called "Being-as-such" in terms of "sense-as-such" and his "Being of beings" in terms of the "meaningfulness of beings," and further, I want to discuss sense and meaningfulness in the language of "giveness" (or as Heidegger prefers, "presence"). This procedure constitutes, *salva reverentia,* a "phenomenological reduction" from beings to their meaningful givenness and finally to sense-as-such as the horizon for all modes of beingness. It likewise entails a "phenomenological construction" of that realm of sense-as-such in terms of interrelating types of givenness (presence and relative absence). Such a translation of Heidegger's richly suggestive, and therefore potentially misleading, lexicon may open the way to understanding how the term *"Ereignis"* emerged from a "phenomenological destruction" of Aristotle's *kinēsis* to become the guiding term in Heidegger's thought.[8]

Epoche [=die Metaphysik] ist die ganze Geschichte des Seins" (377=206.11). "Positively" the central "topic" may be seen as contracting itself into these modes of beingness so that the whole process is the "Geschichte des Seyns selbst" (134=30.38) or even "Geschichte als Ereignis" (190=85.35).

[6]*Philosophy and Phenomenological Research,* VII (1946), 652.

[7]Cf. M. Heidegger, *Die Grundprobleme der Phänomenologie* (1975) pp. 29-31.

[8]Nor is this talk of "sense-as-such" a lapse into consciousness or some sphere of cognition abandoned by Heidegger from the beginning. For Heidegger, Being is accessible only as sense (SZ 152), and all the language of presence and absence in Heidegger refers to givenness in meaning, not to the mere presentness-in-existence of the Scholastic *esse*. If talk of "sense" *risks* falling into epistemology, talk of "Being itself" runs the far greater risk of collapsing into the naive realism that still haunts Heideggerian scholarship. (Cf. SZ 208 on "idealism.") In the Jaspers-essay in this

To begin then: beings are the given, their beingness is their givenness, and all this presupposes a prior horizon within which such
givenness can happen at all. Equally, beings may have meaning, in
which case their beingness is their meaningfulness, all of this presupposing a prior horizon of sense-as-such. The tradition has been clear
enough on the first two moments of this schema (the given and its
givenness, the meaningful and its meaningfulness—the metaphysical
difference) and has given various titles to the experienced givenness
of beings, some of which I listed above. But the horizon or "place" (I
will use the Greek word *topos*) of the whole scenario has gone unheeded, even though it was originally named by the Pre-Socratics and
mentioned in passing by the later Greeks (e.g., *alētheia* in
Metaphysics IX, 10). We may now see the significance of Heidegger's
double claim that essential thinking took a momentous step forward
when Parmenides located the topic worthy of thought in the "well-
rounded" open place in which *noein* and *einai* come together (131,
referring to Fr. I, 28 ff. & Fr. 3)[9] and that since Aristotle the only
advance in awareness of the topic occurred when Kant turned the
philosophical gaze away from things, even away from their
givenness/beingness and for a moment directed it upon the projection
of the topos within which the given and its objective-categorial givenness show up. To be sure, Kant did not go far enough, and from the
beginning Heidegger abjured any location of the topos within transcendental subjectivity, whether Kant's synthetic unity of apperception, Hegel's absolute spirit, or Husserl's constitutive transcendental
ego.[10] From his earliest lectures after World War I Heidegger read the
topos, the horizon within which givenness occurs, as generated in

---

volume Heidegger is quite clear that talk of "Existenz" is talk of "Existenzsinn"
(" 'ist'-Sinn," "(ich) 'bin'-Sinn" p. 29) and talk of "Sein" is talk of "Seinssinn" (30).
Cf. also 366=196.5: " 'das Sein Selbst' ist das Sein in seiner Wahrheit, welche Wahrheit zum Sein gehört, d.h. in welche Wahrheit 'Sein' entschwindet."

[9]Cf. Heidegger's text in Edmund Husserl, *Phänomenologische Psychologie (Husserliana,* IX), ed. W. Biemel, The Hague: Nijhoff, 1968, p. 256.

[10]But cf. Prof. Hans Seigfried's wondrous transformation of Heidegger into a
neo-Kantian who, armed with "a method modeled on that of the sciences," busies
himself with "construction" of phenomena in the interests of a *"Grundlegung der
Wissenschaften"*! H. Seigfried, "Descriptive Phenomenology and Constructivism,"
PPR 37 (1976), 248-261.

"the factical life-experience" (*das faktische Lebenserfahrung, die Faktizität*) or "existence" (*Dasein*) or simply in *Leben* as the *Grundbewegtheit* whose meaning is *Sorge* (1921-22 course on Aristotle). There are other ways of expressing it with various degrees of accuracy, many of them found in these marginalia. In the language of the early Husserl the topos is the empty projection which may be filled in by the presence of beings (SZ 151, 343).[11] In the language of givenness, the topos is the very "giving" of an area within which occurs the meaningfulness of beings—expressed by Heidegger as the *Es gibt* vs. the *Gegebenheit des Gegebenen* and in the present notes by various forms of *gewähren* (114; 188; 306; 372; 479=306.31). Again, the topos may be called *physis* or *Lichtung*, the emergence or "clearing" of the finite area of sense-as-such within which various modes of the meaningfulness of beings are played out and become comprehensible. In the traditional light-metaphor, the topos is *alētheia*, the "outbreak" (*Aus-schlag*, ἐκβολή 249=319.29) of light/ sense-as-such which renders possible all modes of luminosity/ meaningfulness of this or that. Now, whereas the tradition has been quite clear about the metaphysical difference between beingness and beings, it has ignored *the* difference between beingness and the topos which possibilizes it (e.g., 131) Because the tradition has reserved the word "Being" (*einai, ousia, esse, das Sein*) for what Heidegger would prefer to call "beingness" (the meaningful givenness, *Seiendheit*, of beings, their *Washeit*, 306), Heidegger will designate *his* topic, the emerging topos, as the *sense* of being(ness) or as the *clearing* for the presentness of beings (*"Lichtung...von Anwesenheit des Anwesenden*," 184), or as *Seyn* in the sense of *das Einfache von Seiendem und Sein/Seiendheit* (159). To stress the emergent-dynamic character of the topos Heidegger resorts to such striking phrases as *"Entwurf der Wesung der Wahrheit des Seyns"* (132) and *"das Seyende des Seyns"* (134, cf. 127) and, stressing the *-heit* of *Wahrheit: "das Heitere (das Heiternde), das Lichtende"* (179=74.31).

Very little of Heidegger can be understood if we confuse this distinction between the possibilizing topos (*Seyn* or *Sein*, i.e., *Sein* in

---

[11]The new volume has one note on Husserl at 457=285.16 in the Kant-essay: "Dagegen Husserls 'kategoriale Anschauung' *Logische Untersuchungen* VI; aber was heisst für Husserl 'Kategorie'? "

Heidegger's sense) and the various modes of givenness/presentness of beings (*Seiendheit,* i.e., *Sein* in the *tradition's* sense). The confusion becomes well nigh inevitable when Heidegger himself shortens the title of his project from *die Frage nach dem Sinn* (=*Seyn*) *des Seins* (=*Sein des Seienden*) to simply *die Seinsfrage,* as he does in the dedication to this volume. In hopes of avoiding such confusion, I have spoken simply of "the topic," and now we may say: the topic is the topos (*die Sache selbst ist die Lichtung*) and Heidegger's project is a "topology" (447=275.17), a showing of the topos.

Up to now this description of the topos in mostly static, spatial, and horizonal-transcendental terms has neglected two essential factors: (a) the question of man and (b) the question of what possibilizes the possibilizing topos.

(a) The primordial event of the topos—if you will, the event or out-break of the topos—happens only in, with, and "as" essential and proper human existence (*Da-sein*). To discuss the topic without reference to man would be to say too little, in fact nothing at all (SF 407=235.23, cf. WD 74). For Heidegger man is nothing but possibility, not empty pure possibility, but the ability to live into a future and to retain meaning from the past, thereby opening up the sphere of sense-as-such. It is worth pausing over this word "past." Instead of the usual *"Vergangenheit,"* which suggests something by-gone. Heidegger coins *"Gewesenheit"* from the past participle of *sein,* "to be." This has come into English as "having-been-ness"; however, I prefer "alreadiness" in order to stress that the human "past" lies not behind but *in front of man* (SZ 20) precisely by operating in and determining the structure of man's present and future. For example, one's Graeco-Roman, Judeo-Christian, secular-scientific "past"—or for that matter one's Oedipal complex—hardly flows away behind one into the distance. These are already out ahead, setting up the possibilities one might choose. That is why Heidegger speaks of the alreadiness of human existence in terms of throwness or projectedness (*Geworfenheit*) into already determined possibilities, indeed into the most human of all determining possibilities, one's death. On the other hand living into the future does not mean forging possibilities *ex nihilo* but re-opening already operative possibilities, rejecting some, modifying others, in an effort to become what one most properly is. Temporally described, human possibility has a dimension of alreadiness (*Gewesenheit*) and a dimension of retrieving one's proper alreadiness (*Zukünftigkeit*); and to live authentically in and as possibility means, in the words of Pindar which Heidegger likes to quote, to "become what you already [properly] are."[12]

Below I show how this "circular" structure is modeled on and yet transforms the fundamental structure of Aristotelian *kinēsis*. But now it is important to discuss human existence not in the language of the early Heidegger but in the later language of *Ereignis*. All through the marginalia we find variations on this word, but one particular note highlights the relation between this term and the earlier language of thrownness and project. Heidegger glosses a sentence from *"Einleitung zu 'Was ist Metaphysik?',"* viz., "[*Das Verstehen*] *ist der ekstatische, d.h. im Bereich des Offenen innestehende geworfene Entwurf"* with the following: *"Geworfenheit und Ereignis. Werfen, Zu-werfen, Schicken; Ent-Wurf: dem Wurf entsprechen"* (377=206.23). Here he translates the earlier language of projected project into the later one of being-appropriated and resonating. In SZ existence was projected into sense; later, existence is seen as being appropriated unto sense by having sense "sent to" it. Before the turn, understanding meant that existence, as projected forward and opening the horizon, reveals a realm of meaning-fraught relations and references; after the turn understanding is a resonance with the realm of sense which is given to man, or equally, into which man is appropriated. The new volume is suffused with footnotes on the "appropriation" (*Ereignis*) and "employment" (*Brauch*) of man for sense. The interesting texts are those in which both words combine: *Seyn* is the *Ereignis des Brauchs* (312=107.25); the unthought is the *brauchendes Eignen* (459=287.11); man's existential essence is *ereignet-gebrauchte* (375=204.11); when *ereignen* is used transitively, it is called *Brauch* (311=106.16; 369=198.28; 370 c). Compare as well *die Vereignung des Brauchs* (309=105.10). Clearly in both periods the same topic is under discussion: the event in which the topos is opened in conjunction with the opening of essential and proper human existence. In the early period this happens by man's self-appropriation in acts of resolve whereby he becomes what he properly (*eigentlich*) is: the emergent and mortal disclosure of the world of sense. In the later period man's most proper self is had in

---

[12]SZ 145; EM 77.

acceding to being "appropriated" or "employed" for the event of sense. (Thus the later Heidegger returns in a more profound way to the early Husserl's concern for the autonomy of sense over against the concrete acts in which it is performed.)

(b) But what possibilizes the possibilizing topos? In *Vom Wesen der Wahrheit* Heidegger glosses: *"Wesen: 1. quidditas–das Was– κοινόν; 2. Ermöglichung–Bedingung der Möglichkeit; 3. Grund der Ermöglichung"* (178=73.1). In the first set we recognize all modes of traditional beingness, including Aquinas' *ipsum esse,* for these all tell what the state or condition of beings is. In the second we recognize the modern search for the transcendental horizon which possibilizes beingness, and we may assume this includes the language but not the intention of Heidegger's early discussion of existence as "transcendence" and of Being as *"das transcendens schlechthin"* (SZ 38). In the third set we again find the transcendental pattern but in its moment of searching out the "whence" of the transcendental projection. For Kant this would be the transcendental unity of apperception (or in the "A" deduction, the transcendental imagination); for Husserl it would be the constitutive transcendental ego. But for Heidegger what is it? In *Vom Wesen des Grundes,* Heidegger annotates the phrase *"nichts ist ohne Grund"* with *". . .Gründung überall wo Seyn. Welchen Wesens ist Seyn, dass zu ihm Gründung gehört . . .? Wo liegt die Notwendigkeit für Gründung? Im Ab- und Un-Grund. Und wo dieses? Im Da-sein"* (127=24.9). In this distinction between *Gründung* and *Ab-Grund* or equally between *Seyn* and *Seyn* (306 note "g") we come upon the issue of the so called *"lēthē"*—dimension of the topos. The clearest text in that regard is found in the *"Einleitung zu 'Was ist Metaphysik?' "* where Heidegger says: "Whenever unhiddenness emerges, that which essentially become present in this unhiddenness, viz., hiddenness itself, remains absent precisely so that the unhidden thing can appear as a being" (370=199.22 f.) In this text we can distinguish four moments which then reduce to two: (1) the thing which appears as meaningful, *das Unverborgene;* (2) the meaningfulness of that meaningful thing, *die Unverborgenheit des Unverborgenen;* (3) the emergence-dimension of the realm of sense-as-such, *das Aufgehen der Unverborgenheit;* and (4) the submergence-dimension of that same realm, *das Ausbleiben der Verborgenheit in dieser Unverborgenheit.* Now by combining the first two and the last two, the fourfold structure collapses into two: first, there is that-which-appears-in-its-state-of-meaningfulness, and secondly, there is the possibilizing topos with the two dimensions of submergence and emergence, *lēthē* and *alētheia, Enteignis* and *Ereignis* (328=159.25; 370). What is this? Having defined the topos as *alētheia,* we now seem to meet something behind or deeper than *alētheia,* viz., *"das Wesende in dieser [Unverborgenheit], nämlich die Verborgenheit,"* which Heidegger glosses as *"Λήθη als Verbergung."* Were we mistaken in identifying the topic with *Seyn* and *alētheia?* Deeper than these, is the topic *Seyn* and *lēthē?* And what would that possibly mean?

These questions can not be answered without considering why Heidegger calls his topic *Ereignis* and specifically, whence he derives that word. For now we may retain this much: (1) that the topic seems to be the emergent topos which possibilizes all modes of beingness; (2) that the topos happens only in and "as" essential, proper human existence, whether seen in terms of resolve's self-appropriation of what one properly is or as being-appropriated and employed for the emergence of sense-as-such; and (3) that somehow the topos has a bi-dimensionality of presence and absence whereby *both* these moments must be given, although in different ways, insofar as both constitute the topos which itself is sense.

Having shown what Heidegger's topic is not and provisionally what it is, we may now ask why it is called *Ereignis.* In order to show the Aristotelian "basis" of the term I shall draw upon the 1939 text *"Vom Wesen und Begriff der φύσις. Aristoteles Physik B, 1"* and the unpublished 1928 seminar *"Phänomenologische Übungen: Interpretation von Aristoteles, Physik II."*[13] I will show briefly (1) the phenomenological implications of understanding *kinēsis* as *energeia atelēs;* (2) that *in formal terms* the pattern operative in *kinēsis* is that of retrieve; and (3) that the pattern of the movement of retrieve is the pattern which finds expression in the word *Ereignis.*

Because for Aristotle experience in the broadest sense is always experience of beingness, it is therefore always of the presentness of beings in their stable *telos* or *ergon* (cf. *en-tel-echeia, en-erg-eia*). Movement, however, is the very lack of stable presentness and ful-

---

[13]Although this is the title in Richardson, *op. cit.,* 666, the seminar actually dealt with *Physics* III.

fillment, and for that reason would seem to be excluded from beingness (cf. *Physics*, III, 2, 201b 20f.: *mē on*). But the genius of Aristotle,
as Heidegger likes to repeat,[14] is precisely that he grasped movement
as a kind of beingness (*energeia tis,* 201b 30f.), the condition of a
being which at once stands in its *telos (en-tel-echeia)* without having
fully arrived there (*tou dynatou hēi dynaton,* 201 b 5), the state of a
being which is present in partial appearance, yet absent in relative
non-appearance (*energeia atelēs,* 201 b 32).

"Relative non-appearance"—that is, non-appearance *for the sake
of* appearance—is what Heidegger takes Aristotle to mean by
dynamis; indeed, this *dynamis* is the possibilizing condition for a
moving being's partial and negatived appearance. Precisely this
"atelic" quality of a moving being is what allows it to remain in
movement, for were the *dynamis* brought forward into the *telos*, the
being would be achieved and the movement would cease. This atelic
presentness constitutes a unique interplay of presence and absence,
for along with its limited presence, a moving being's non-presence or
possibilizing absence *also becomes present* in a special way. For
example, the *absence* of Pierre from the café and of my stolen bicycle
from the rack are indeed present and given, even when the absent
beings are not. Likewise in a growing natural being, the relative
non-appearance of the source of growth indirectly becomes present in
allowing the flower to appear.[15] To spell out *dynamis* in terms of
presence and relative absence is to lay out the geneologically most
primitive form of "retrieve" (*Wiederholung*). Indeed if it may be said
that Heidegger's topic is the emergent topos (*physis*) and if, as
Heidegger argues, *physis* is *kinēsis* or *energeia atelēs,* and if this atelic
presence has the fundamental structure of drawing *dynamis* finitely
into *energeia* while ever allowing *dynamis* its non-appearance, then
we may begin to see anew the unity and simplicity in Heidegger's
thought precisely by discovering its Aristotelian roots.

A natural moving being, for example a plant, must maintain and
not abolish its absence, preserve and not fully actualize its *dynamis,*

---

[14]"On the Being and Conception of *Physis,*" *Man and World* IX (1976), 225, In *In-
terpretationen aus der antiken Philosophie,* SS 1931, Heidegger dealt in the third lecture (May 5, 1931) with the "introduction" of non-being into being in Plato and Aristotle.

[15]"On the Being and Conception of *Physis,*" p. 266.

if it is to remain what it is. While using *dynamis* as power for presence (*entelecheia* ...), a moving being conserves it *as* possibility (...*tou dynatou hēi dynaton*). There are various ways of expressing this. We may say that the plant constantly "goes back into" its *dynamis (Insichzurückgehen)*[16] as it comes forth into appearance. Or we may say that the plant again and again seeks (re-peats) and draws upon (re-trieves) its *dynamis* in order to appear. In order to name this process of drawing upon *dynamis* for the sake of *energeia* while allowing *dynamis* to remain relatively absent, Heidegger comes up with "*Eignung*," "appropriation." *This is Heidegger's proper title for movement, and it is the basic model of the concept of Ereignis.* But there is a lot of mileage between Aristotelian *kinēsis* and the unique "movement" that is the emergent topos. Three examples will illustrate how this *Eignung* respectively (a) operates externally in the movement of constructing an artifact, (b) takes on the *formal* pattern of "retrieve" in natural movement, and (c) is radically transformed into the pattern of retrieve *stricte dicta* in resolve, temporality and historicity.[17]

(a) While underway and unfinished, the process of constructing a table is the on-going appropriation (*Eignung*) of the appropriate wood (*das Geeignete, to dynamei on*) unto the incompletely attained *eidos* "table." Note that in the generation of artifacts the appropriation-process is external to the product and does not provide its own appropriate material. The *eidos prohaireton* "table," which is the guiding force of the movement of construction, does not provide any wood but sends the carpenter to the lumberyard to buy it. (b) By contrast the movement of natural beings introduces a new element into the appropriation-process. In the growth of a plant the very process of generation is a "self"-provision of the appropriate material. The plant "orders up" (*bestellt*) its own seed which develops naturally into a flower which in turn "orders up" a new seed. This process of "ordering up" is the most primitive form of "retrieve." The becoming of a plant is the plant's appropriation of its own *dynamis* unto its own *energeia*. In so doing, the plant takes over what it properly is (*to ti ēn einai, Wesen, Gewesenheit*), i.e., it appropriates what it *already* is in *dynamis* by *becoming* it in incom-

---

[16]*Ibid.*, 268.
[17]*Ibid.*, 254-263.

plete *energeia•Kinēsis* (and therefore *physis*) is already a primordial structure of retrieve, namely, becoming what one already is. (c) The appropriation-process is radically transformed when the movement that is *physis* becomes the movement that is *logos* in the human existence. In his 1922 course on Aristotle Heidegger first pointed out how for the Greeks *logos* is a form of *kinēsis,* but a unique one, as he indicates four years later: "The movedness [*Bewegtheit*] of existence is not the motion [*Bewegung*] of something present-at-hand" (SZ 374 f.). Human existence is that unique form of movement which, by stretching ahead of itself towards its death, opens the realm of sense-as-such. In its ordinary condition, however, existence hides this movement from itself and falls back on various forms of stability, such as accepting handed down meanings rather than waking up to the generation of sense-as-such. The act of resolve is the self-appropriating insight or self-disclosive retrieval whereby existence accepts and understandingly becomes the most proper possibility it already is, its dying. This constitutes a "retrieve of itself" (*Wiederholung ihrer selbst,* SZ 308), a "coming back to what one already properly is" (*Zurückkommen auf das eigenste Gewesen,* SZ 326), a "return to the possibilities one already is" (*Rückgang in Möglichkeiten des dagewesenen Daseins,* SZ 385). In that dimension of retrieve called historicity Heidegger speaks of a "*Sichüberliefern der Möglichkeiten*" (SZ 383 f.), which is not the "handing down" of possibilities as the existing English translation has it, but a "freeing up" of possibilities for oneself, a destruction-retrieve *formally* homologous with the classical therapeutic process delineated by Freud and with the process of reactualization of archetypes in primitive cultures. To draw upon proper possibility in the act of resolve or in historical retrieve is not to pull *dynamis* into full present appearance (cf. "... *nicht, um es abermals zu verwicklichen*" SZ 385), but rather to bring it indirectly into presense precisely by leaving it possible, i.e., in absence. In resolve one lets the possibilizing absence be present when one chooses the dying, hence finitely present, self that one is. Anticipation thus constitutes the "revering" of the "repeatable possibilities of existence" (SZ 391).

A marginal note in the *Humanismusbrief* gets right to the topic. At 330=161.21 Heidegger glosses the phrase "*die eigentliche Würde des Menschen*" with: "*Die ihm eigene, d.h. zu-geeignete, er-eignete Würde. Eignung und Ereignis.*" In the early period the "value proper to man," his openness whereby sense-as-such is generated, was concretely taken over when man appropriated his being-ahead-of-himself-unto-death (*die Übernahme der Geworfenheit*, SZ 325). The later position in the gloss states that this same value of aheadness and openness, while remaining proper to man, is not appropriated by him so much as apportioned to him as his possibility. Most important of all, this apportionment happens in the pattern called *Eignung und Ereignis*. To state it baldly these two name the same thing: the *energeia atelēs* that is movement; indeed at one point in his 1928 seminar on the *Physics* Heidegger combines both words into *Ereignung*. In that seminar he defines movement as "*Sich-ereignen*" in the sense of *die Anwesenheit des Geeigneten in seiner Eignung*, the presentness which something appropriated has precisely in its state of being appropriated—a perfect translation of Aristotle's *entelecheia tou dynatou hēi dynaton*. But that definition states only what movement is in Aristotle. The unique atelic presence which is *Ereignis* in Heidegger's thought is the happening of the event of sense, not the mere "thereness" (*Vorhandenheit*) of Aristotelian movement; it is the on-going retrieval of power for the meaningful givenness of beings amidst unsense, non-sense, and no-longer-sense; it is the continual actualization of the finite realm of sense-as-such from out of its own potentiality for appearance. This fundamental movement is *Sinn* as *Wegrichtung* (377=206.27) which happens only in man's essential proper existence. Projected ahead of himself (*geworfen* in SZ) or drawn beyond himself (*angezogen* in WD), man experiences the "wonder of all wonders," the partially open, partially closed emergence of the topos within which beings have meaningful presence. Heidegger's topic is the event of sense, the movement of *alētheia* where the *lēthē*-dimension functions as the withdrawn but present power for the meaningful appearance of things.

Thomas J. Sheehan
Loyola University of Chicago

APPENDIX: SELECTED MARGINALIA

(I) Improvements of the Text. 114=12.4: vor das Seiende → vor Sein des Seienden, vor den Unterschied. 223=129.25: Wahrheit → im Sinne des Wahren. 373=202.26: Stelle → die sterblich bewohnte Ortschaft, die sterbliche Gegend der Ortschaft. 378=206.32: möglichen → ermöglichenden. 331=162.14: weiter → Weite: aber nicht die des Umgreifens, sondern der ereignenden Ortschaft; als die Weite der Lichtung. (N.B.: the new text adds "wesenhaft" before "weiter.") 334=164.33: Räumliche → Raum weder neben Zeit, noch in Zeit aufgelöst, noch aus Zeit deduziert. 342=172.29: des Seins → besser: im Sein qua Ereignis. 327=159.10: Bezug zur Lichtung → ekstatisches Innestehen in der Lichtung. 190=85.34 f.: geschichtlich → unzureichend; Wesen der Geschichte aus Geschichte als Ereignis. 164=59.31: Menschen → Umgekehrt: Das Dasein besteht das Walten, besser das Wesen der Wahrheit und gründet so die Möglichkeit des Menschseins als Menschsein *im* Dasein!

(II) Explanations of the Text. 114=12.1: Ermöglichung → d.h. Sein. 179=74.32: macht → machen—her-stellen—hervorgehen lassen in die Lichtung. 188=83.21f.: Sein-lassen → 1. nicht negativ, sondern gewähren—Wahrnis; 2. nicht als ontisch gerichtetes Wirken. Achten, er-achten das Sein als Seyn. 237=143.20: Unverborgenheit → Die *Alētheia* ist ein Name für *esse*, nicht für *veritas*. 326=158.11: Hin-aus-stehen → hin in das Aus des Auseinander des Unterschieds (das Da), nicht "hinaus" aus einem Innen. 332=163.14: Verhältnis → Verhältnis aus Verhaltenheit (Vor-enthalt) der Verweigerung (des Entzugs). 332=163.31: Eigentlichkeit → aus dem Eignen des Er-eignens zu denken. 331=162.4: Geschick → Ge-schick: Versammlung der Epochen des brauchenden Anwesenlassens. 333=164.7: Nähe → im Sinne der Nahnis: lichtend bereithalten, halten als hüten. 338=169.19: Nähe zum Sein → Als diese Nähe verwahrt und birgt sich das Sein selbst. 359=189.35: seiender → insofern Sein Seiendes "sein" lässt. 237=143.21: Grundzug des Seienden → d.h. als das Seyn. 450=277.29 & 31: allgemeinen & höchste → *koinon – koinotaton; koinon – katholou (theion).* 188=83.32: Sicheinlassen auf das Seiende → dem Anwesenden sein Anwesen lassen und nichts anderes dazu und dazwischen bringen. 328=159.15: das Ganze → im Was und Wie des Denkwürdigen und des Denkens. 328=159.17: Sagen → Sichzeigenlassen. 328=159.22: Standpunktes → d.h. der Seinsfrage. 328=159.25: Seinsvergessenheit → Vergessenheit—Lēthē—Verbergung —Entzug—Enteignis: Ereignis. 328=160.1 f.: Unterscheidung → Diese Unterscheidung ist aber nicht identisch mit der ontologischen Differenz. Innerhalb dieser gehört jene Unterscheidung auf die 'Seite' des Seins.

(III) Some notes from "Vom Wesen des Grundes": 126=24 title: Das Problem des Grundes → Der Ansatz der Wahrheit des Seyns ist hier noch ganz im Rahmen der überlieferten Metaphysik vollzogen und in einfacher und wiederholender Entsprechung zur Wahrheit des Seienden und Unverborgenheit des Seienden und Enthülltheit der Seiendheit. Seiendheit als *idea* selbst Enthülltheit. *Ein* Weg zur Ueberwindung der "Ontologie" als solcher ist hier eingeschlagen (vgl. III), aber die Ueberwindung ist nicht ursprünglich aus dem Erreichten her vollzogen und aufgebaut. 131=28.24f.: *ontologische Wahrheit* → Unklar! Ontologische Wahrheit ist

Enthüllen der Seiendheit—durch die Kategorien—aber Seiendheit als solche bereits *eine* bestimmte Wahrheit des Seyns, Lichtung seiner Wesung. Diese Unterscheidung "ontisch-ontologische Wahrheit" ist nur eine Verdoppelung der Unverborgenheit und bleibt zunächst im Platonischen Ansatz stecken. Damit nur aus dem Bisherigen her die Richtung der Ueberwindung gewiesen, aber nicht eine Ueberwindung aus ihrem eigenen Grunde vollzogen und gegründet. 163=59 title: Vom Wesen des Grundes → Entsprechend dem Wesen des Grundes herausstellen das ursprüngliche *Ergründen*. Ergründung vor aller Begründung. Ergründung in Philosophie und Kunst, nicht aber in der Religion.—In III. der Ansatz zur Destruktion von I., d.h. der ontologischen Differenz; ontisch-ontologische Wahrheit. In III. der Schritt in einen Bereich, der die Zerstörung des Bisherigen erzwingt und eine völlige Umkippung [=Kehre; note from von Herrmann] notwendig macht. In III. das Wesen des Willens als Da-sein, Aufhebung und Ueberwindung aller Vermögen. 175 = 70.31: Seinsverfassung → Der Sprung in den Ursprung! (Da-sein) Ursprung—Freiheit—Zeitlichkeit; Endlichkeit des Daseins nicht identisch mit der Endlichkeit des Menschen, anders zu fassen: Ursprungscharakter!

(IV) Some Notes from the altered "Nachwort zu: 'Was ist Metaphysik?' " The text and footnotes here are very complicated. The 1943 version of the most controversial text reads: "dass das Sein wohl west ohne das Seiende, dass niemals aber ein Seiendes ist ohne das Sein." The 1949 emendation reads: "dass das Sein nie west ohne das Seiende, dass niemals ein Seiendes ist ohne das Sein" (306=102.13f.). First of all Heidegger's 1943 copy glosses "wohl" with: "In der Wahrheit des Seins west das Seyn qua Wesen der Differenz; dieses Seyn qua Seyn ist vor der Differenz das Ereignis und deshalb *ohne* Seiendes." The same 1943 copy glosses "das Sein" with: "im Sinne von Seyn." Heidegger's 1949 copy glosses "west" with: "Wesen von Sein: Seyn, Unterschied; 'Wesen' von Sein mehrdeutig: 1. Ereignis, nicht durch Seiendes bewirkt, Ereignis—Gewährende; 2. Seiendheit—Washeit: während, dauernd, *aei*." Finally the 1949 copy glosses "wohl" again: "Vordeutung aus Seyn qua Ereignis, aber dort (in der 4. Auflage [1943]) nicht verständlich." Good luck!

(V) Some Others: 181=77.2: Schöpfungsordnung → Kein doppeltes Uebereinkommen, sondern *eines,* aber mehrfach gefügtes: Weil Uebereinkunft mit dem Schöpfer, deshalb (als Geschaffenes in gewisser Weise Göttliches) *unter sich;* die "Entsprechung" in einem wesentlicheren Sinne, als ihn die grobe, ungedachte, von Aristoteles übernommene *analogia entis* der Scholastik meint. 193=88.31: Verborgenheit → Zwischen 5. und 6. der Sprung in die (im Ereignis wesende) Kehre. 313=145 title: Brief ueber den "Humanismus" → Das hier Gesagte ist nicht erst zur Zeit der Niederschrift ausgedacht, sondern beruht auf dem Gang eines Weges, der 1936 begonnen wurde, im "Augenblick" eines Versuches, die Wahrheit des Seins einfach zu sagen.—Der Brief spricht immer noch in der Sprache der Metaphysik, und zwar wissentlich. Die andere Sprache bleibt im Hintergrund.

(VI) New and Different Information in the "Nachweise." On p. 481 Heidegger cites at length from the preface (1925, 3rd ed.) of Jaspers' *Psychologie der Welt-*

anschauung, which he takes as Jaspers' response to Heidegger's 1919/21 essay, although Heidgger is not explicitly named. There is a strange shift of information concerning PLW. In the 1947 edition which combined PLW and HB, Heidegger said that the text of PLW was "written" (*geschrieben*) in 1940 for an address to a small circle, then published in 1942. He says there that it was first delivered in his course of WS 1930/31 (a mistake: it actually was delivered in WS 1931/32, but Heidegger is notoriously inaccurate when referring to his own courses; cf. *Heraklit,* p. 100, US 91f., 128) and 1933/34. The 1967 edition of *Wegmarken* dropped the word "*geschrieben,*" repeated the error about 1930/31 and dropped the reference to 1933/34. The 1976 edition of *Wegmarken* substitutes "*zusammengestellt*" for "*geschrieben,*" repeats the error about 1930/31 (but corrects it in the Table of Contents) and likewise drops reference to 1933/34.

(*VII*) *Some Errata.* P. 127 note "b": close parentheses after *physis.*
P. 370 note "a": Read "Lēthē" instead of "*Dēthē.*" P. 378: Shift "207" to left margin. The greatest erratum in this volume is the lack of an index to the marginalia.

NOTES ON CONTRIBUTORS

J. L. Mehta is currently Professor at the Center for the Study of World Religions at Harvard University. He is the author of a major book on Heidegger's work, *Martin Heidegger: The Vision and the Way*.

Werner Marx, Director of Philosophisches Seminar I at the University of Freiburg, holds the chair previously held by Heidegger. He is the author not only of a major study of Heidegger, *Heidegger and the Tradition,* but also of books on Aristotle, on Schelling and on Hegel.

Otto Pöggeler, Ruhr-Universität Bochum, is Director of the Hegel-Archiv and author of two books on Heidegger, *Der Denkweg Martin Heideggers* and *Heidegger und die Politik.*

John Sallis, Duquesne University, is the author of several books in the areas of Phenomenology, Greek philosophy, and German Idealism. He is the editor of *Research in Phenomenology* and of the book *Heidegger and the Path of Thinking.*

Jacques Taminiaux, University of Louvain, is associated with the Husserl Archives. He is the author of several studies of modern German philosophy including the book *La Nostalgie de la Grèce à l'aube de l'idealisme allemand.*

John D. Caputo, Villanova University, has published several studies dealing with Heidegger's relation to medieval philosophy. He is the author of a book on Heidegger and German mysticism.

Joseph J. Kockelmans, Pennsylvania State University, is editor of *Heidegger on Language* and author of numerous publications on recent Continental philosophy, including *Martin Heidegger: A First Introduction.*

Karsten Harries, Yale University, is the author of *The Meaning of Modern Art* and of various papers on Heidegger including the recent study "Heidegger as a Political Thinker."

Joan Stambaugh, Hunter College, is co-editor of the English edition of Heidegger's *Works*. She has translated several volumes by Heidegger

317

and is presently preparing a new translation of Heidegger's major work *Being and Time.*

Theodore Kisiel, Northern Illinois University, has published numerous papers on Heidegger and on philosophy of science. He is co-author and co-editor of *Phenomenology and the Natural Sciences.*

Manfred Frings, DePaul University, is general editor of the German edition of the works of Max Scheler. He is also co-editor of the Heidegger *Gesamtausgabe* and editor of *Heidegger and the Quest for Truth.*

Parvis Emad, DePaul University, is the author of several studies dealing with Heidegger's thought.

Hugh J. Silverman, SUNY at Stony Brook, has translated and commented extensively on several major texts by Merleau-Ponty. He is also the author of various other studies in the areas of recent Continental philosophy, philosophical psychology, and aesthetics.

André Schuwer, Duquesne University, is Associate Editor of *Research in Phenomenology.* He has published several papers on the thought of Heidegger.

David Farrell Krell, University of Mannheim, is editor of *Martin Heidegger: Basic Writings.* He is co-translator of Heidegger's *Early Greek Thinking* and is now editing and co-translating Heidegger's monumental two-volume work, *Nietzsche.*

Michael E. Zimmerman, Tulane University, has published several papers dealing with Heidegger's thought.

Kenneth Maly, presently at Winona State University, has been a member of the Philosophy Department at the University of Freiburg and has written extensively on Heidegger.

Thomas J. Sheehan, Loyola University of Chicago, has edited *Heidegger, the Man and the Thinker* and has published various translations of and critical essays on Heidegger.